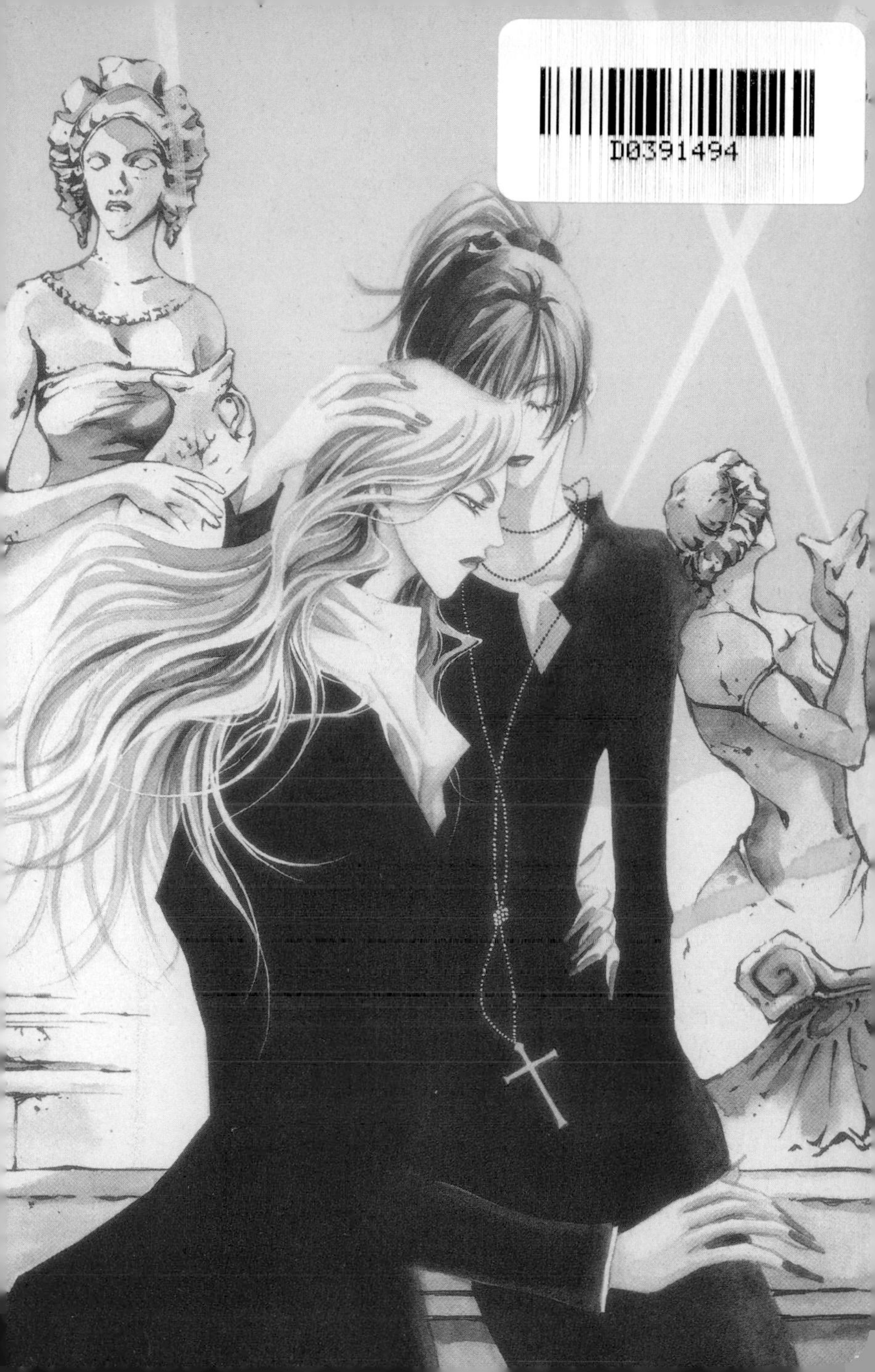

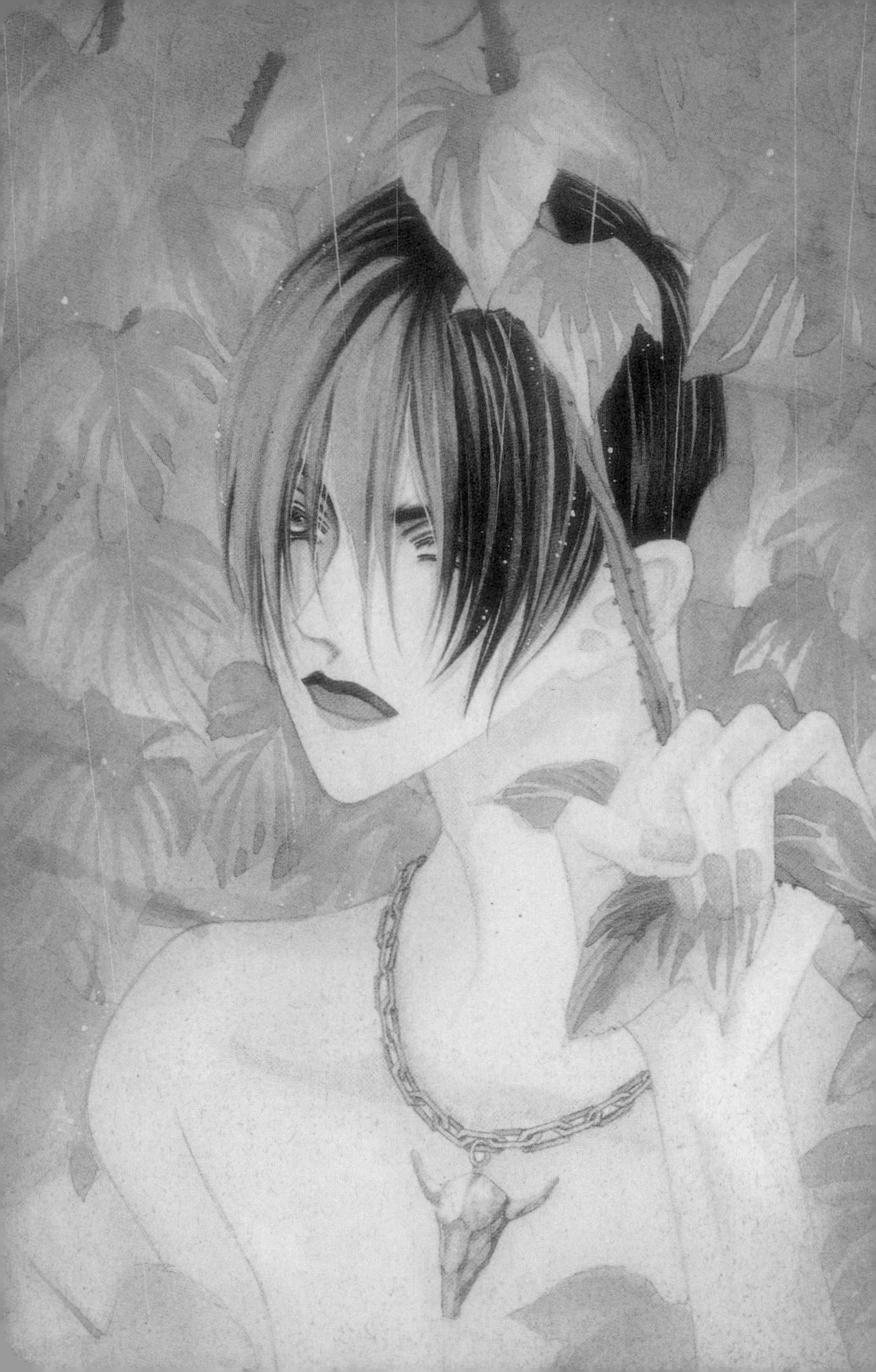

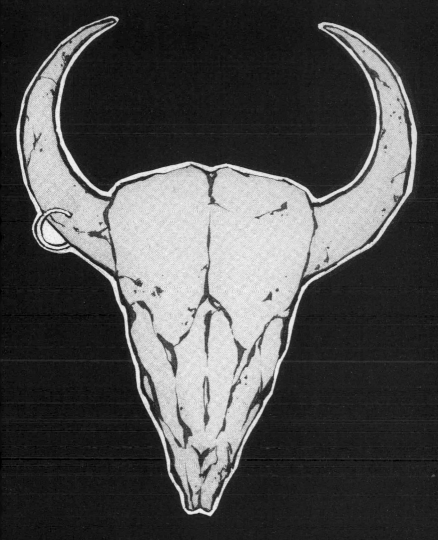

MODEL

ALSO AVAILABLE FROM 🐾 TOKYOPOP®

**For more
information visit
www.TOKYOPOP.com**

03.30.04T

Translator - Lauren Na
English Adaptation - Sam Stormcrow Hayes
Retouch and Lettering - Joseph Mariano
Cover Layout - Anna Kernbaum
Graphic Designer - Vicente Rivera, Jr.

Editor - Bryce P. Coleman
Digital Imaging Manager - Chris Buford
Pre-Press Manager - Antonio DePietro
Production Managers - Jennifer Miller, Mutsumi Miyazaki
Art Director - Matt Alford
Managing Editor - Jill Freshney
VP of Production - Ron Klamert
President & C.O.O. - John Parker
Publisher & C.E.O. - Stuart Levy

E-mail: info@TOKYOPOP.com
Come visit us online at www.TOKYOPOP.com

A  Manga

TOKYOPOP Inc.
5900 Wilshire Blvd. Suite 2000
Los Angeles, CA 90036

Model Vol. 2

ISBN: 1-59182-712-4

First TOKYOPOP printing: July 2004

10 9 8 7 6 5 4
Printed in the USA

VOLUME TWO

BY
LEE SO-YOUNG

TOKYOPOP®

LOS ANGELES • TOKYO • LONDON • HAMBURG

MODEL: TWO

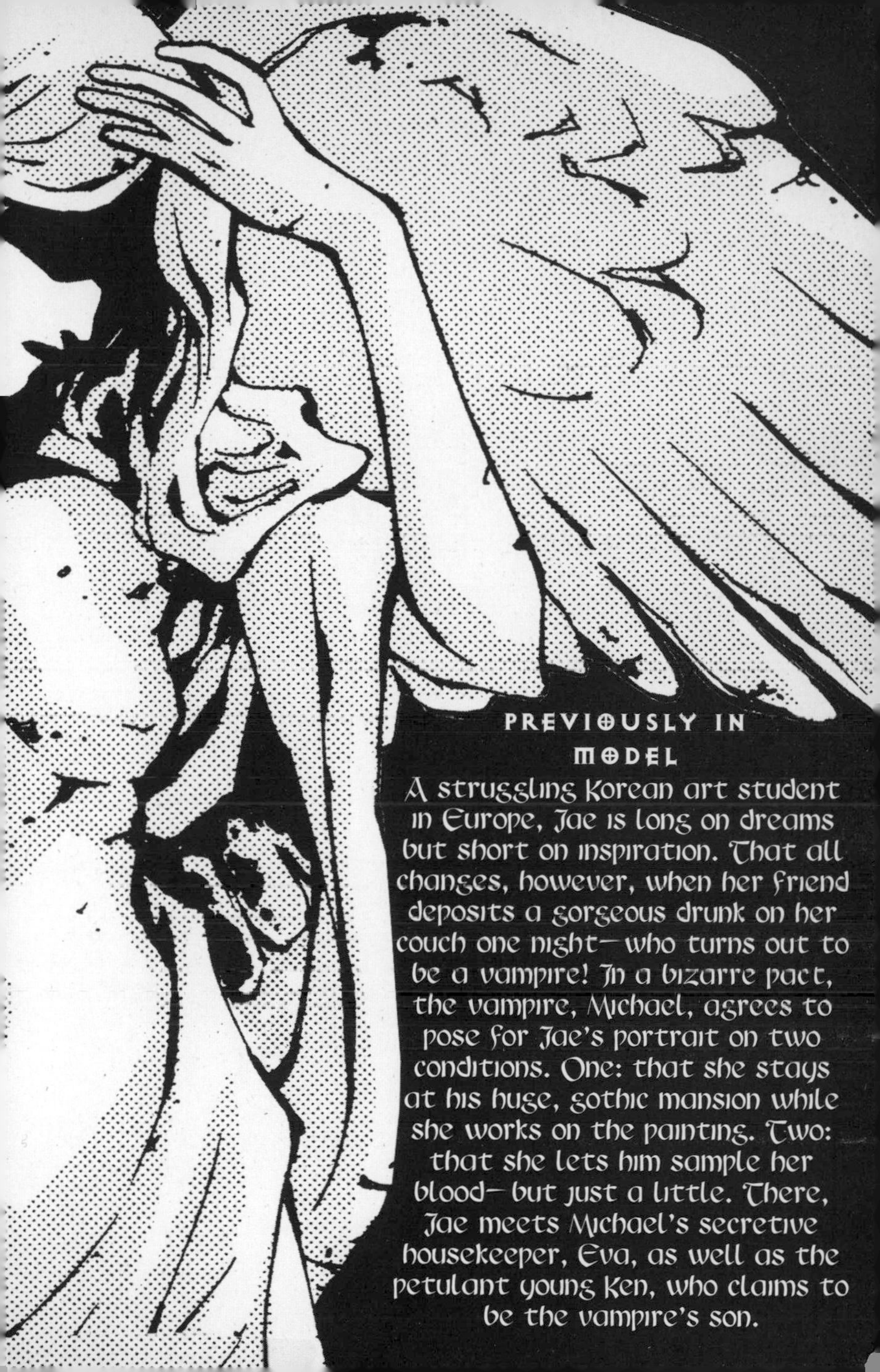

PREVIOUSLY IN MODEL

A struggling Korean art student in Europe, Jae is long on dreams but short on inspiration. That all changes, however, when her friend deposits a gorgeous drunk on her couch one night—who turns out to be a vampire! In a bizarre pact, the vampire, Michael, agrees to pose for Jae's portrait on two conditions. One: that she stays at his huge, gothic mansion while she works on the painting. Two: that she lets him sample her blood—but just a little. There, Jae meets Michael's secretive housekeeper, Eva, as well as the petulant young Ken, who claims to be the vampire's son.

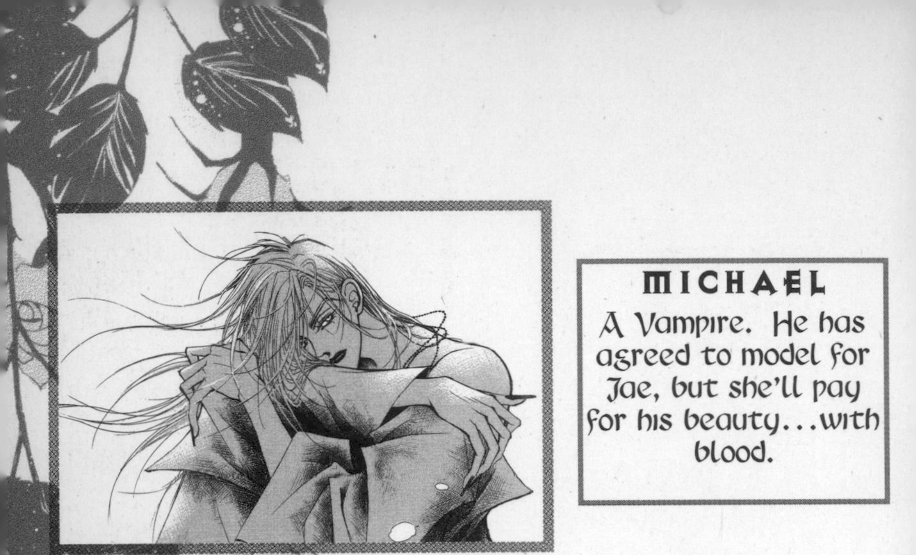

MICHAEL

A Vampire. He has agreed to model for Jae, but she'll pay for his beauty...with blood.

KEN

A Youth. A member of the household who may, or may not, be Michael's prodigal son.

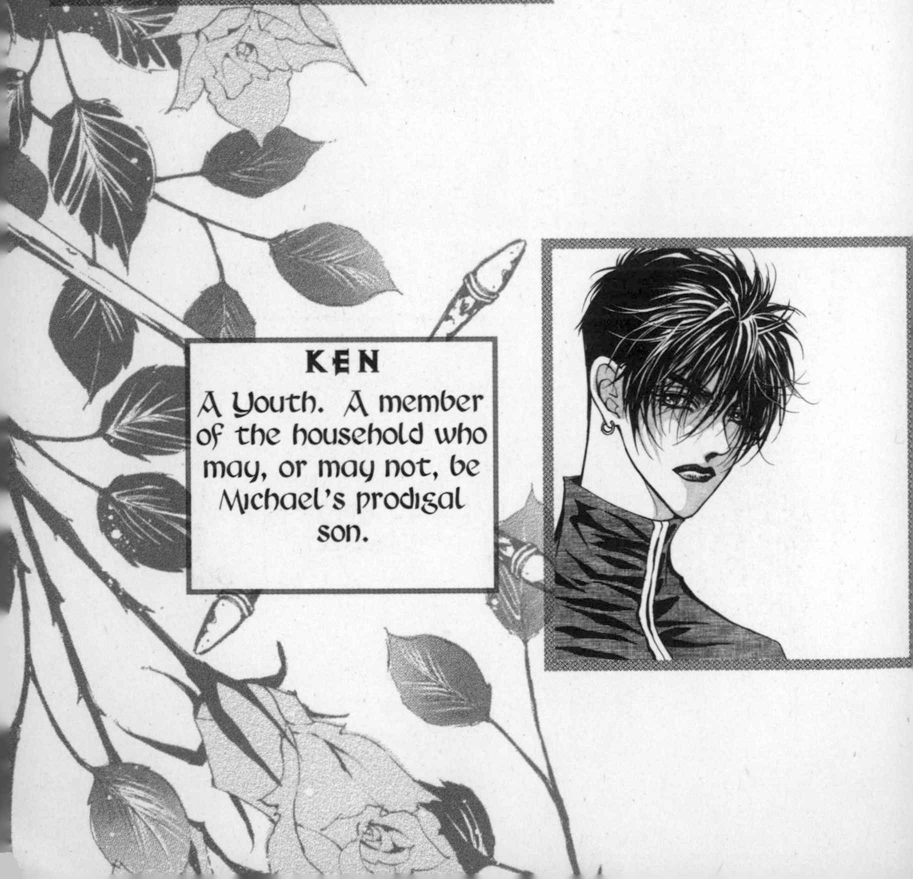

JAE

An Artist. She may have found her muse in Michael, but is he her inspiration or her damnation?

EVA

The Housekeeper. She serves only Michael. But she hasn't always called the vampire "Master."

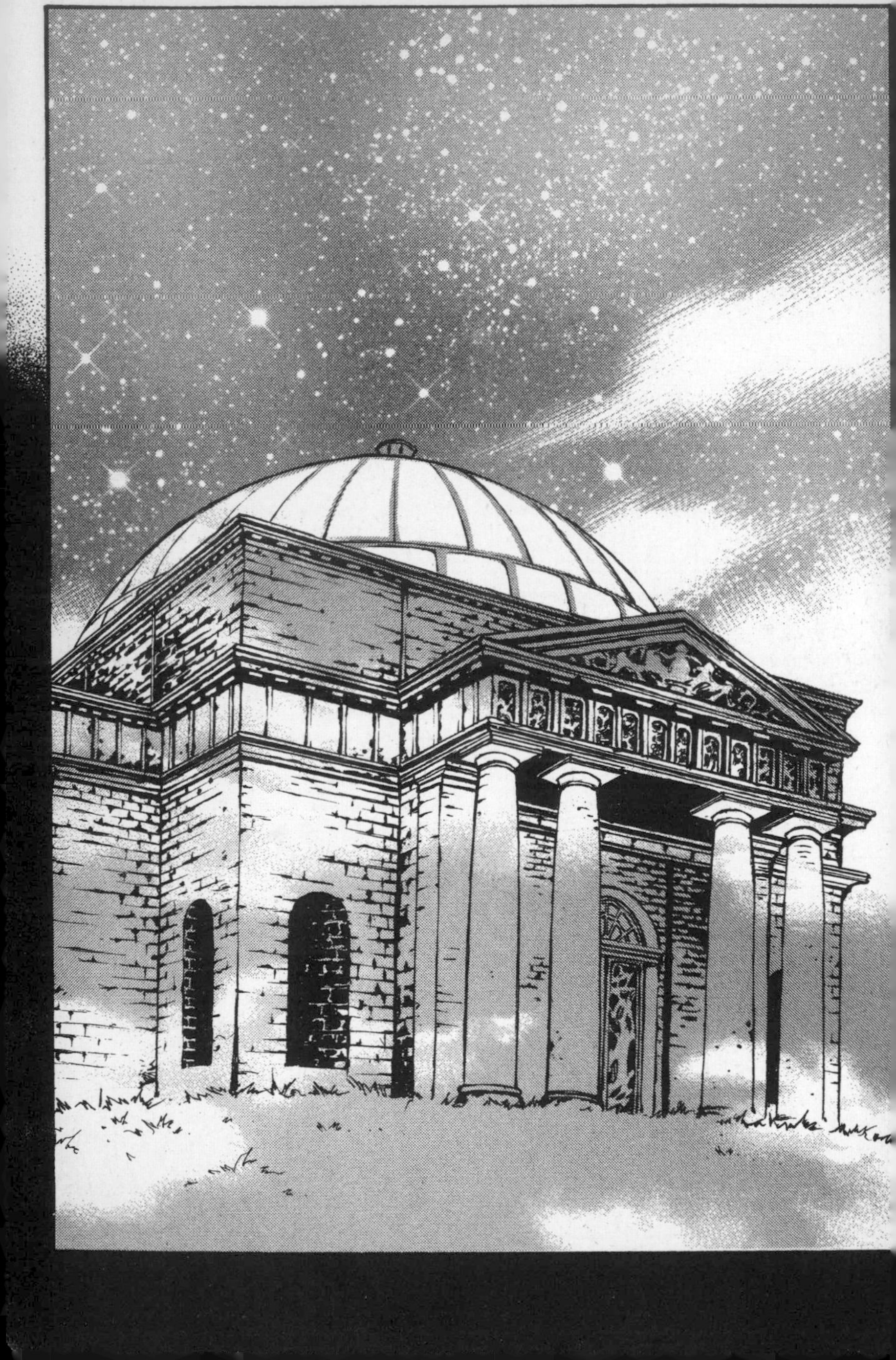

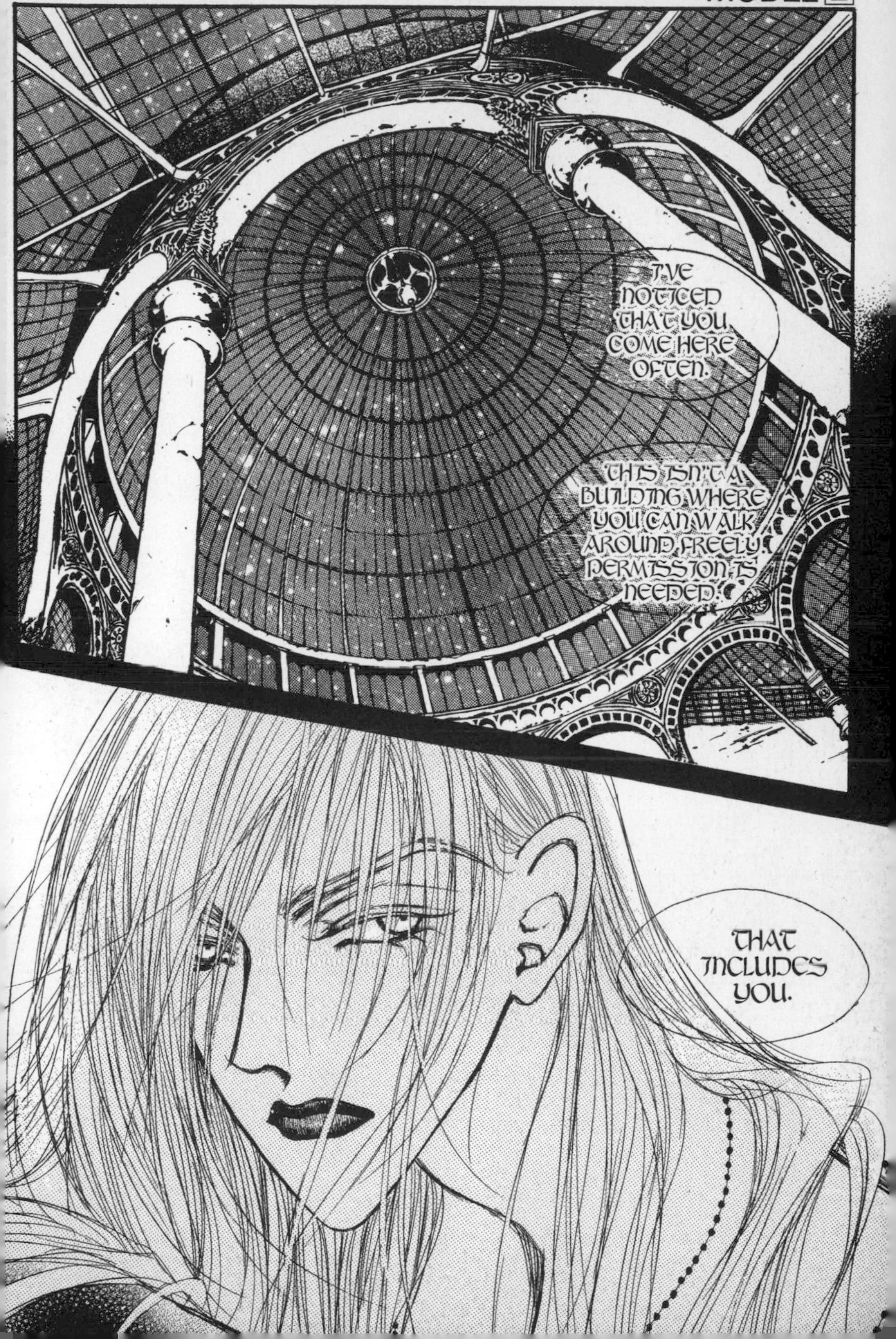
I'VE NOTICED THAT YOU COME HERE OFTEN.
THIS ISN'T A BUILDING WHERE YOU CAN WALK AROUND FREELY. PERMISSION IS NEEDED.
THAT INCLUDES YOU.

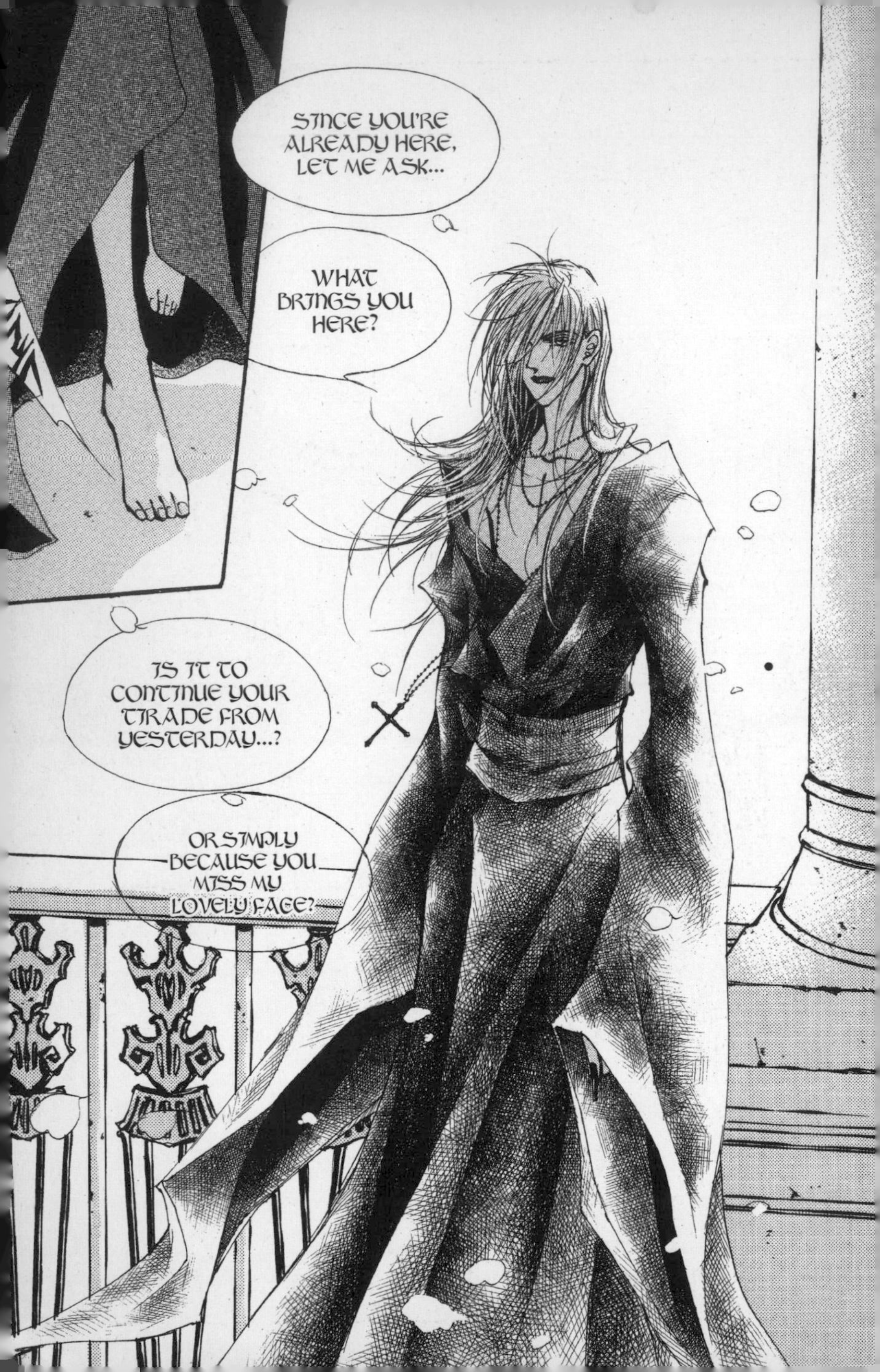
SINCE YOU'RE ALREADY HERE, LET ME ASK...
WHAT BRINGS YOU HERE?
IS IT TO CONTINUE YOUR TIRADE FROM YESTERDAY...?
OR SIMPLY BECAUSE YOU MISS MY LOVELY FACE?

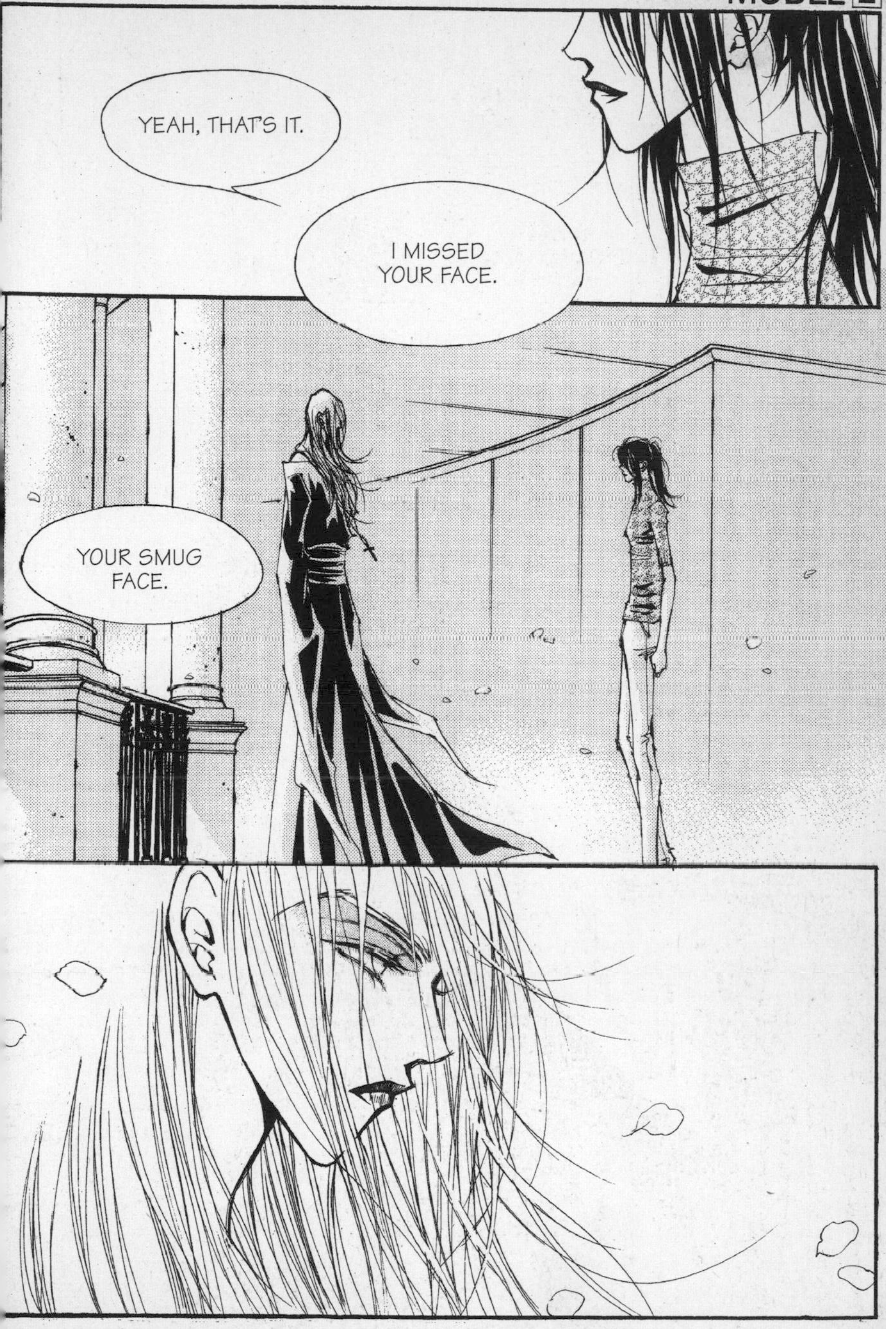
YEAH, THAT'S IT.
I MISSED YOUR FACE.
YOUR SMUG FACE.

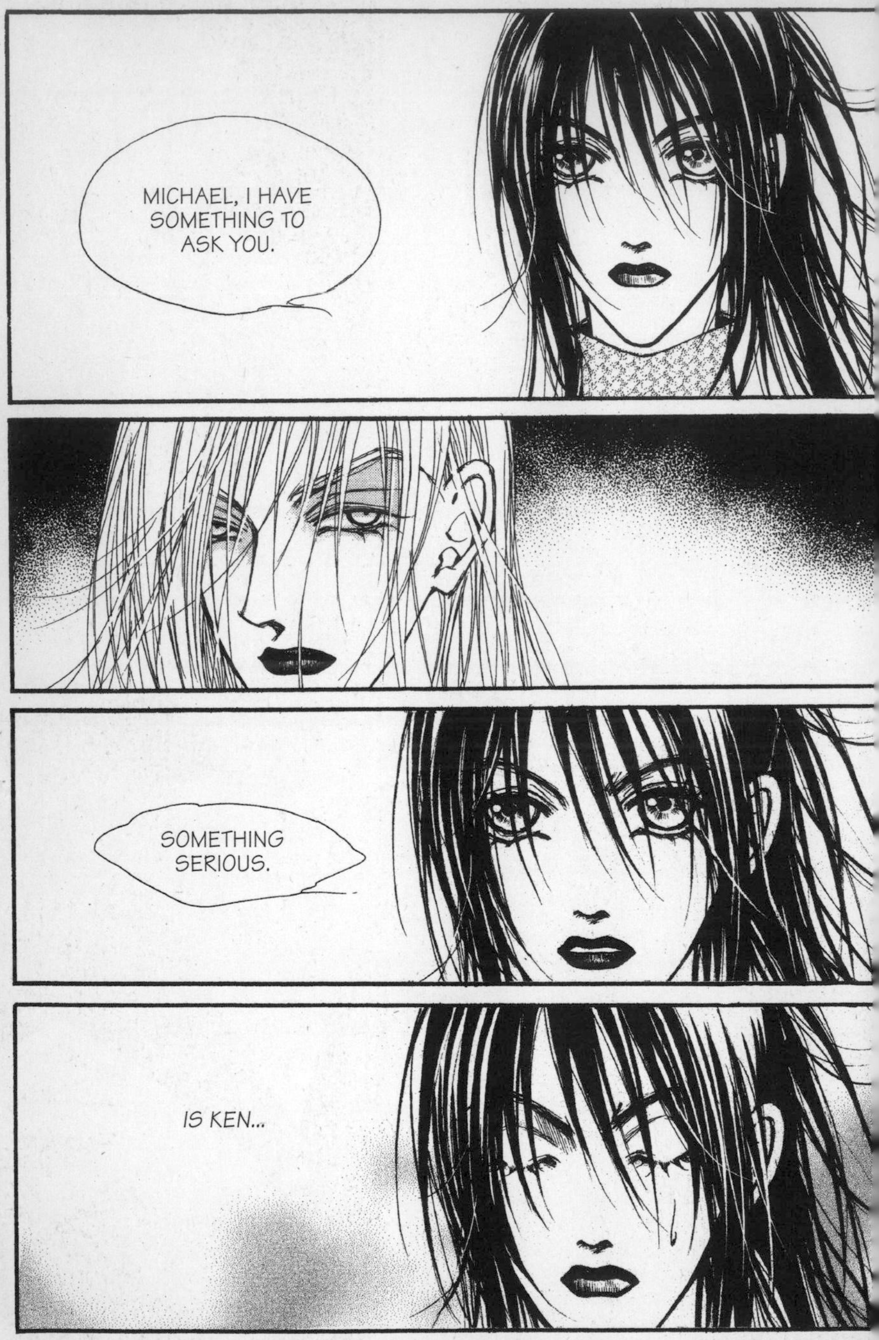
MICHAEL, I HAVE SOMETHING TO ASK YOU.
SOMETHING SERIOUS.
IS KEN...

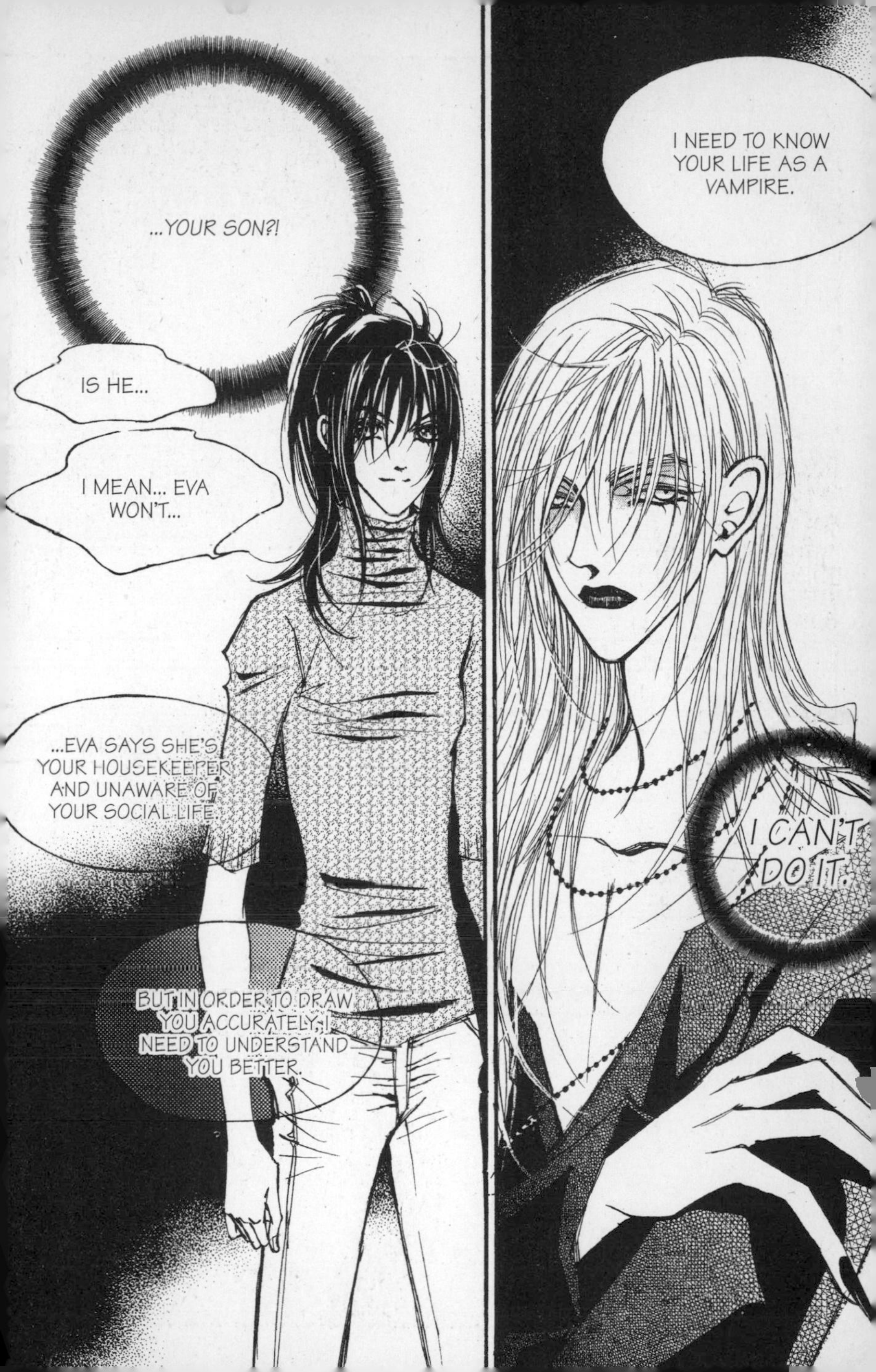
...YOUR SON?!
IS HE...
I MEAN... EVA WON'T...
...EVA SAYS SHE'S YOUR HOUSEKEEPER AND UNAWARE OF YOUR SOCIAL LIFE.
BUT IN ORDER TO DRAW YOU ACCURATELY, I NEED TO UNDERSTAND YOU BETTER.
I NEED TO KNOW YOUR LIFE AS A VAMPIRE.
I CAN'T DO IT.

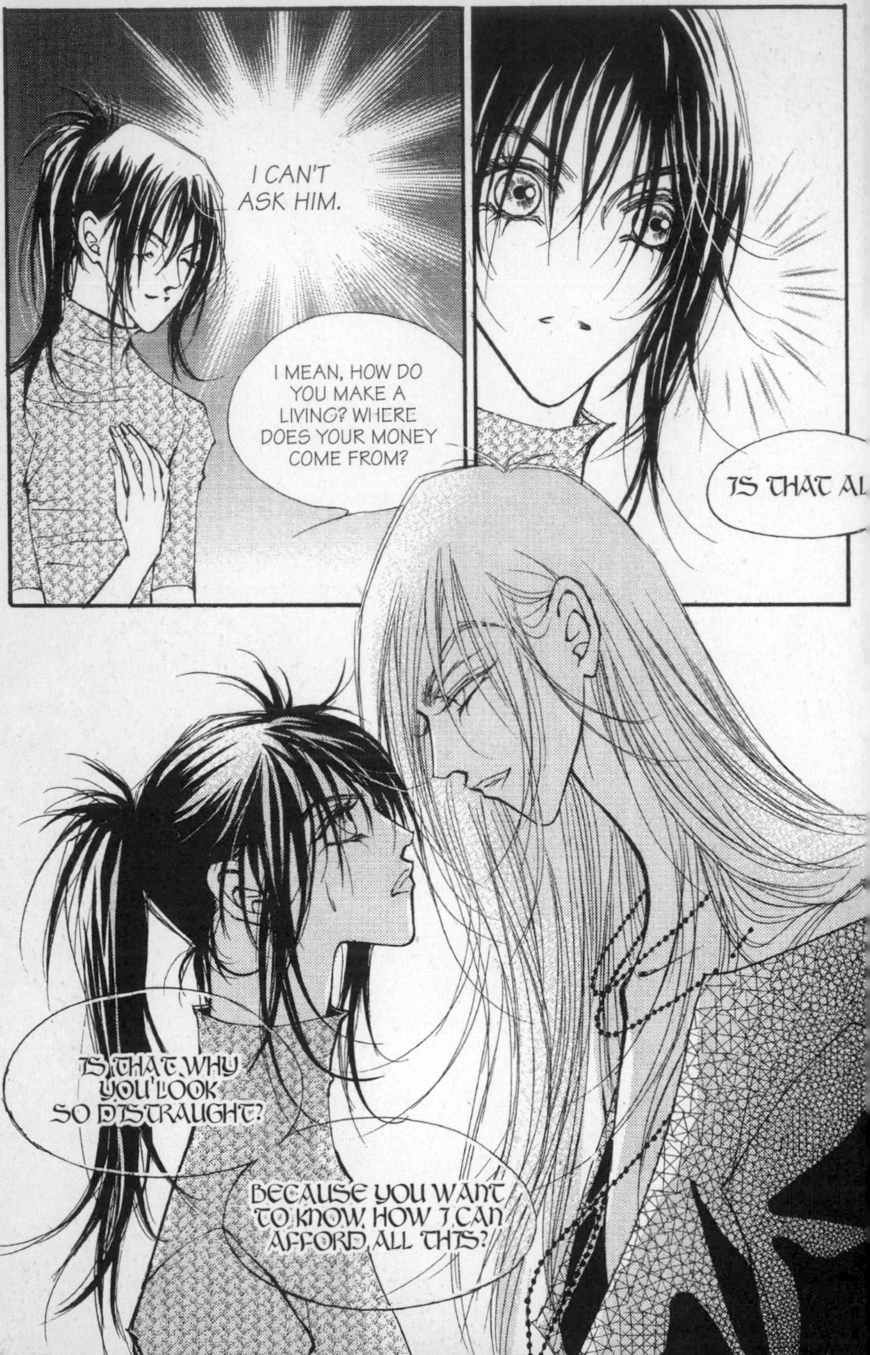
I CAN'T ASK HIM.
I MEAN, HOW DO YOU MAKE A LIVING? WHERE DOES YOUR MONEY COME FROM?
IS THAT AL
IS THAT WHY YOU LOOK SO DISTRAUGHT?
BECAUSE YOU WANT TO KNOW HOW I CAN AFFORD ALL THIS?

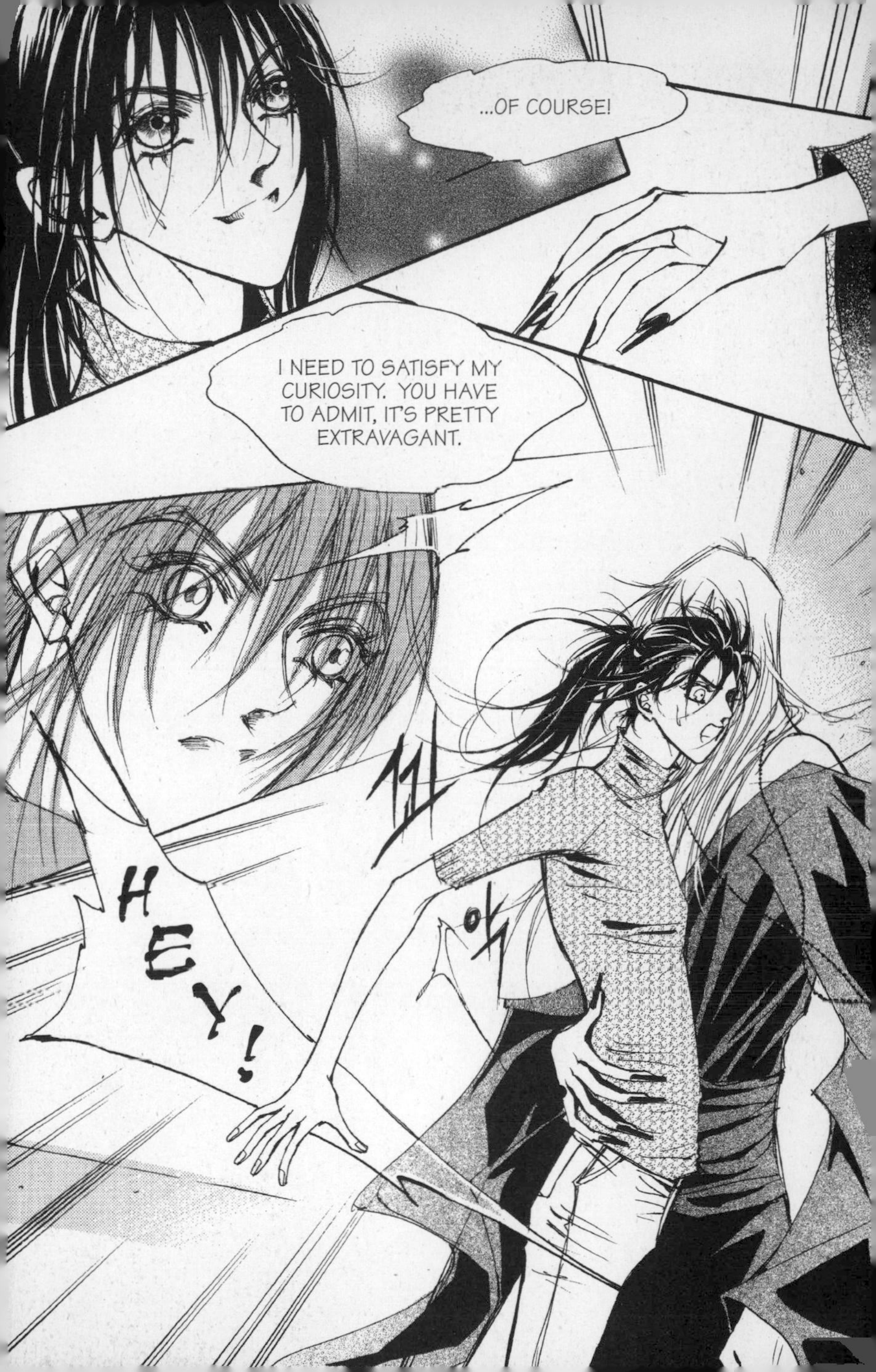
...OF COURSE!
I NEED TO SATISFY MY CURIOSITY. YOU HAVE TO ADMIT, IT'S PRETTY EXTRAVAGANT.
HEY!

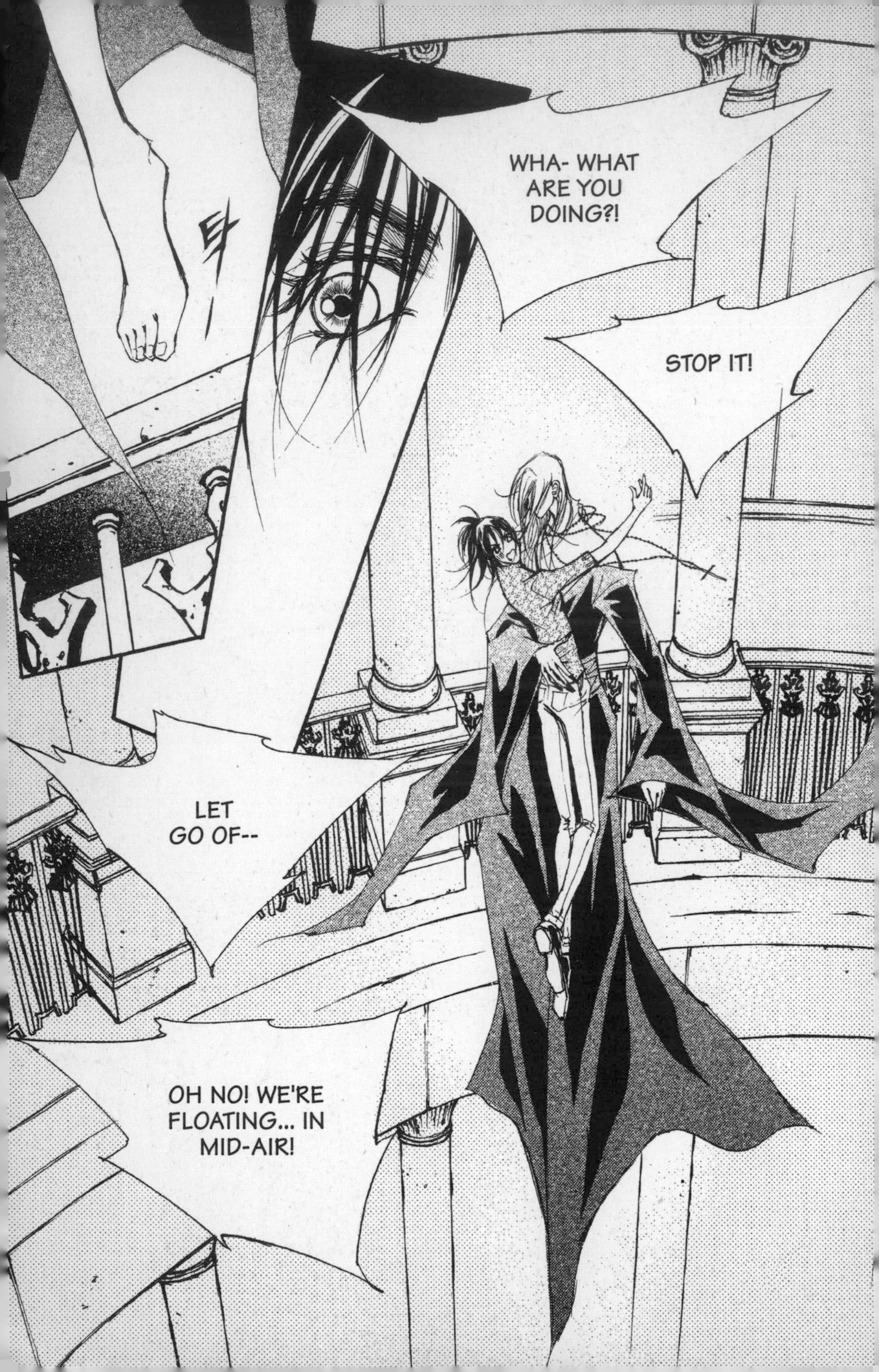
WHA- WHAT ARE YOU DOING?!
STOP IT!
LET GO OF--
OH NO! WE'RE FLOATING... IN MID-AIR!

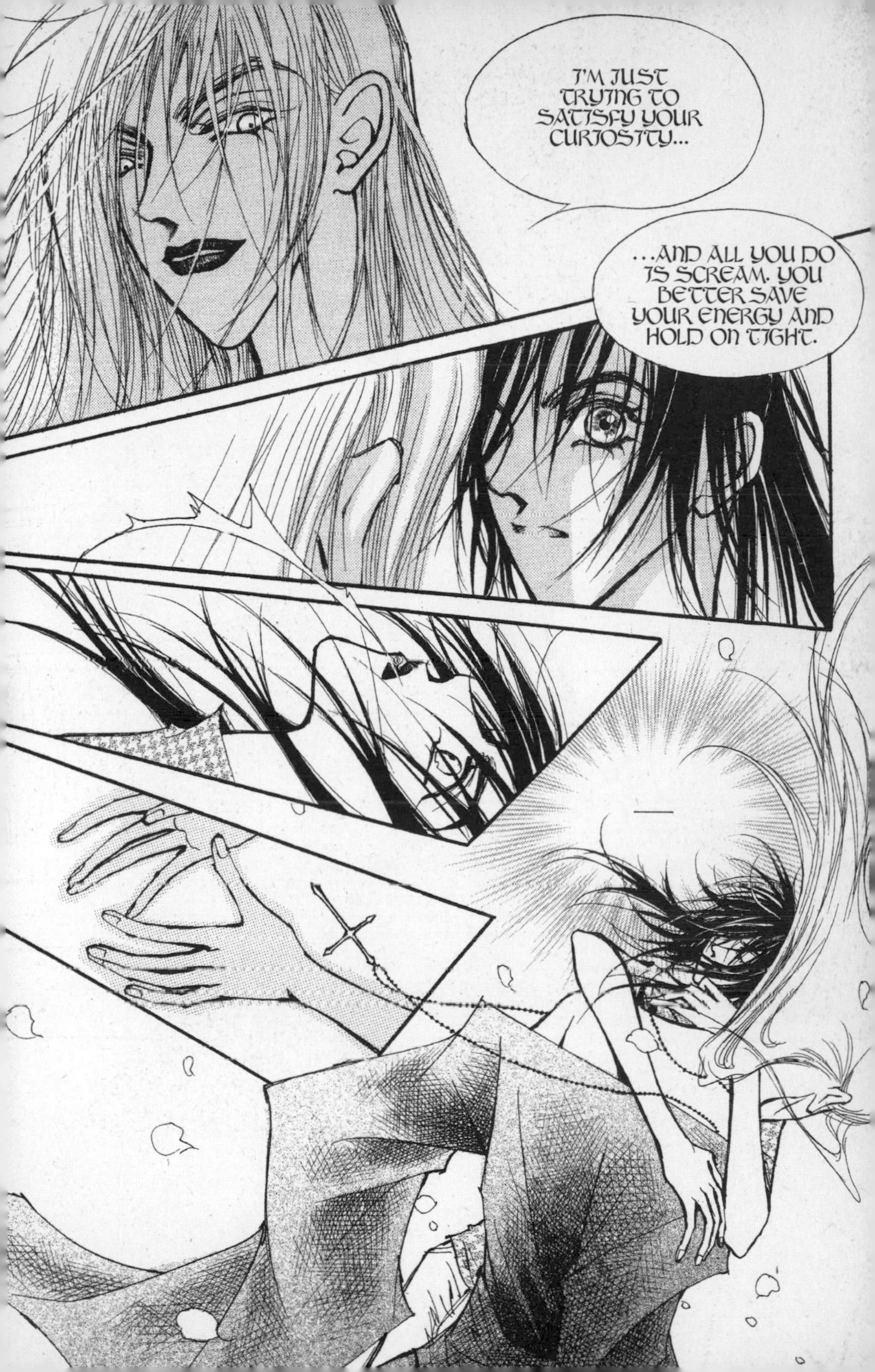
I'M JUST TRYING TO SATISFY YOUR CURIOSITY...
...AND ALL YOU DO IS SCREAM. YOU BETTER SAVE YOUR ENERGY AND HOLD ON TIGHT.

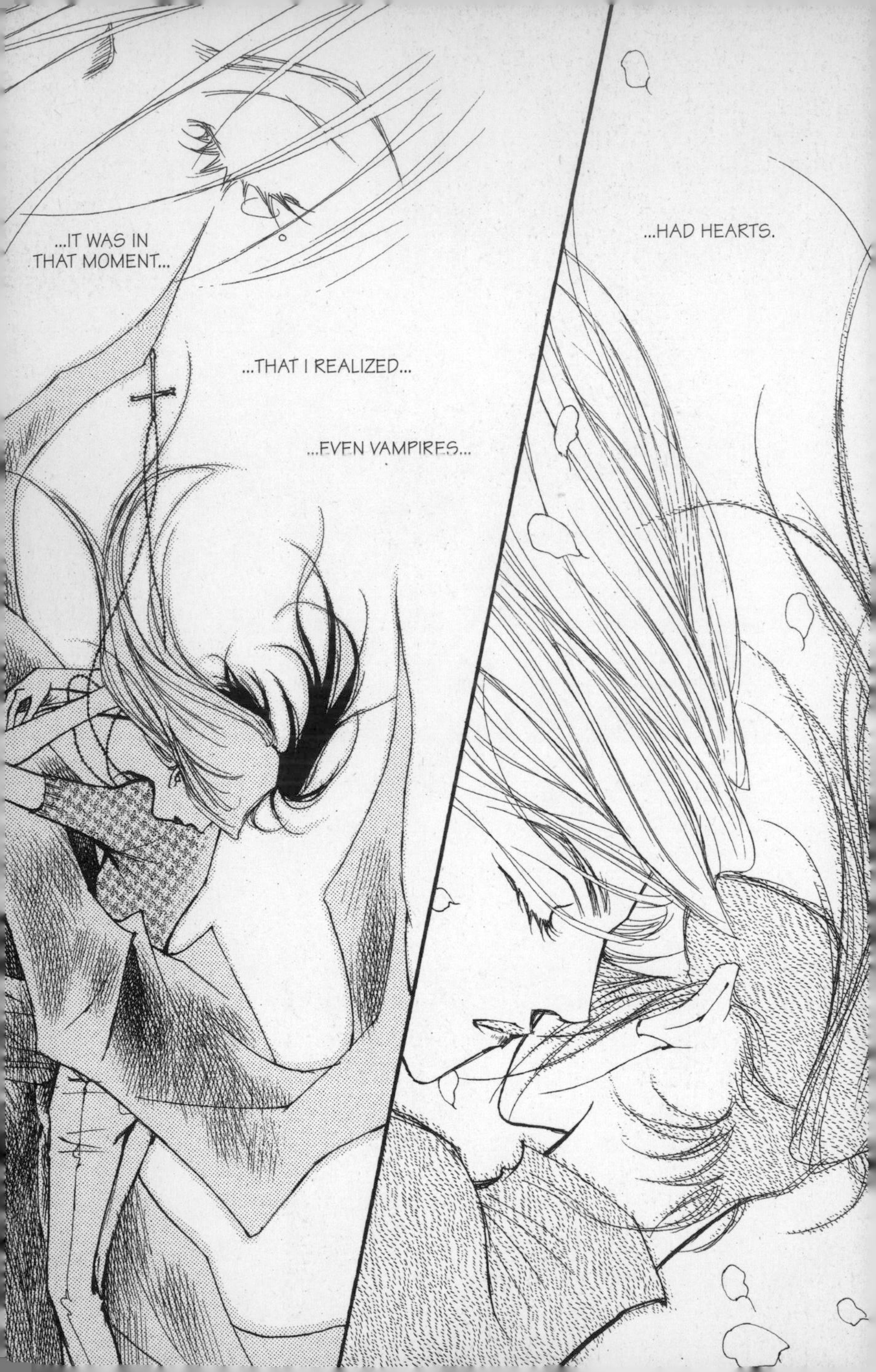
...IT WAS IN THAT MOMENT...
...THAT I REALIZED...
...EVEN VAMPIRES...
...HAD HEARTS.

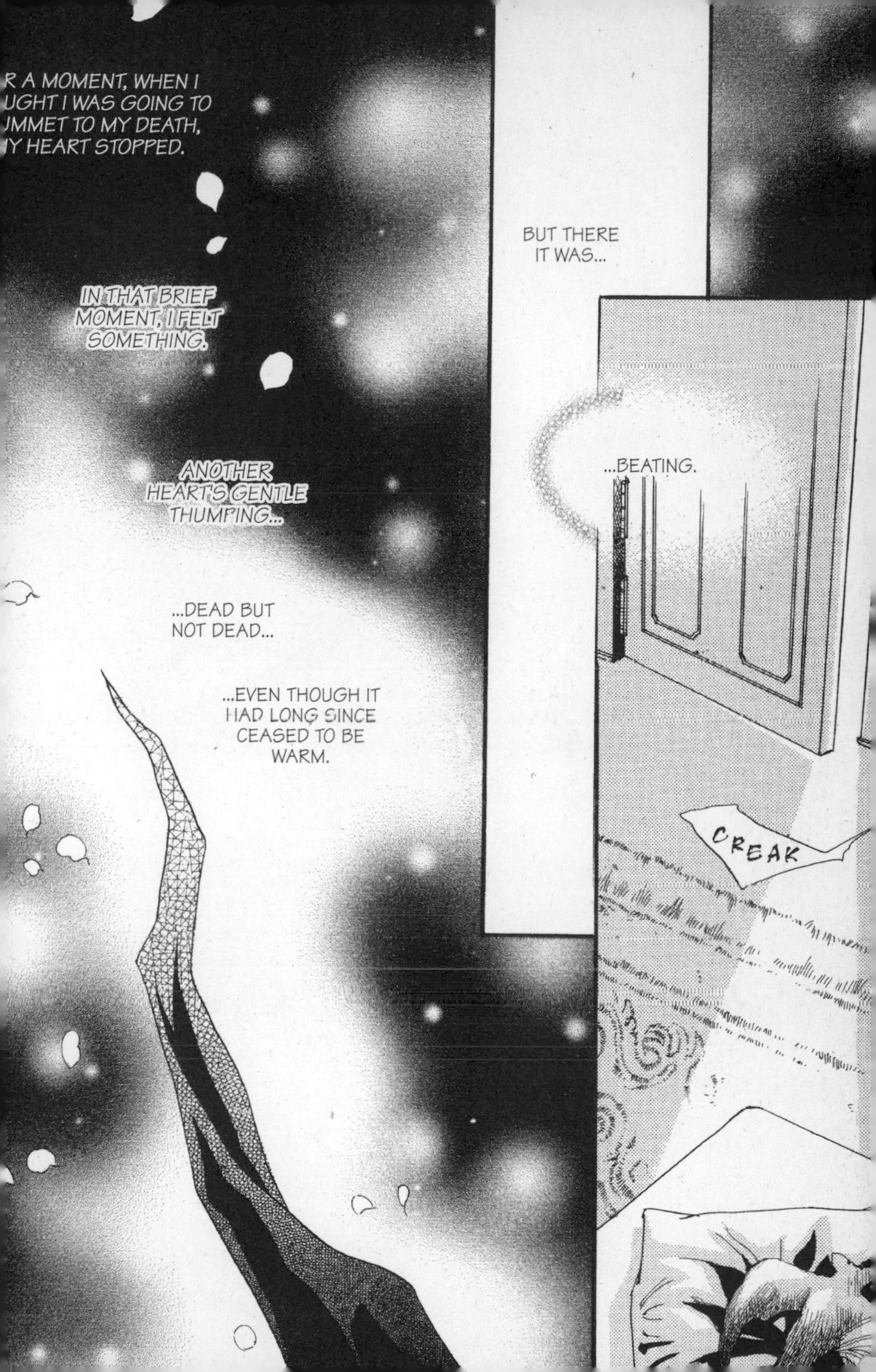
R A MOMENT, WHEN I UGHT I WAS GOING TO UMMET TO MY DEATH, Y HEART STOPPED.
IN THAT BRIEF MOMENT, I FELT SOMETHING.
ANOTHER HEART'S GENTLE THUMPING...
...DEAD BUT NOT DEAD...
...EVEN THOUGH IT HAD LONG SINCE CEASED TO BE WARM.
BUT THERE IT WAS...
...BEATING.
CREAK

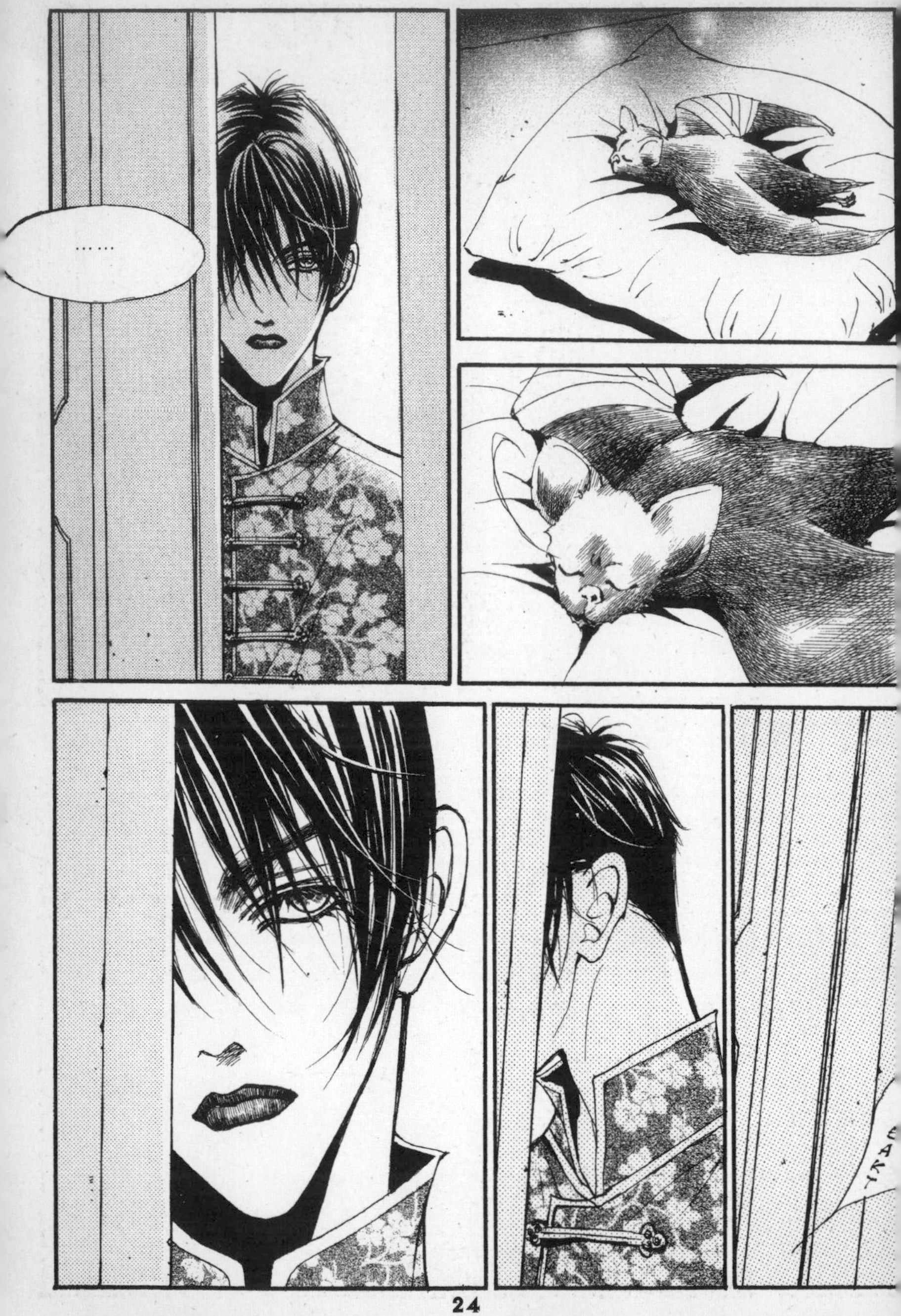

......
EAK

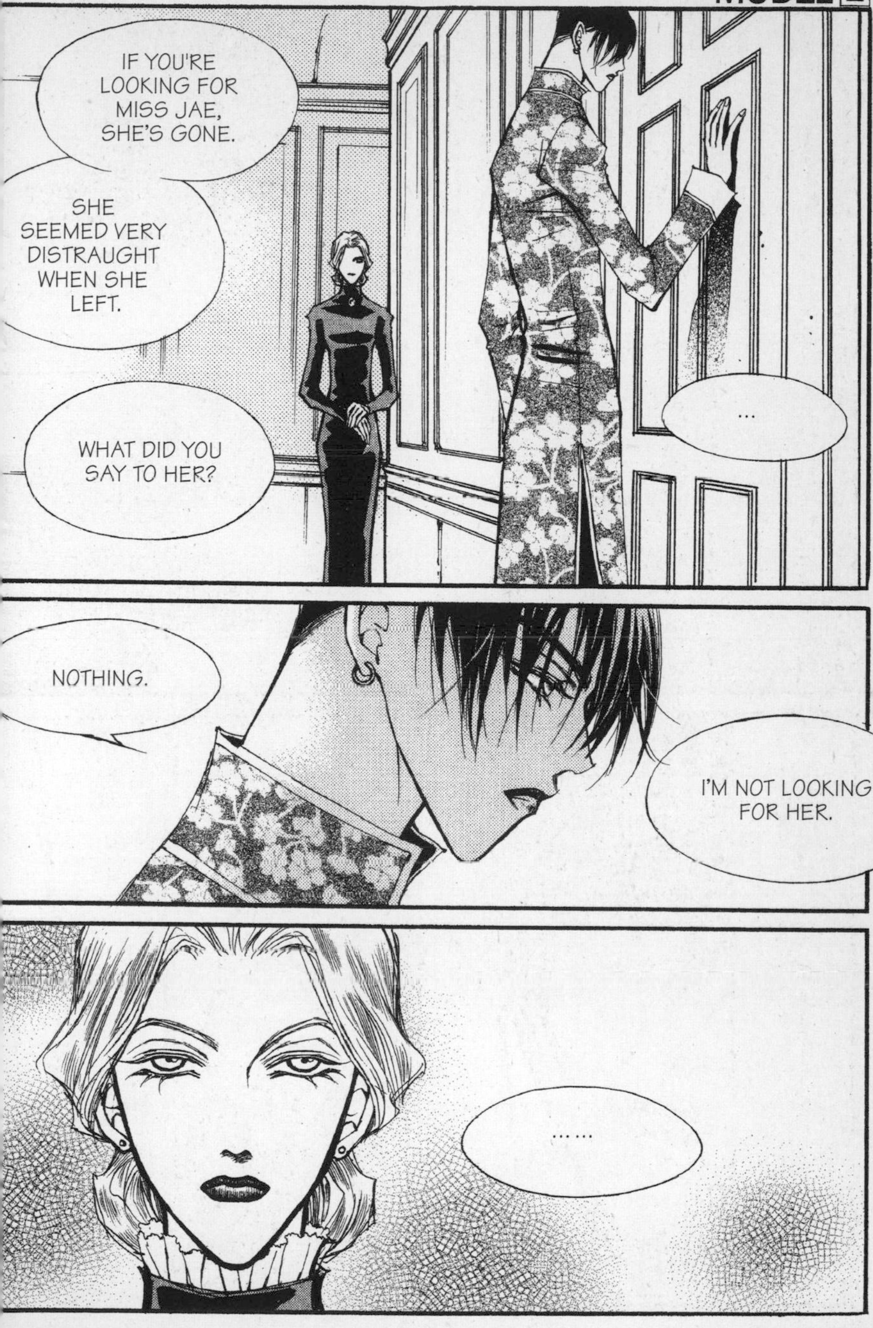
IF YOU'RE LOOKING FOR MISS JAE, SHE'S GONE.
SHE SEEMED VERY DISTRAUGHT WHEN SHE LEFT.
WHAT DID YOU SAY TO HER?
...
NOTHING.
I'M NOT LOOKING FOR HER.
......

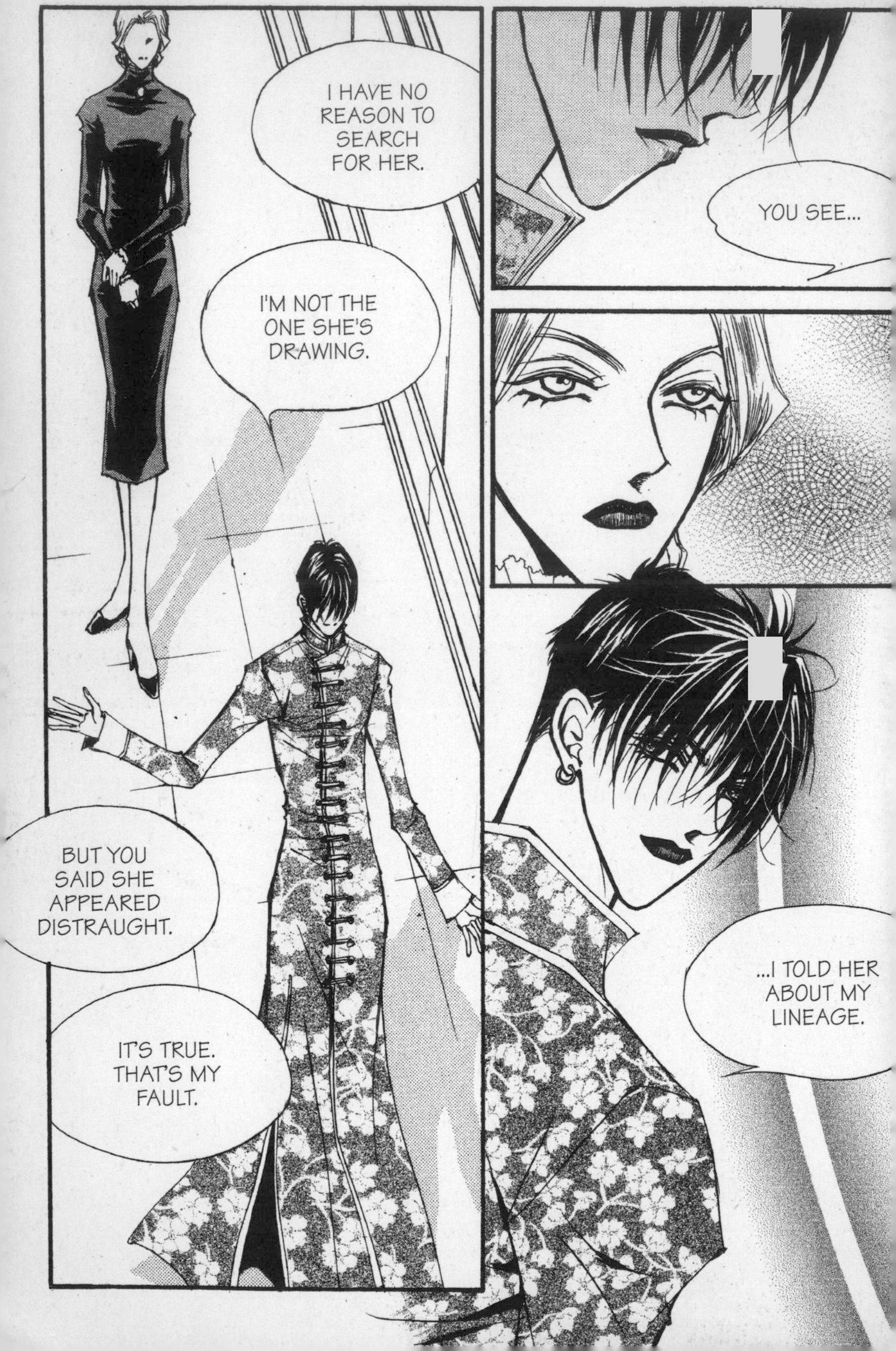
I HAVE NO REASON TO SEARCH FOR HER.
I'M NOT THE ONE SHE'S DRAWING.
BUT YOU SAID SHE APPEARED DISTRAUGHT.
IT'S TRUE. THAT'S MY FAULT.
YOU SEE...
...I TOLD HER ABOUT MY LINEAGE.

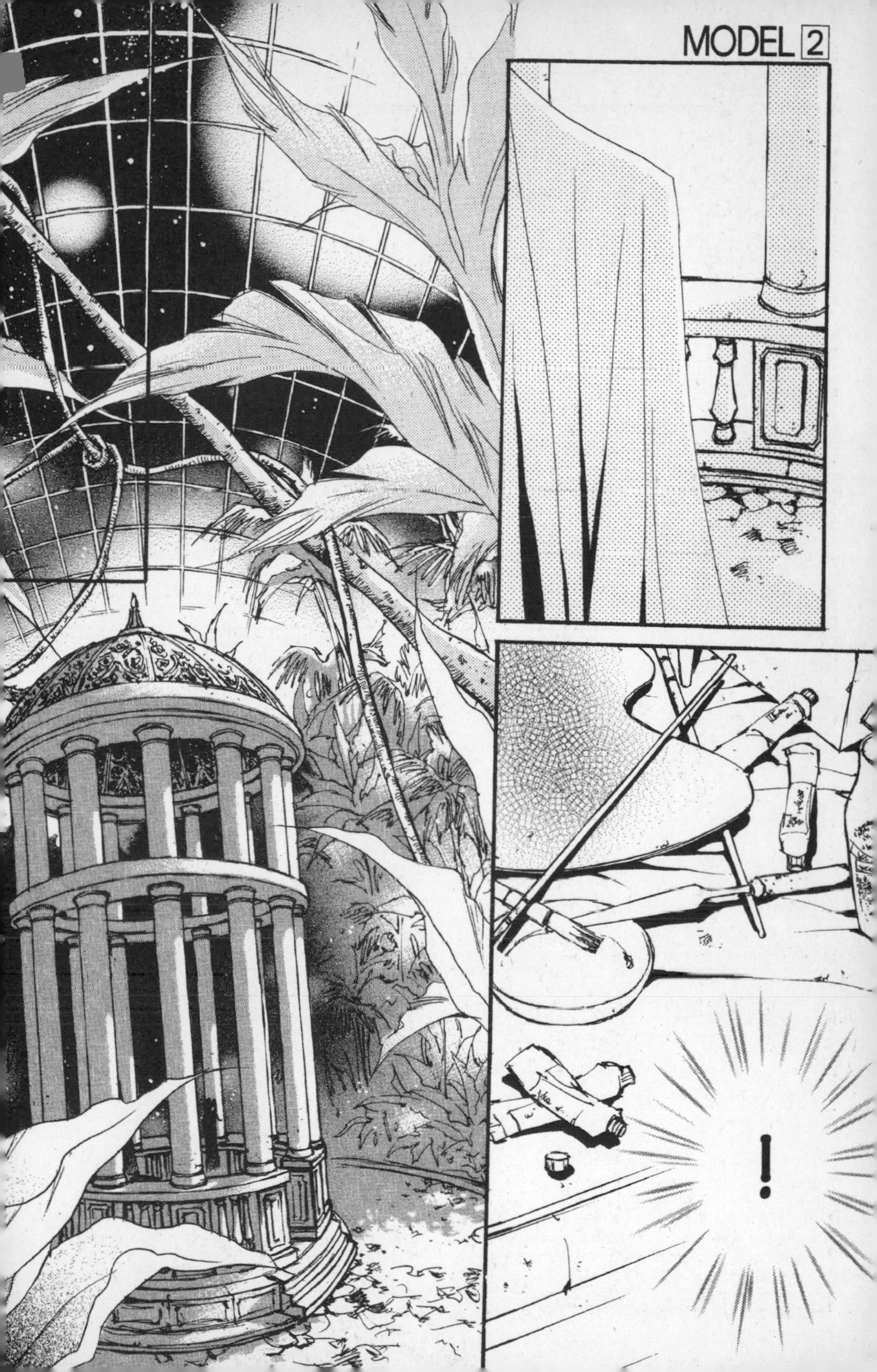
!

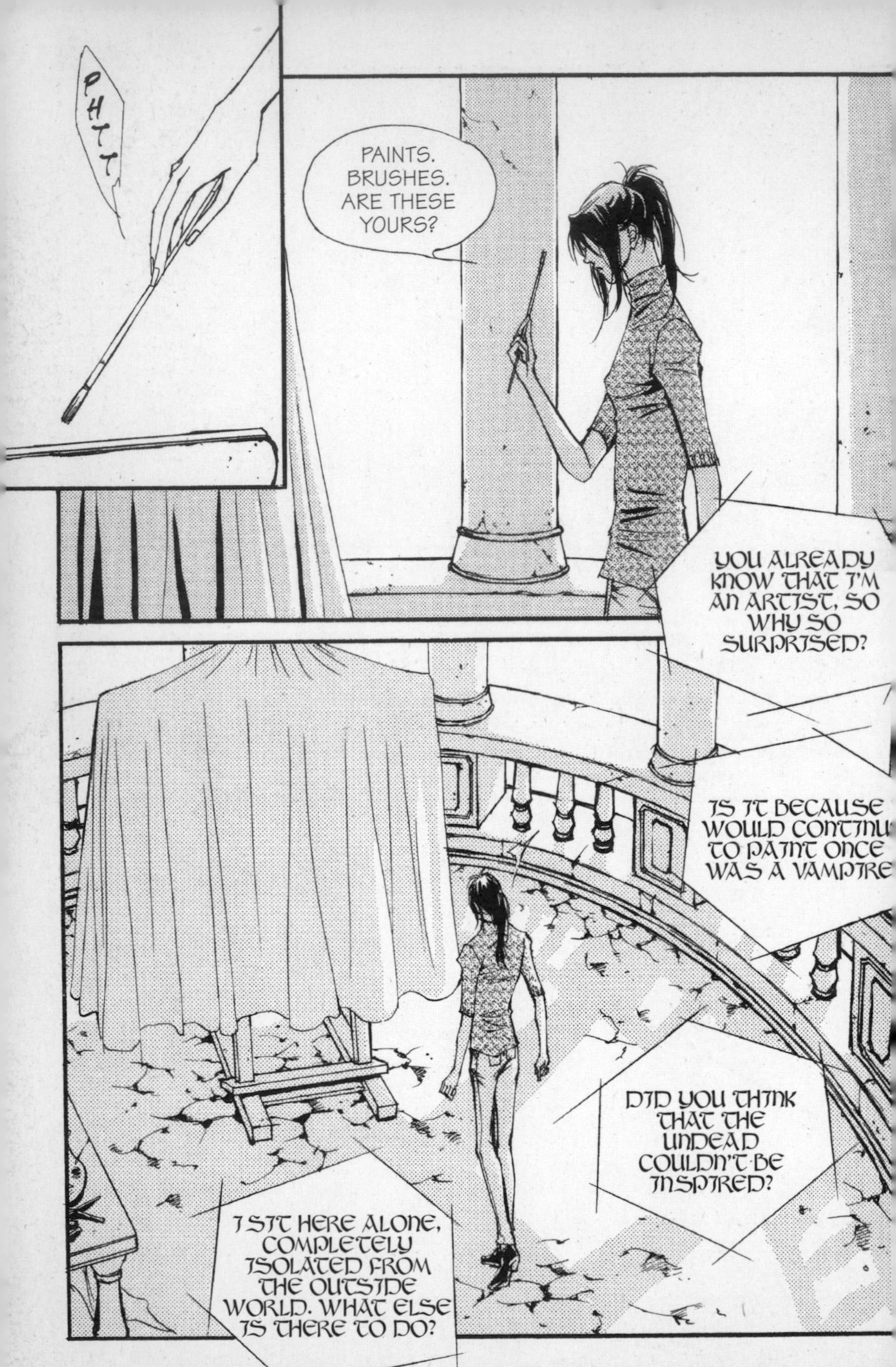
PHTT
PAINTS. BRUSHES. ARE THESE YOURS?
YOU ALREADY KNOW THAT I'M AN ARTIST, SO WHY SO SURPRISED?
IS IT BECAUSE WOULD CONTINU TO PAINT ONCE WAS A VAMPIRE
DID YOU THINK THAT THE UNDEAD COULDN'T BE INSPIRED?
I SIT HERE ALONE, COMPLETELY ISOLATED FROM THE OUTSIDE WORLD. WHAT ELSE IS THERE TO DO?

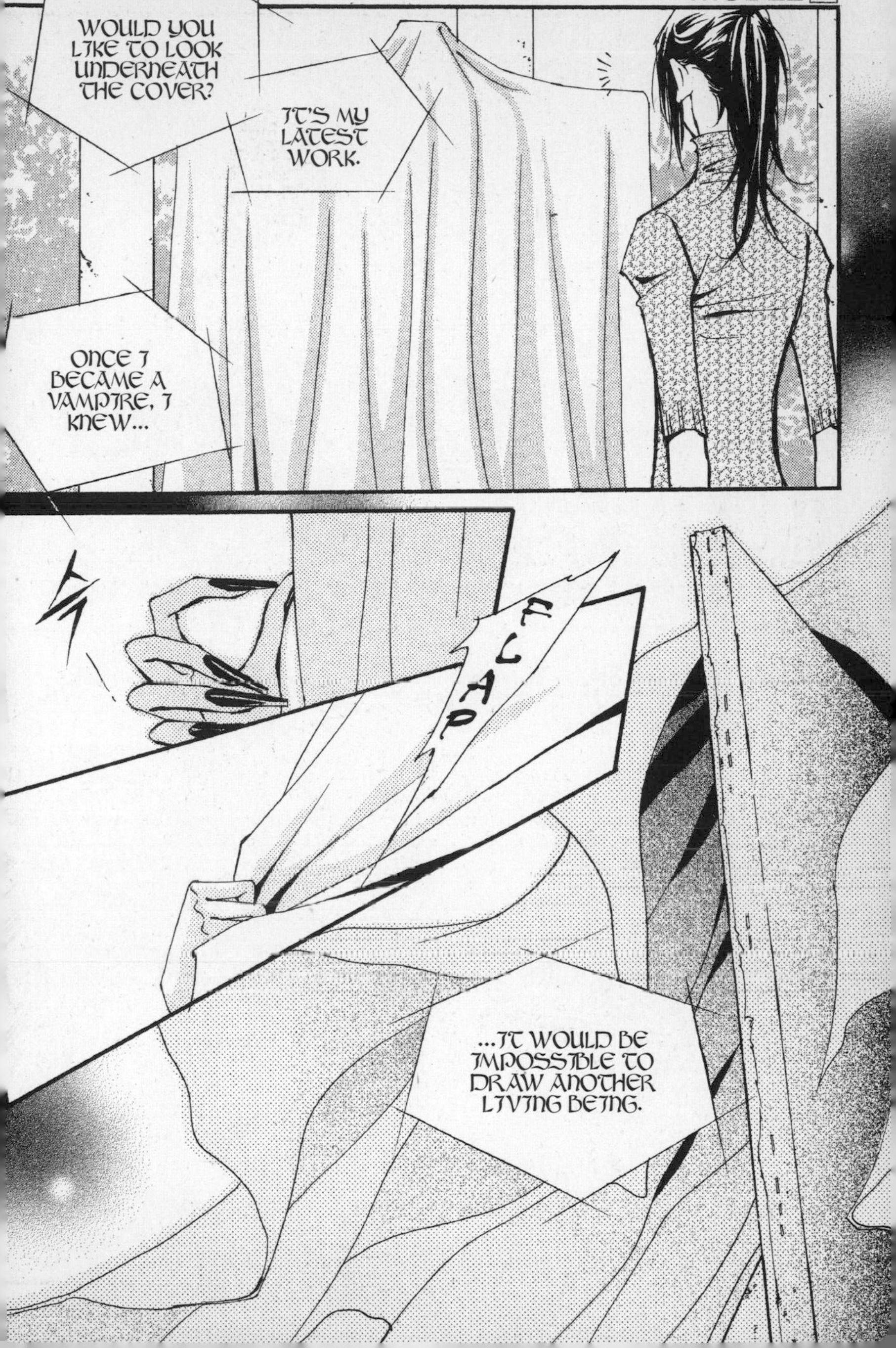
WOULD YOU LIKE TO LOOK UNDERNEATH THE COVER?
IT'S MY LATEST WORK.
ONCE I BECAME A VAMPIRE, I KNEW...
FLAP
...IT WOULD BE IMPOSSIBLE TO DRAW ANOTHER LIVING BEING.

CHAPTER TWO
MARY

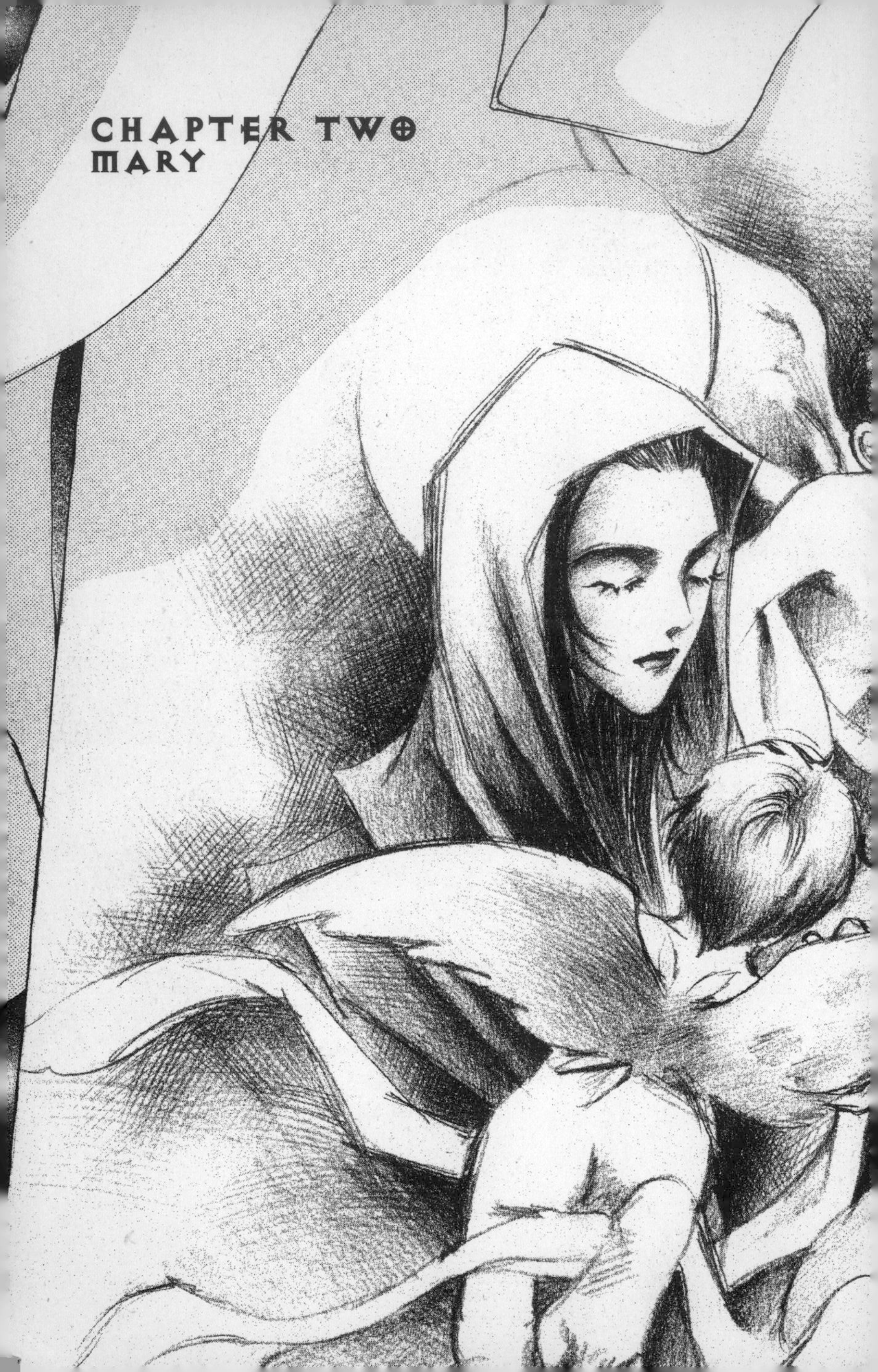

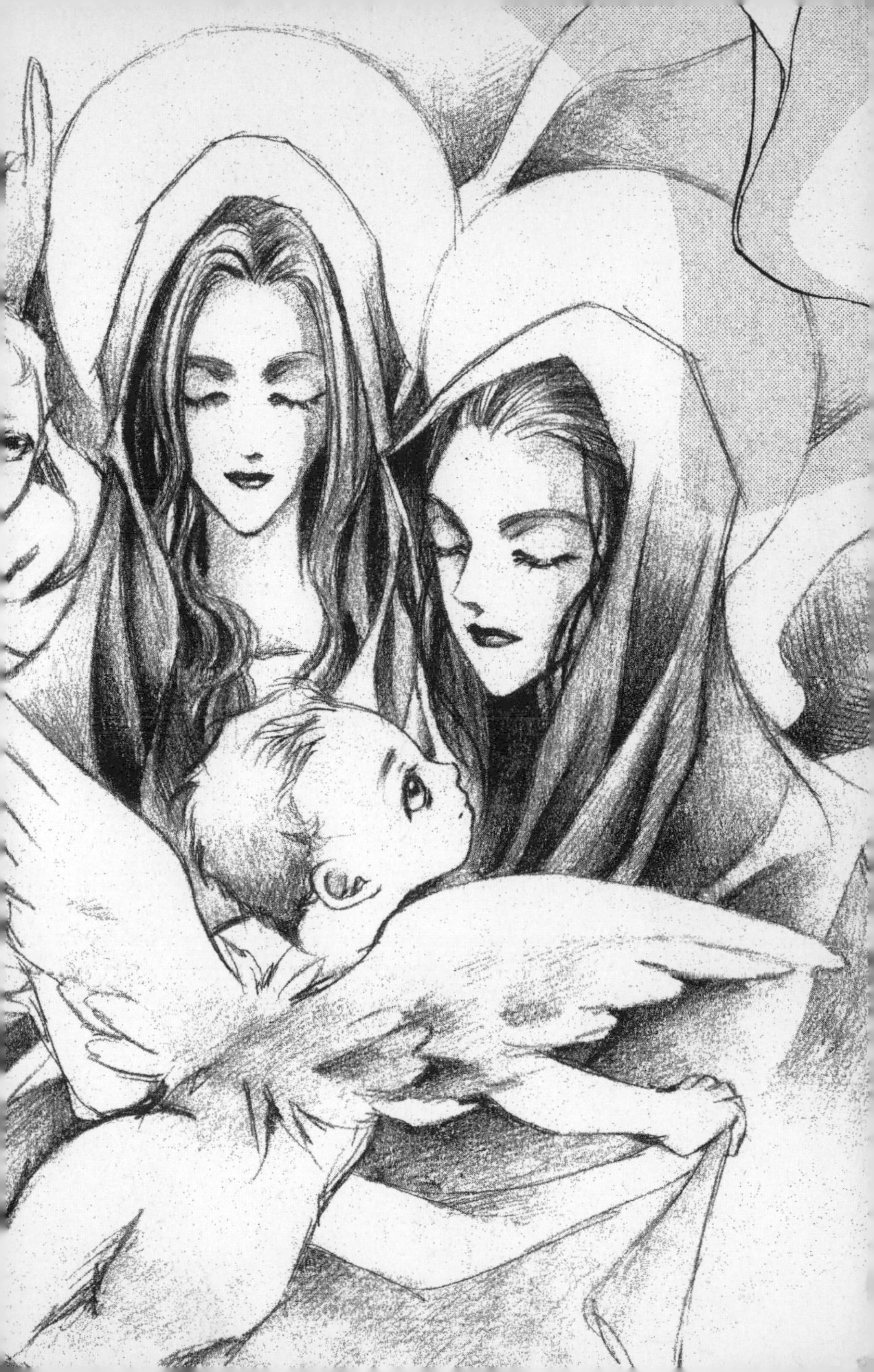

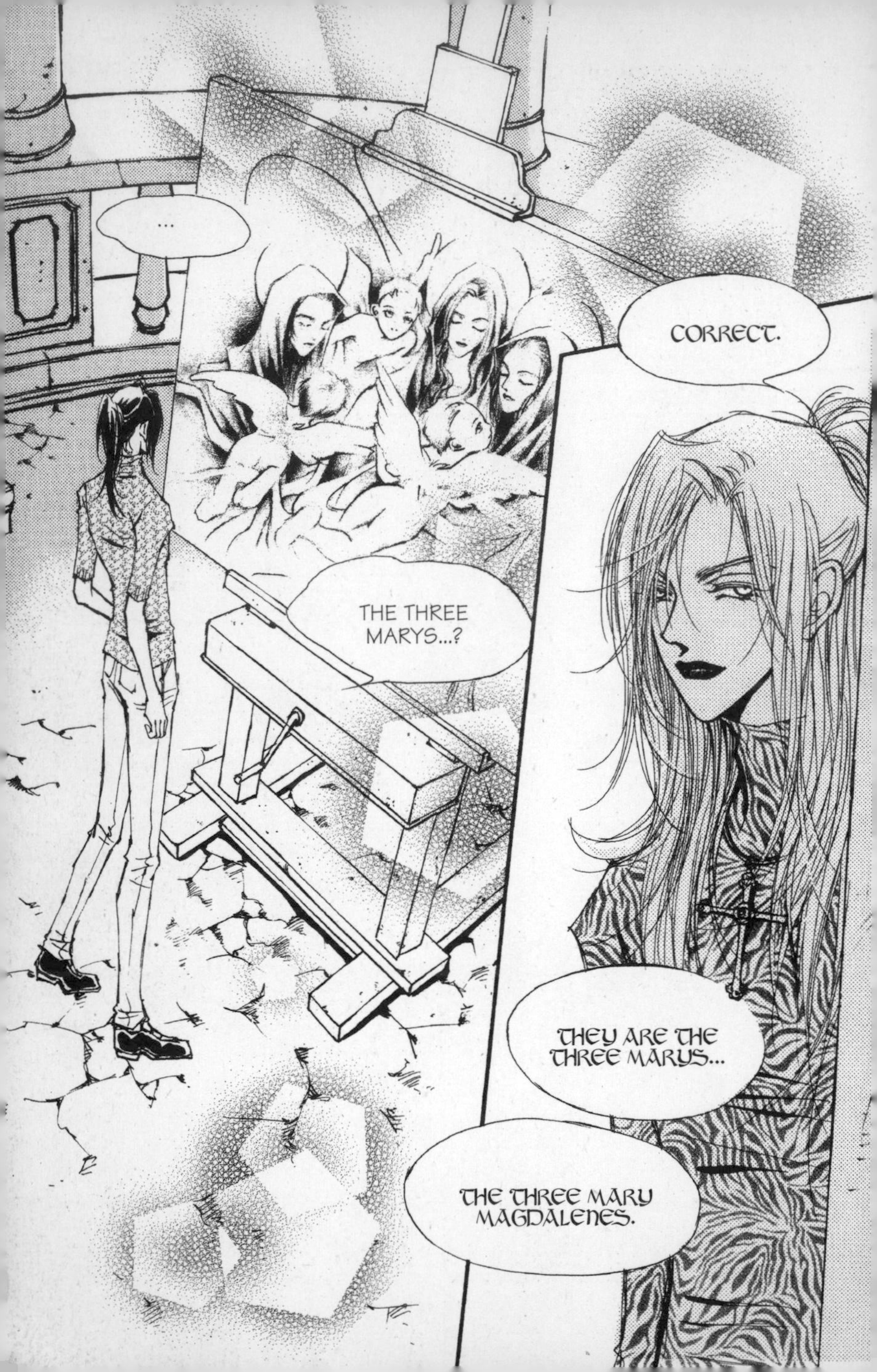
...
THE THREE MARYS...?
CORRECT.
THEY ARE THE THREE MARYS...
THE THREE MARY MAGDALENES.

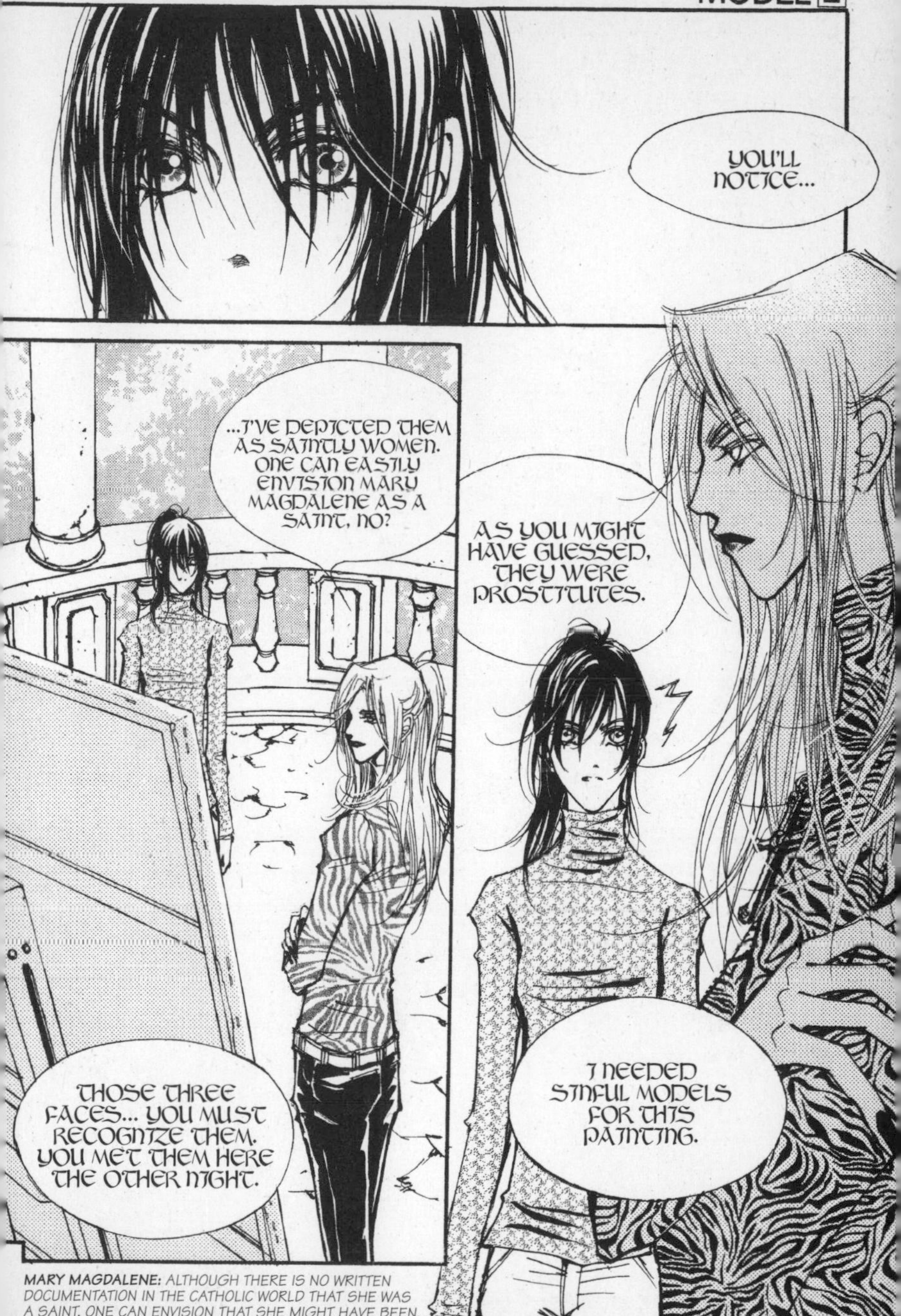
YOU'LL NOTICE...
...I'VE DEPICTED THEM AS SAINTLY WOMEN. ONE CAN EASILY ENVISION MARY MAGDALENE AS A SAINT, NO?
THOSE THREE FACES... YOU MUST RECOGNIZE THEM. YOU MET THEM HERE THE OTHER NIGHT.
AS YOU MIGHT HAVE GUESSED, THEY WERE PROSTITUTES.
I NEEDED SINFUL MODELS FOR THIS PAINTING.

MARY MAGDALENE: *ALTHOUGH THERE IS NO WRITTEN DOCUMENTATION IN THE CATHOLIC WORLD THAT SHE WAS A SAINT, ONE CAN ENVISION THAT SHE MIGHT HAVE BEEN.*

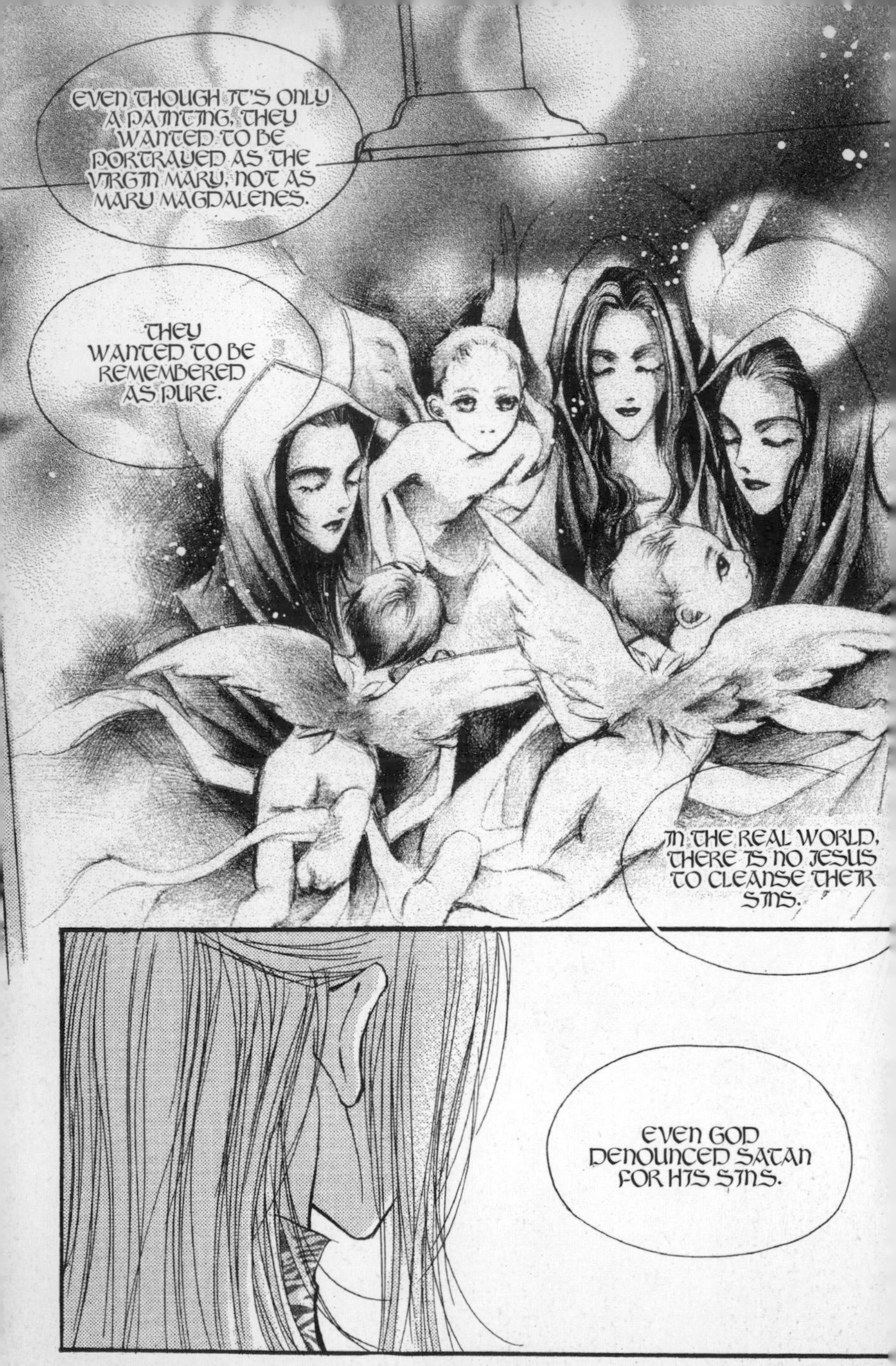
EVEN THOUGH IT'S ONLY A PAINTING, THEY WANTED TO BE PORTRAYED AS THE VIRGIN MARY, NOT AS MARY MAGDALENES.
THEY WANTED TO BE REMEMBERED AS PURE.
IN THE REAL WORLD, THERE IS NO JESUS TO CLEANSE THEIR SINS.
EVEN GOD DENOUNCED SATAN FOR HIS SINS.

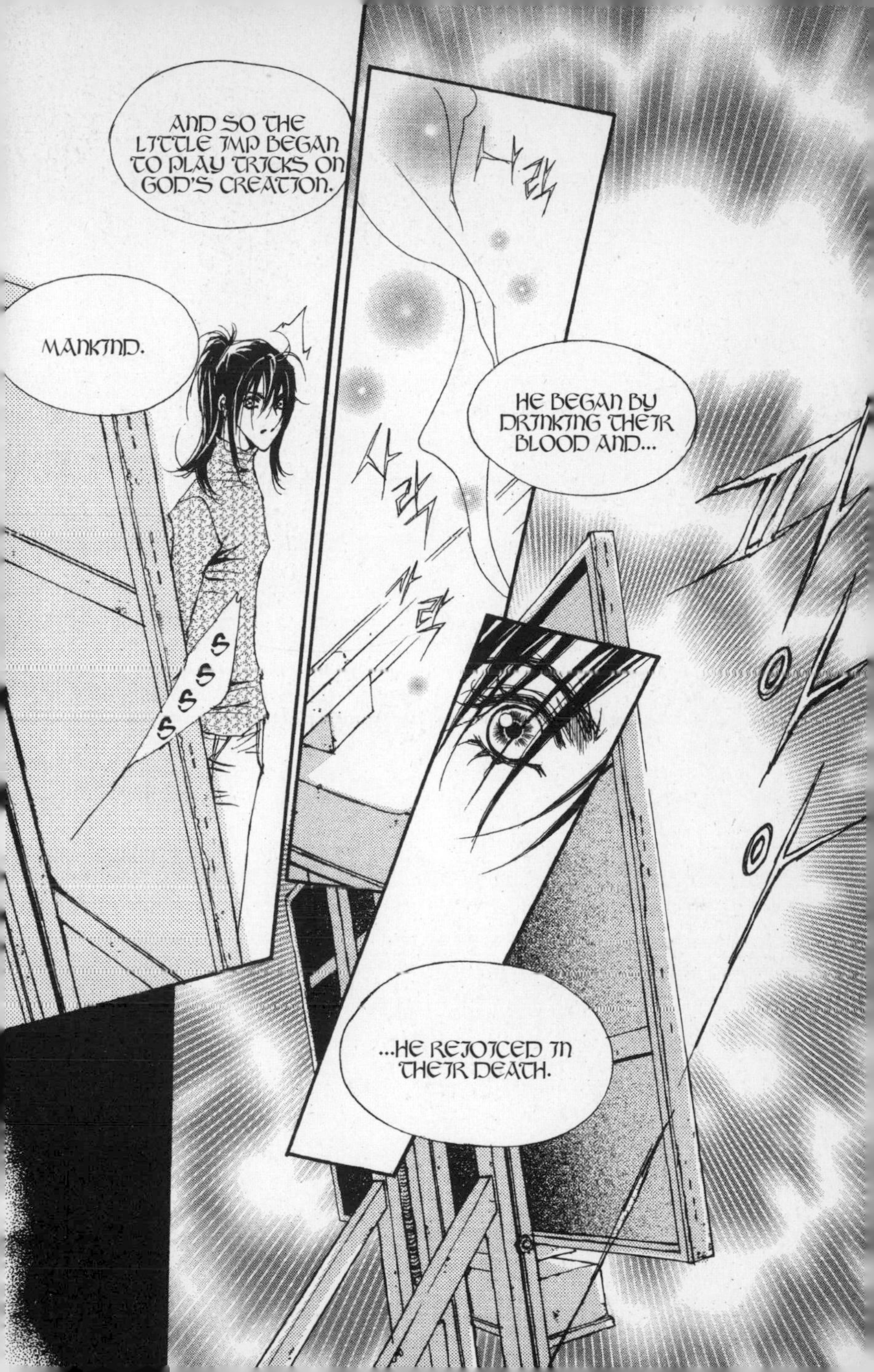
AND SO THE LITTLE IMP BEGAN TO PLAY TRICKS ON GOD'S CREATION.
MANKIND.
SSSS
HE BEGAN BY DRINKING THEIR BLOOD AND...
...HE REJOICED IN THEIR DEATH.

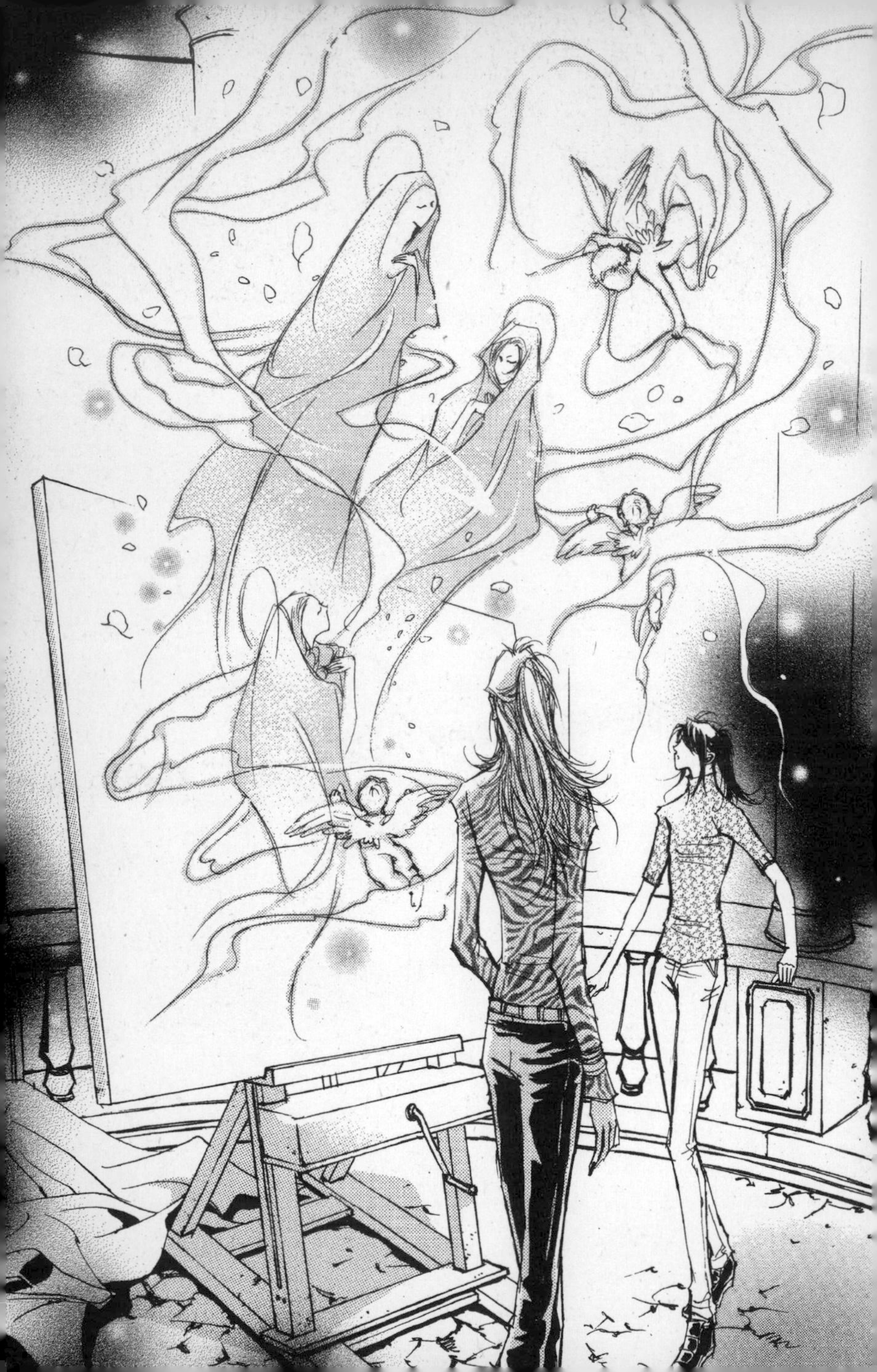

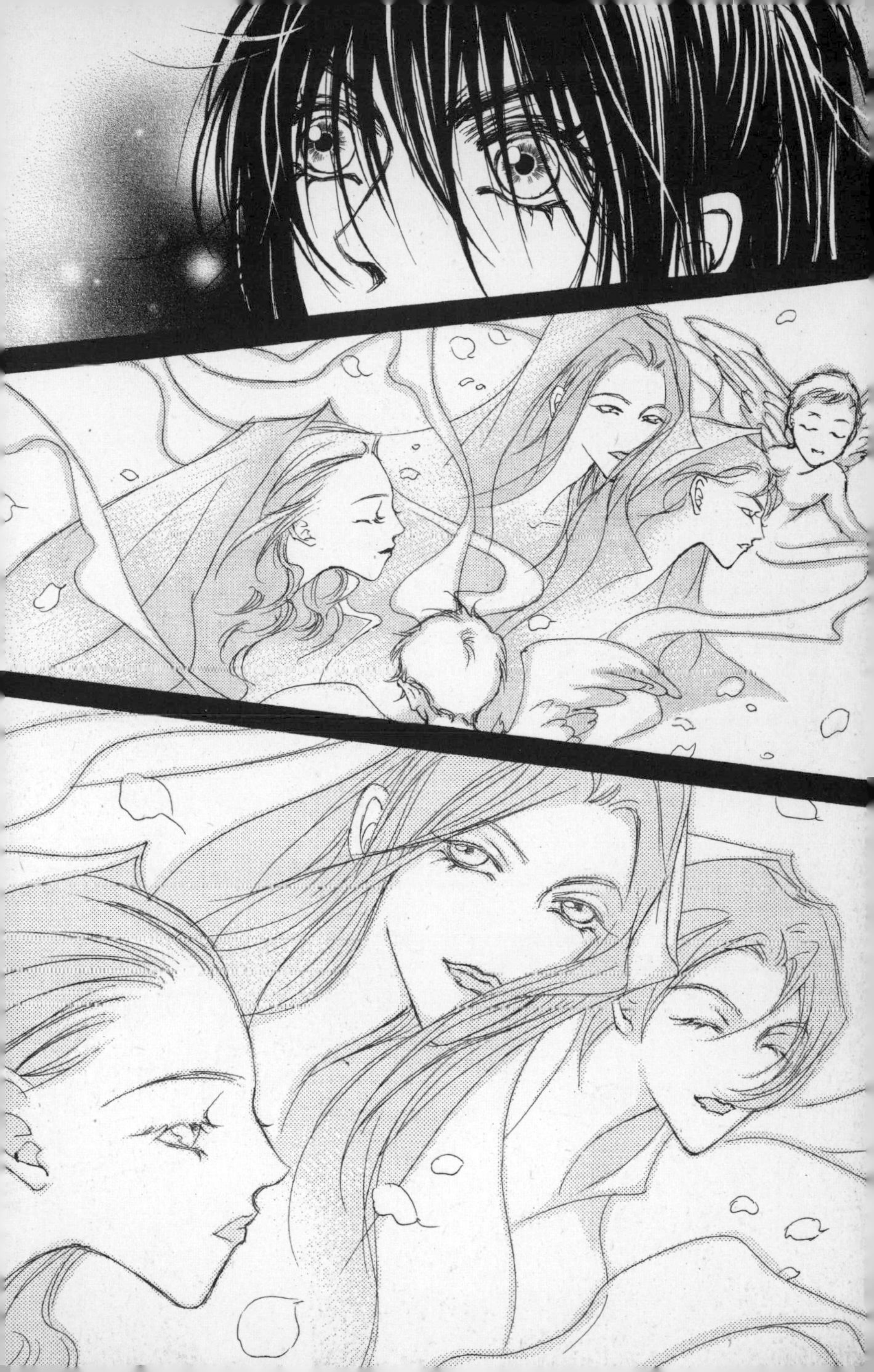

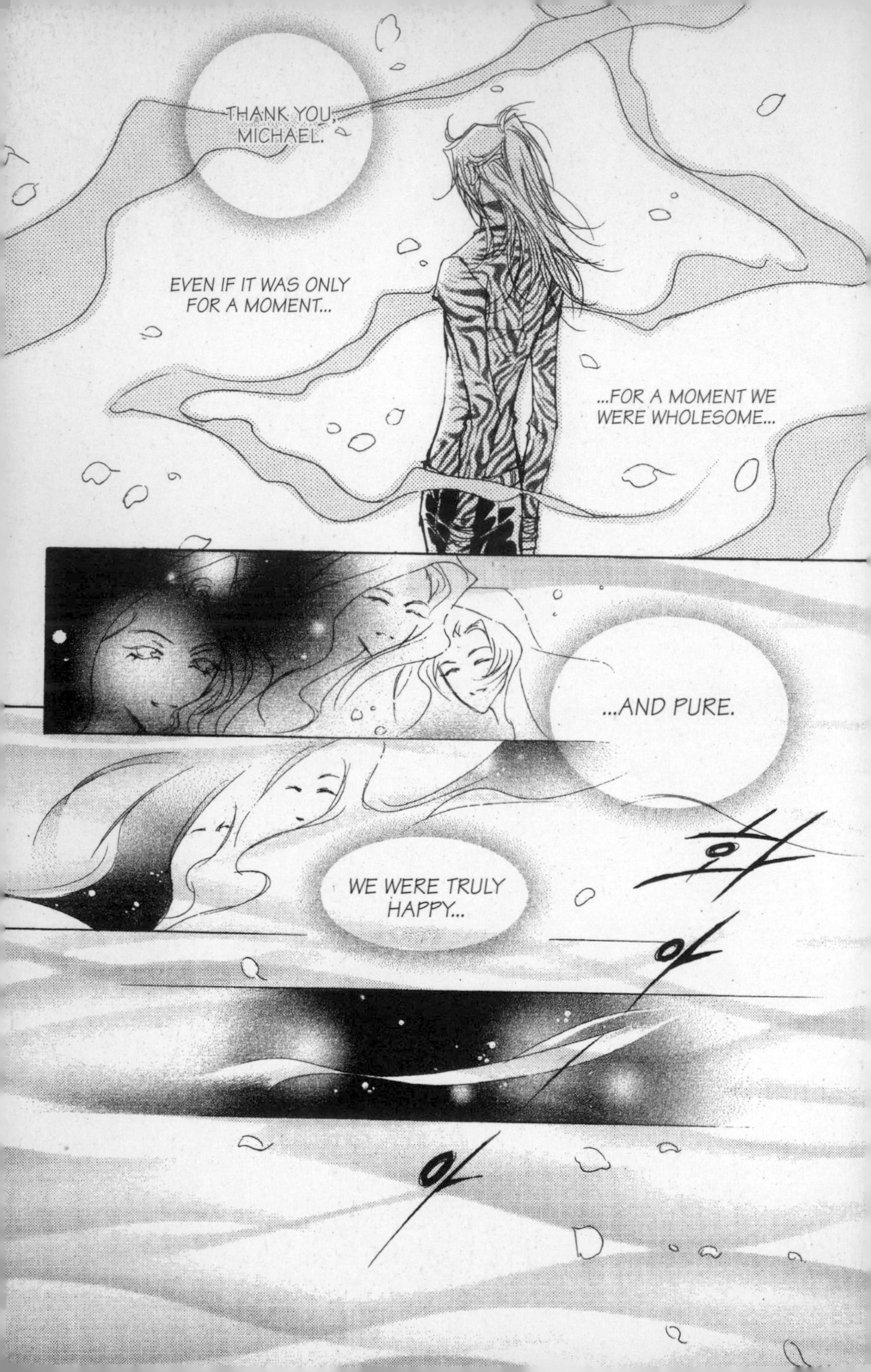
THANK YOU, MICHAEL.
EVEN IF IT WAS ONLY FOR A MOMENT...
...FOR A MOMENT WE WERE WHOLESOME...
...AND PURE.
WE WERE TRULY HAPPY...

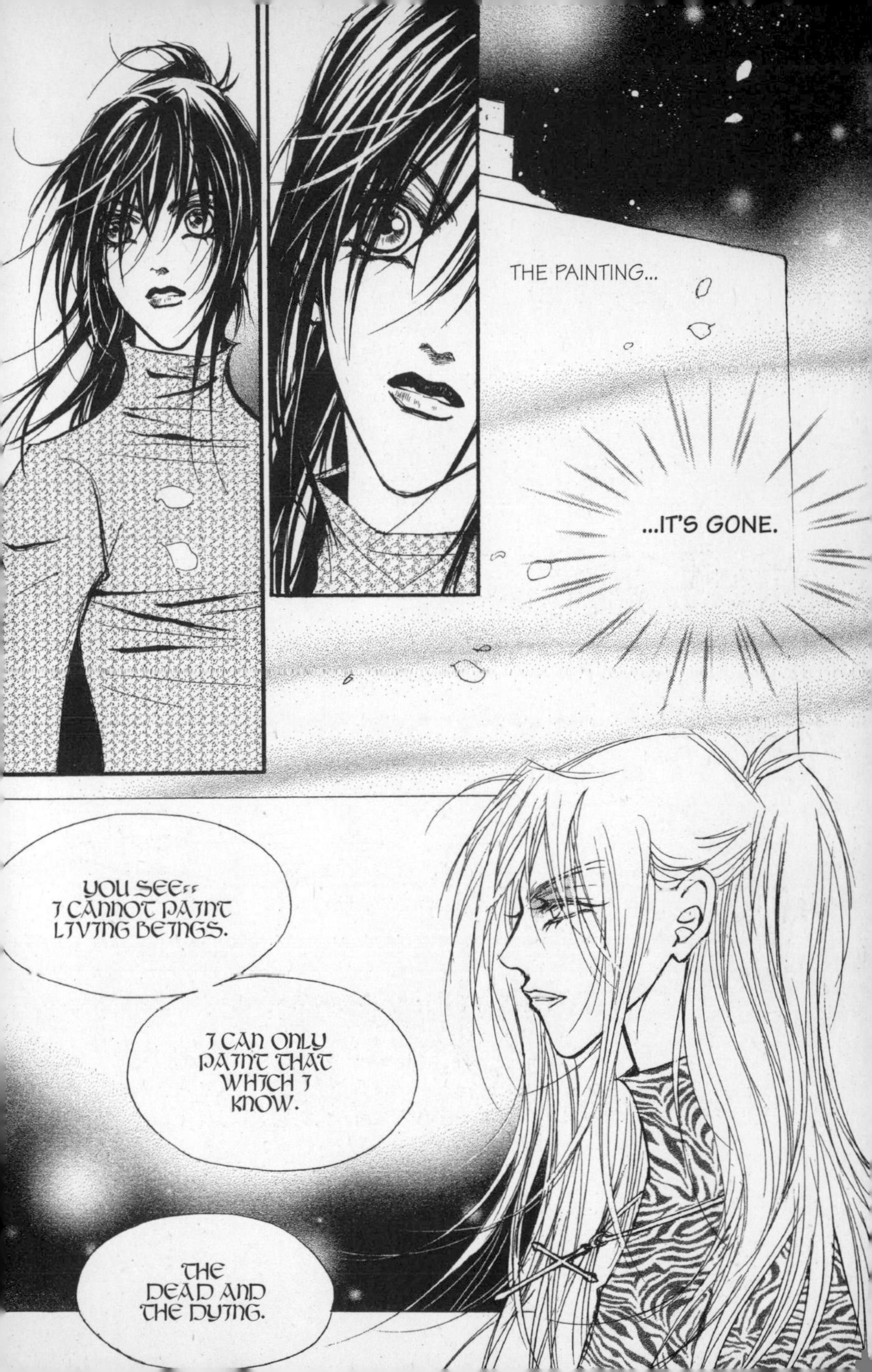
THE PAINTING...
...IT'S GONE.
YOU SEE.. I CANNOT PAINT LIVING BEINGS.
I CAN ONLY PAINT THAT WHICH I KNOW.
THE DEAD AND THE DYING.

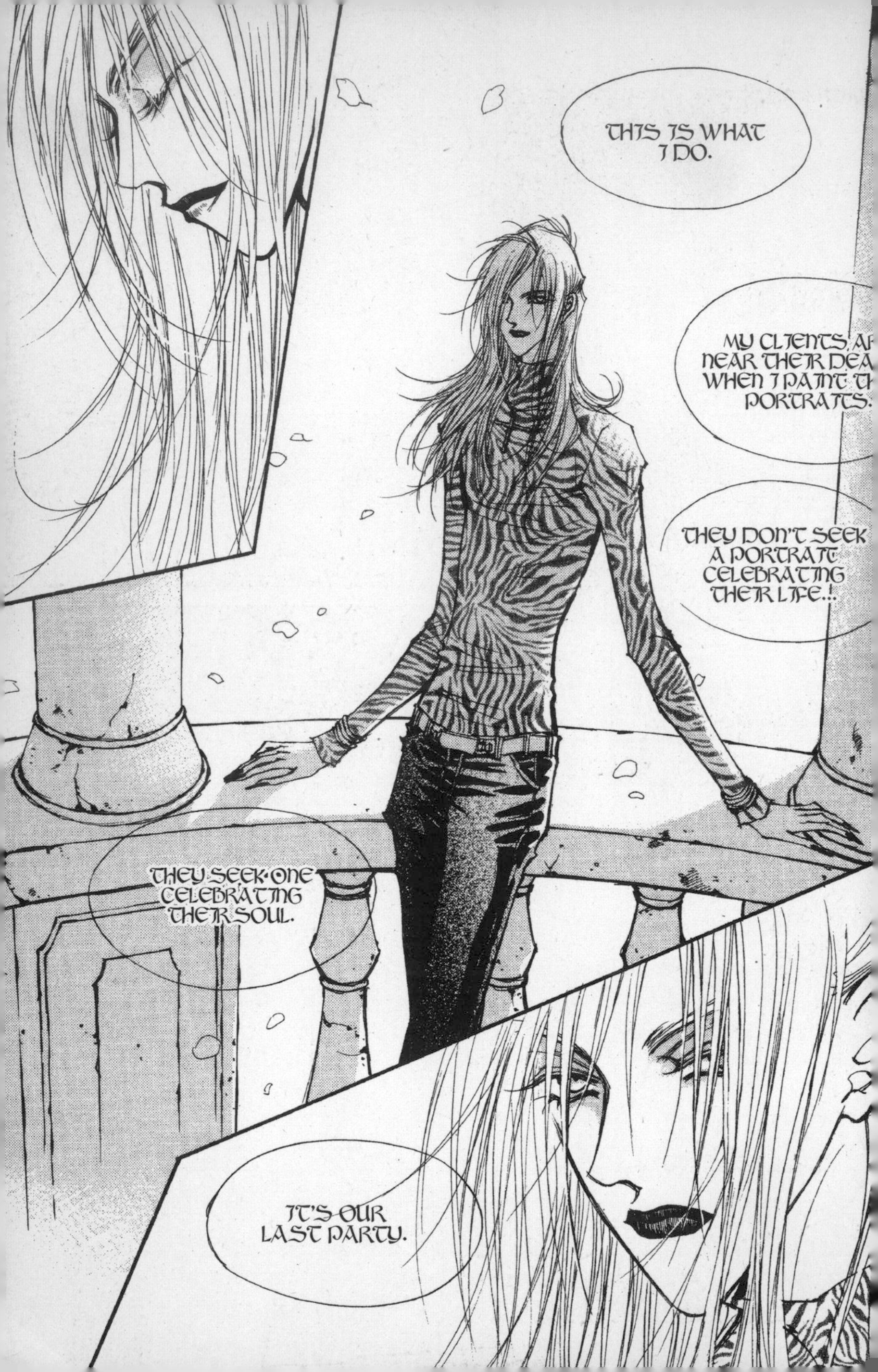
THIS IS WHAT I DO.
MY CLIENTS AR NEAR THEIR DEA WHEN I PAINT TH PORTRAITS.
THEY DON'T SEEK A PORTRAIT CELEBRATING THEIR LIFE...
THEY SEEK ONE CELEBRATING THEIR SOUL.
IT'S OUR LAST PARTY.

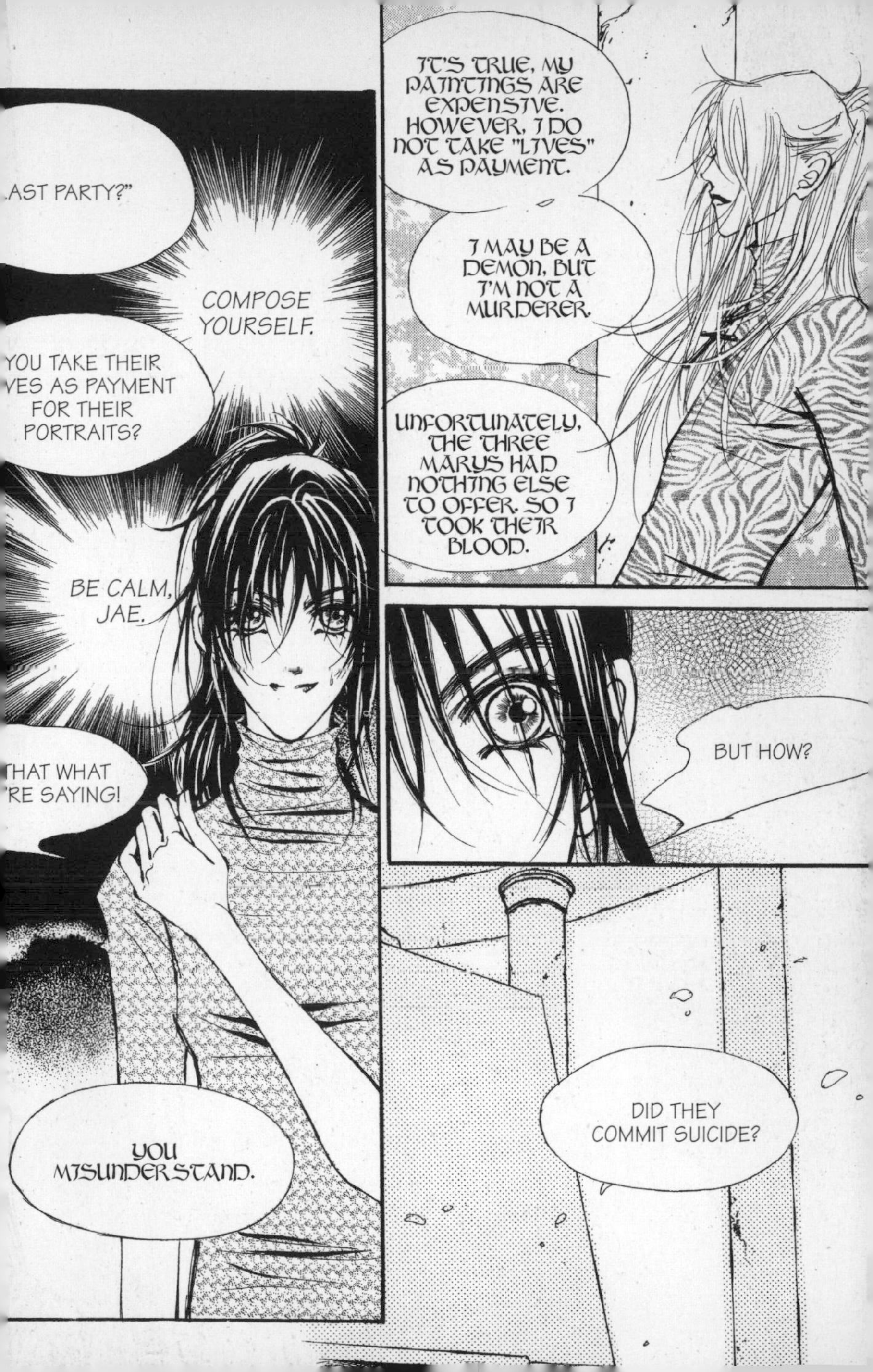
AST PARTY?"
COMPOSE YOURSELF.
YOU TAKE THEIR VES AS PAYMENT FOR THEIR PORTRAITS?
BE CALM, JAE.
THAT WHAT 'RE SAYING!
YOU MISUNDERSTAND.
IT'S TRUE, MY PAINTINGS ARE EXPENSIVE. HOWEVER, I DO NOT TAKE "LIVES" AS PAYMENT.
I MAY BE A DEMON, BUT I'M NOT A MURDERER.
UNFORTUNATELY, THE THREE MARYS HAD NOTHING ELSE TO OFFER. SO I TOOK THEIR BLOOD.
BUT HOW?
DID THEY COMMIT SUICIDE?

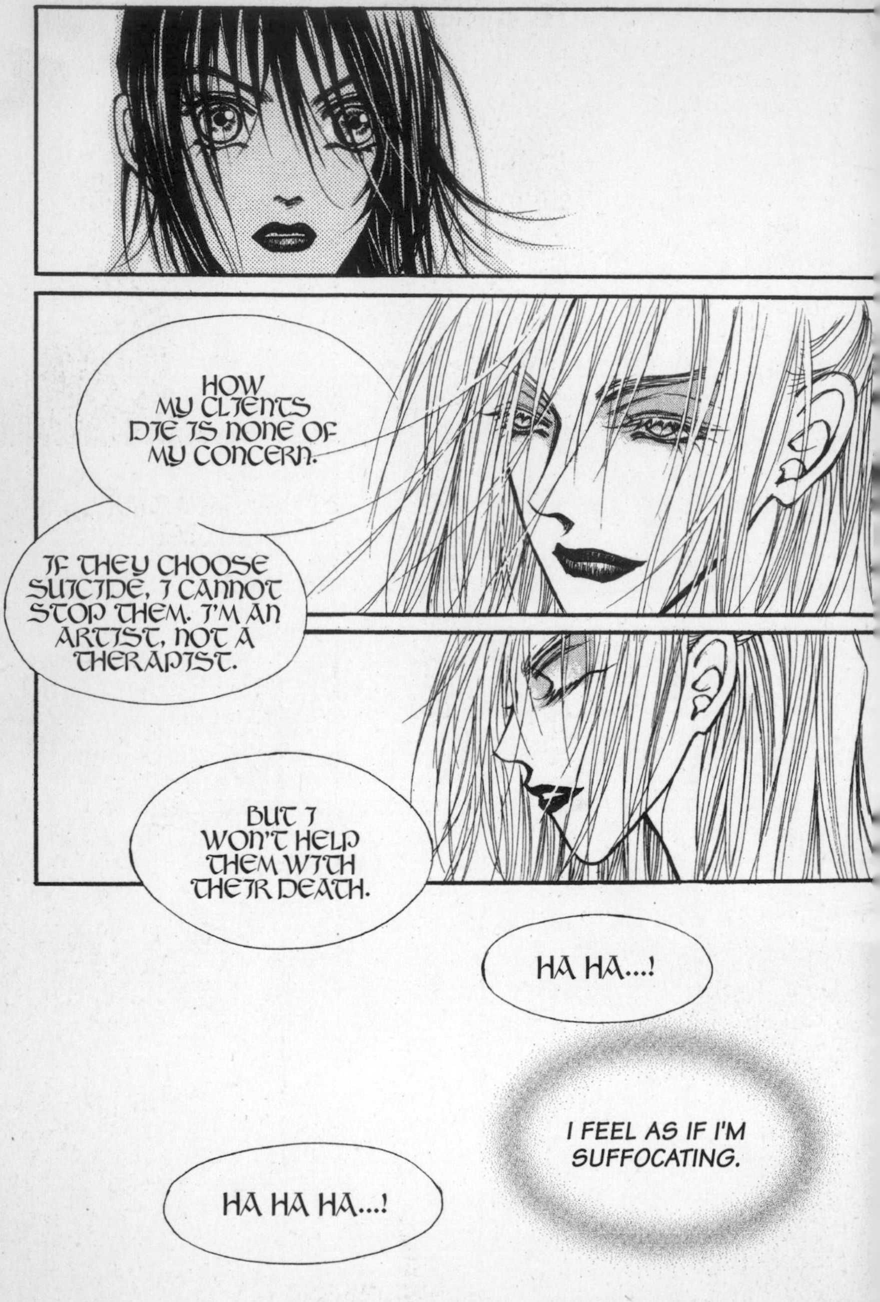
HOW MY CLIENTS DIE IS NONE OF MY CONCERN.
IF THEY CHOOSE SUICIDE, I CANNOT STOP THEM. I'M AN ARTIST, NOT A THERAPIST.
BUT I WON'T HELP THEM WITH THEIR DEATH.
HA HA...!
I FEEL AS IF I'M SUFFOCATING.
HA HA HA...!

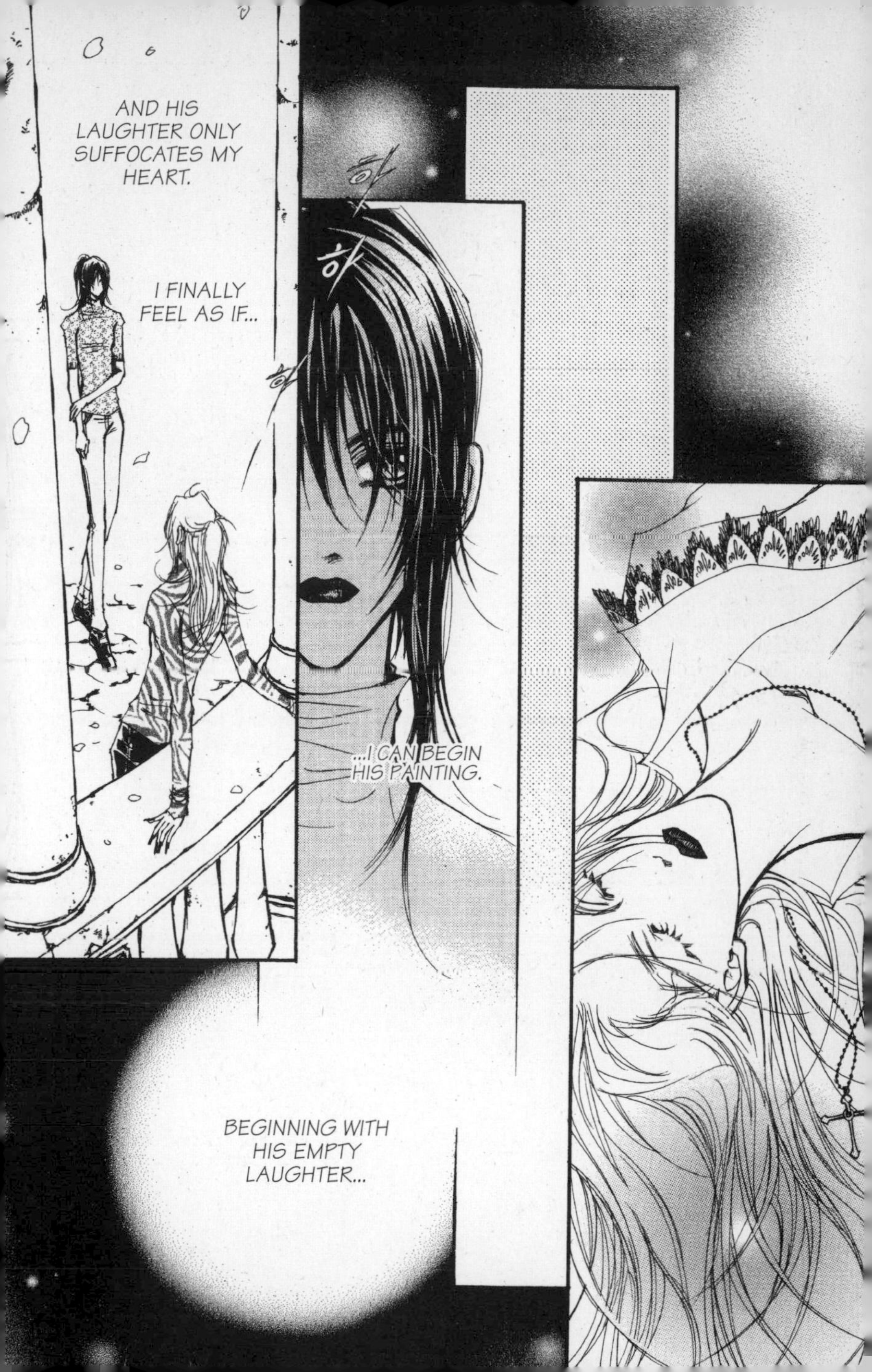
AND HIS LAUGHTER ONLY SUFFOCATES MY HEART.
I FINALLY FEEL AS IF...
하
하
하
...I CAN BEGIN HIS PAINTING.
BEGINNING WITH HIS EMPTY LAUGHTER...

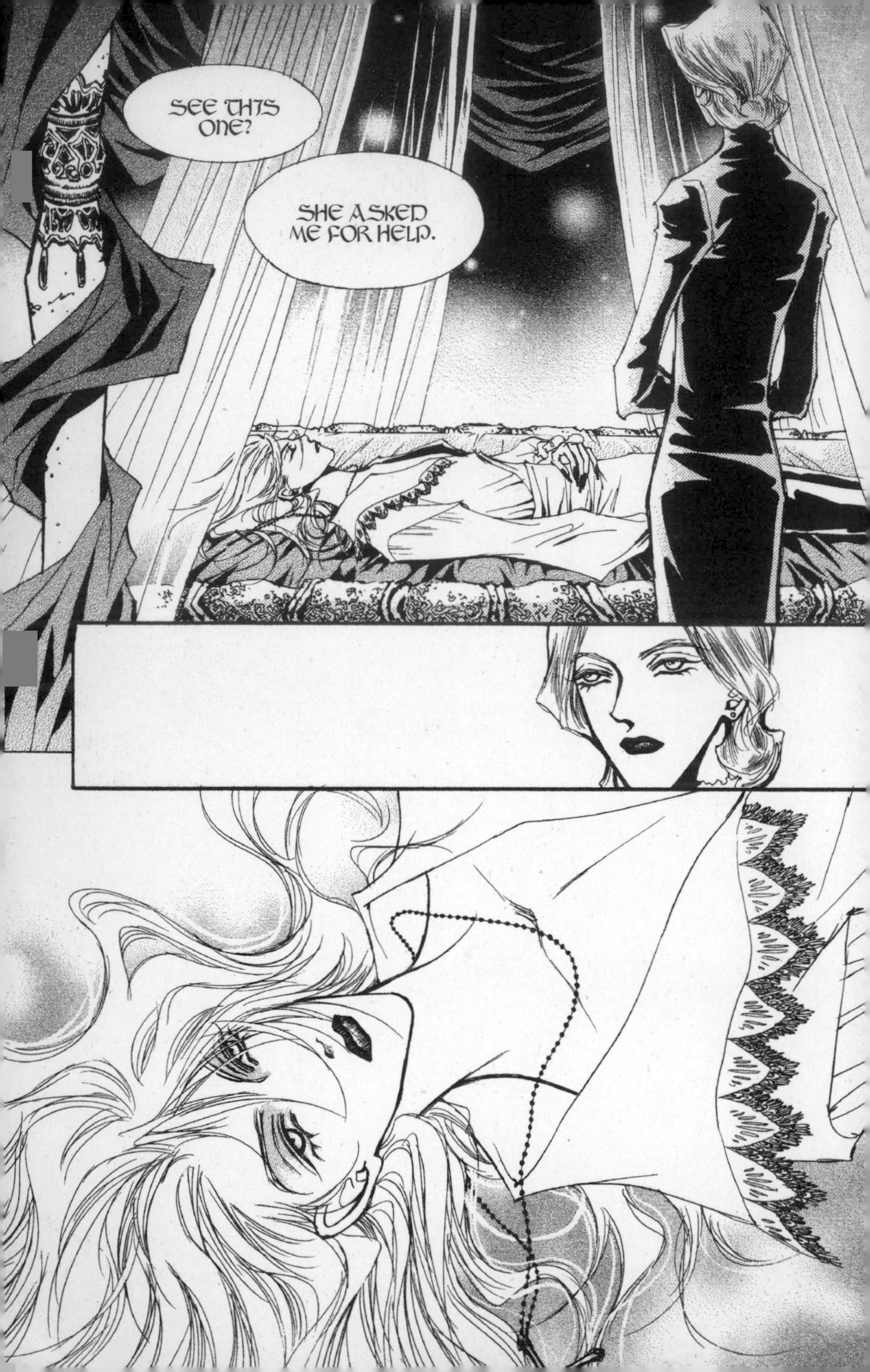
SEE THIS ONE?
SHE ASKED ME FOR HELP.

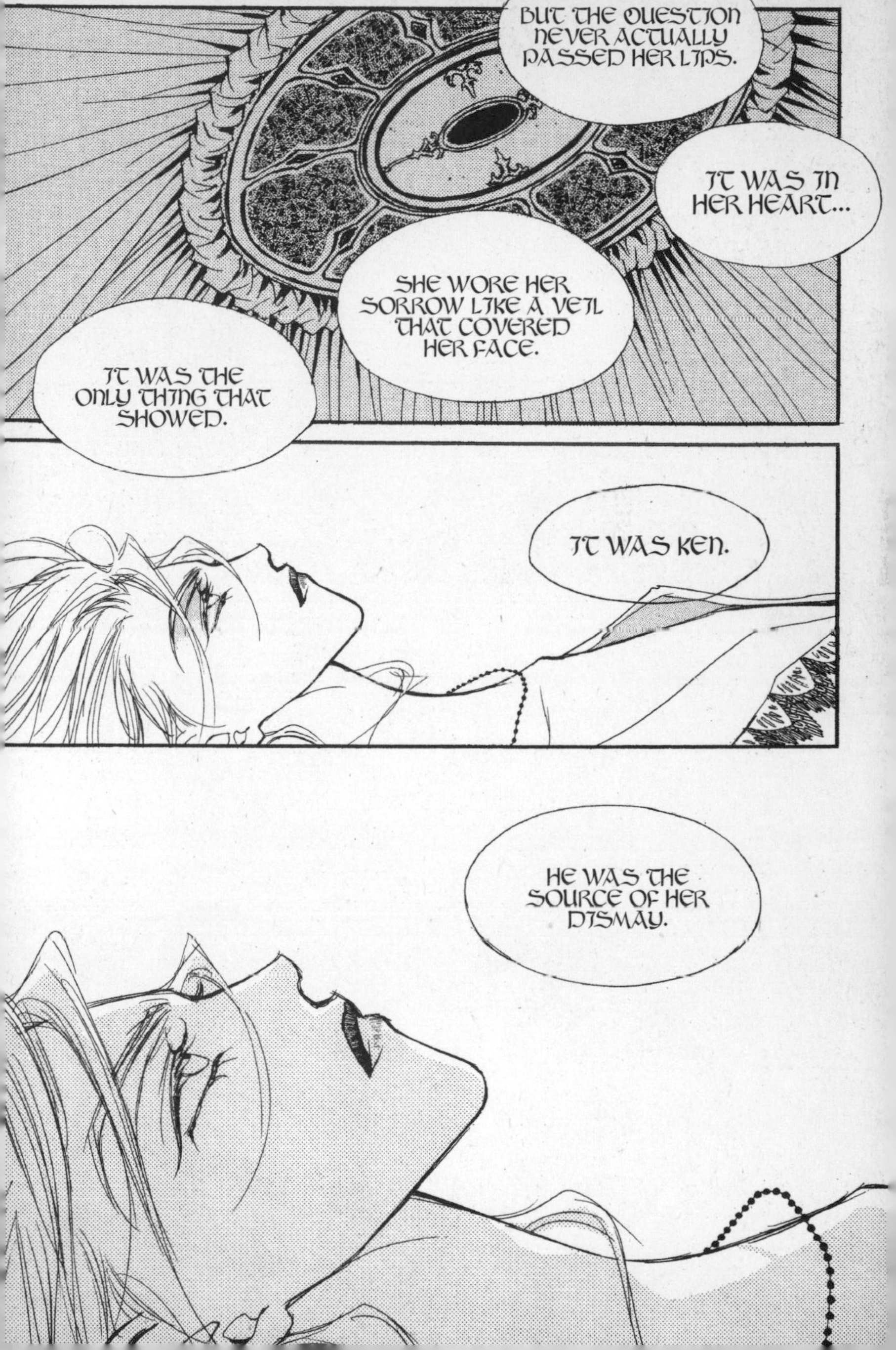
BUT THE QUESTION NEVER ACTUALLY PASSED HER LIPS.
IT WAS IN HER HEART...
SHE WORE HER SORROW LIKE A VEIL THAT COVERED HER FACE.
IT WAS THE ONLY THING THAT SHOWED.
IT WAS KEN.
HE WAS THE SOURCE OF HER DISMAY.

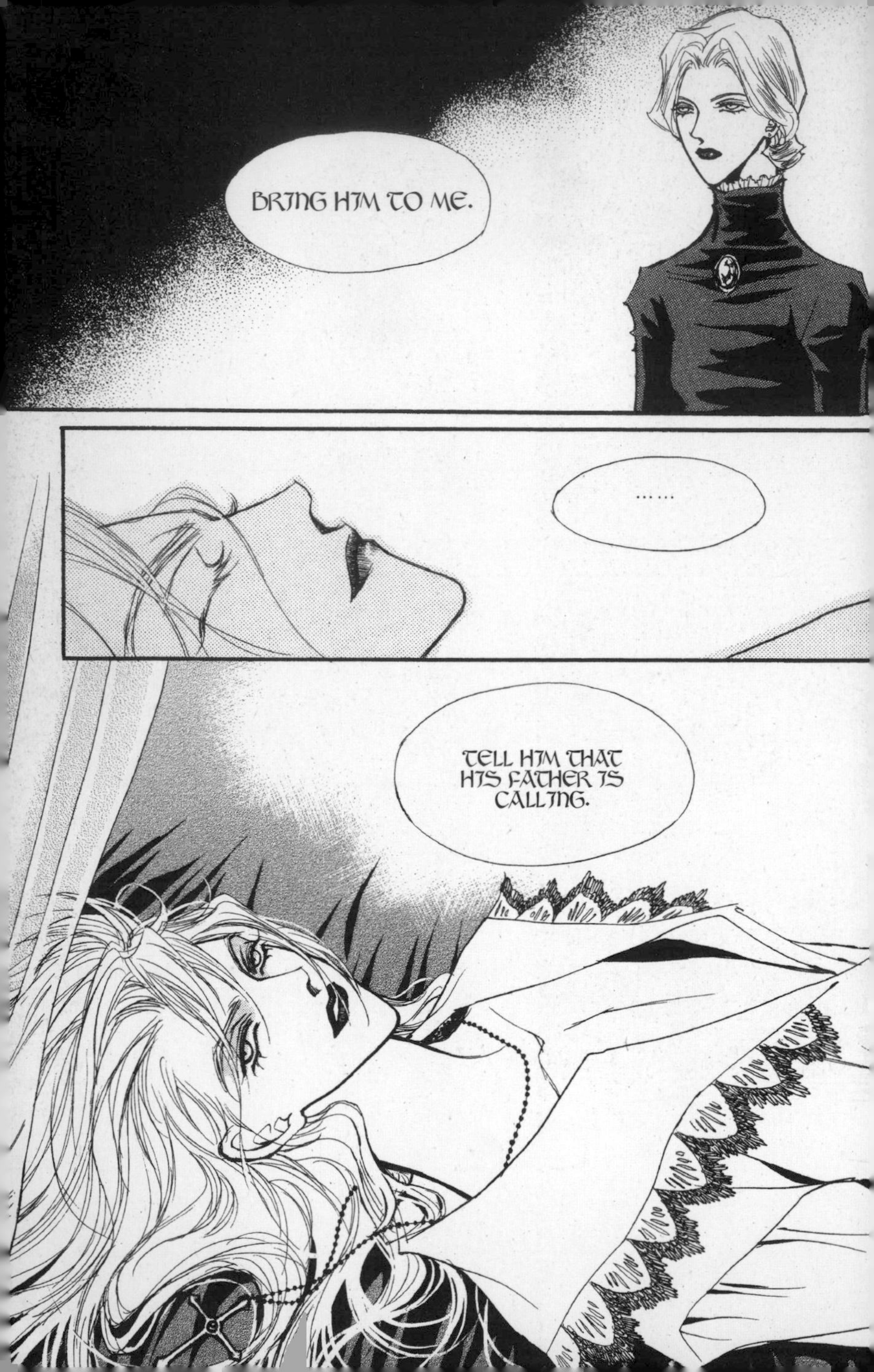
BRING HIM TO ME.
......
TELL HIM THAT HIS FATHER IS CALLING.

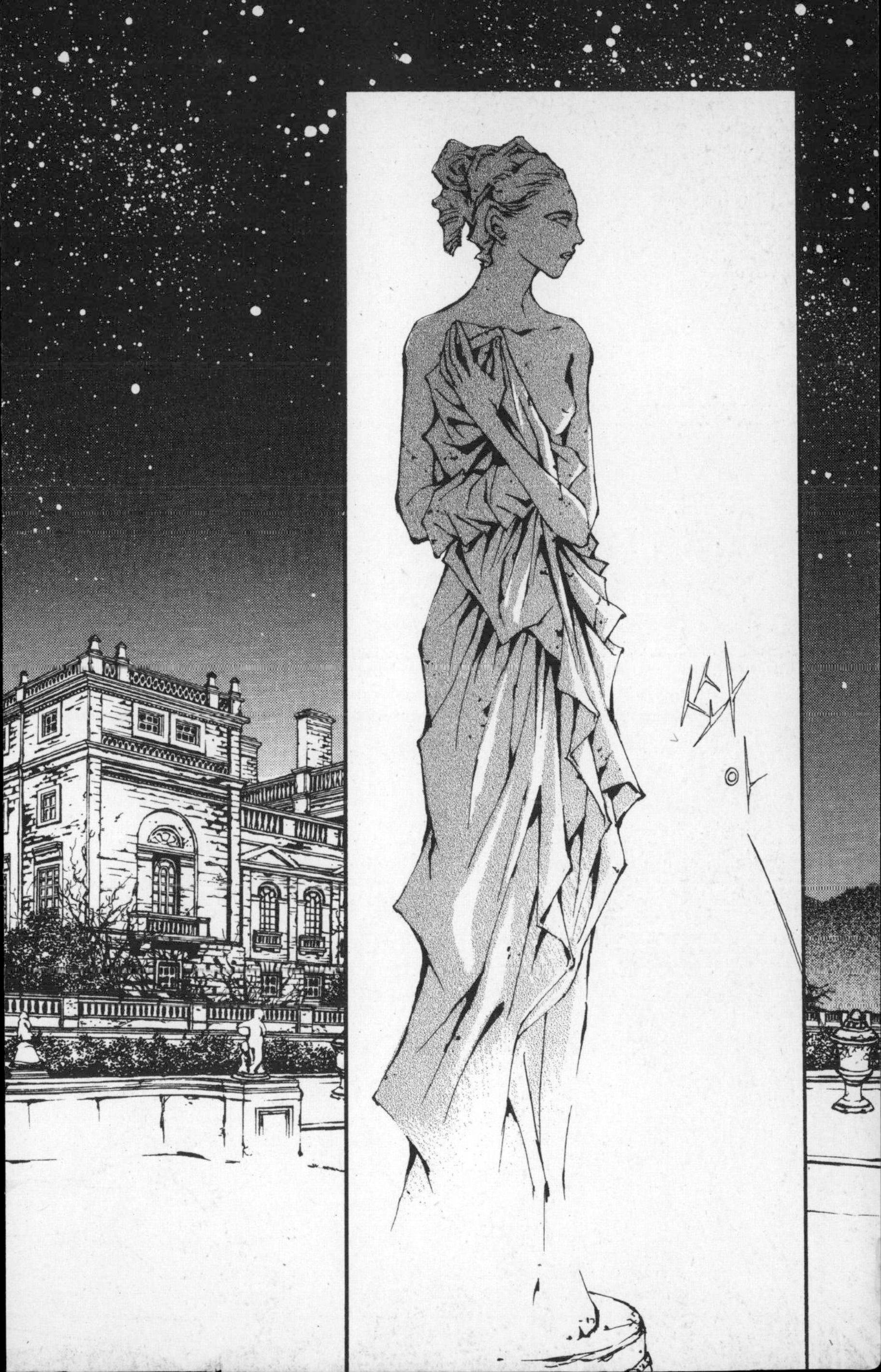
쏴아

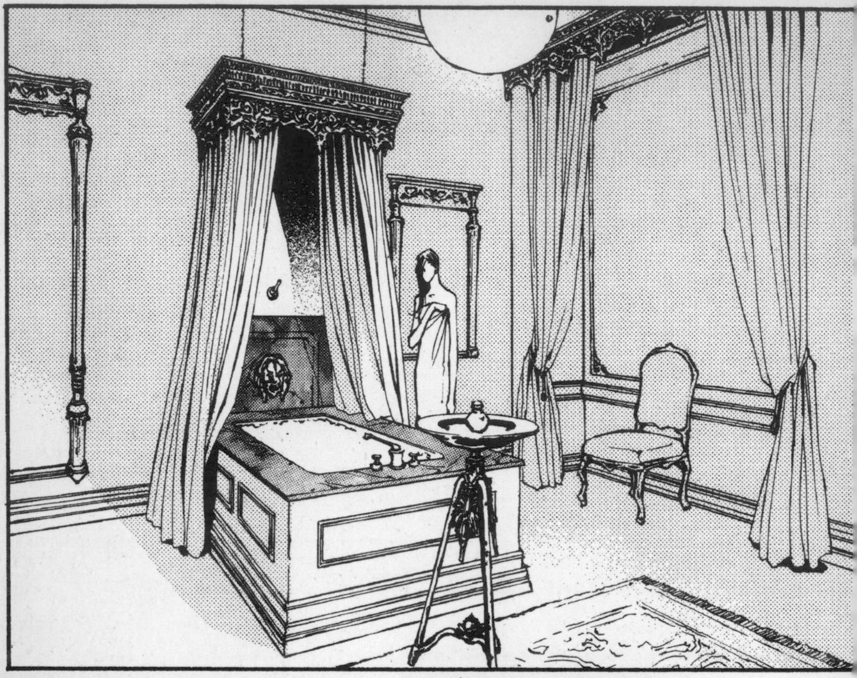

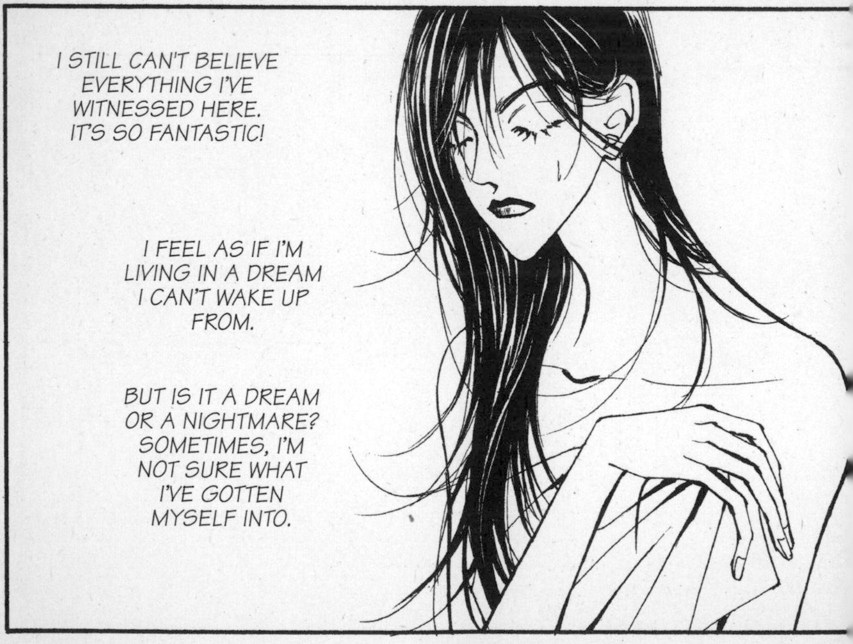
I STILL CAN'T BELIEVE EVERYTHING I'VE WITNESSED HERE. IT'S SO FANTASTIC!
I FEEL AS IF I'M LIVING IN A DREAM I CAN'T WAKE UP FROM.
BUT IS IT A DREAM OR A NIGHTMARE? SOMETIMES, I'M NOT SURE WHAT I'VE GOTTEN MYSELF INTO.

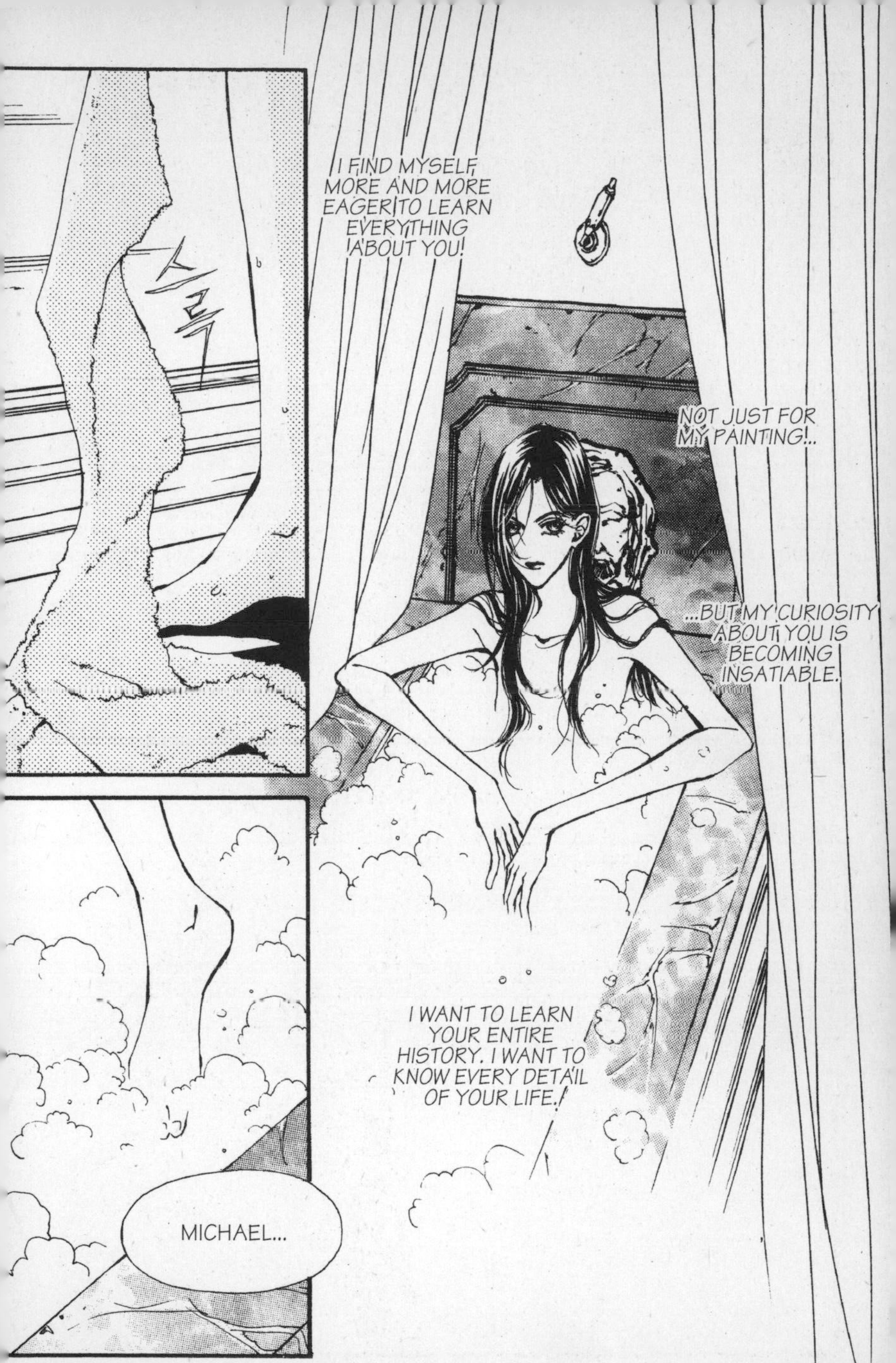
스르륵
MICHAEL...
I FIND MYSELF MORE AND MORE EAGER TO LEARN EVERYTHING ABOUT YOU!
NOT JUST FOR MY PAINTING...
...BUT MY CURIOSITY ABOUT YOU IS BECOMING INSATIABLE.
I WANT TO LEARN YOUR ENTIRE HISTORY. I WANT TO KNOW EVERY DETAIL OF YOUR LIFE.

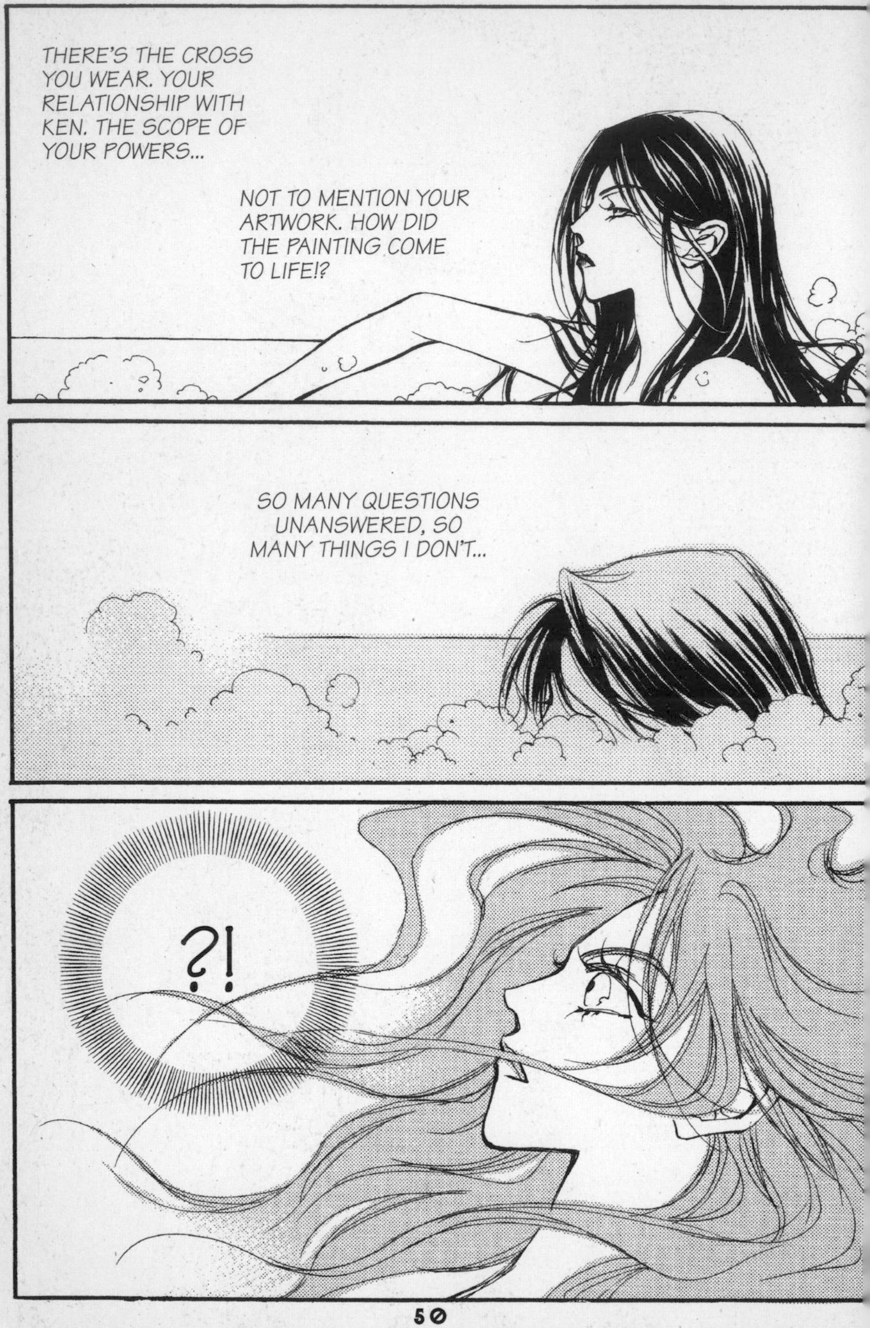
THERE'S THE CROSS YOU WEAR. YOUR RELATIONSHIP WITH KEN. THE SCOPE OF YOUR POWERS...
NOT TO MENTION YOUR ARTWORK. HOW DID THE PAINTING COME TO LIFE!?
SO MANY QUESTIONS UNANSWERED, SO MANY THINGS I DON'T...
?!

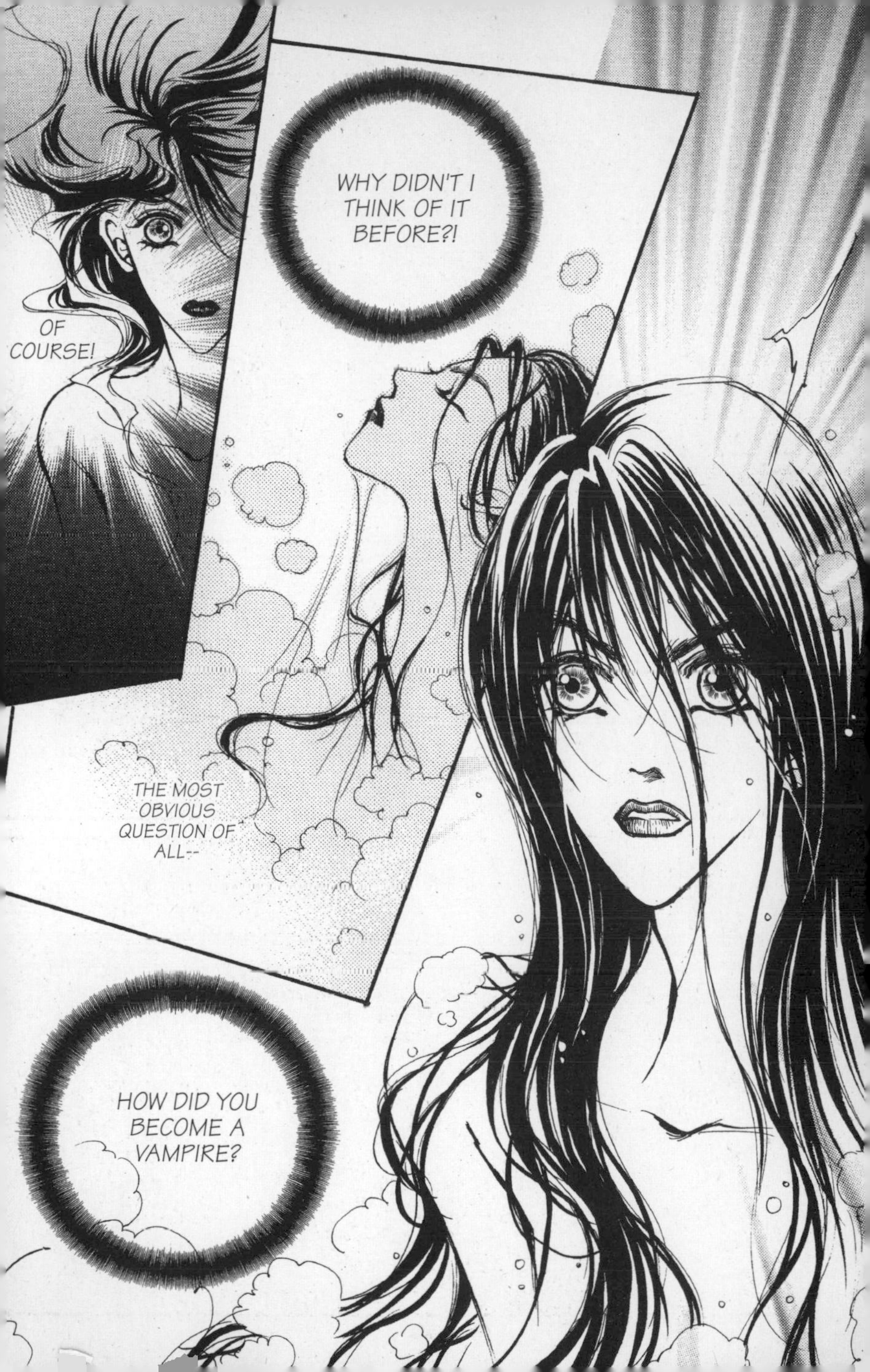
OF COURSE!
WHY DIDN'T I THINK OF IT BEFORE?!
THE MOST OBVIOUS QUESTION OF ALL--
HOW DID YOU BECOME A VAMPIRE?

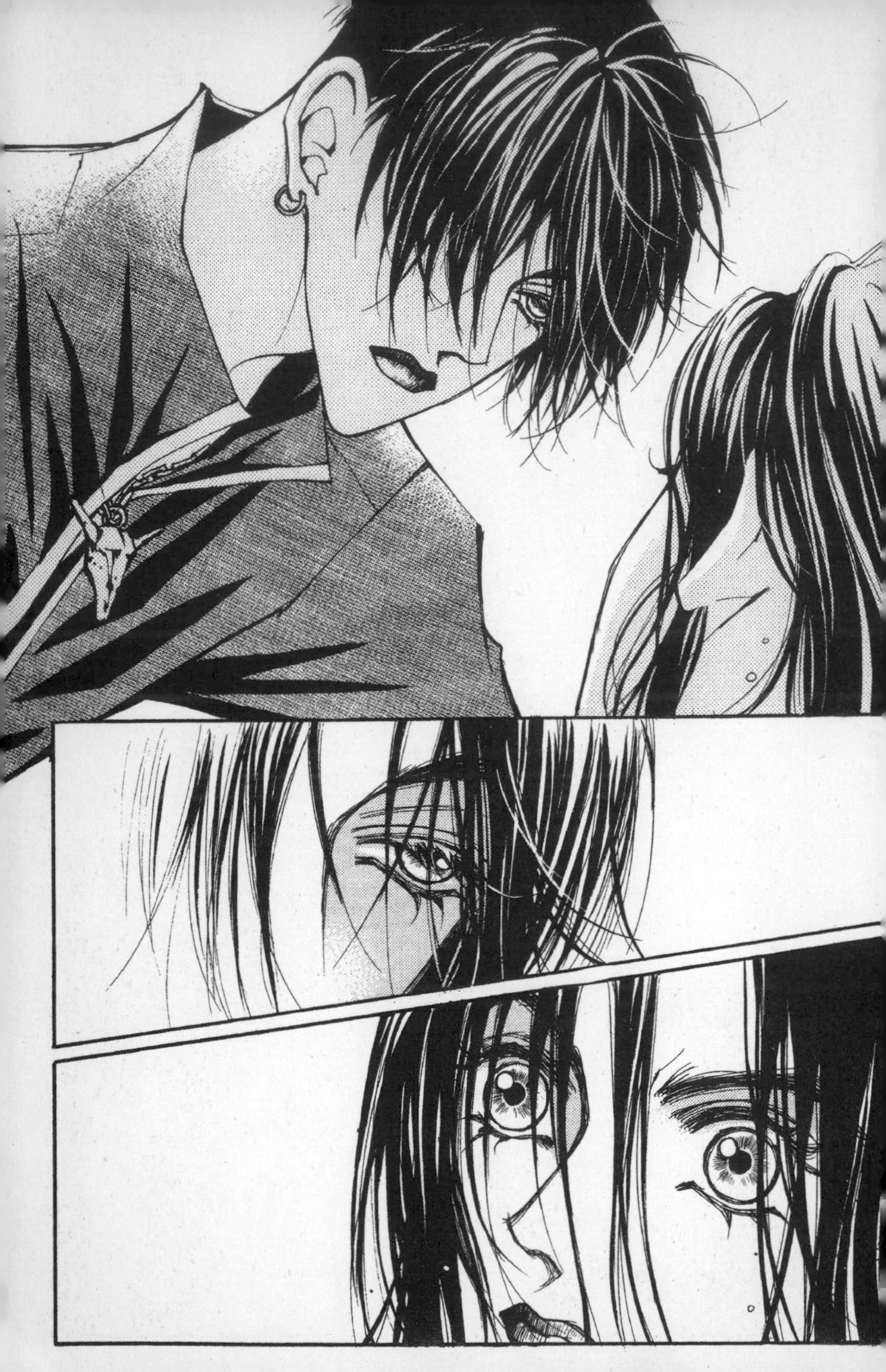

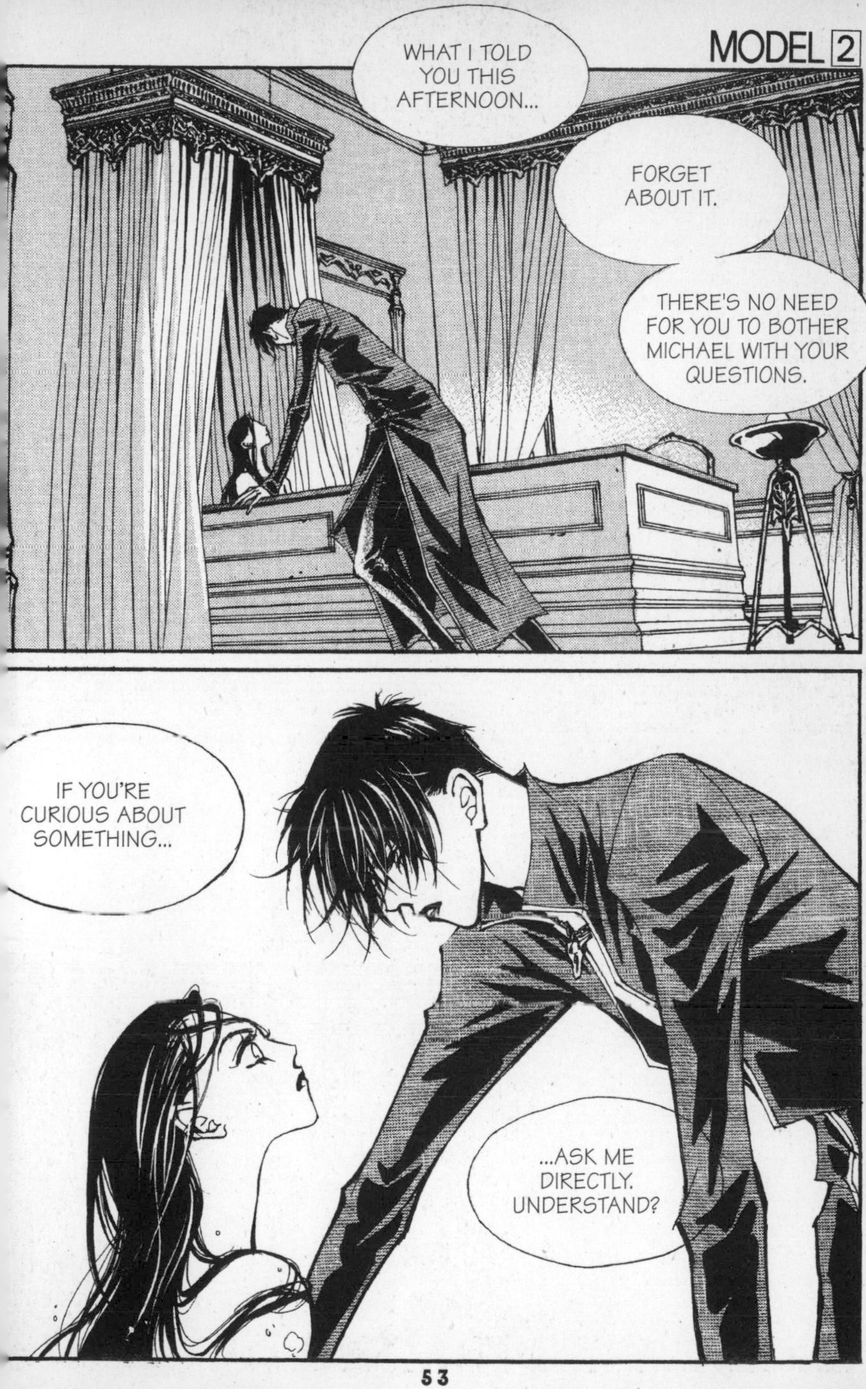
WHAT I TOLD YOU THIS AFTERNOON...
FORGET ABOUT IT.
THERE'S NO NEED FOR YOU TO BOTHER MICHAEL WITH YOUR QUESTIONS.
IF YOU'RE CURIOUS ABOUT SOMETHING...
...ASK ME DIRECTLY. UNDERSTAND?

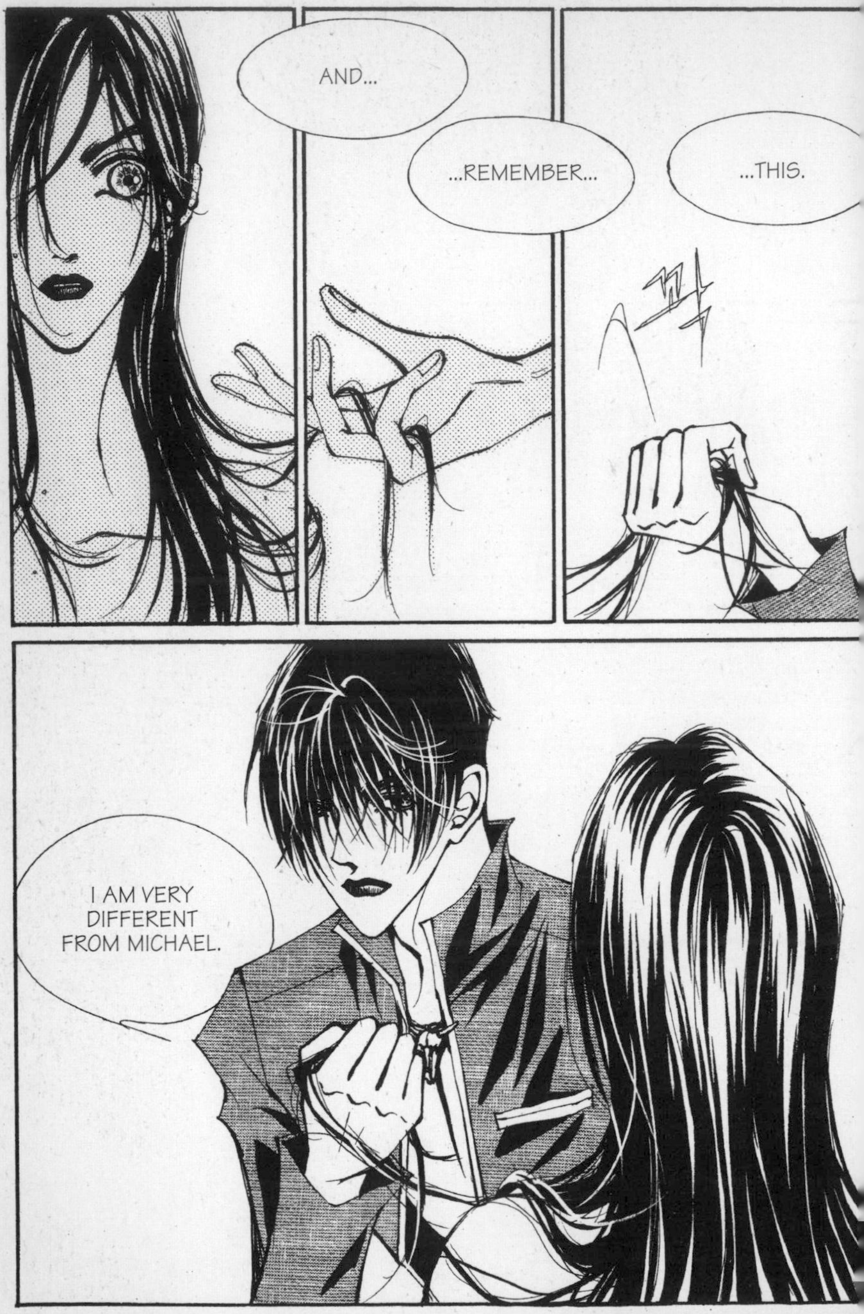
AND...
...REMEMBER...
...THIS.
I AM VERY DIFFERENT FROM MICHAEL.

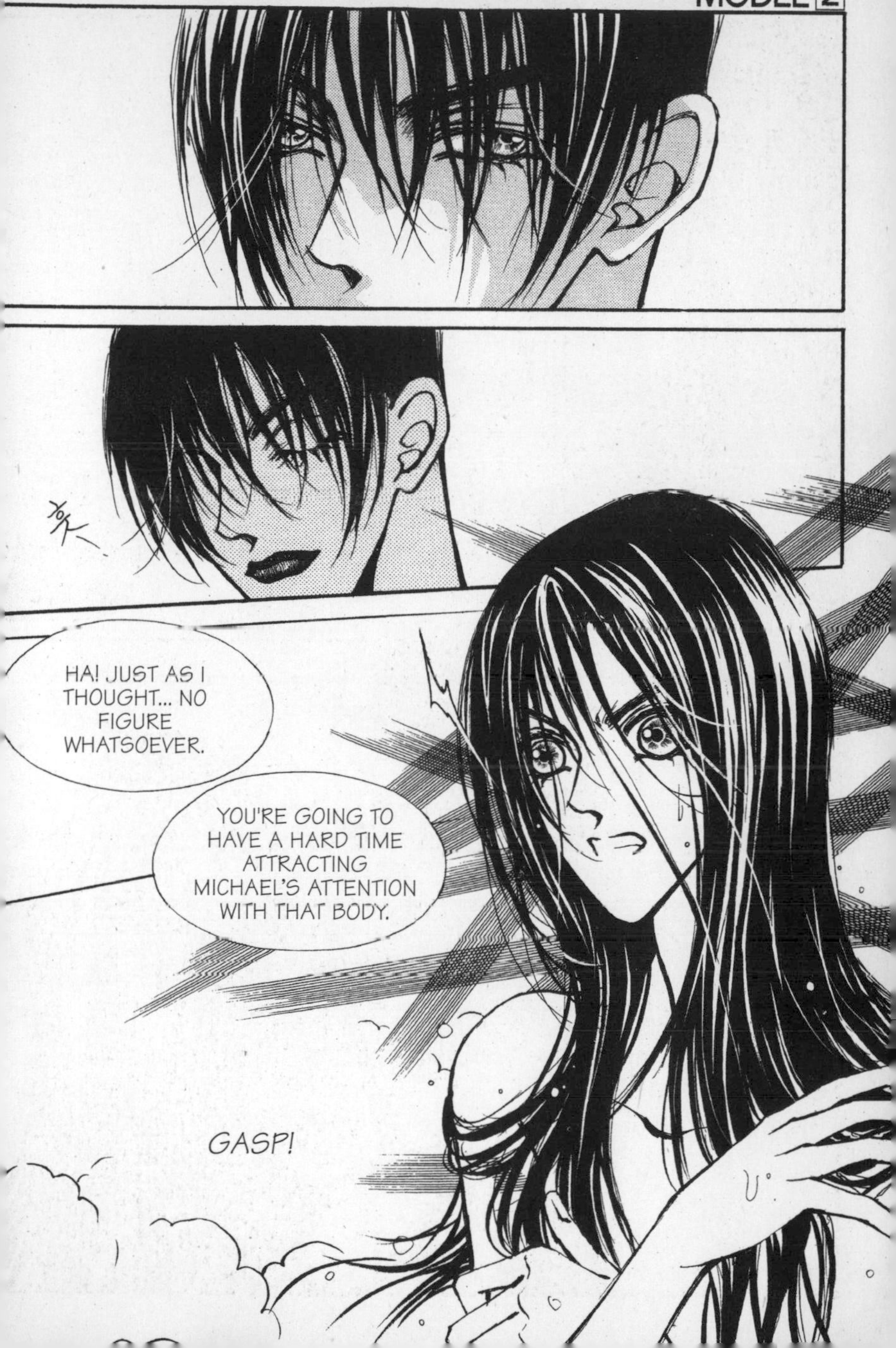
HA! JUST AS I THOUGHT... NO FIGURE WHATSOEVER.
YOU'RE GOING TO HAVE A HARD TIME ATTRACTING MICHAEL'S ATTENTION WITH THAT BODY.
GASP!

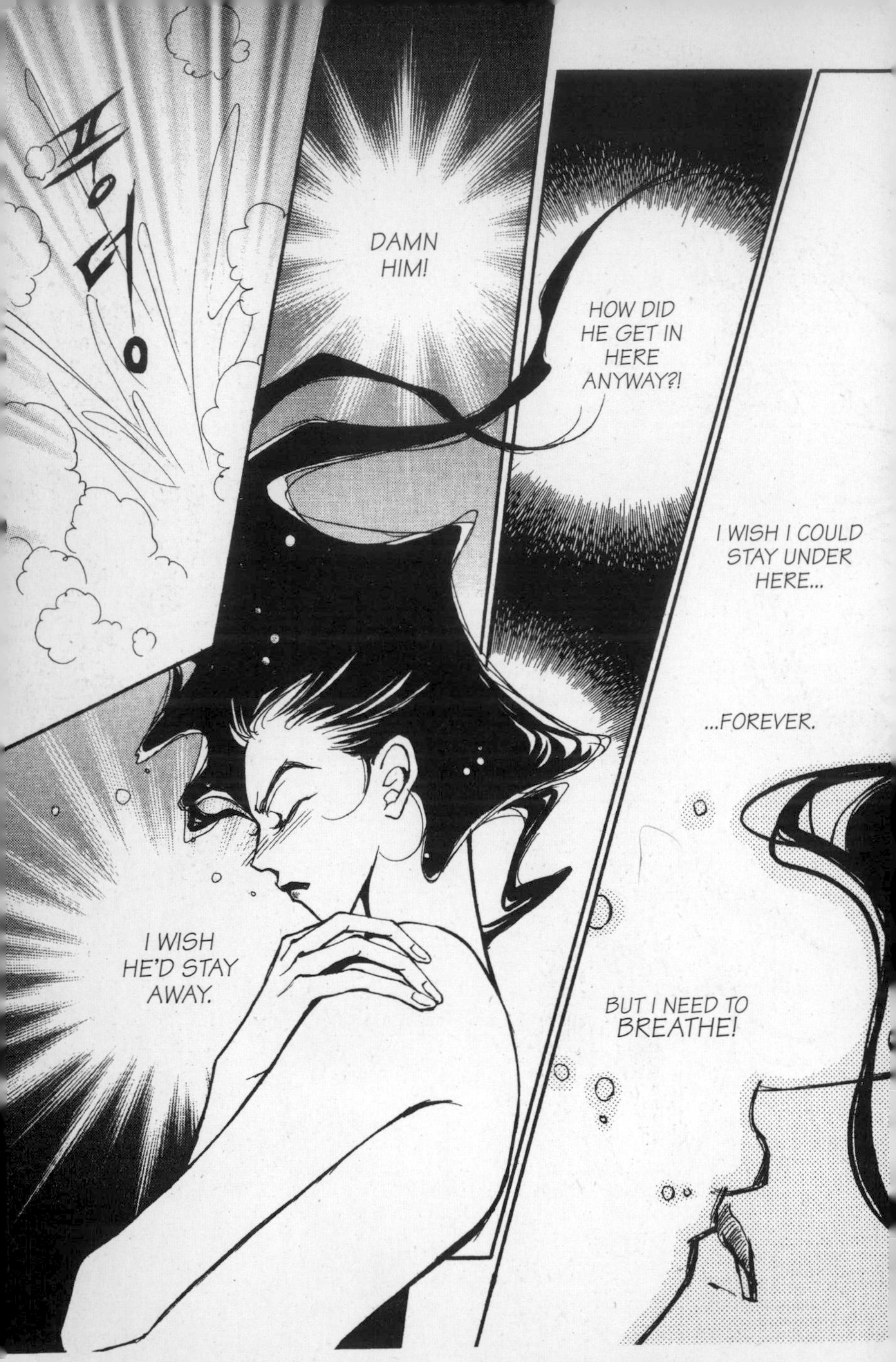
풍덩
DAMN HIM!
HOW DID HE GET IN HERE ANYWAY?!
I WISH I COULD STAY UNDER HERE...
...FOREVER.
I WISH HE'D STAY AWAY.
BUT I NEED TO BREATHE!

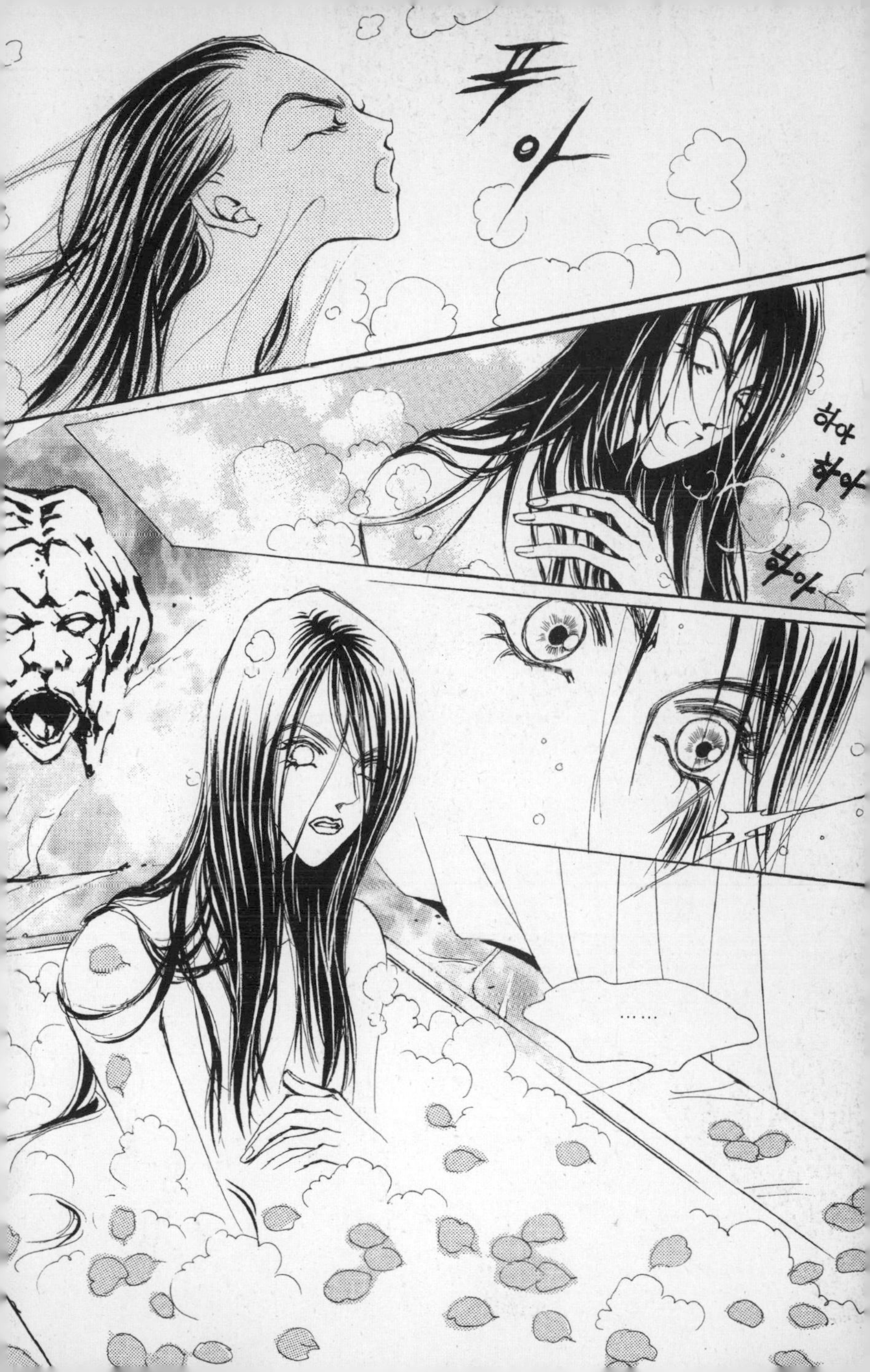

푸아
하아
하아
하아
......

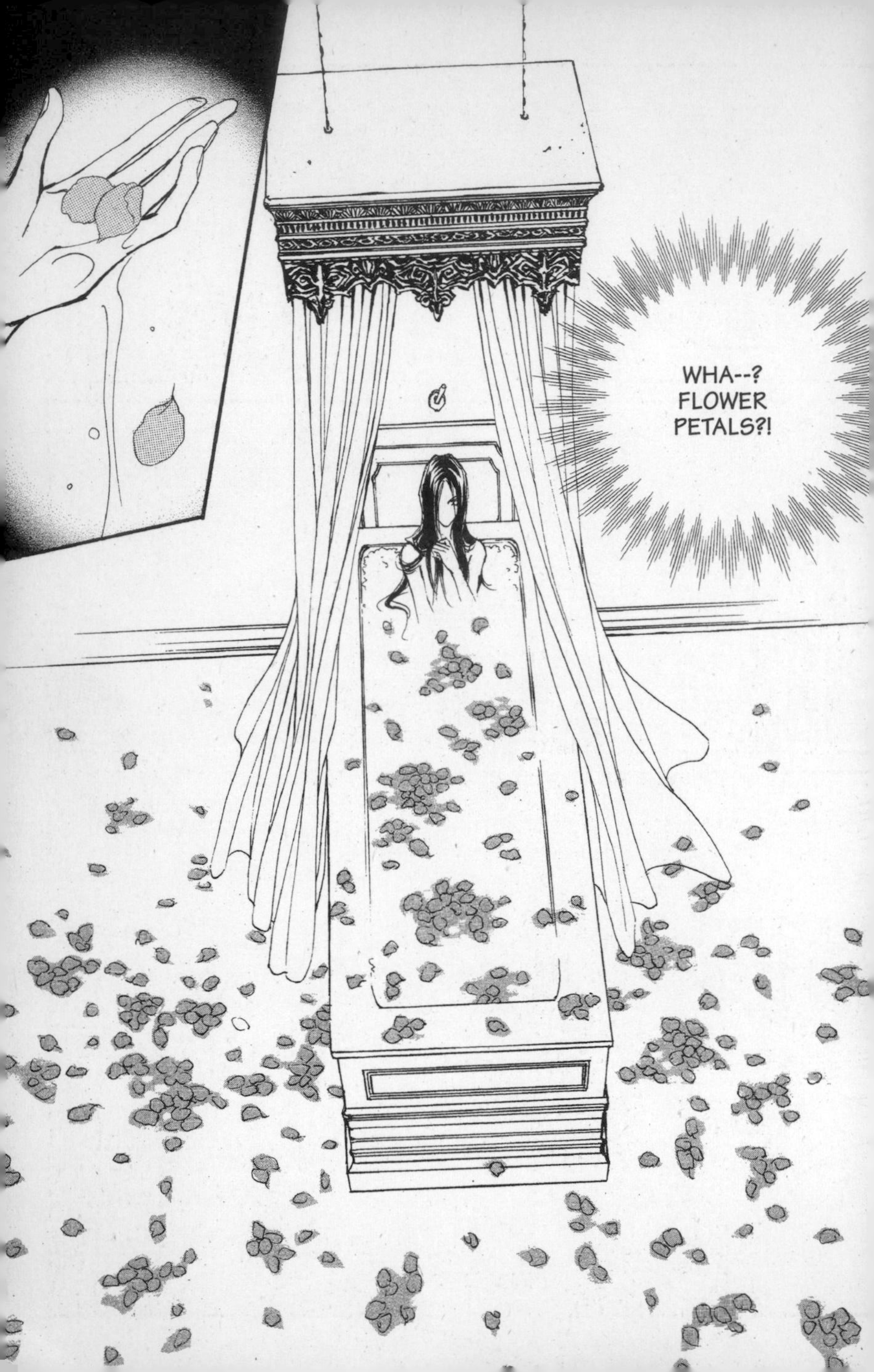
WHA--? FLOWER PETALS?!

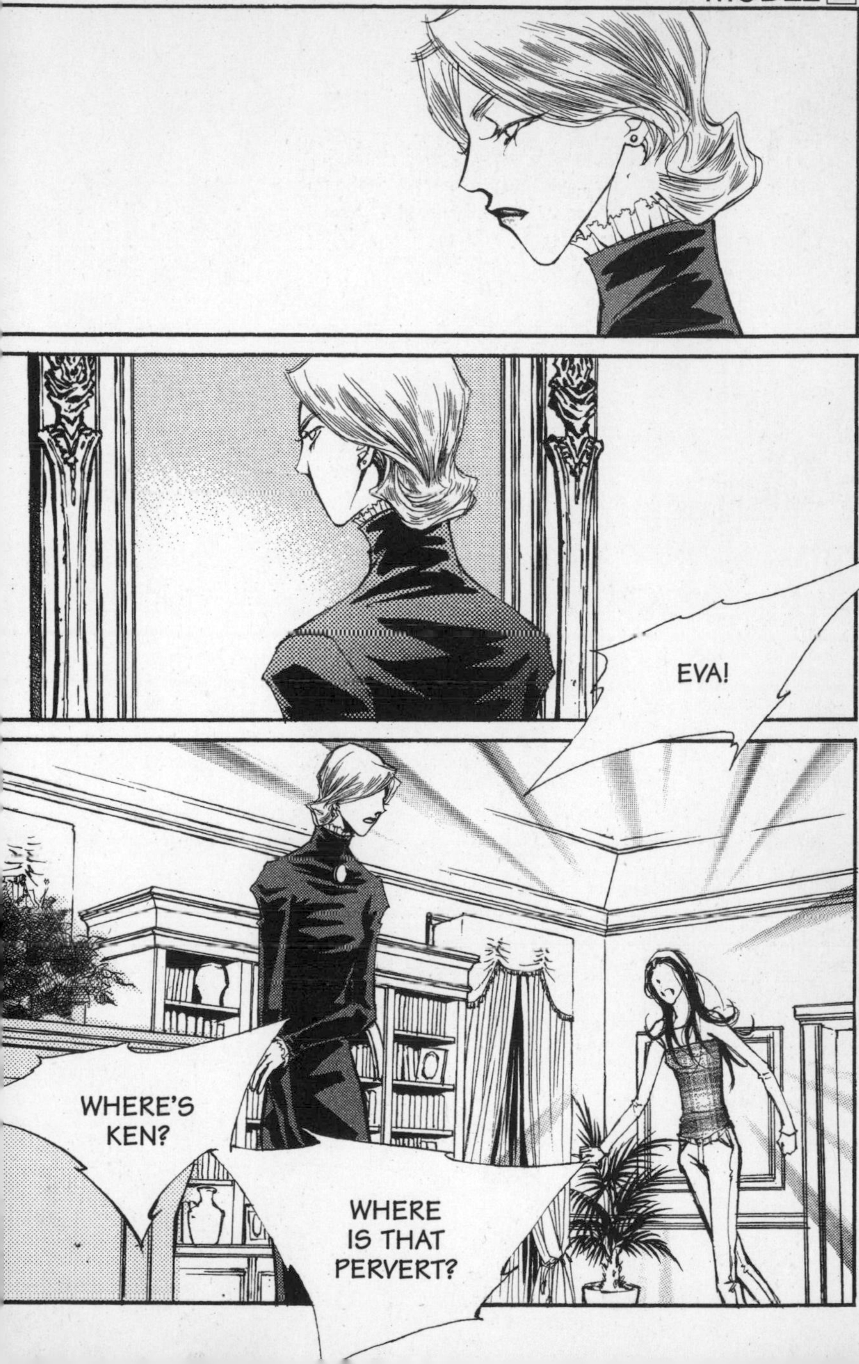
EVA!
WHERE'S KEN?
WHERE IS THAT PERVERT?

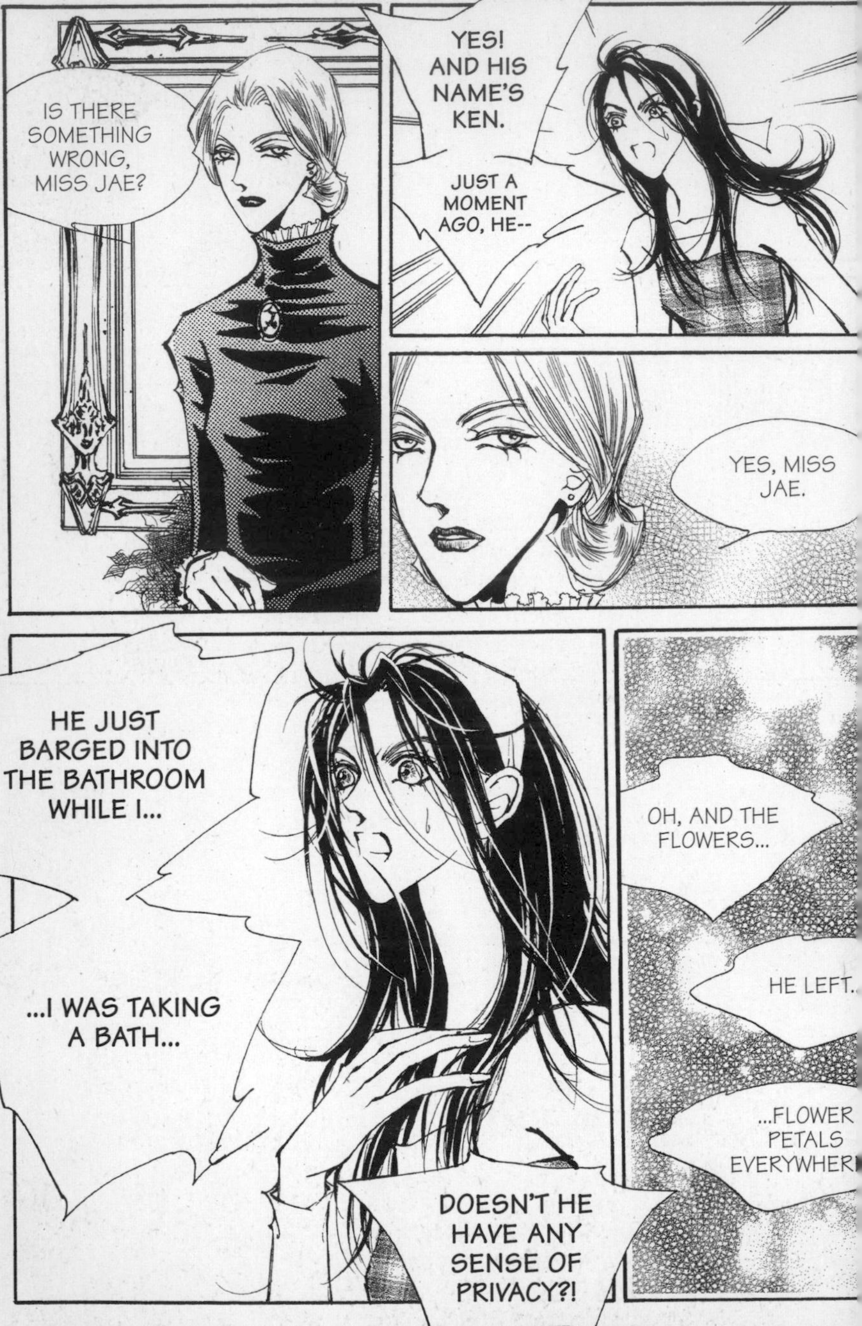
IS THERE SOMETHING WRONG, MISS JAE?
YES! AND HIS NAME'S KEN.
JUST A MOMENT AGO, HE--
YES, MISS JAE.
HE JUST BARGED INTO THE BATHROOM WHILE I...
...I WAS TAKING A BATH...
DOESN'T HE HAVE ANY SENSE OF PRIVACY?!
OH, AND THE FLOWERS...
HE LEFT...
...FLOWER PETALS EVERYWHER

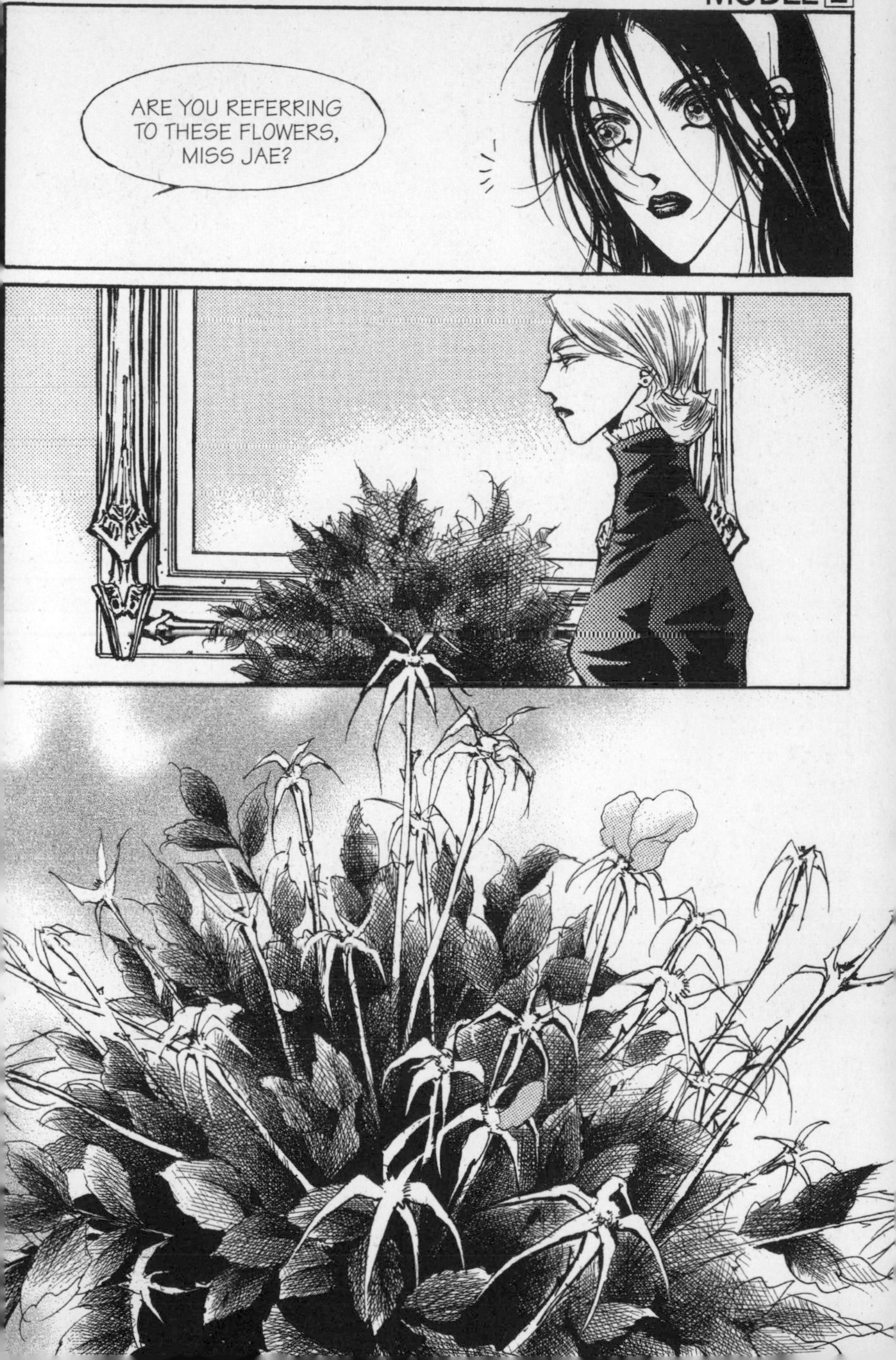
ARE YOU REFERRING TO THESE FLOWERS, MISS JAE?

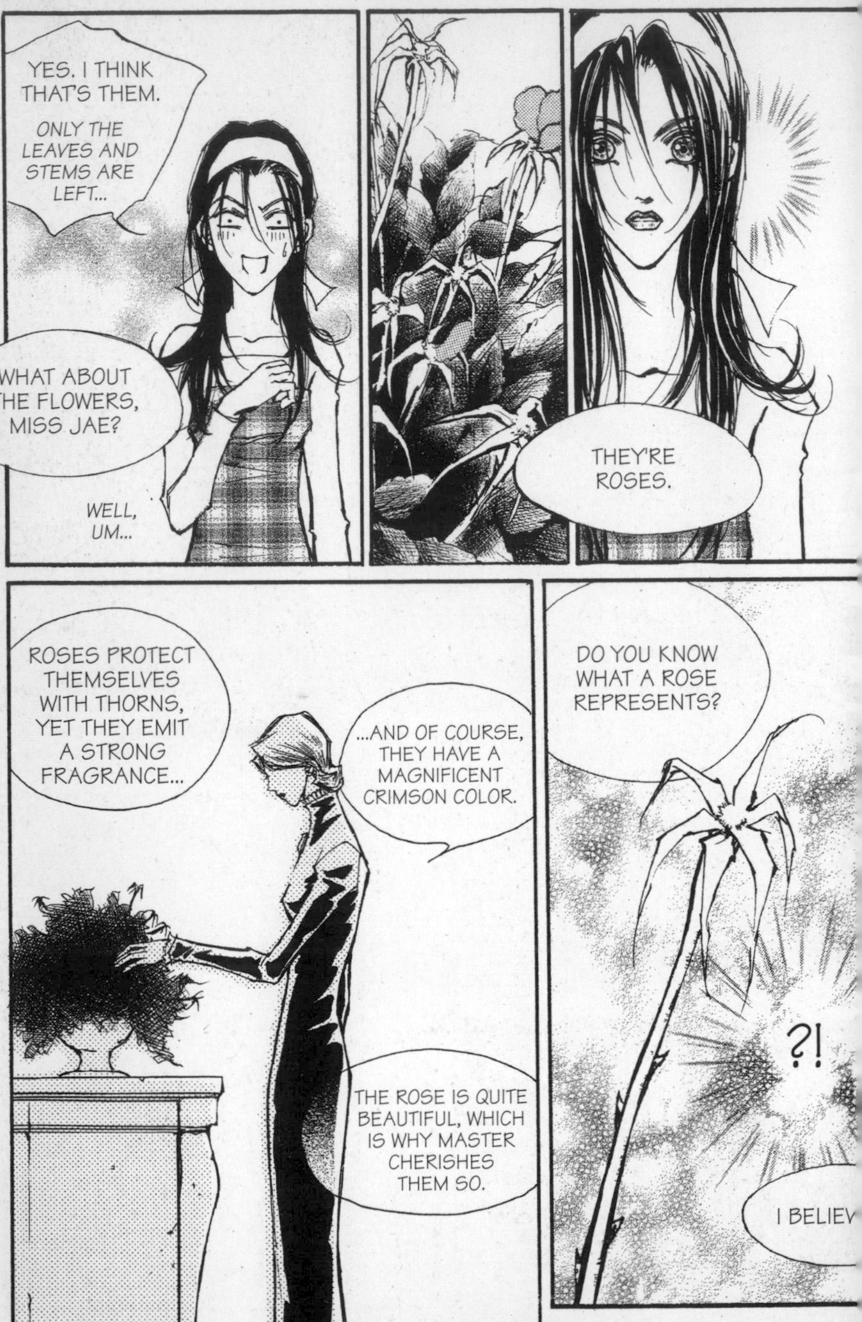
YES. I THINK THAT'S THEM.
ONLY THE LEAVES AND STEMS ARE LEFT...
WHAT ABOUT THE FLOWERS, MISS JAE?
WELL, UM...
THEY'RE ROSES.
ROSES PROTECT THEMSELVES WITH THORNS, YET THEY EMIT A STRONG FRAGRANCE...
...AND OF COURSE, THEY HAVE A MAGNIFICENT CRIMSON COLOR.
THE ROSE IS QUITE BEAUTIFUL, WHICH IS WHY MASTER CHERISHES THEM SO.
DO YOU KNOW WHAT A ROSE REPRESENTS?
?!
I BELIEV

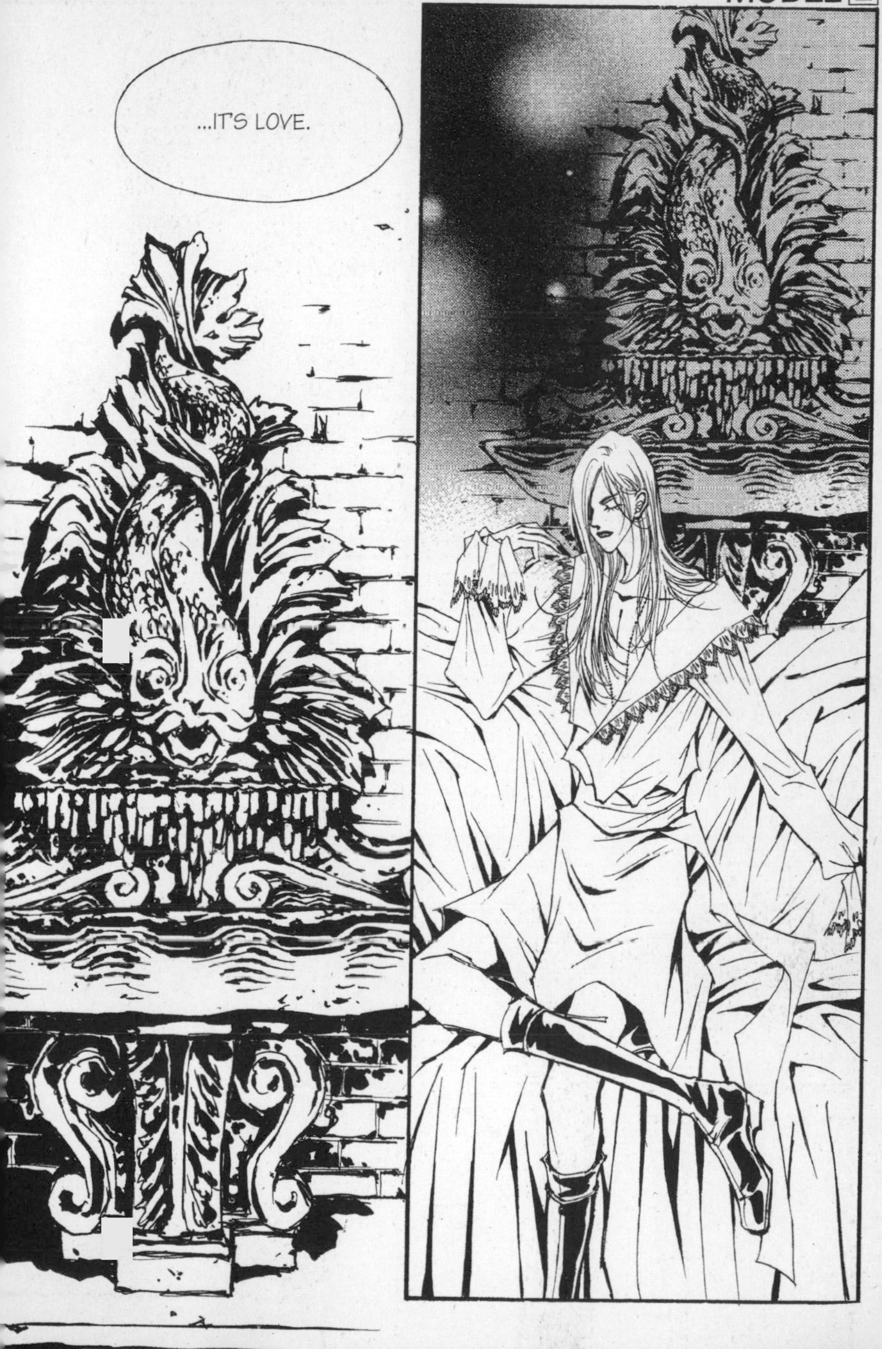
...IT'S LOVE.

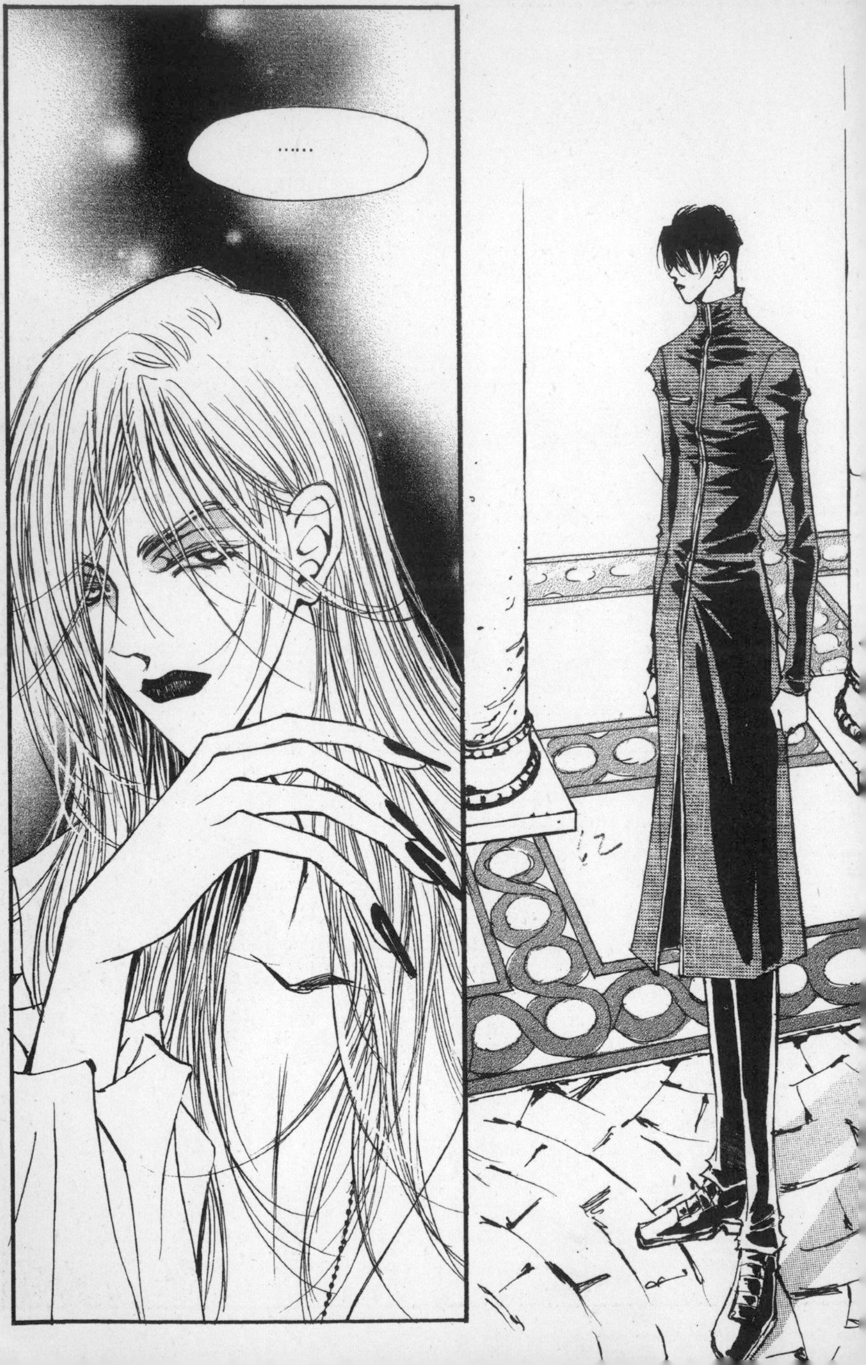
……

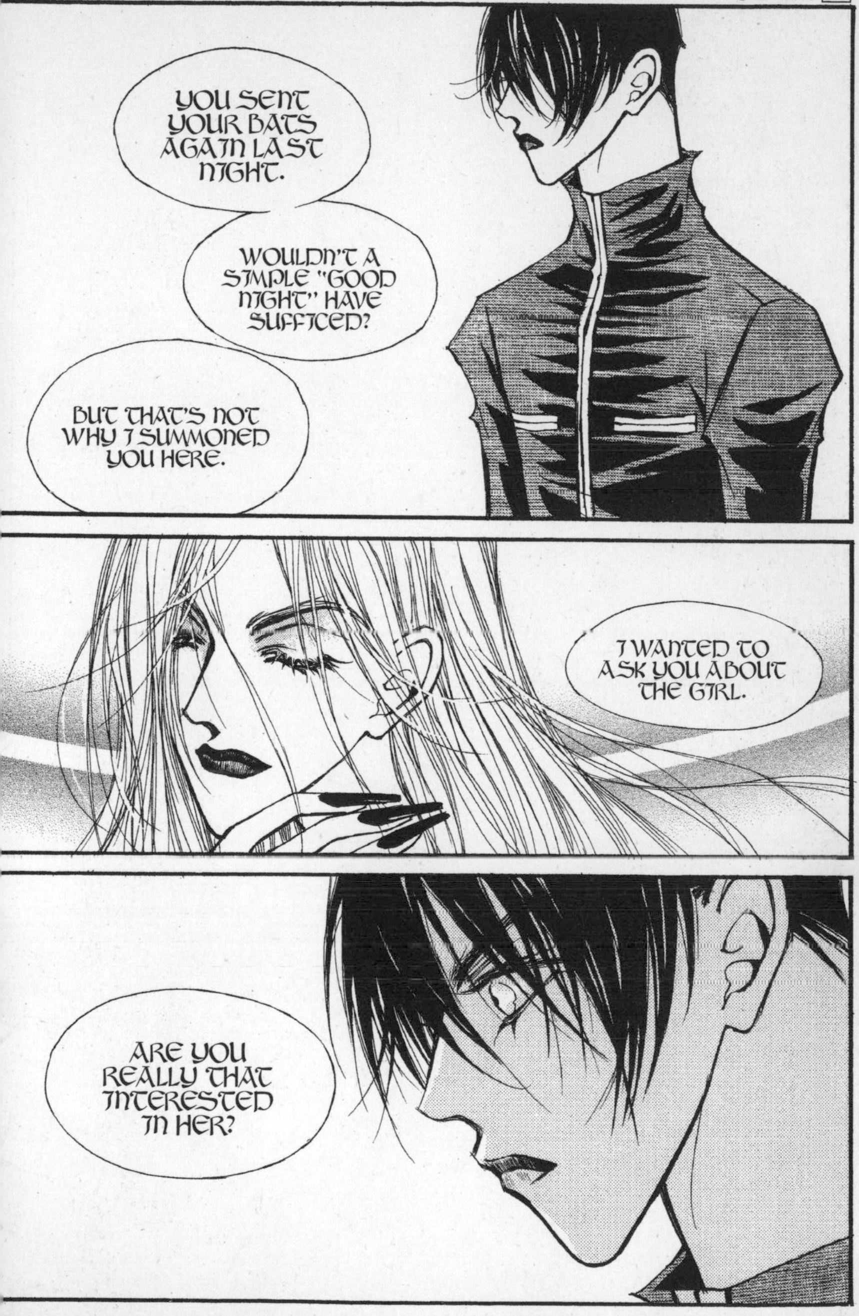
YOU SENT YOUR BATS AGAIN LAST NIGHT.
WOULDN'T A SIMPLE "GOOD NIGHT" HAVE SUFFICED?
BUT THAT'S NOT WHY I SUMMONED YOU HERE.
I WANTED TO ASK YOU ABOUT THE GIRL.
ARE YOU REALLY THAT INTERESTED IN HER?

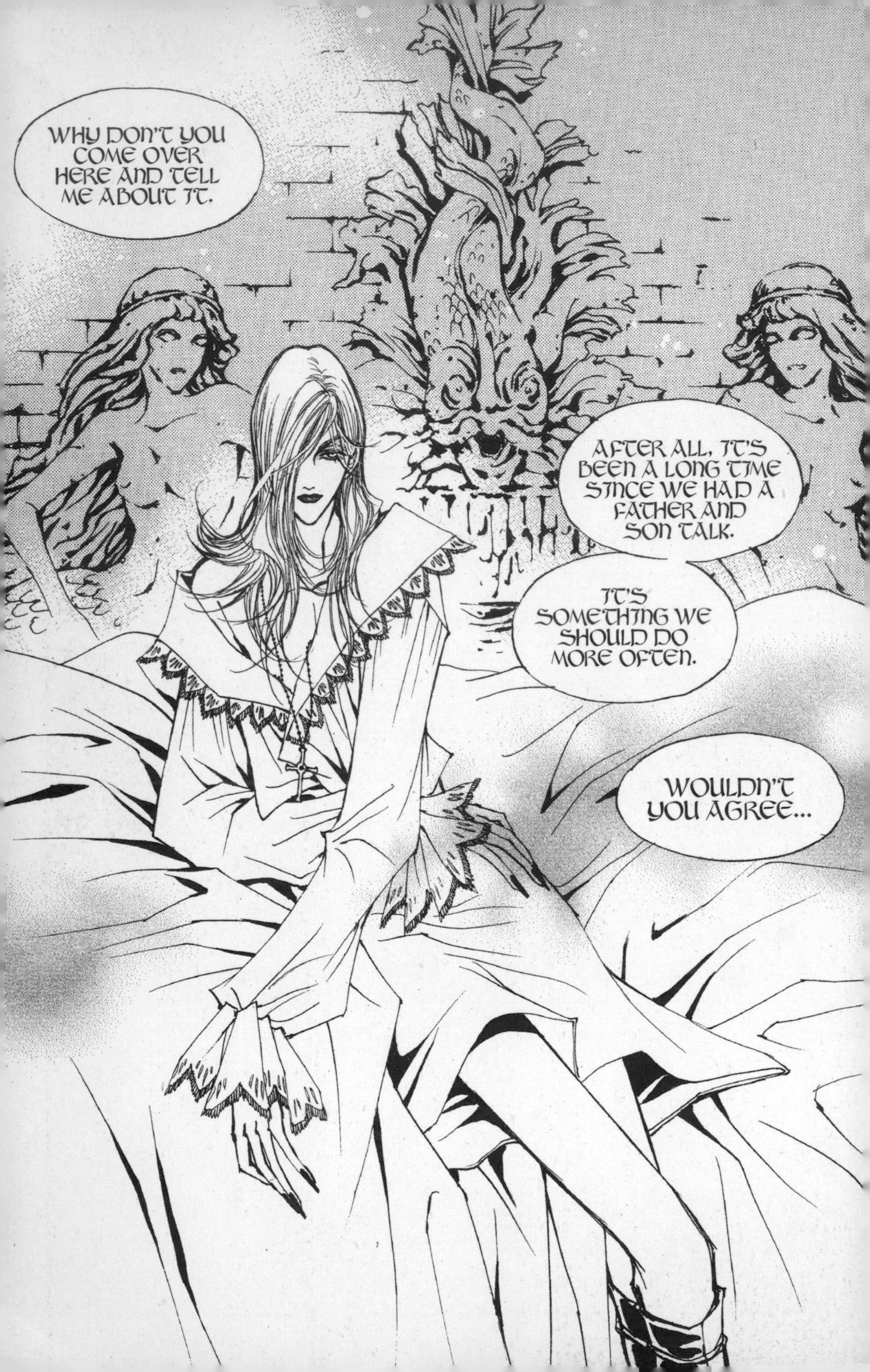
WHY DON'T YOU COME OVER HERE AND TELL ME ABOUT IT.
AFTER ALL, IT'S BEEN A LONG TIME SINCE WE HAD A FATHER AND SON TALK.
IT'S SOMETHING WE SHOULD DO MORE OFTEN.
WOULDN'T YOU AGREE...

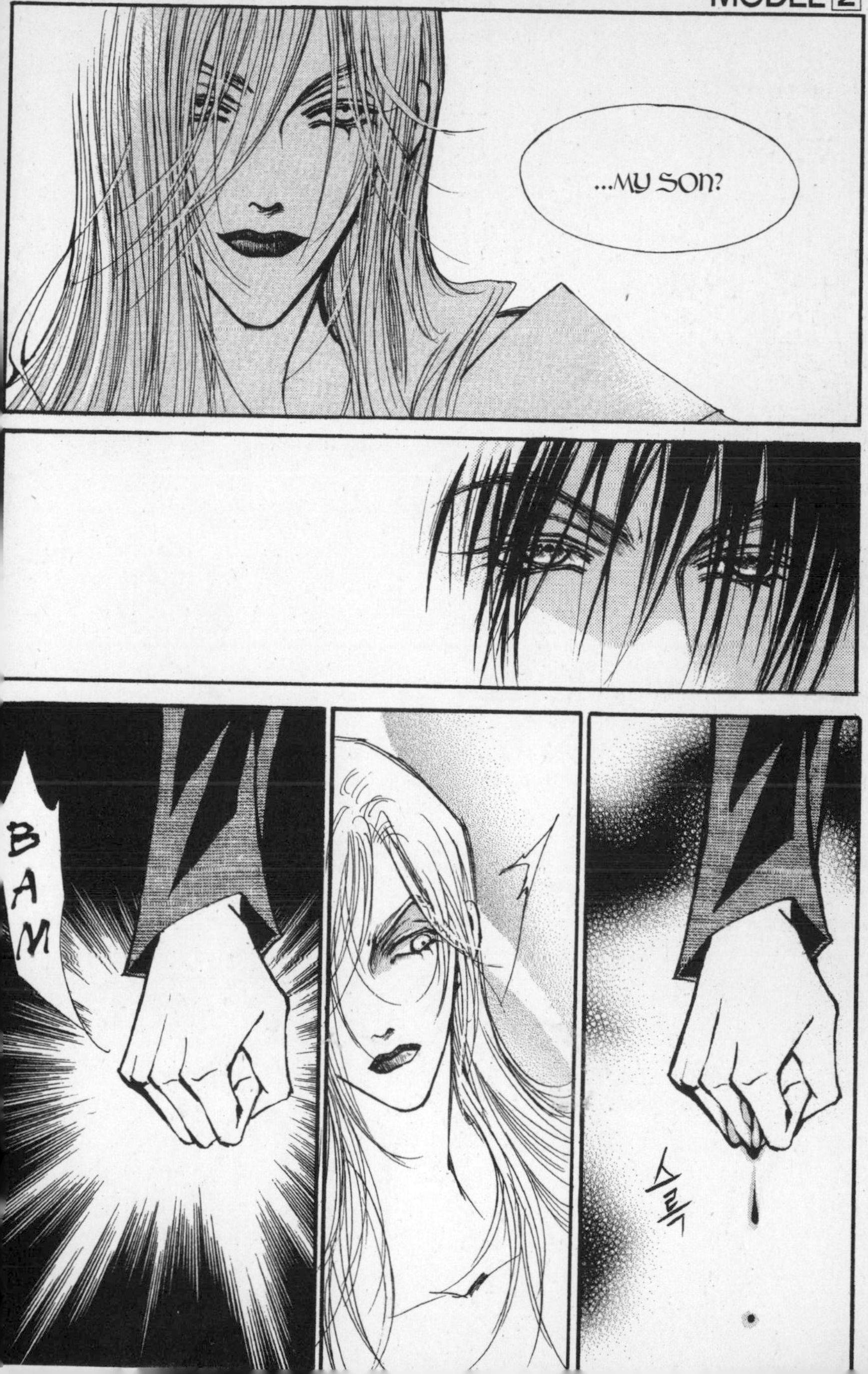
...MY SON?
BAM
스륵

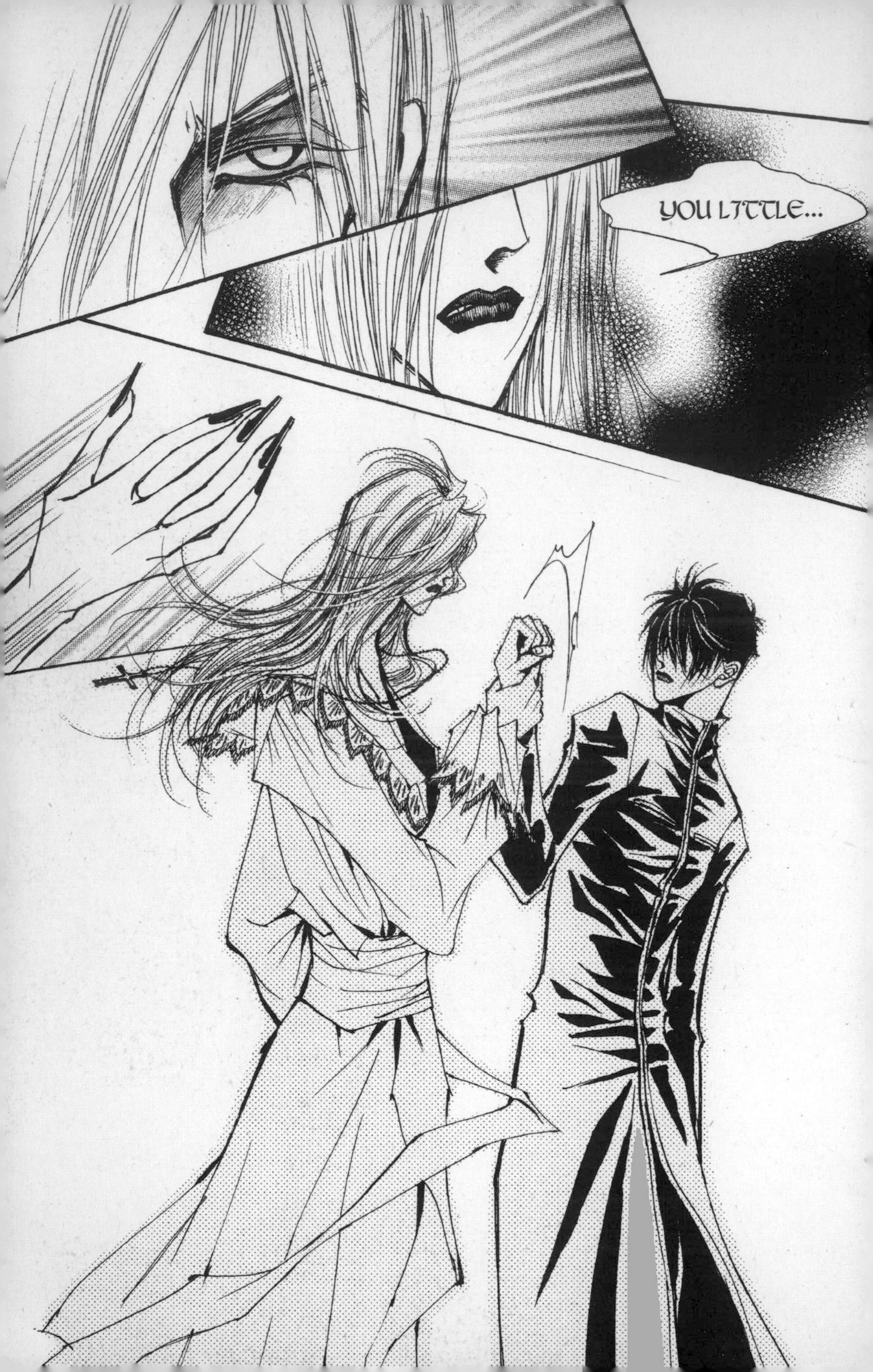
YOU LITTLE...

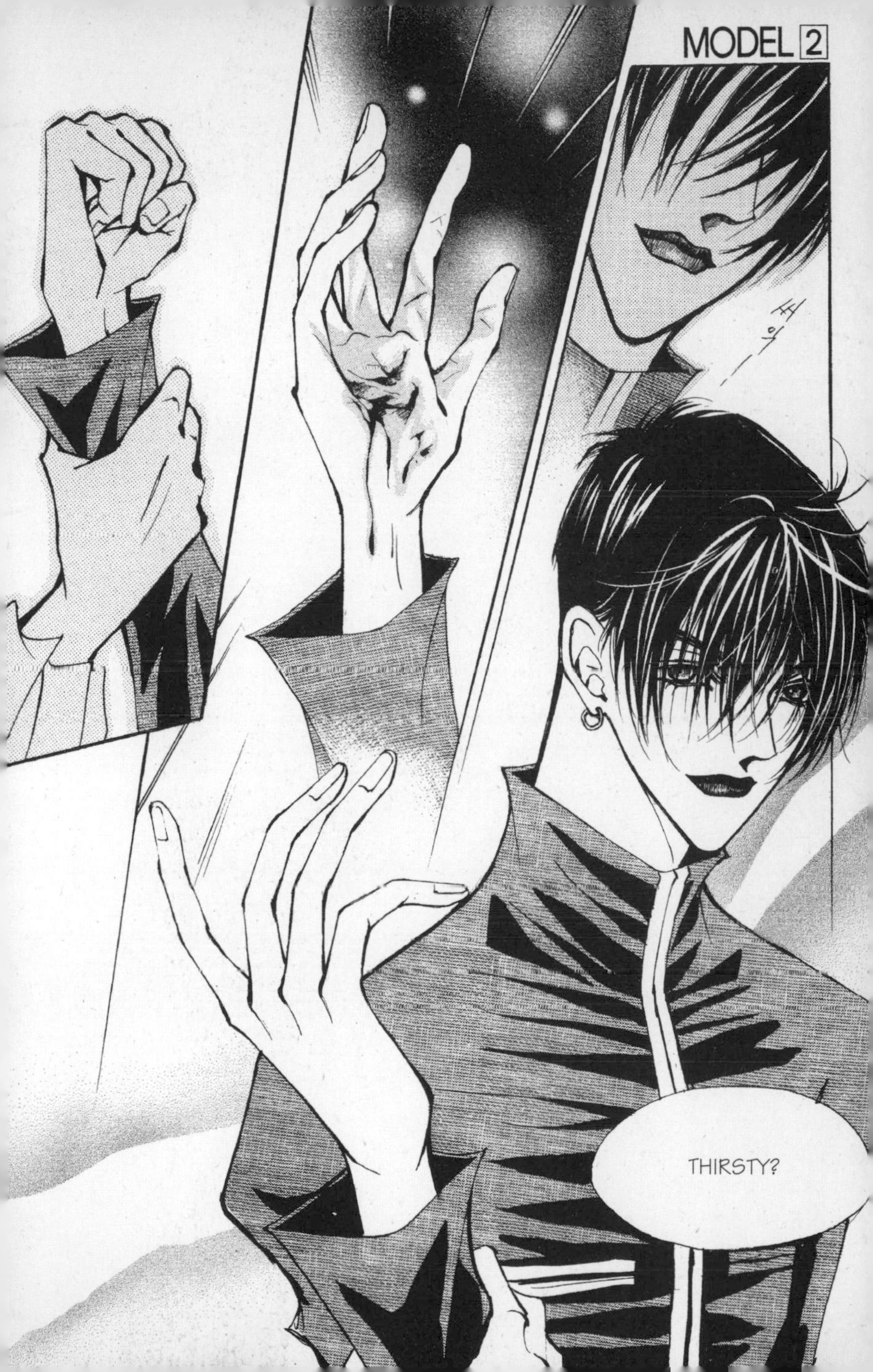
THIRSTY?

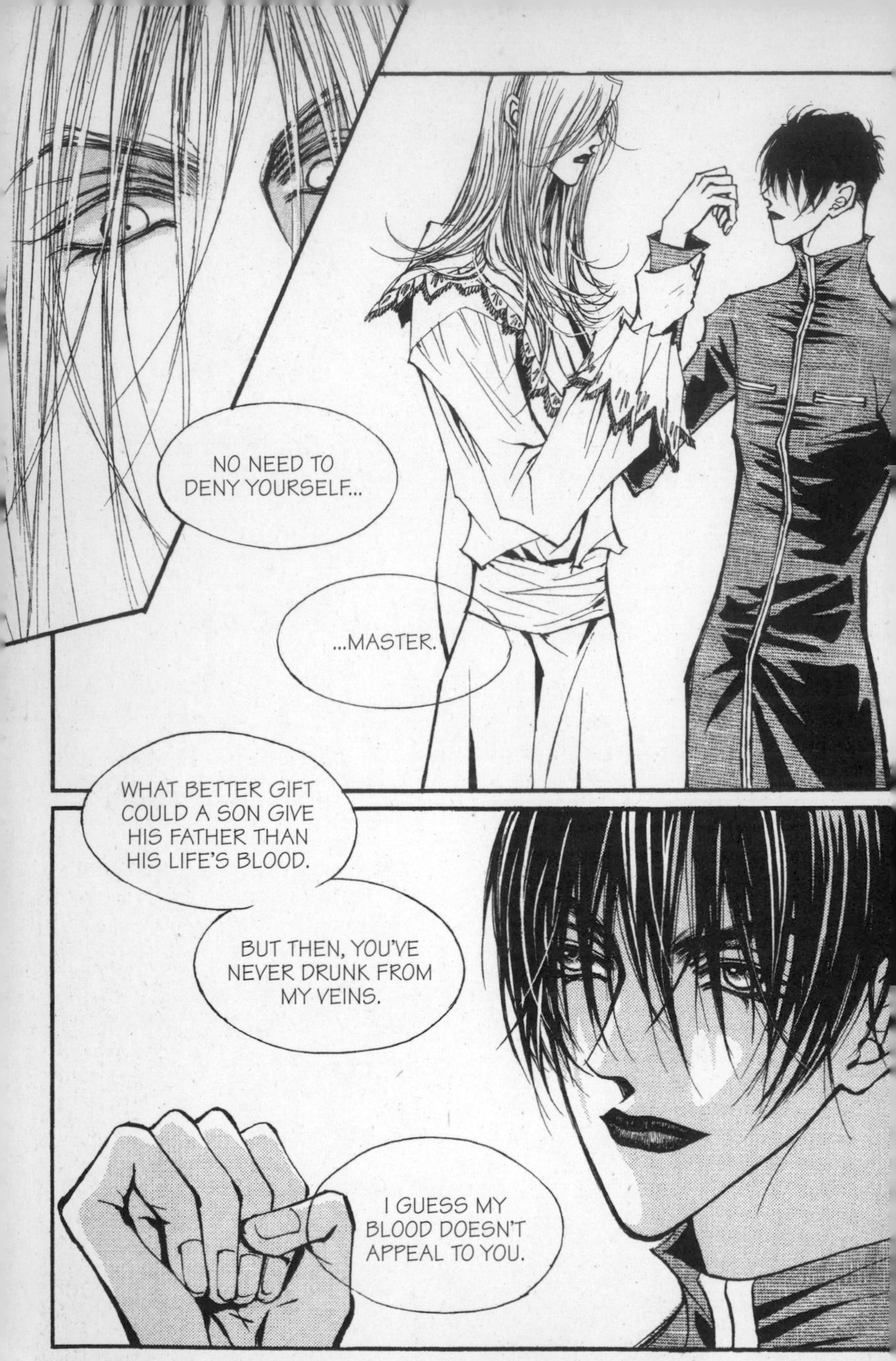
NO NEED TO DENY YOURSELF...
...MASTER.
WHAT BETTER GIFT COULD A SON GIVE HIS FATHER THAN HIS LIFE'S BLOOD.
BUT THEN, YOU'VE NEVER DRUNK FROM MY VEINS.
I GUESS MY BLOOD DOESN'T APPEAL TO YOU.

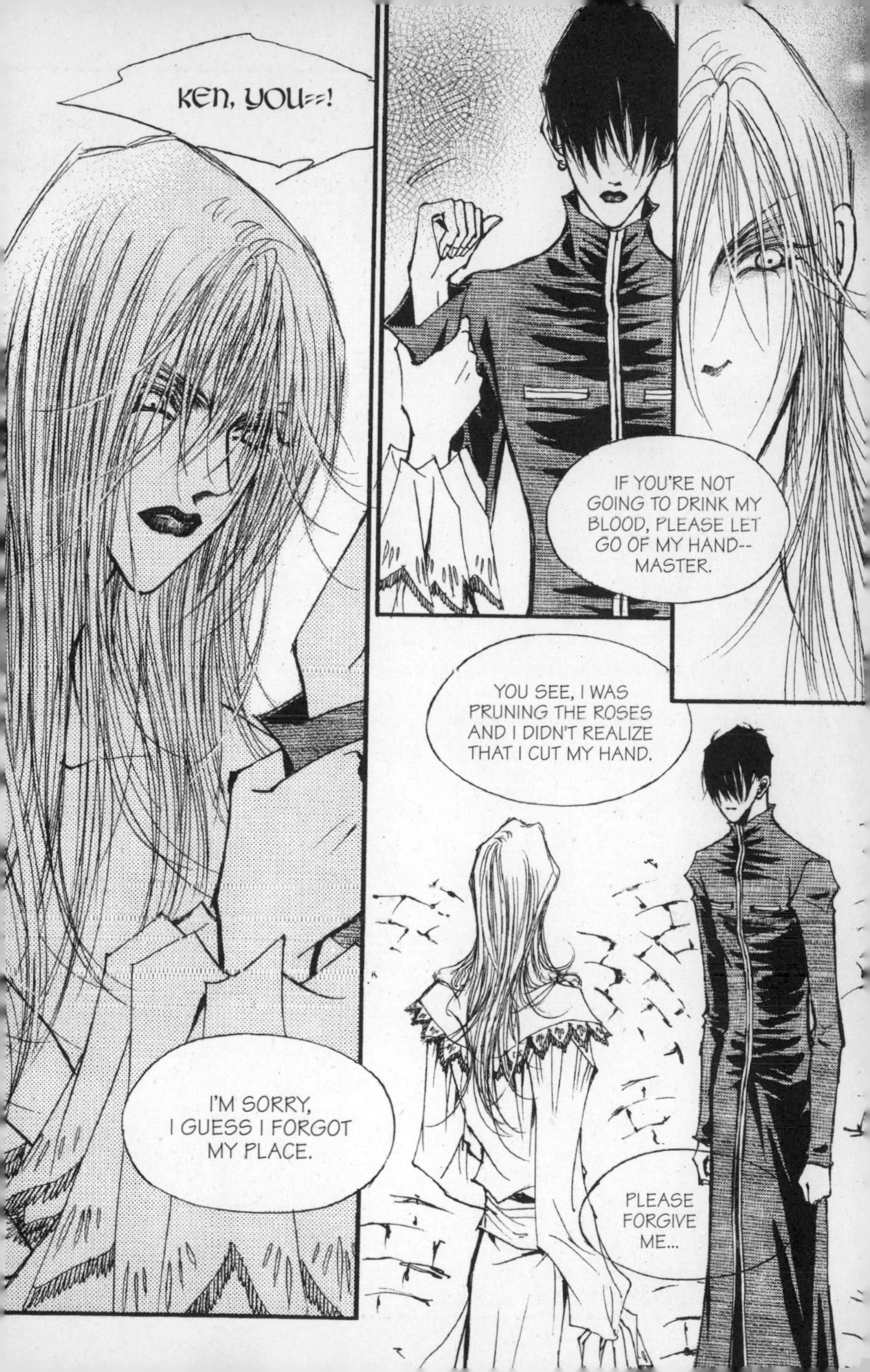
KEN, YOU==!
I'M SORRY, I GUESS I FORGOT MY PLACE.
IF YOU'RE NOT GOING TO DRINK MY BLOOD, PLEASE LET GO OF MY HAND-- MASTER.
YOU SEE, I WAS PRUNING THE ROSES AND I DIDN'T REALIZE THAT I CUT MY HAND.
PLEASE FORGIVE ME...

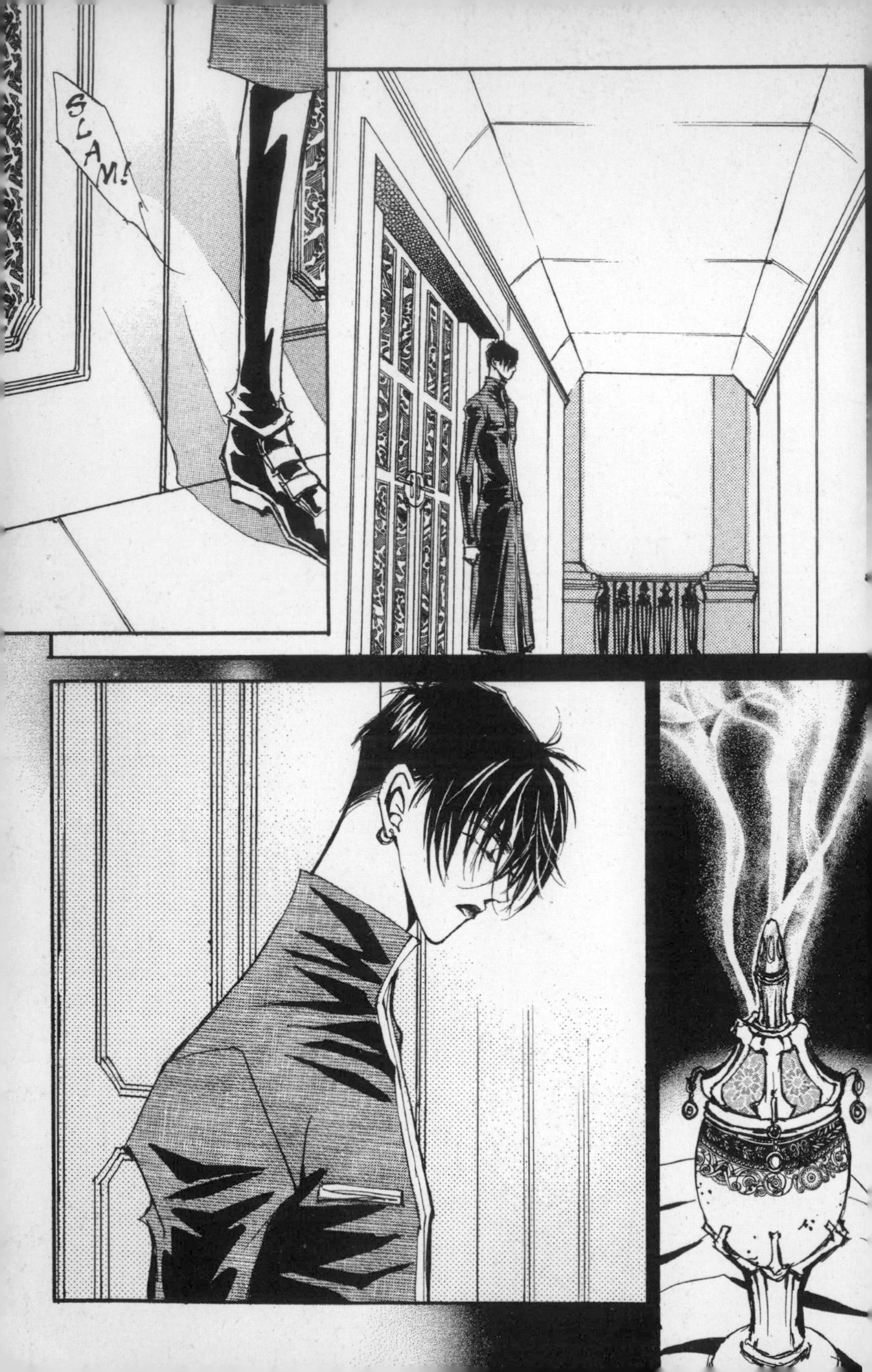
SLAM!

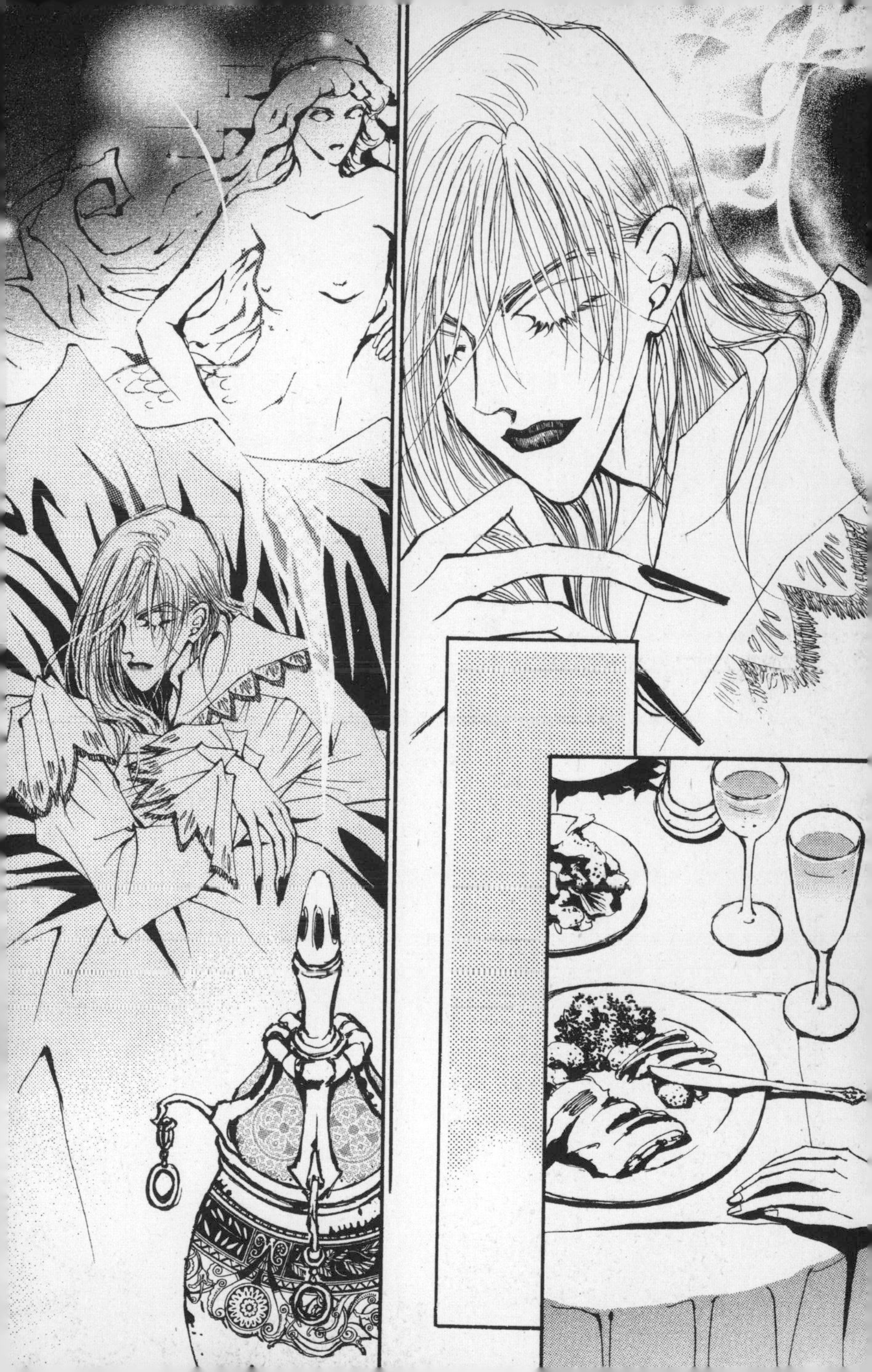

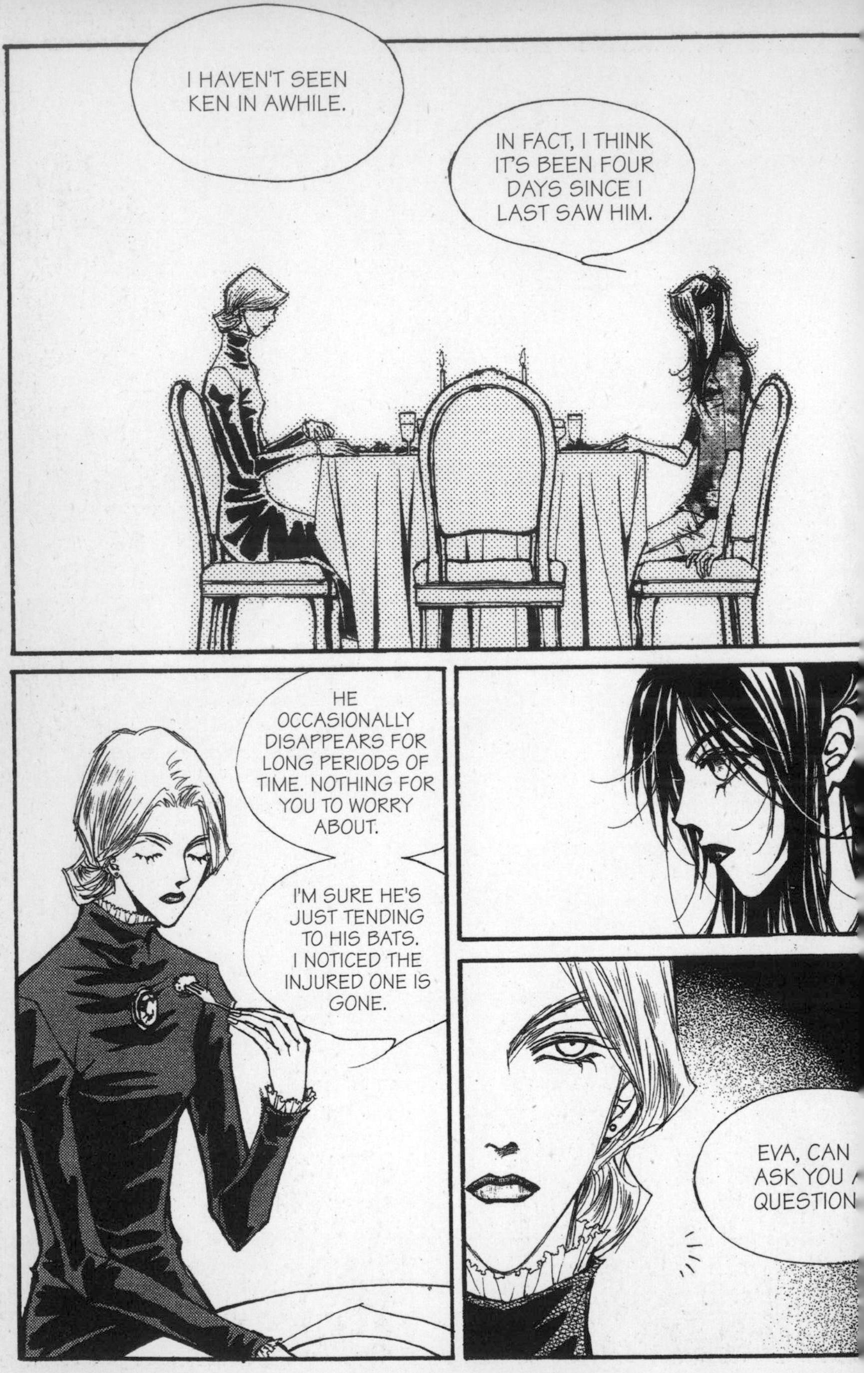
I HAVEN'T SEEN KEN IN AWHILE.
IN FACT, I THINK IT'S BEEN FOUR DAYS SINCE I LAST SAW HIM.
HE OCCASIONALLY DISAPPEARS FOR LONG PERIODS OF TIME. NOTHING FOR YOU TO WORRY ABOUT.
I'M SURE HE'S JUST TENDING TO HIS BATS. I NOTICED THE INJURED ONE IS GONE.
EVA, CAN
ASK YOU
QUESTION

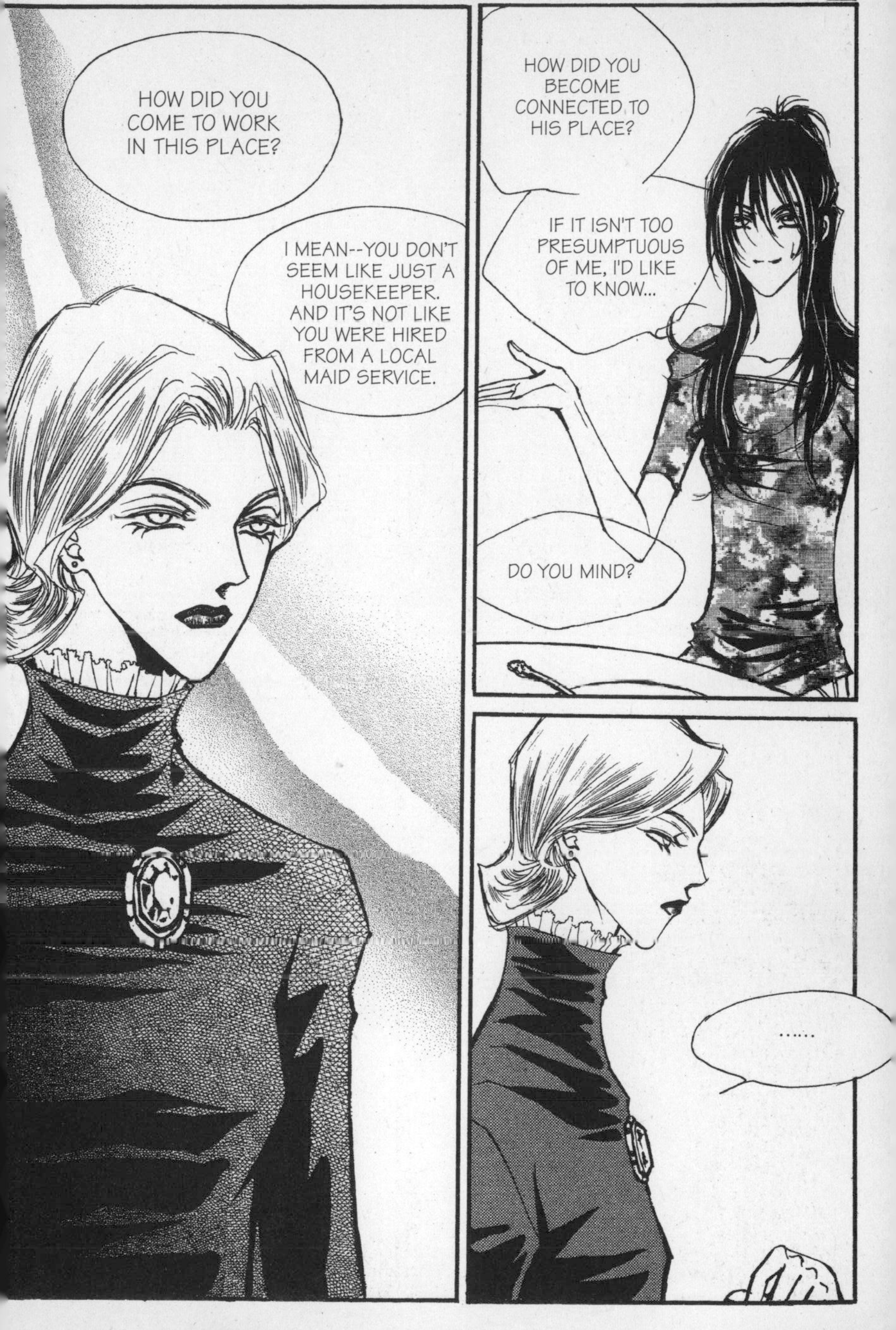
HOW DID YOU COME TO WORK IN THIS PLACE?
I MEAN--YOU DON'T SEEM LIKE JUST A HOUSEKEEPER. AND IT'S NOT LIKE YOU WERE HIRED FROM A LOCAL MAID SERVICE.
HOW DID YOU BECOME CONNECTED TO HIS PLACE?
IF IT ISN'T TOO PRESUMPTUOUS OF ME, I'D LIKE TO KNOW...
DO YOU MIND?
......

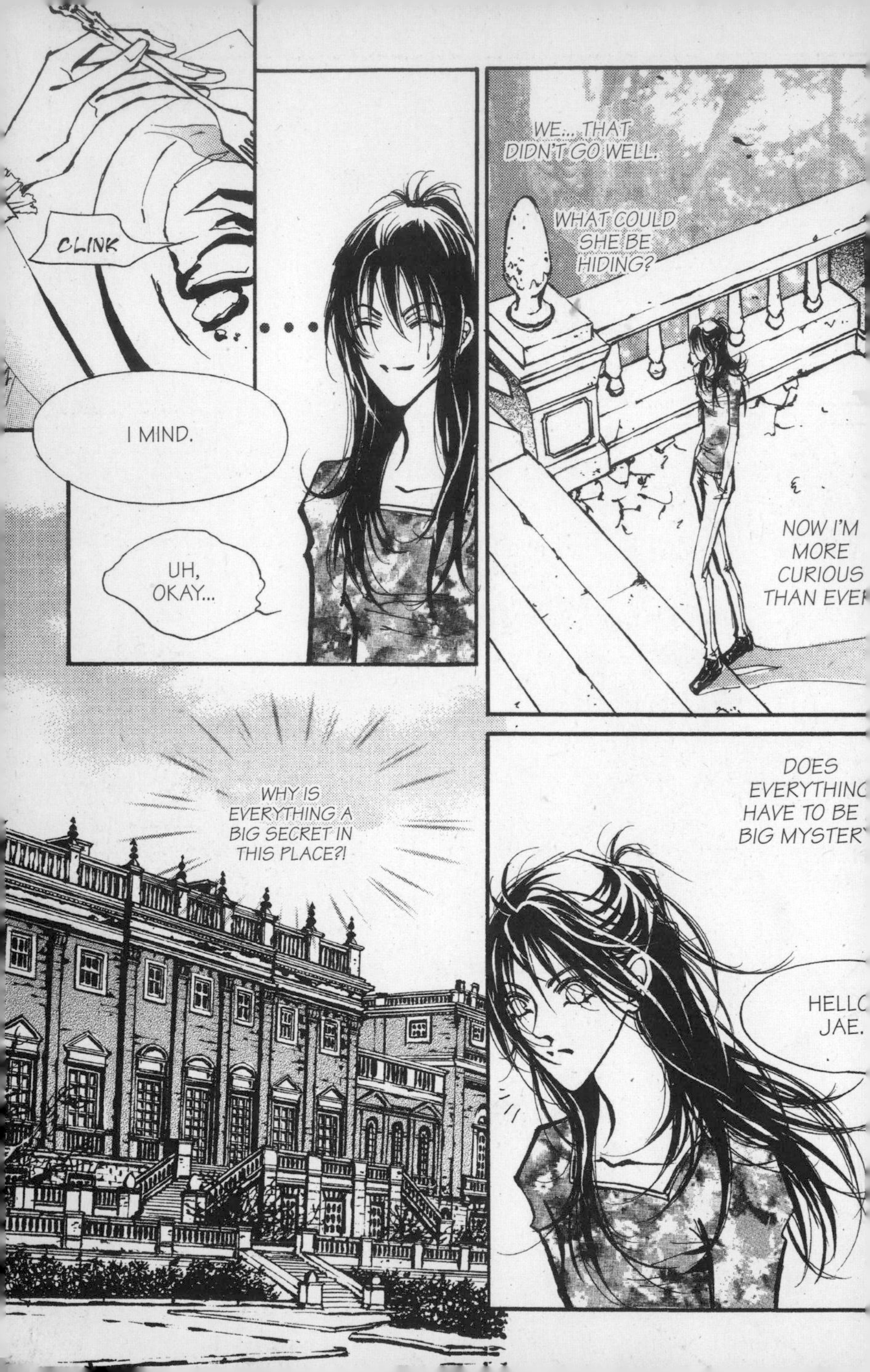
CLINK
I MIND.
UH, OKAY...
WE... THAT DIDN'T GO WELL.
WHAT COULD SHE BE HIDING?
NOW I'M MORE CURIOUS THAN EVER
WHY IS EVERYTHING A BIG SECRET IN THIS PLACE?!
DOES EVERYTHING HAVE TO BE BIG MYSTERY
HELLO JAE.

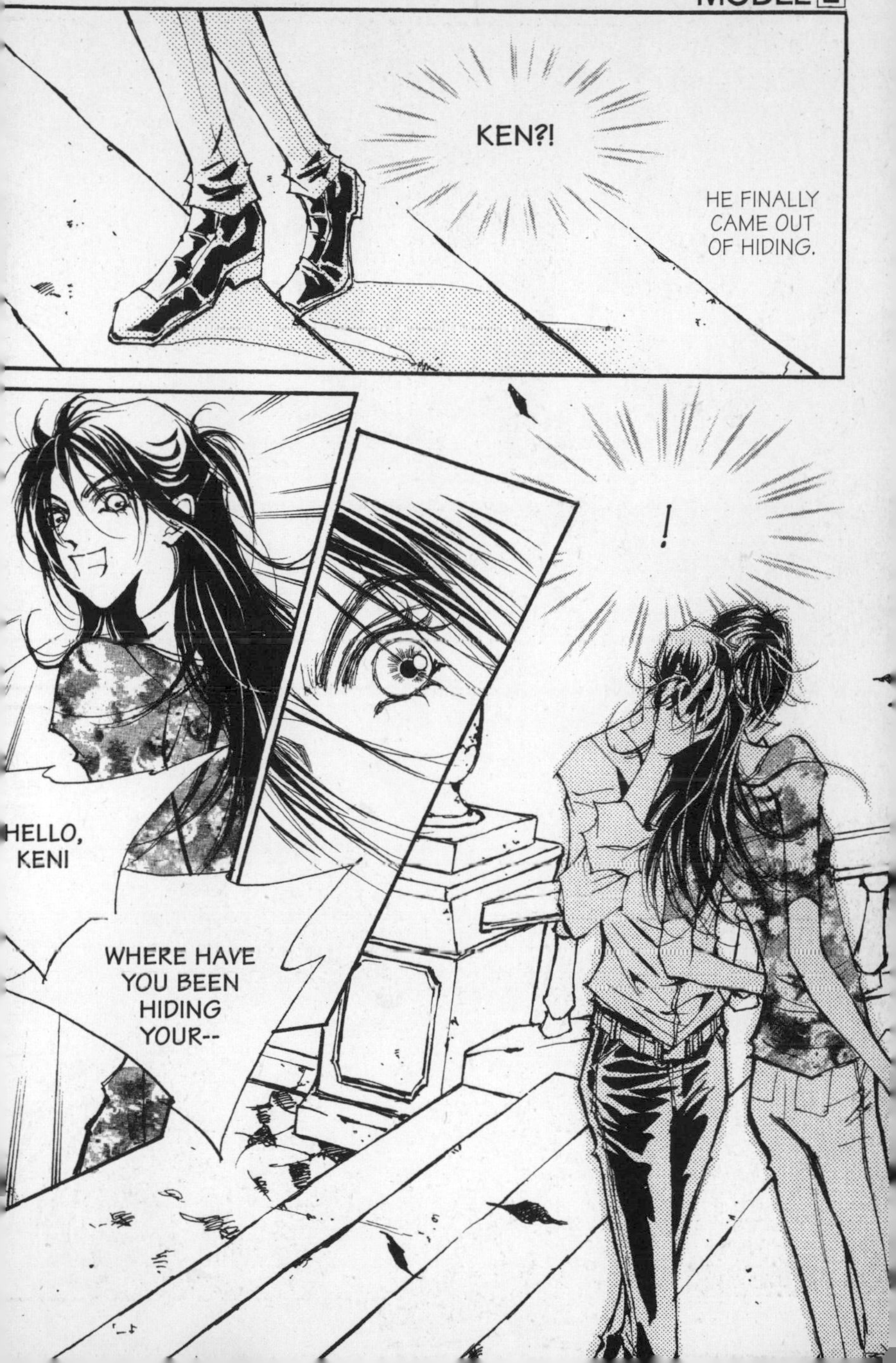
KEN?!
HE FINALLY CAME OUT OF HIDING.
HELLO, KEN!
WHERE HAVE YOU BEEN HIDING YOUR--
!

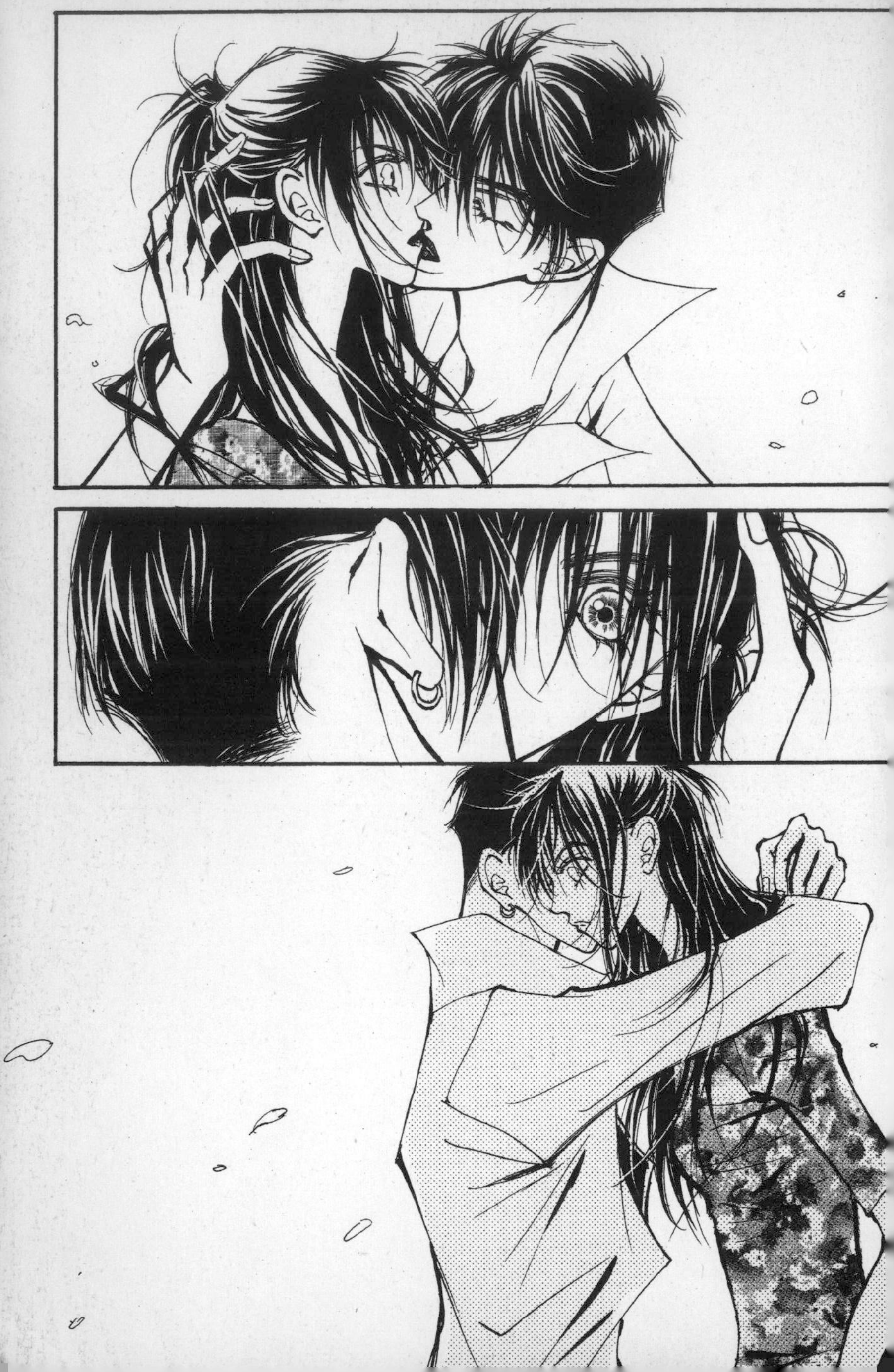

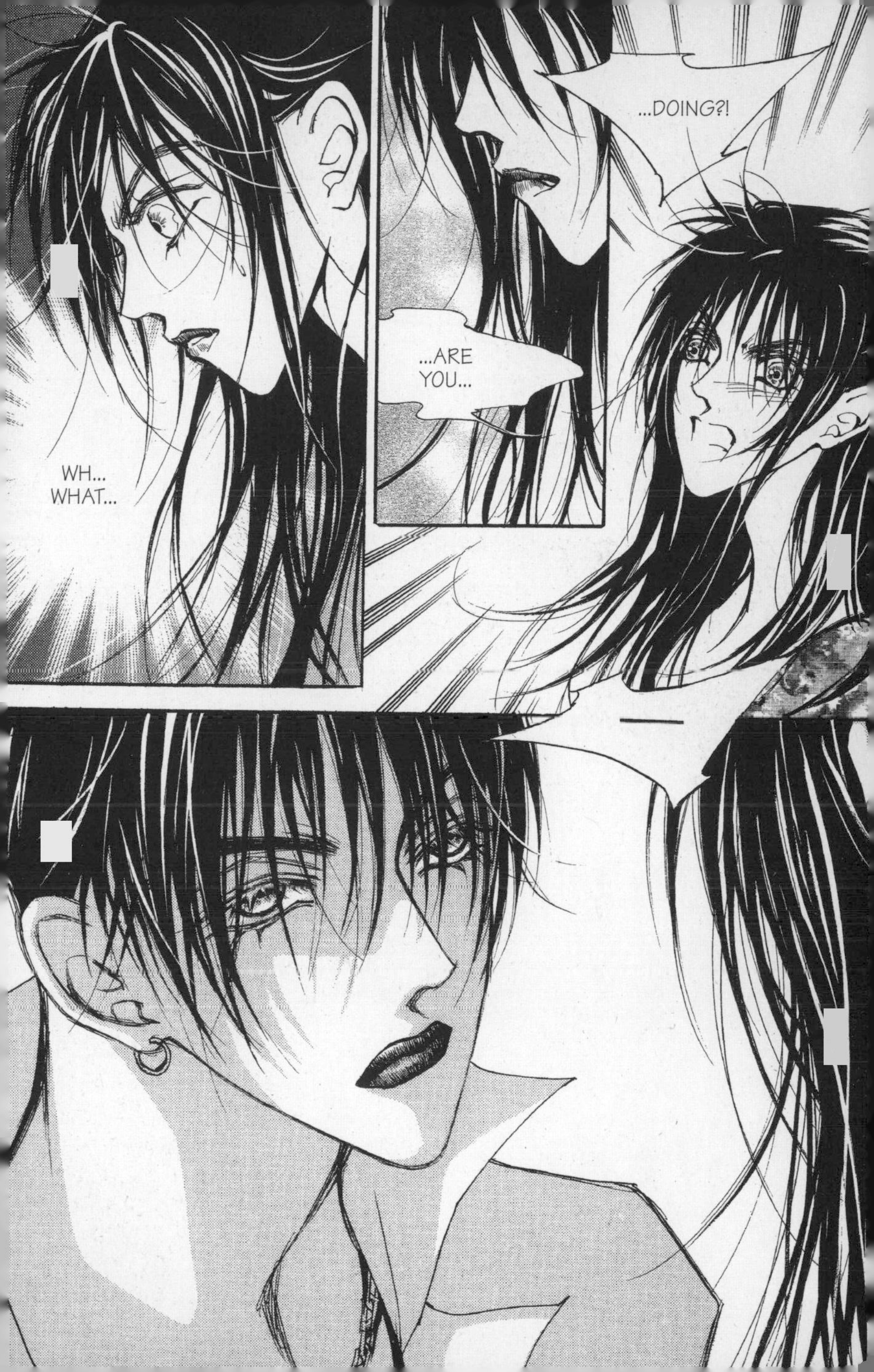
WH...
WHAT...
...ARE
YOU...
...DOING?!
—

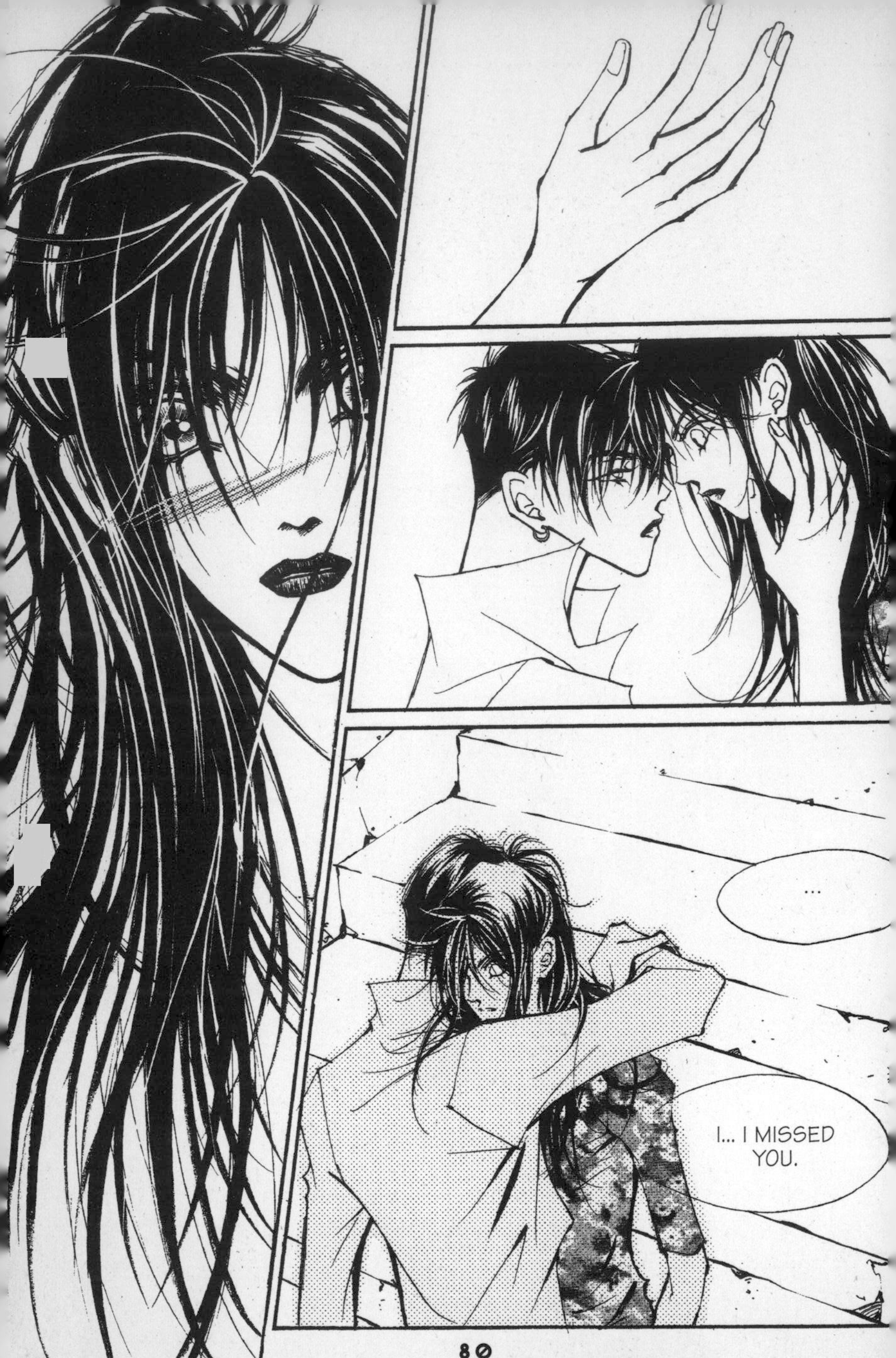
...
I... I MISSED YOU.

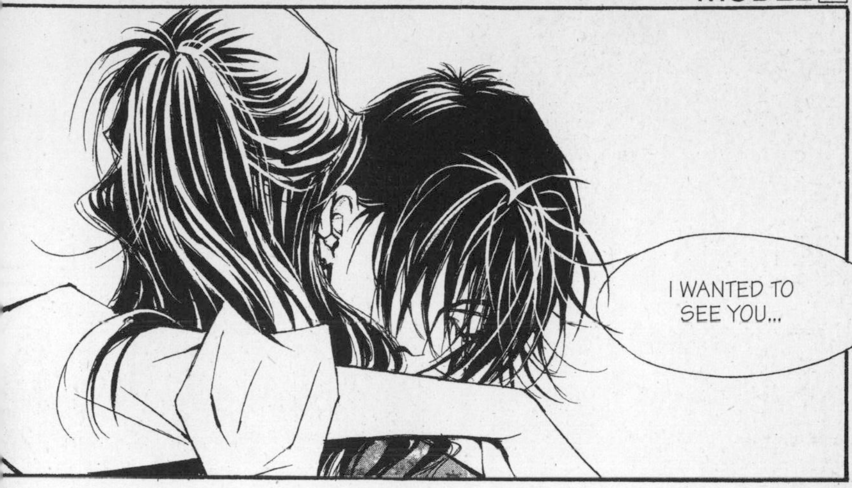
I WANTED TO SEE YOU...

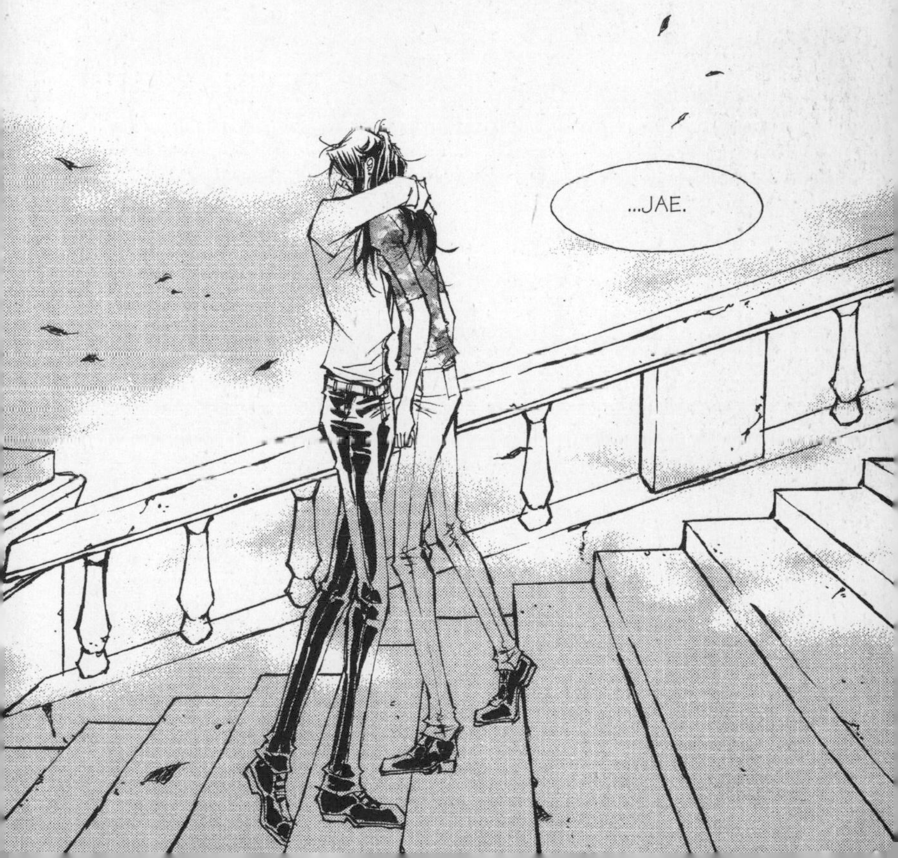
...JAE.

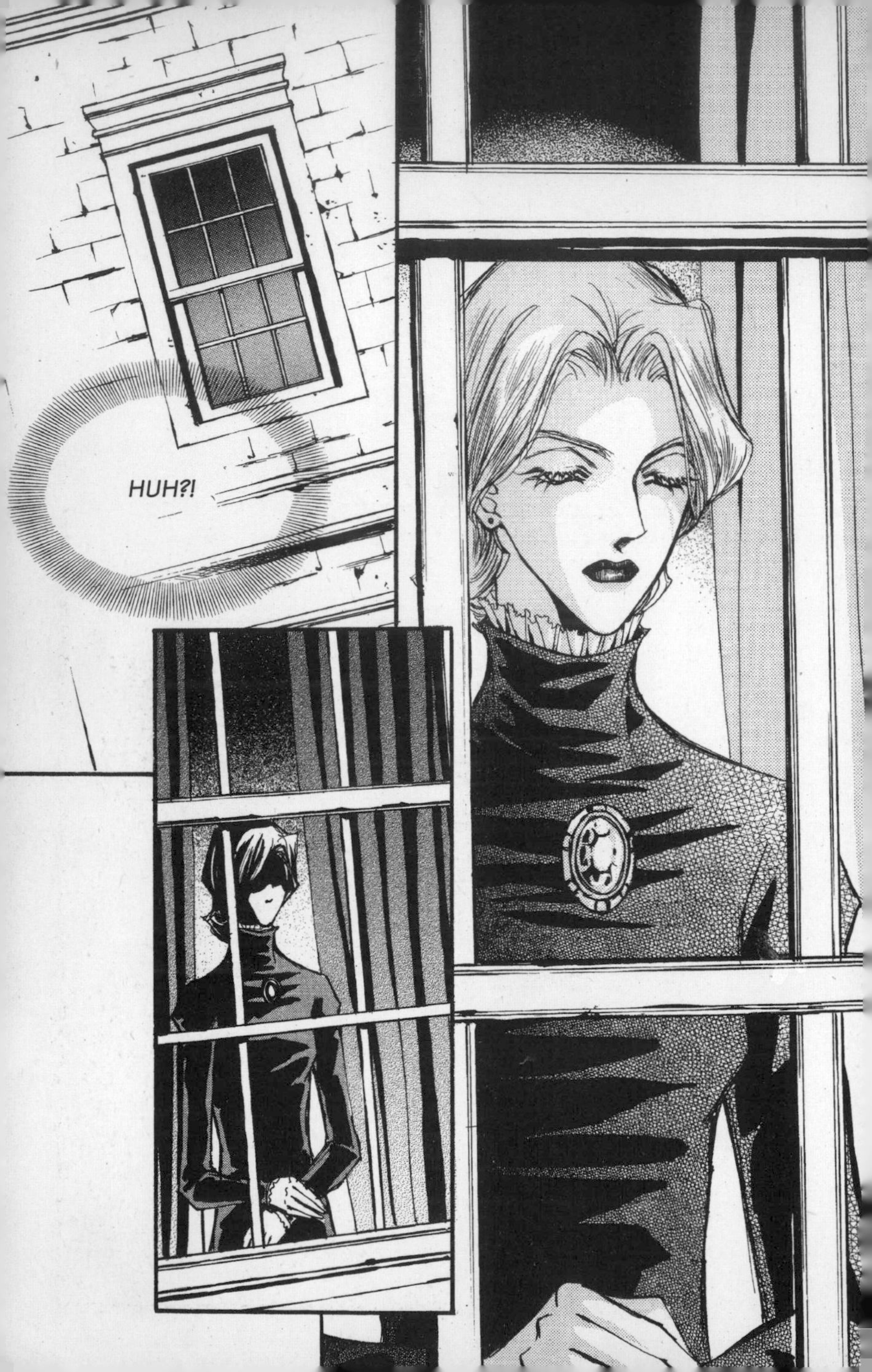
HUH?!

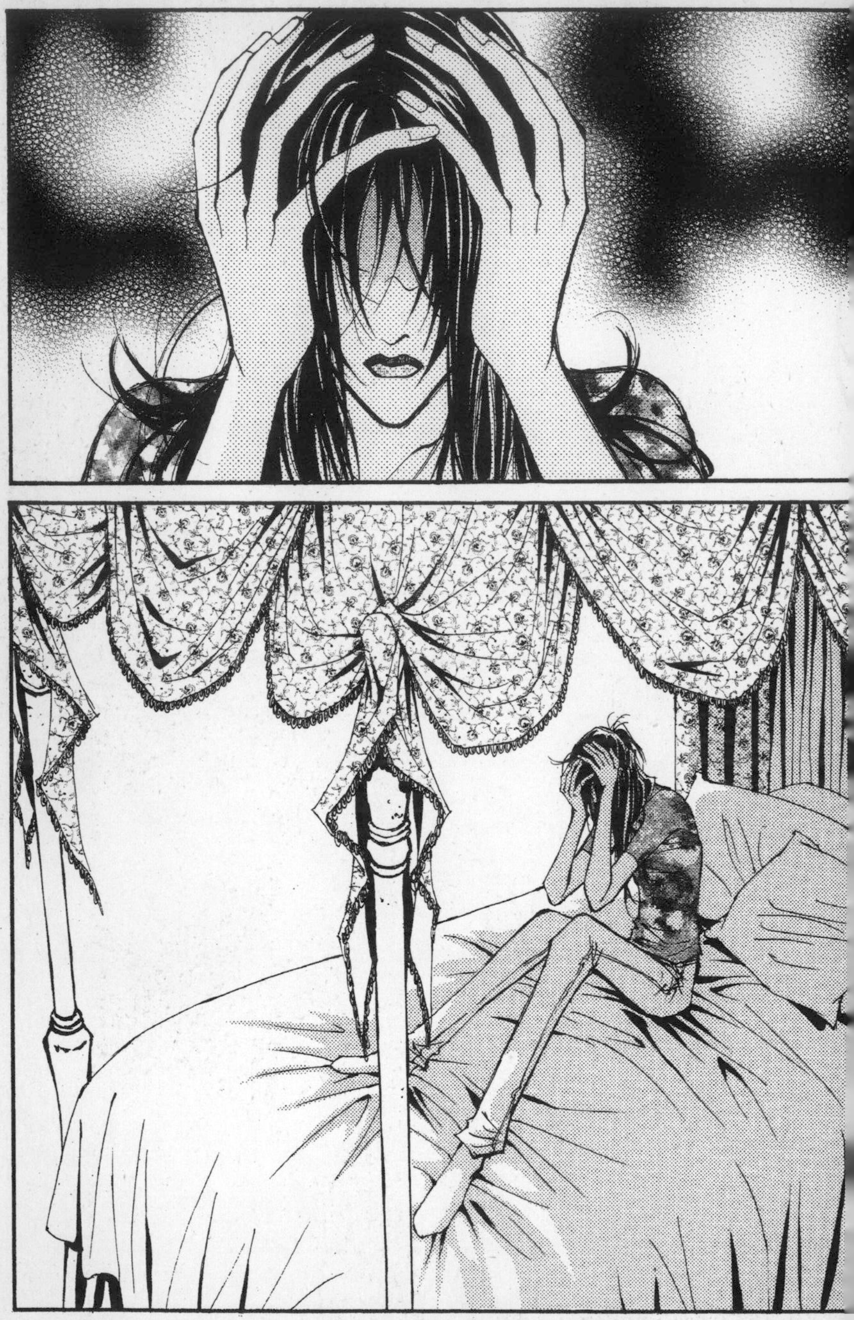

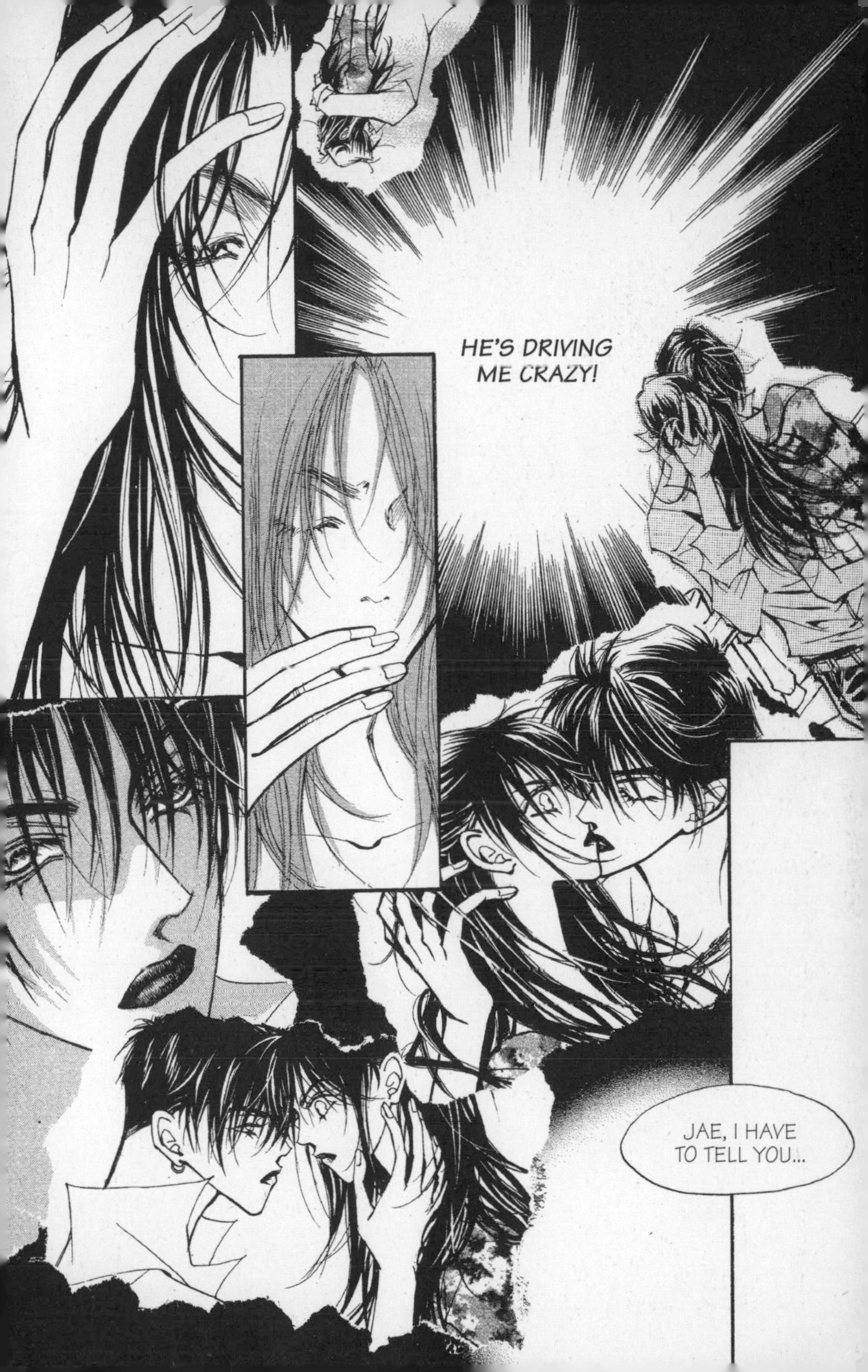
HE'S DRIVING ME CRAZY!
JAE, I HAVE TO TELL YOU...

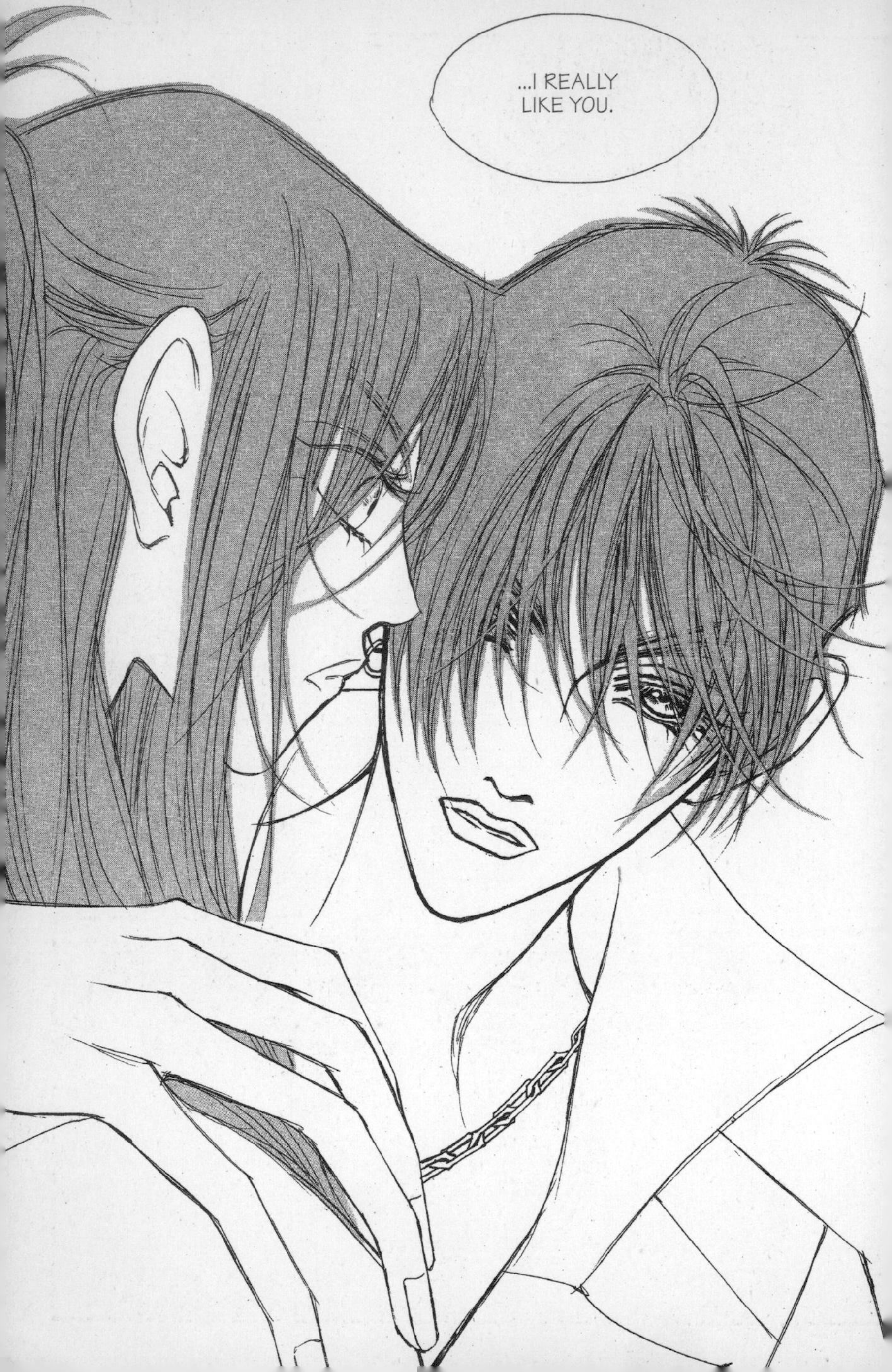
...I REALLY LIKE YOU.

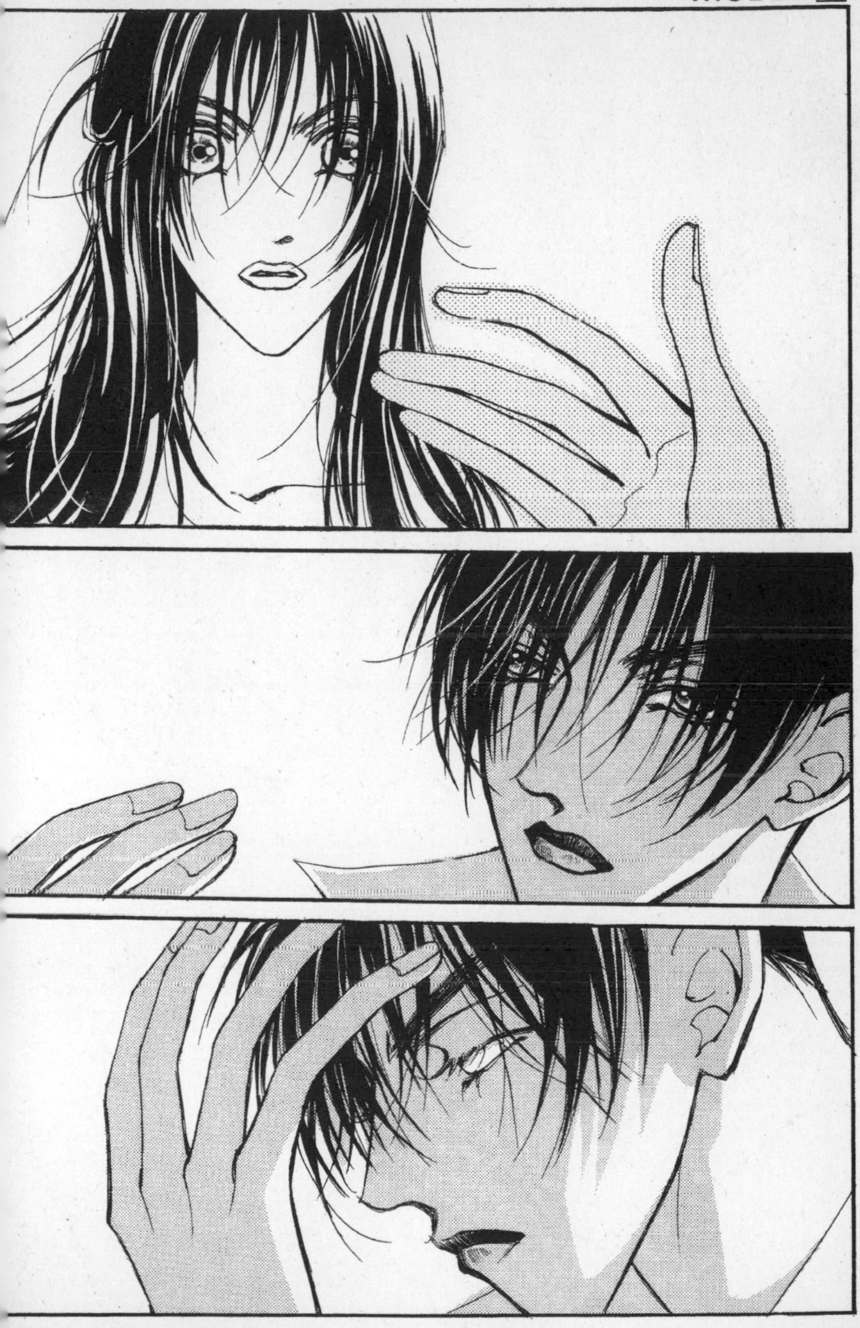

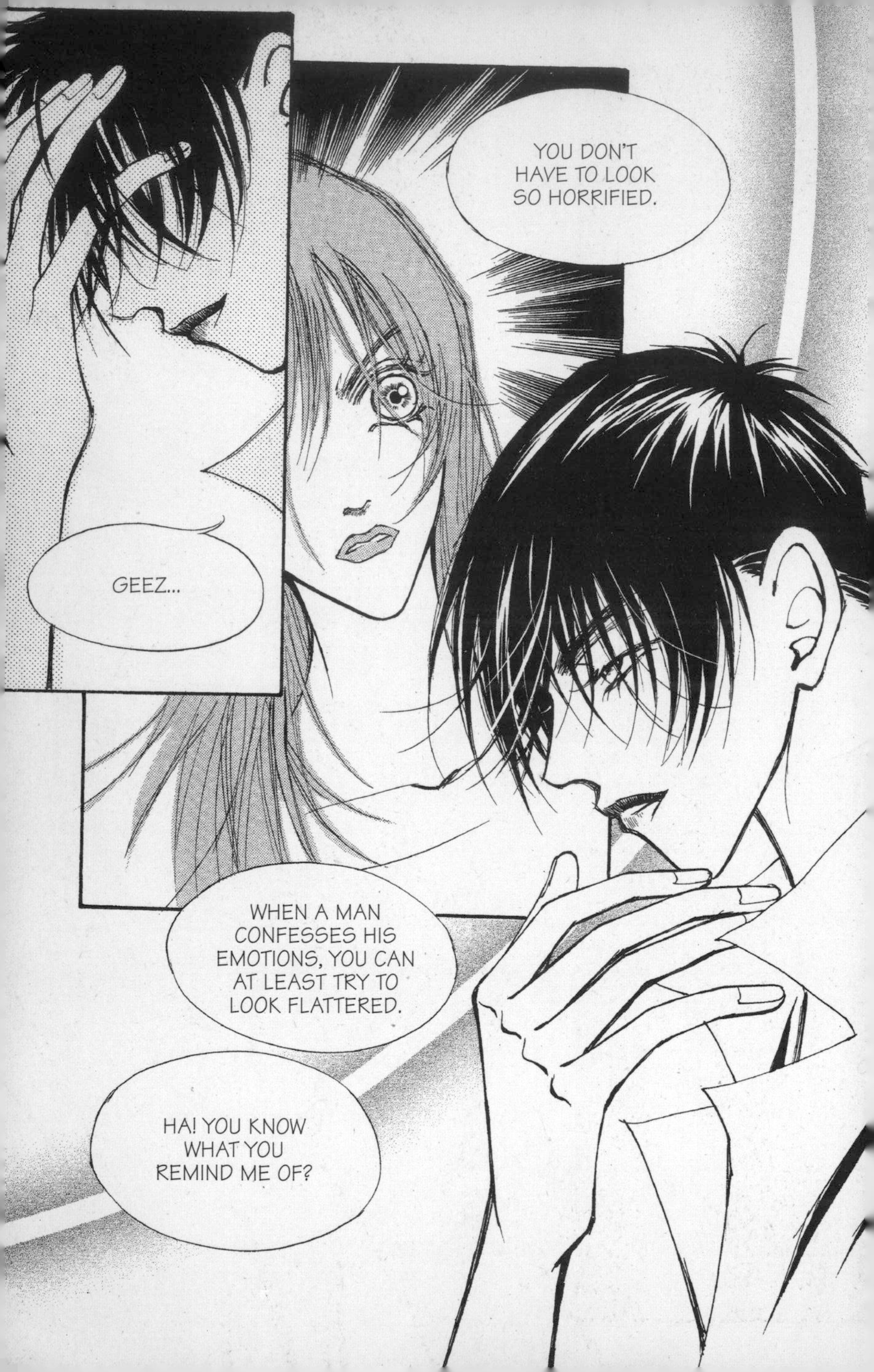

YOU DON'T HAVE TO LOOK SO HORRIFIED.
GEEZ...
WHEN A MAN CONFESSES HIS EMOTIONS, YOU CAN AT LEAST TRY TO LOOK FLATTERED.
HA! YOU KNOW WHAT YOU REMIND ME OF?

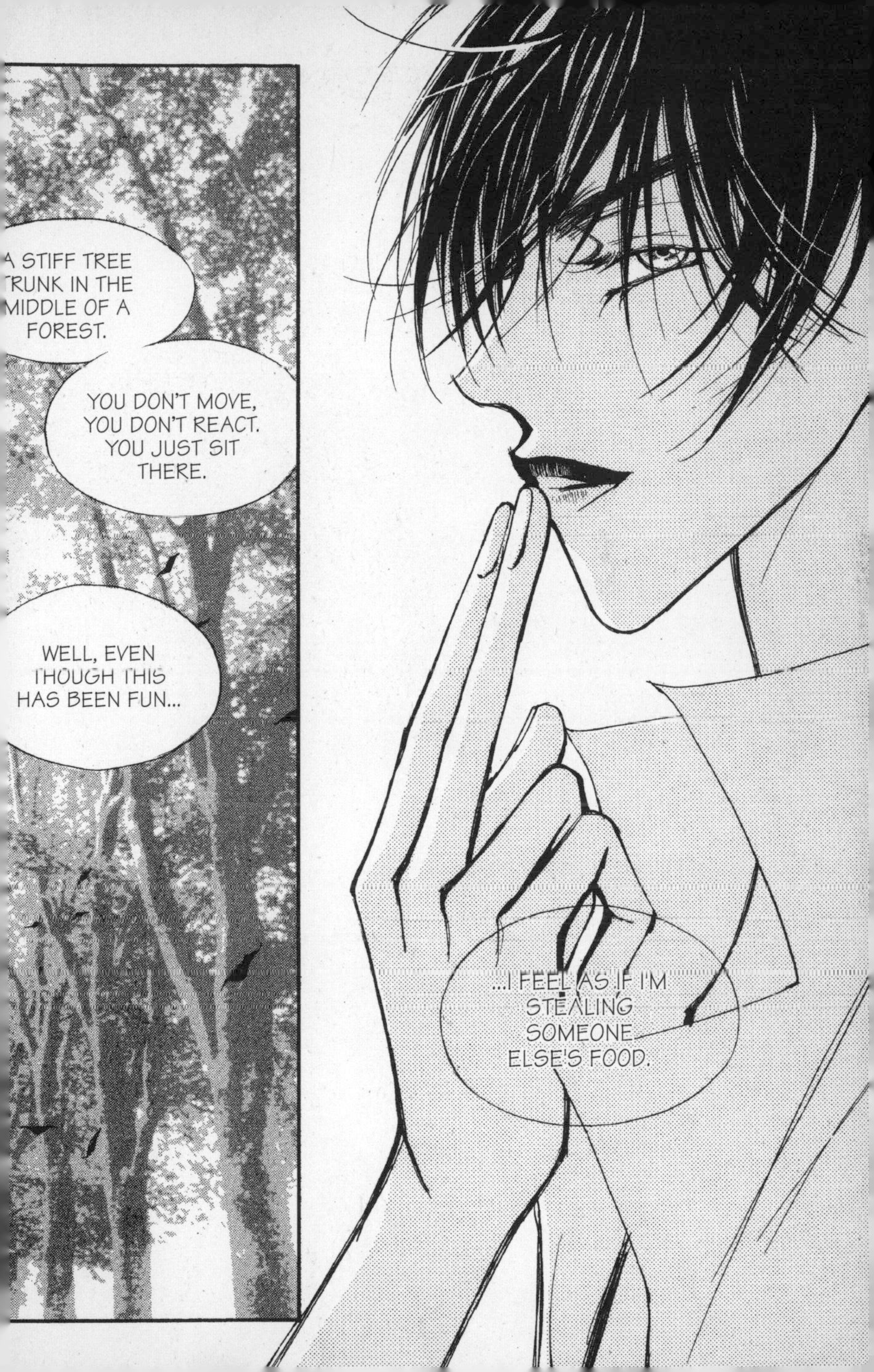
A STIFF TREE TRUNK IN THE MIDDLE OF A FOREST.
YOU DON'T MOVE, YOU DON'T REACT. YOU JUST SIT THERE.
WELL, EVEN THOUGH THIS HAS BEEN FUN...
...I FEEL AS IF I'M STEALING SOMEONE ELSE'S FOOD.

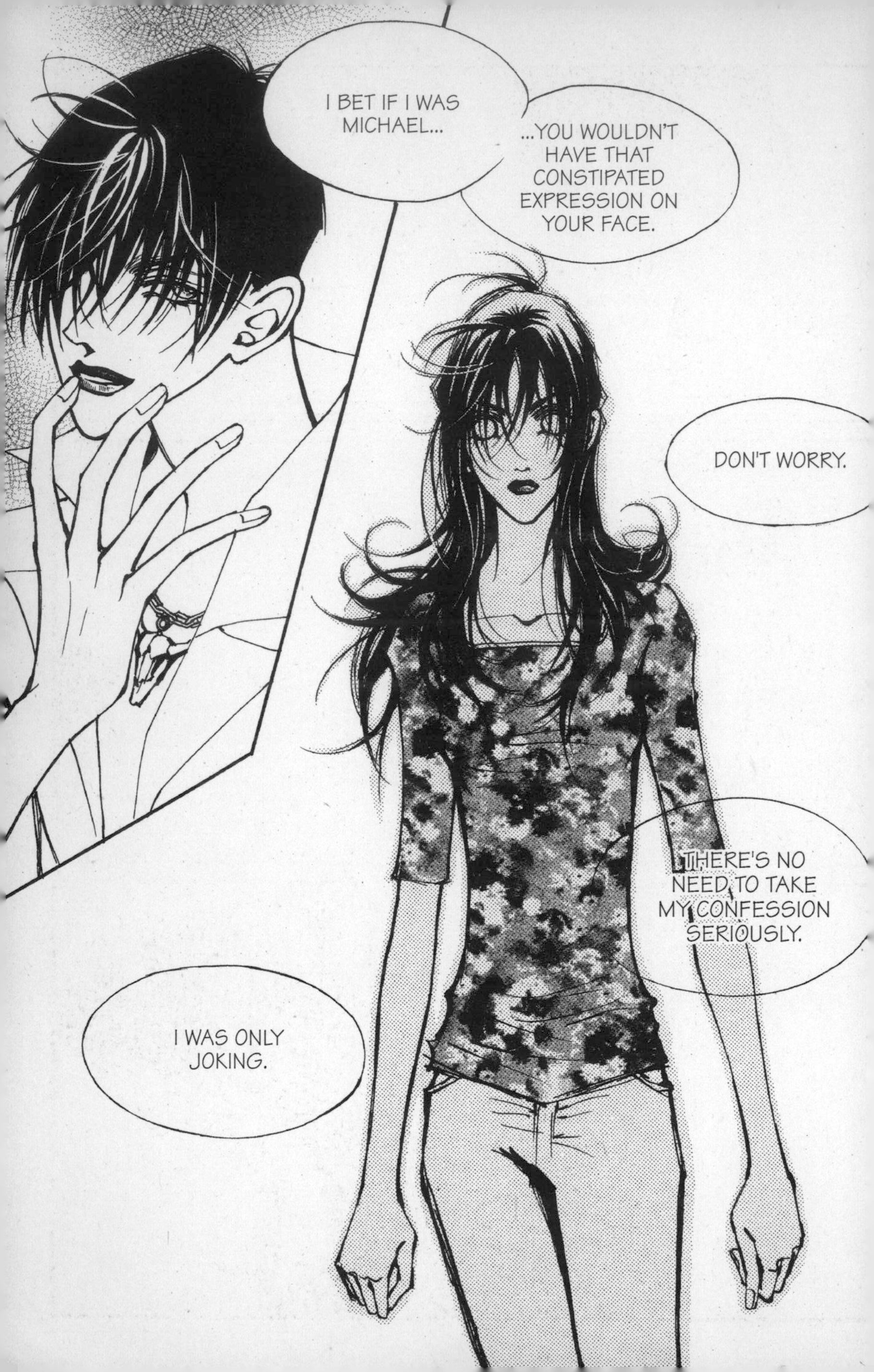
I BET IF I WAS MICHAEL...
...YOU WOULDN'T HAVE THAT CONSTIPATED EXPRESSION ON YOUR FACE.
DON'T WORRY.
THERE'S NO NEED TO TAKE MY CONFESSION SERIOUSLY.
I WAS ONLY JOKING.

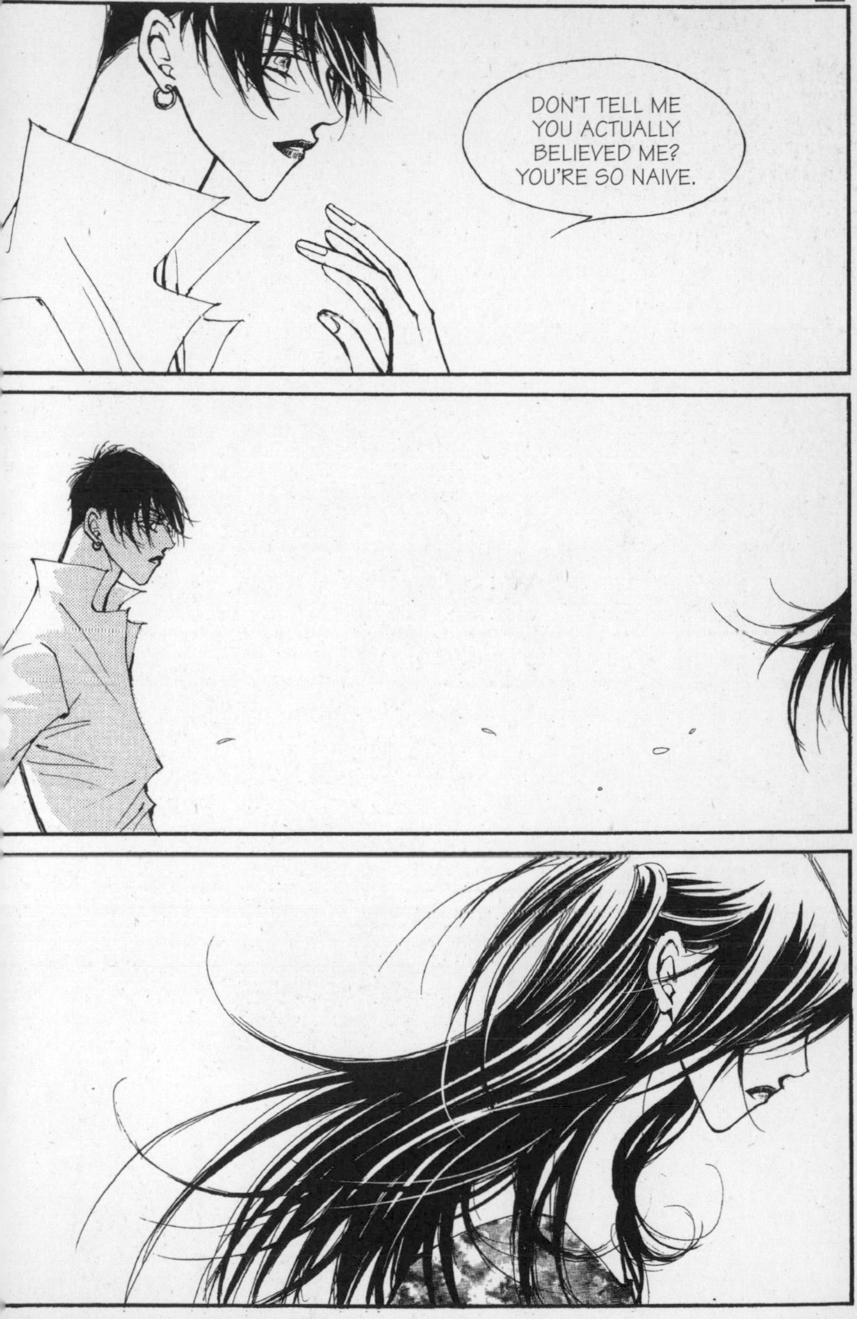
DON'T TELL ME YOU ACTUALLY BELIEVED ME? YOU'RE SO NAIVE.

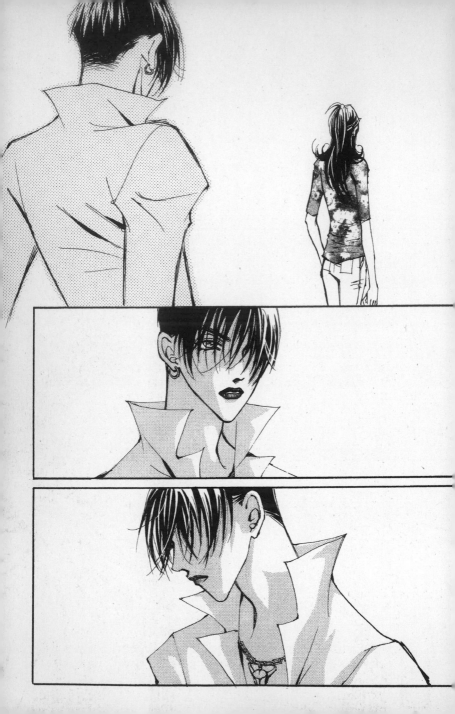

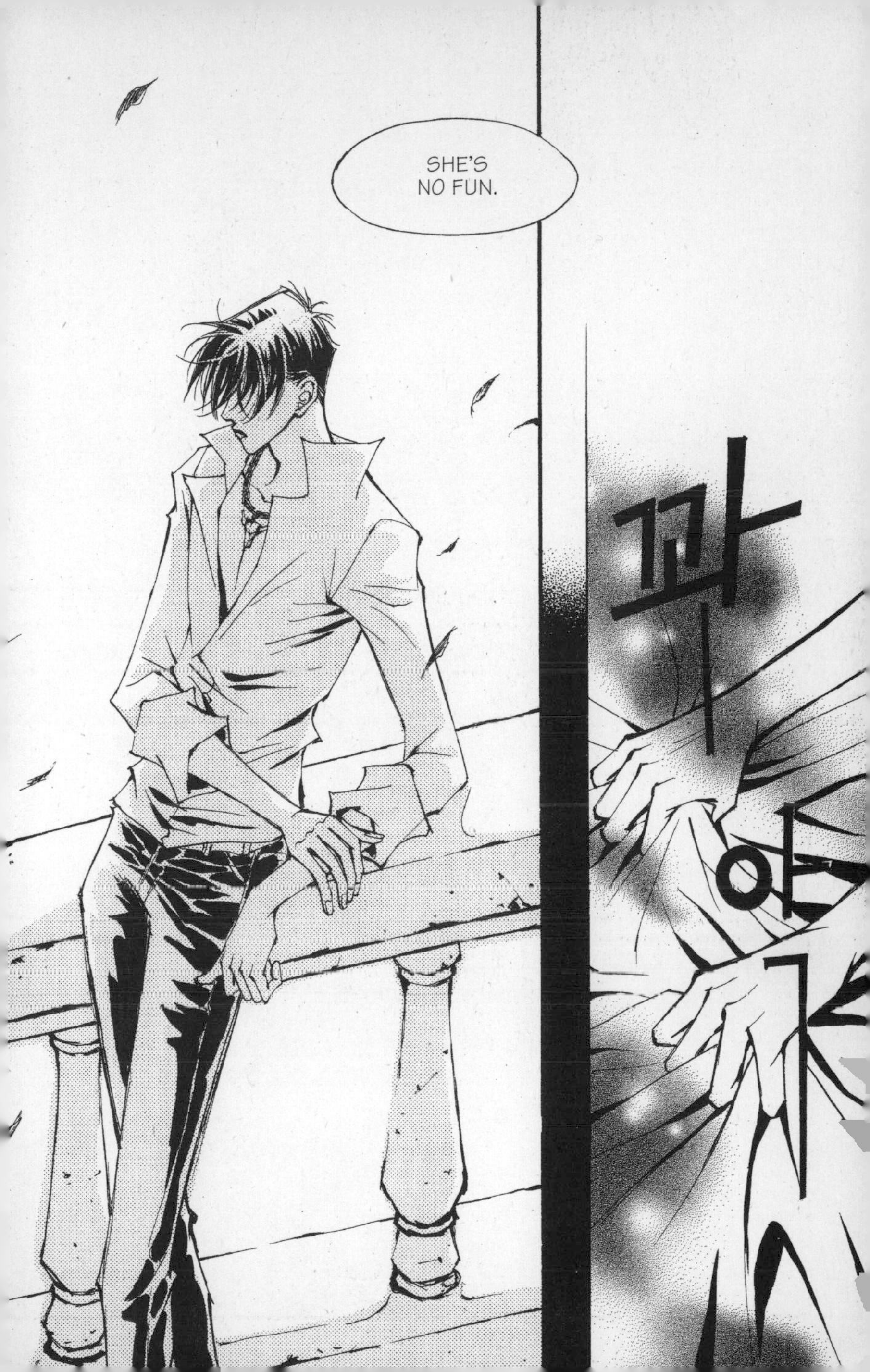
SHE'S NO FUN.
꽈악

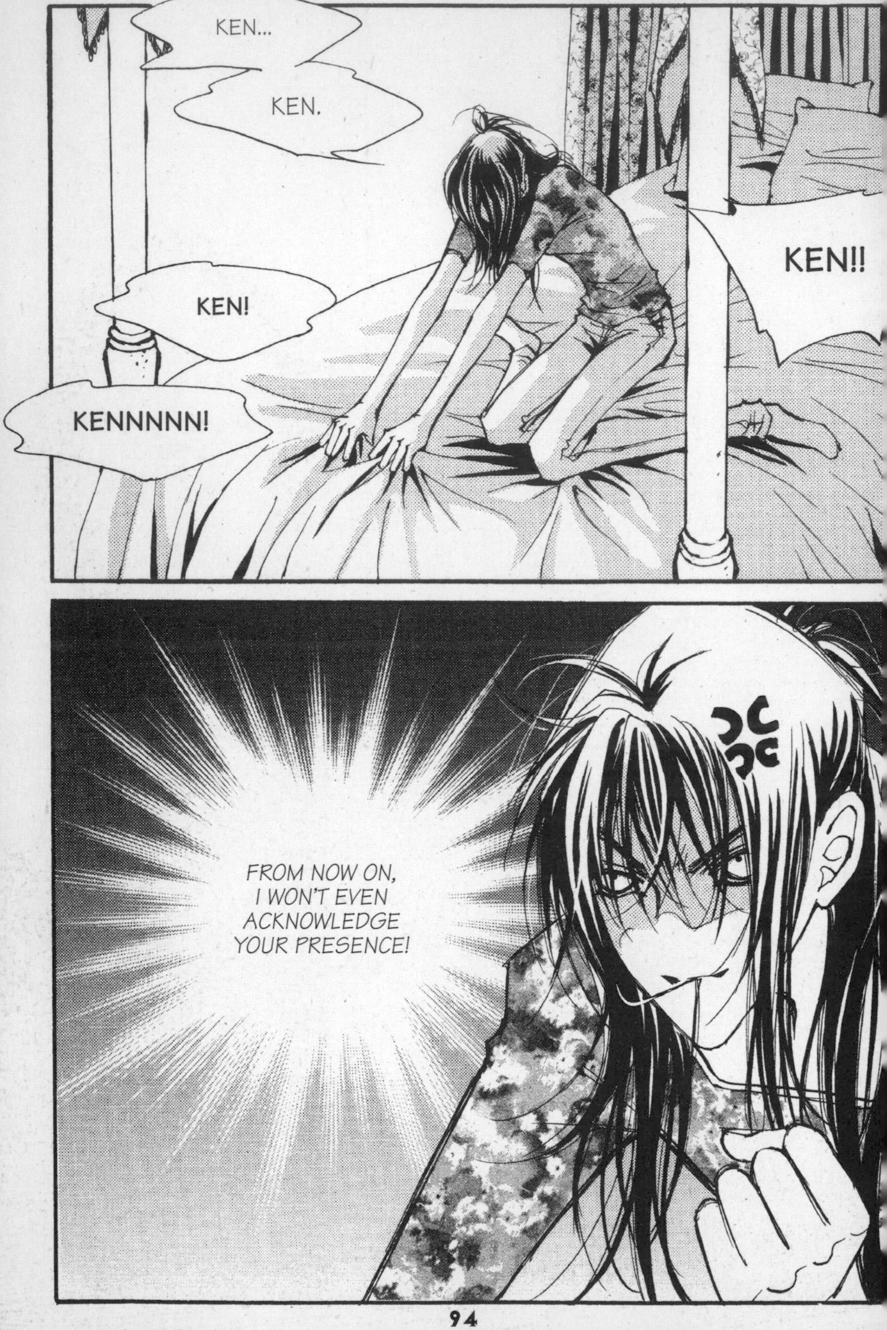
KEN...
KEN.
KEN!
KENNNNN!
KEN!!
FROM NOW ON, I WON'T EVEN ACKNOWLEDGE YOUR PRESENCE!

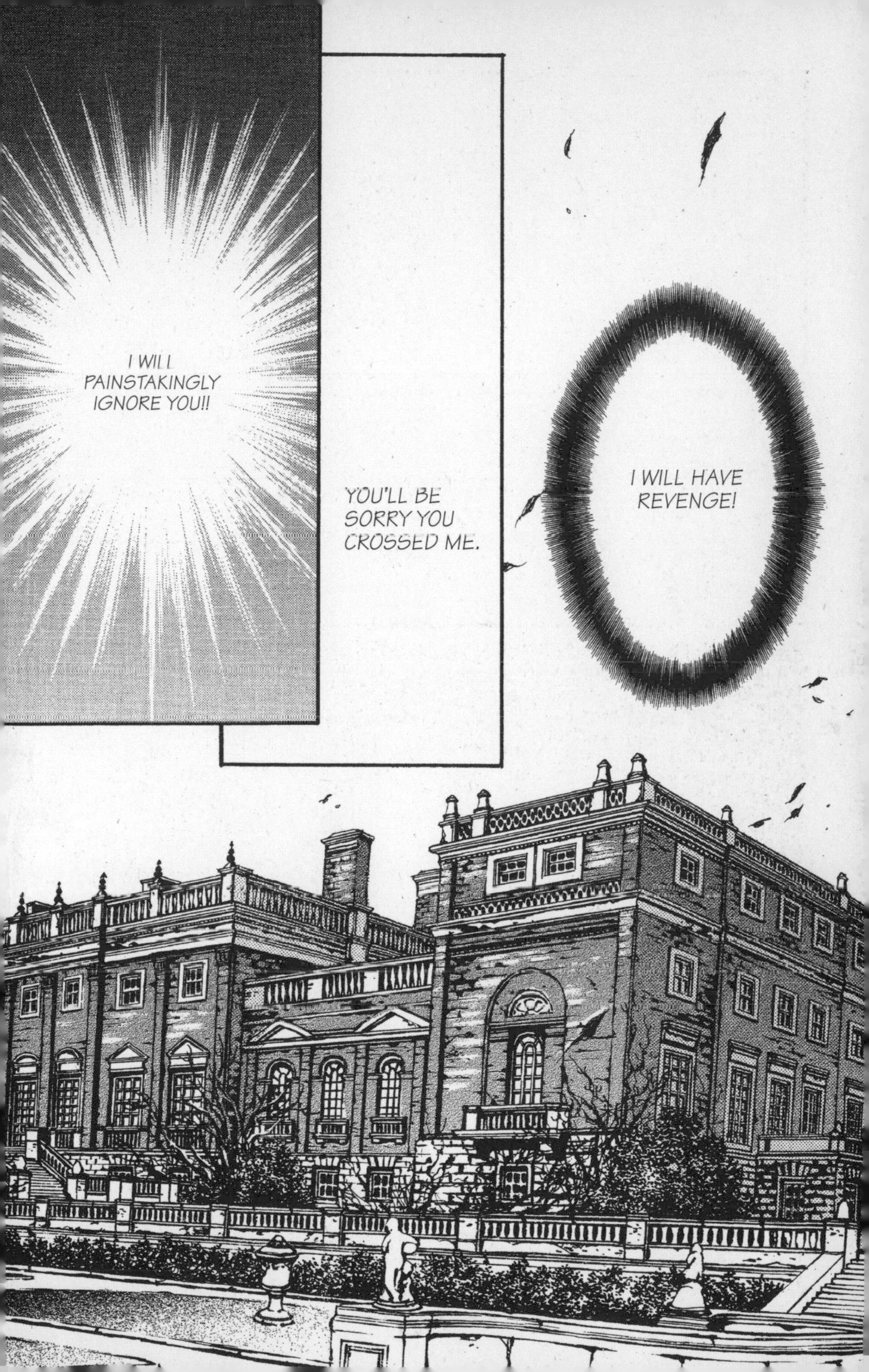
I WILL PAINSTAKINGLY IGNORE YOU!!
YOU'LL BE SORRY YOU CROSSED ME.
I WILL HAVE REVENGE!

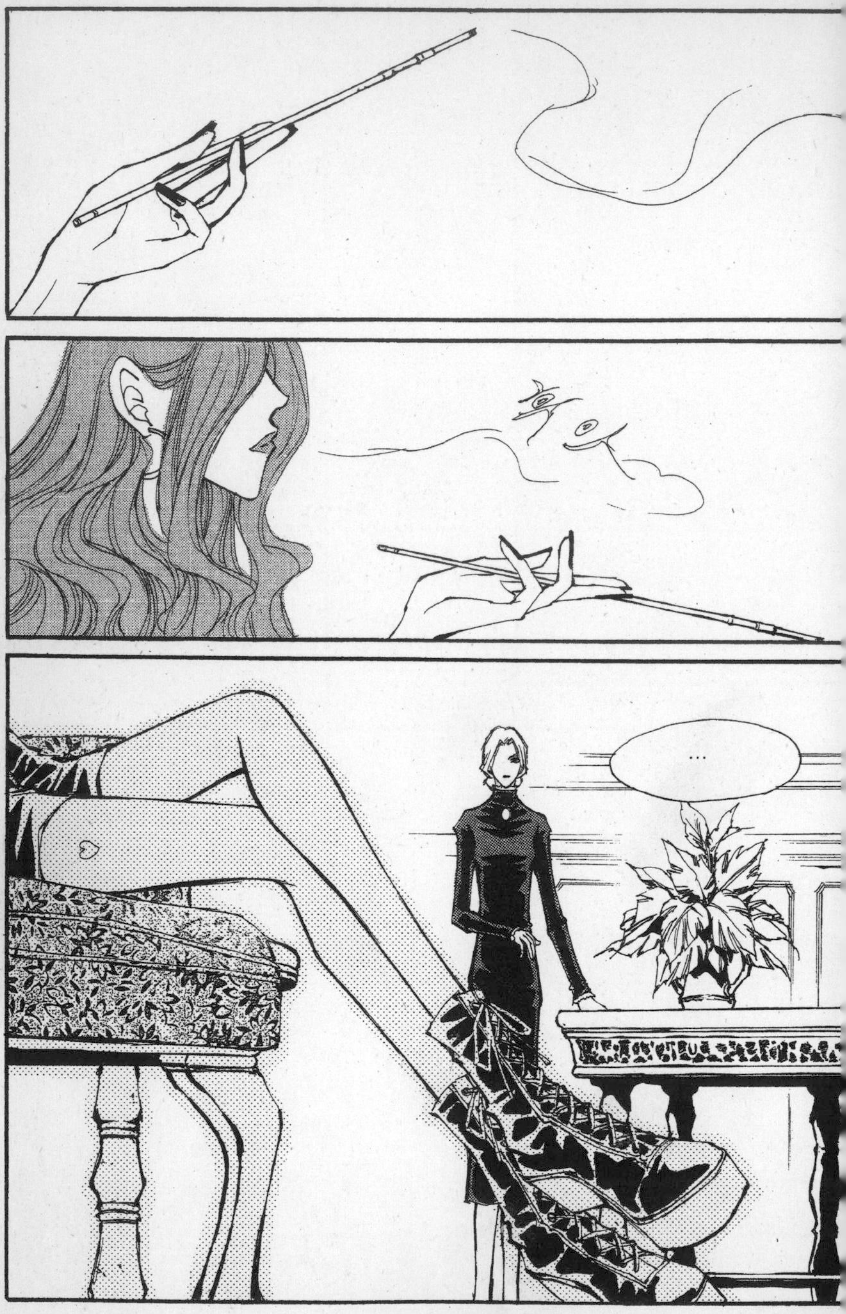
후우
...

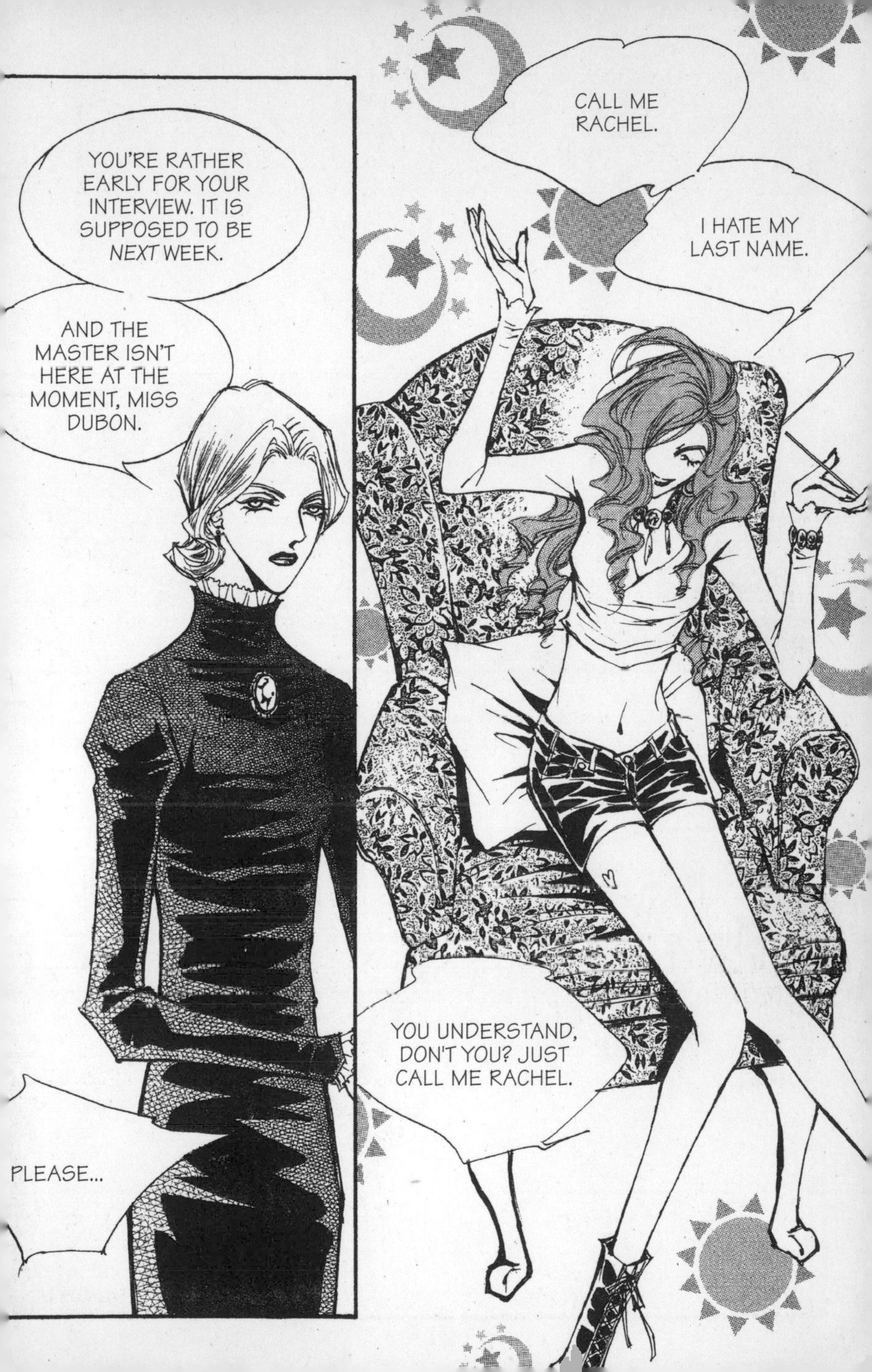
YOU'RE RATHER EARLY FOR YOUR INTERVIEW. IT IS SUPPOSED TO BE *NEXT* WEEK.
AND THE MASTER ISN'T HERE AT THE MOMENT, MISS DUBON.
PLEASE...
CALL ME RACHEL.
I HATE MY LAST NAME.
YOU UNDERSTAND, DON'T YOU? JUST CALL ME RACHEL.

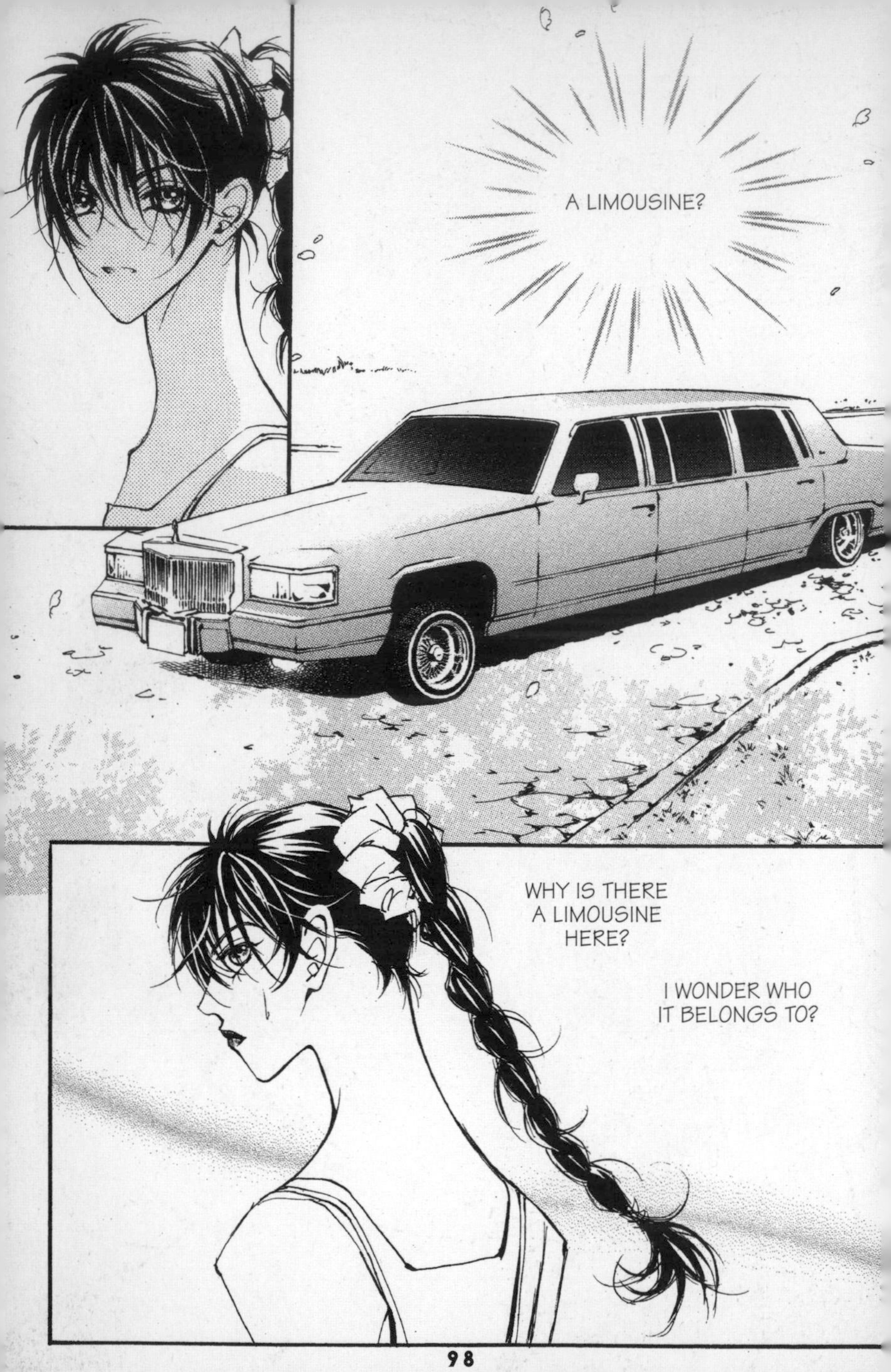
A LIMOUSINE?
WHY IS THERE A LIMOUSINE HERE?
I WONDER WHO IT BELONGS TO?

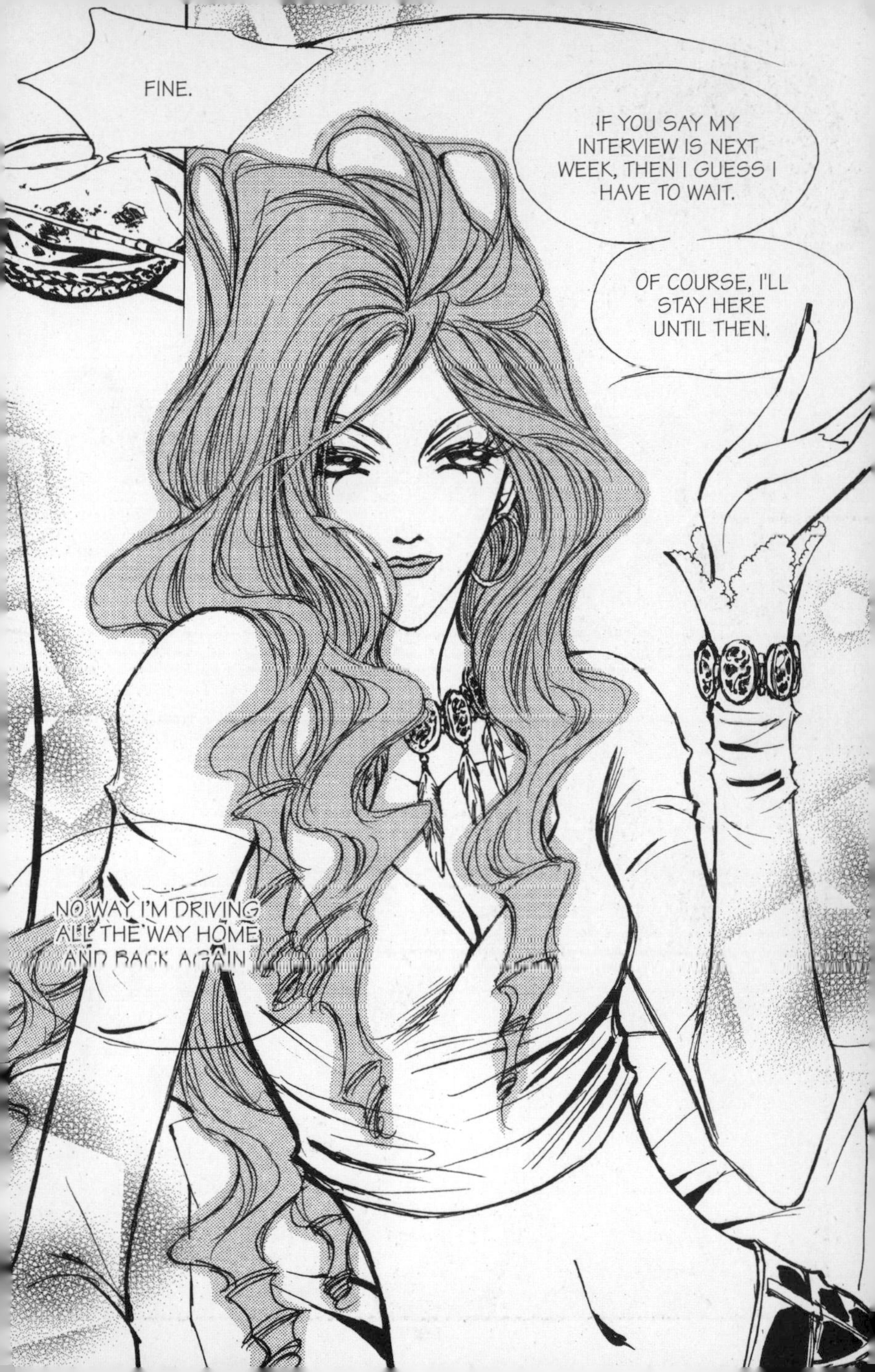
FINE.
IF YOU SAY MY INTERVIEW IS NEXT WEEK, THEN I GUESS I HAVE TO WAIT.
OF COURSE, I'LL STAY HERE UNTIL THEN.
NO WAY I'M DRIVING ALL THE WAY HOME AND BACK AGAIN.

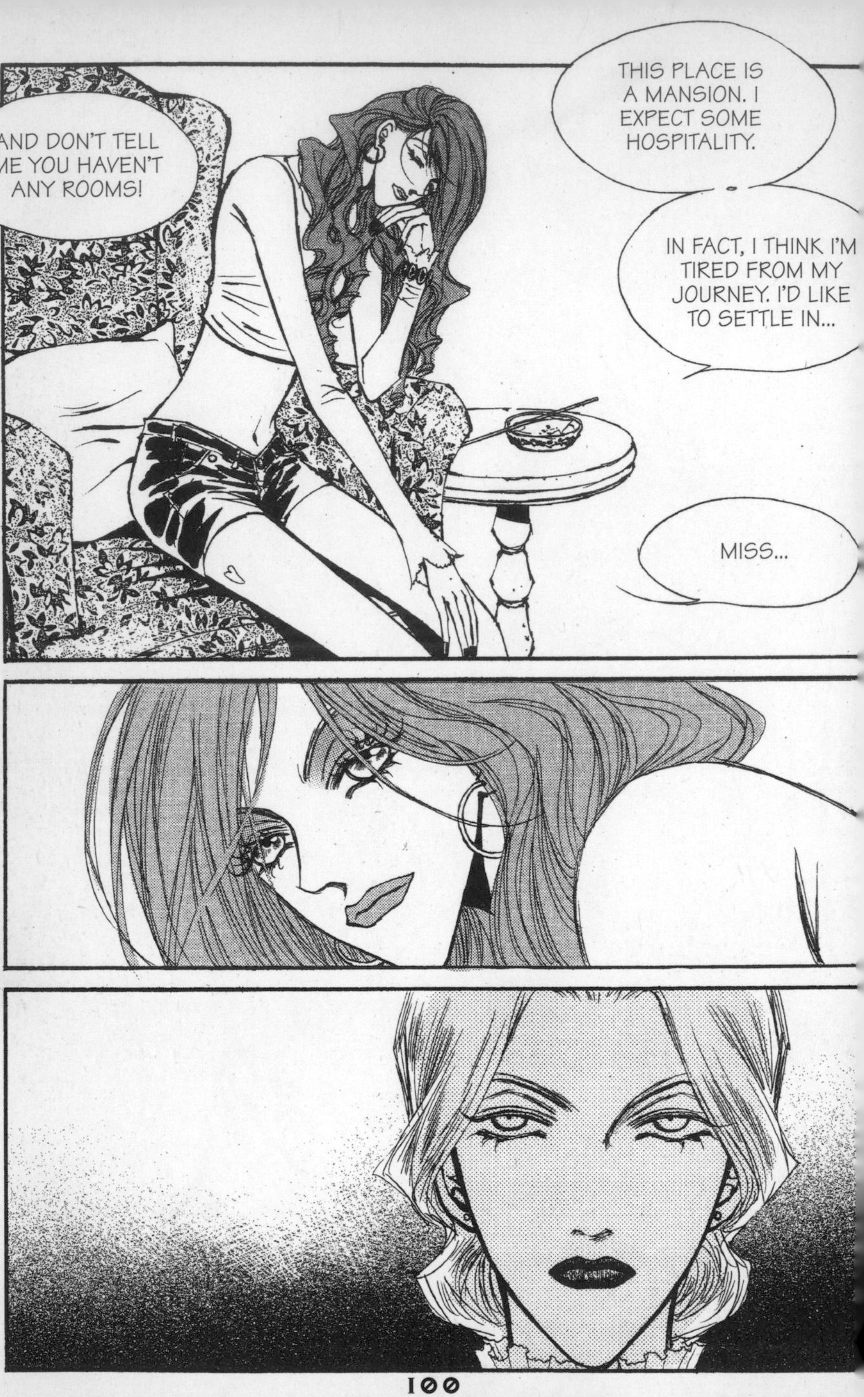
AND DON'T TELL ME YOU HAVEN'T ANY ROOMS!
THIS PLACE IS A MANSION. I EXPECT SOME HOSPITALITY.
IN FACT, I THINK I'M TIRED FROM MY JOURNEY. I'D LIKE TO SETTLE IN...
MISS...

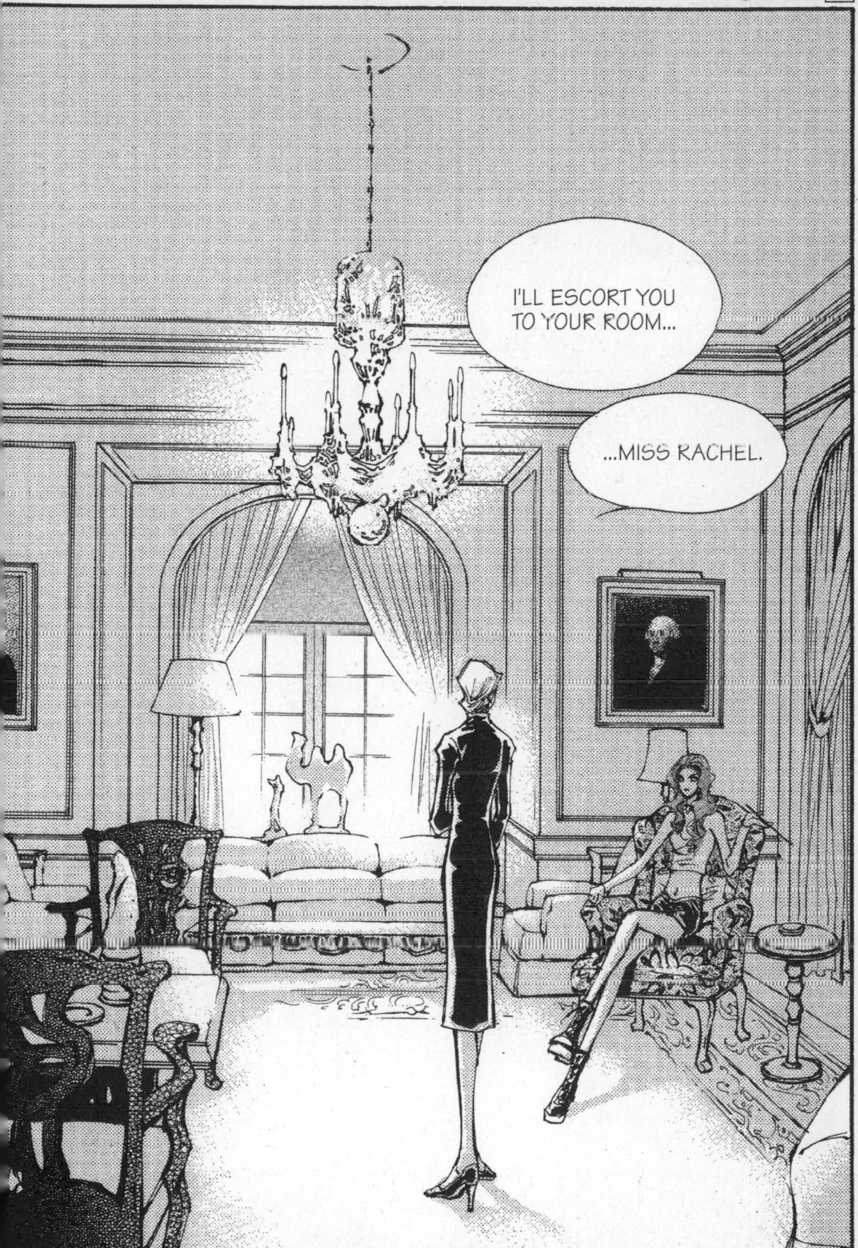
I'LL ESCORT YOU TO YOUR ROOM...
...MISS RACHEL.

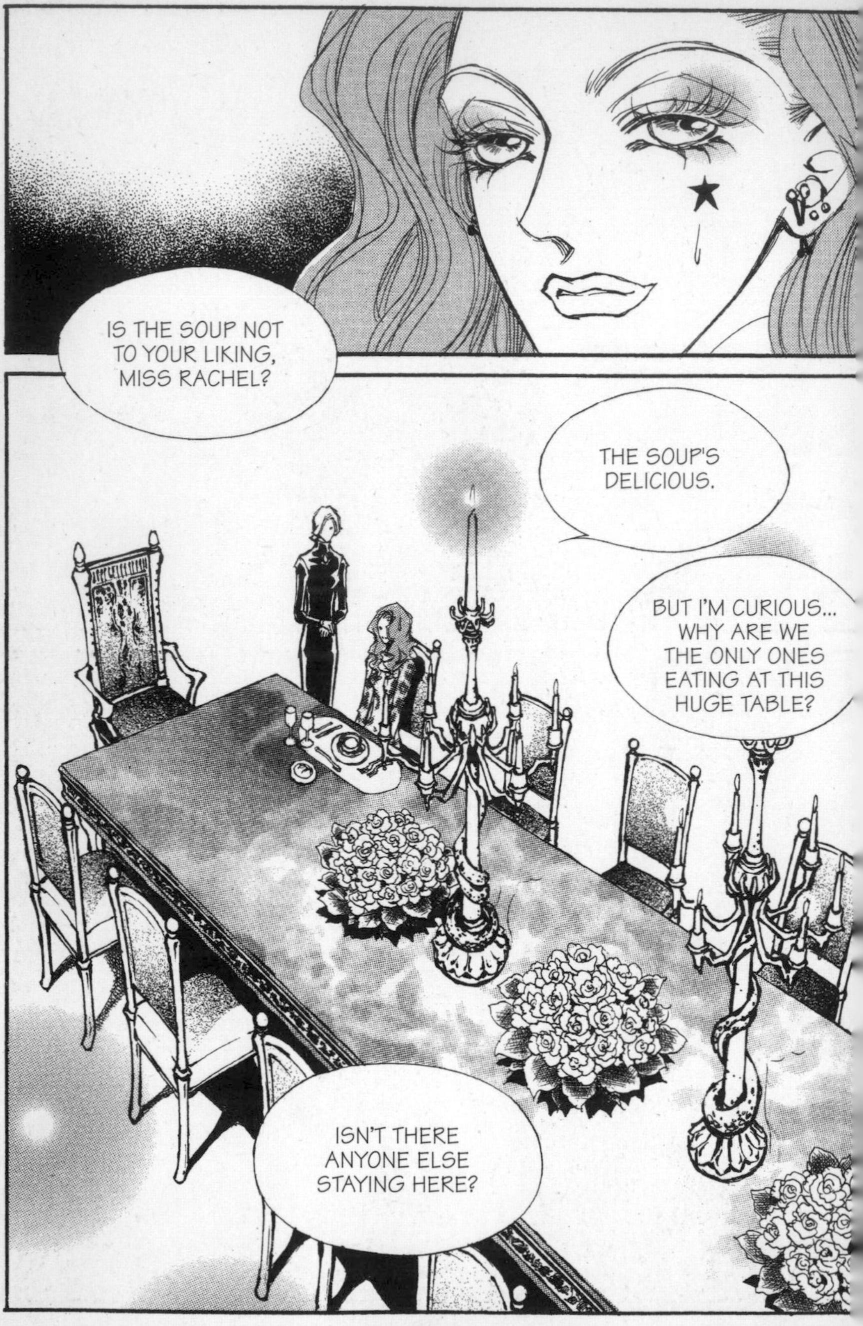
IS THE SOUP NOT TO YOUR LIKING, MISS RACHEL?
THE SOUP'S DELICIOUS.
BUT I'M CURIOUS... WHY ARE WE THE ONLY ONES EATING AT THIS HUGE TABLE?
ISN'T THERE ANYONE ELSE STAYING HERE?

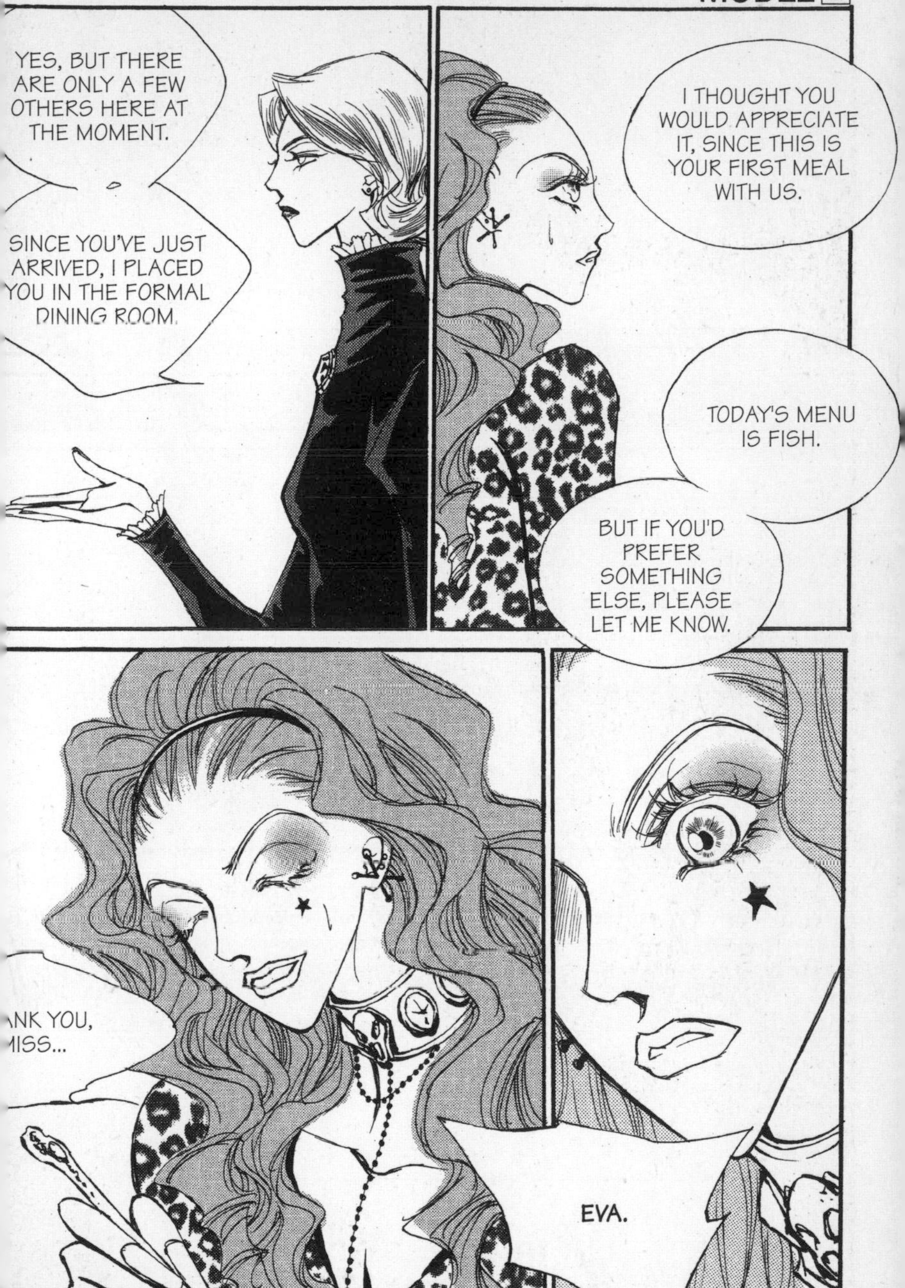
YES, BUT THERE ARE ONLY A FEW OTHERS HERE AT THE MOMENT.
SINCE YOU'VE JUST ARRIVED, I PLACED YOU IN THE FORMAL DINING ROOM.
I THOUGHT YOU WOULD APPRECIATE IT, SINCE THIS IS YOUR FIRST MEAL WITH US.
TODAY'S MENU IS FISH.
BUT IF YOU'D PREFER SOMETHING ELSE, PLEASE LET ME KNOW.
NK YOU, ISS...
EVA.

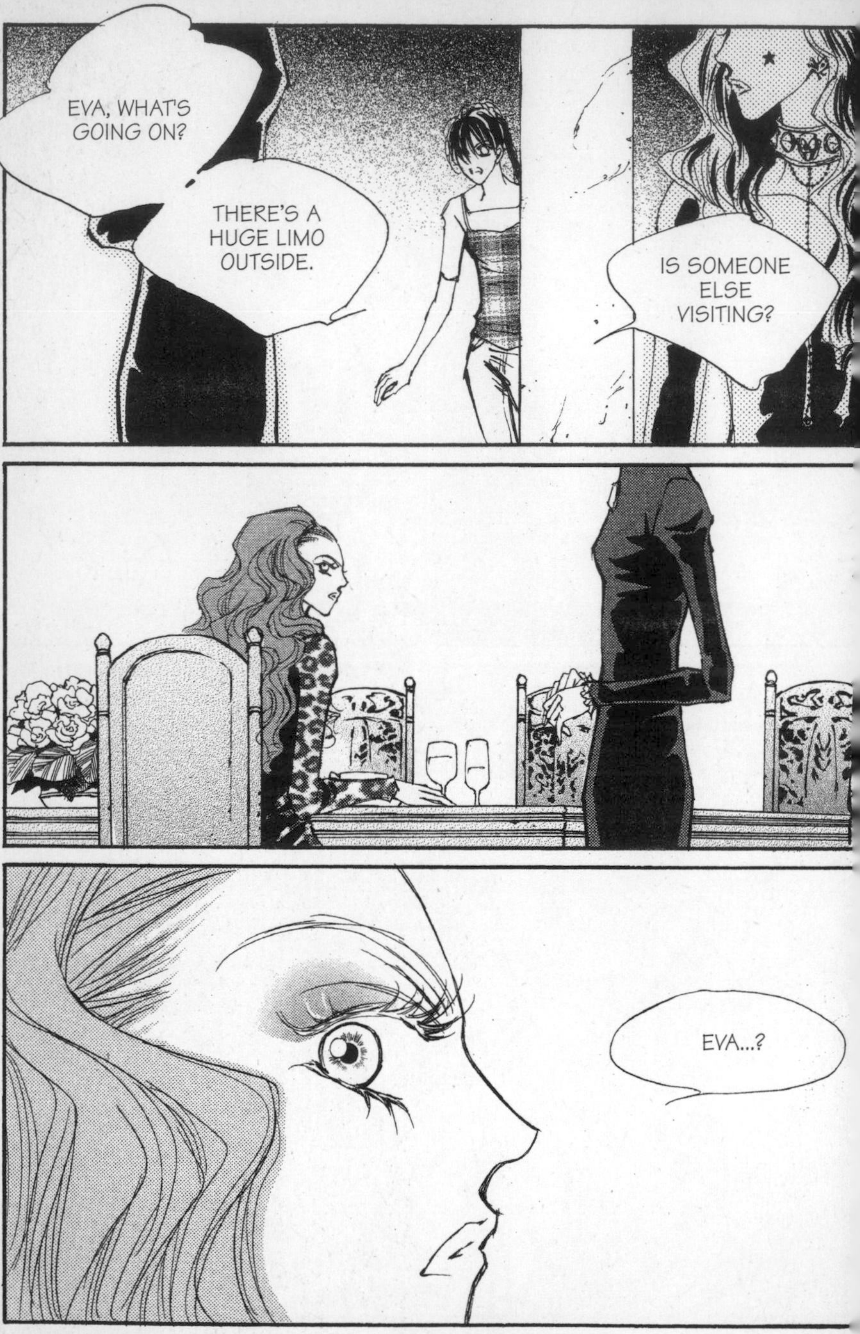
EVA, WHAT'S GOING ON?
THERE'S A HUGE LIMO OUTSIDE.
IS SOMEONE ELSE VISITING?
EVA...?

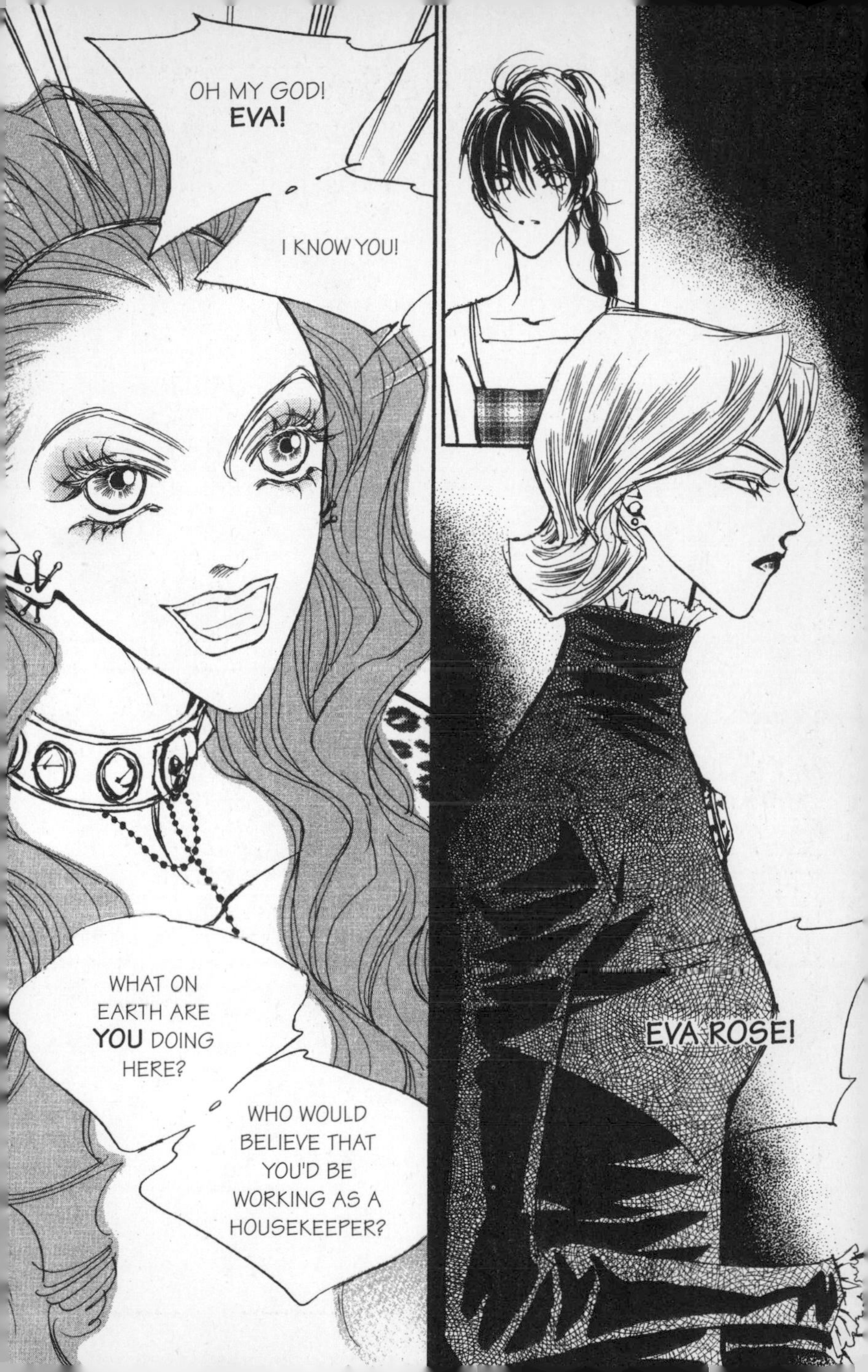
OH MY GOD! **EVA!**
I KNOW YOU!
WHAT ON EARTH ARE **YOU** DOING HERE?
WHO WOULD BELIEVE THAT YOU'D BE WORKING AS A HOUSEKEEPER?
EVA ROSE!

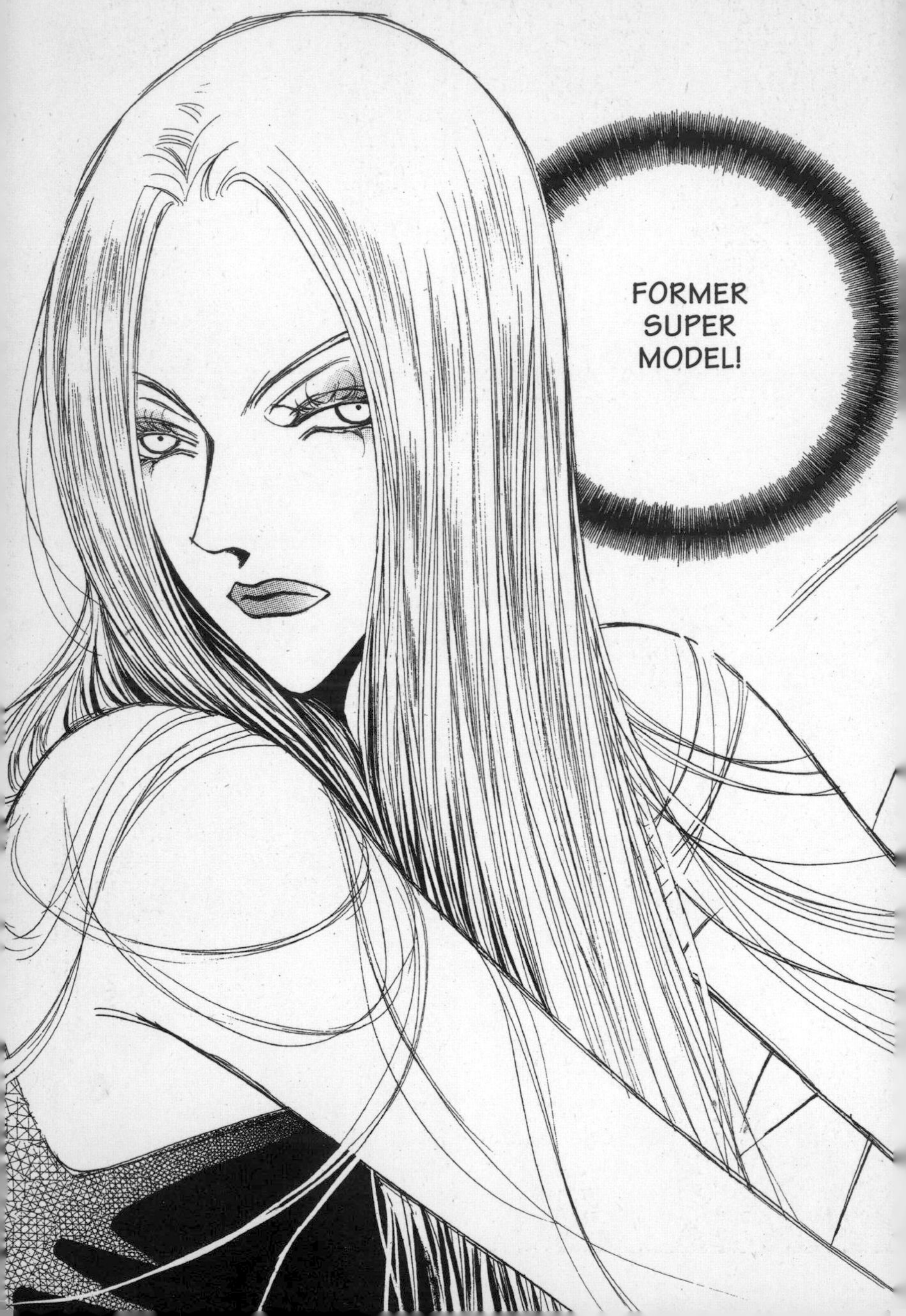
FORMER SUPER MODEL!

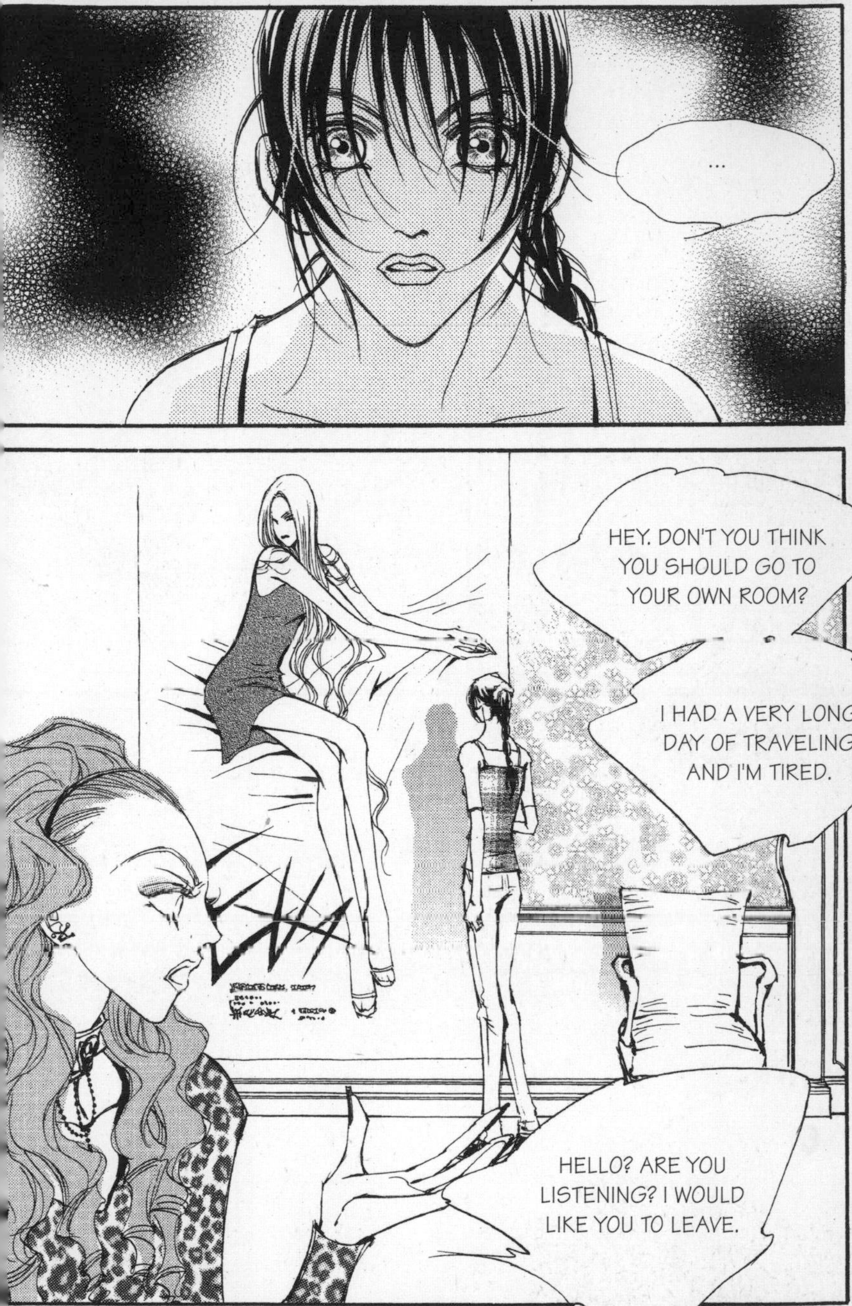
...
HEY. DON'T YOU THINK YOU SHOULD GO TO YOUR OWN ROOM?
I HAD A VERY LONG DAY OF TRAVELING AND I'M TIRED.
HELLO? ARE YOU LISTENING? I WOULD LIKE YOU TO LEAVE.

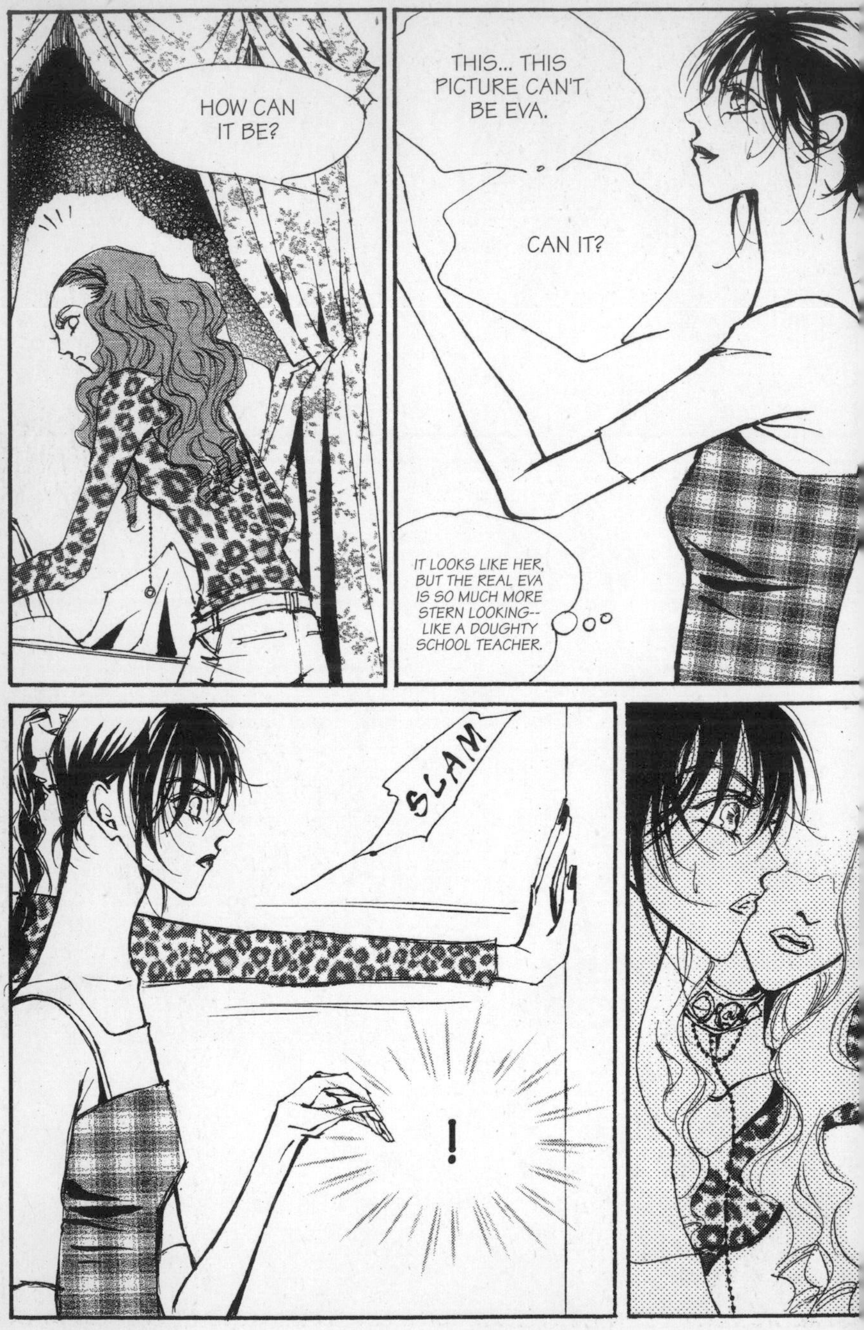
HOW CAN IT BE?
THIS... THIS PICTURE CAN'T BE EVA.
CAN IT?
IT LOOKS LIKE HER, BUT THE REAL EVA IS SO MUCH MORE STERN LOOKING-- LIKE A DOUGHTY SCHOOL TEACHER.
SLAM
!

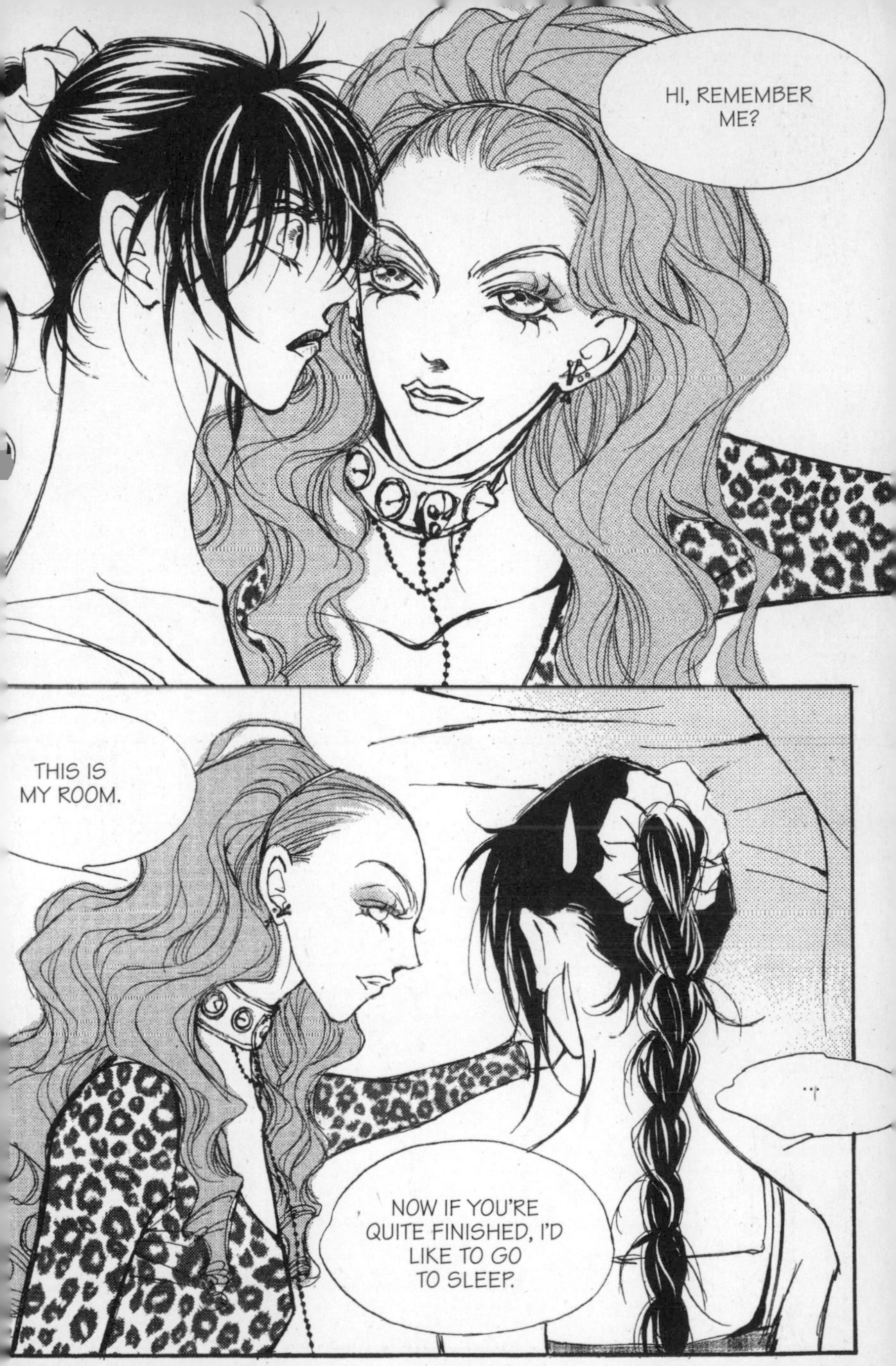
HI, REMEMBER ME?
THIS IS MY ROOM.
NOW IF YOU'RE QUITE FINISHED, I'D LIKE TO GO TO SLEEP.
...

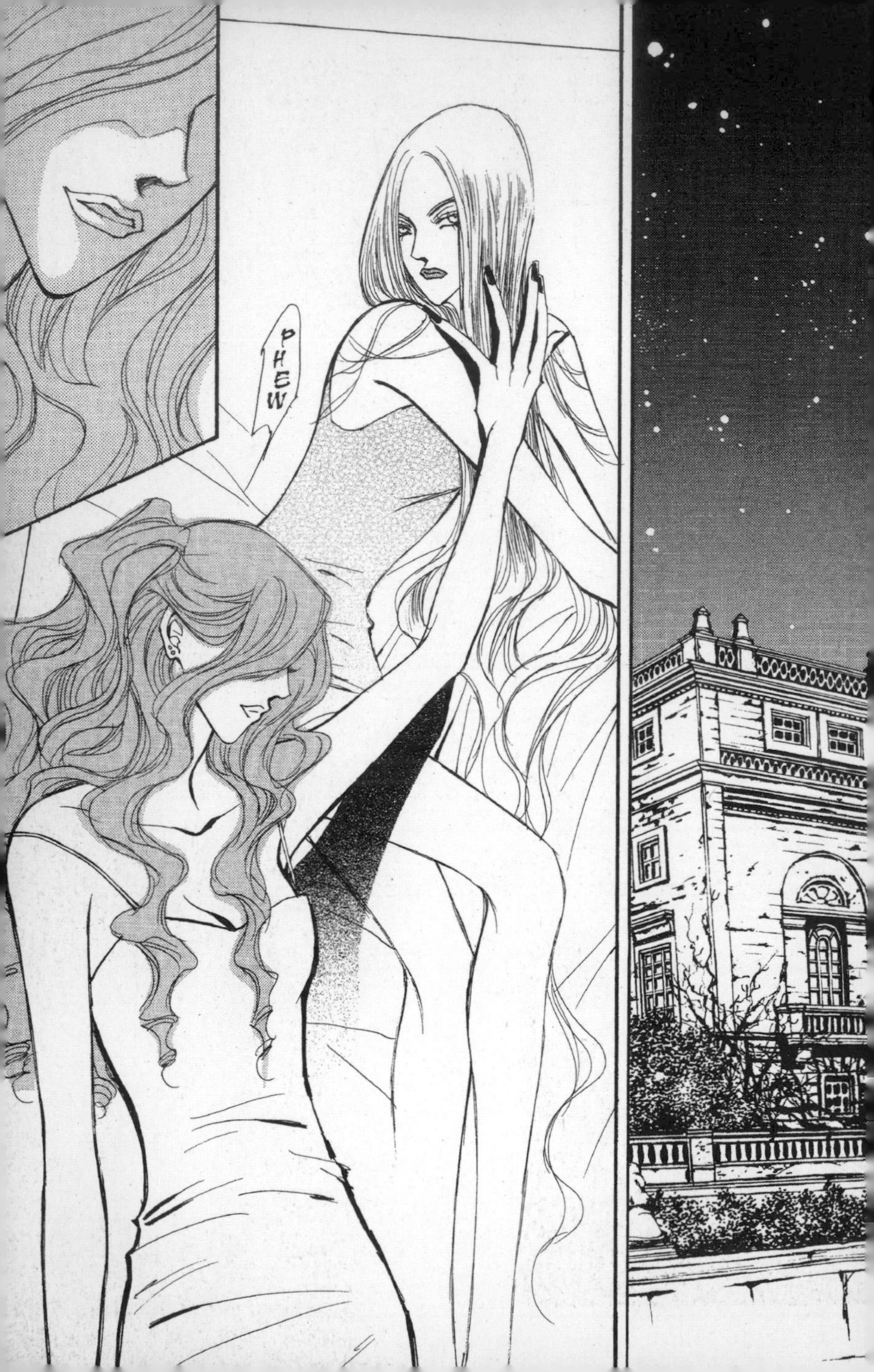
PHEW

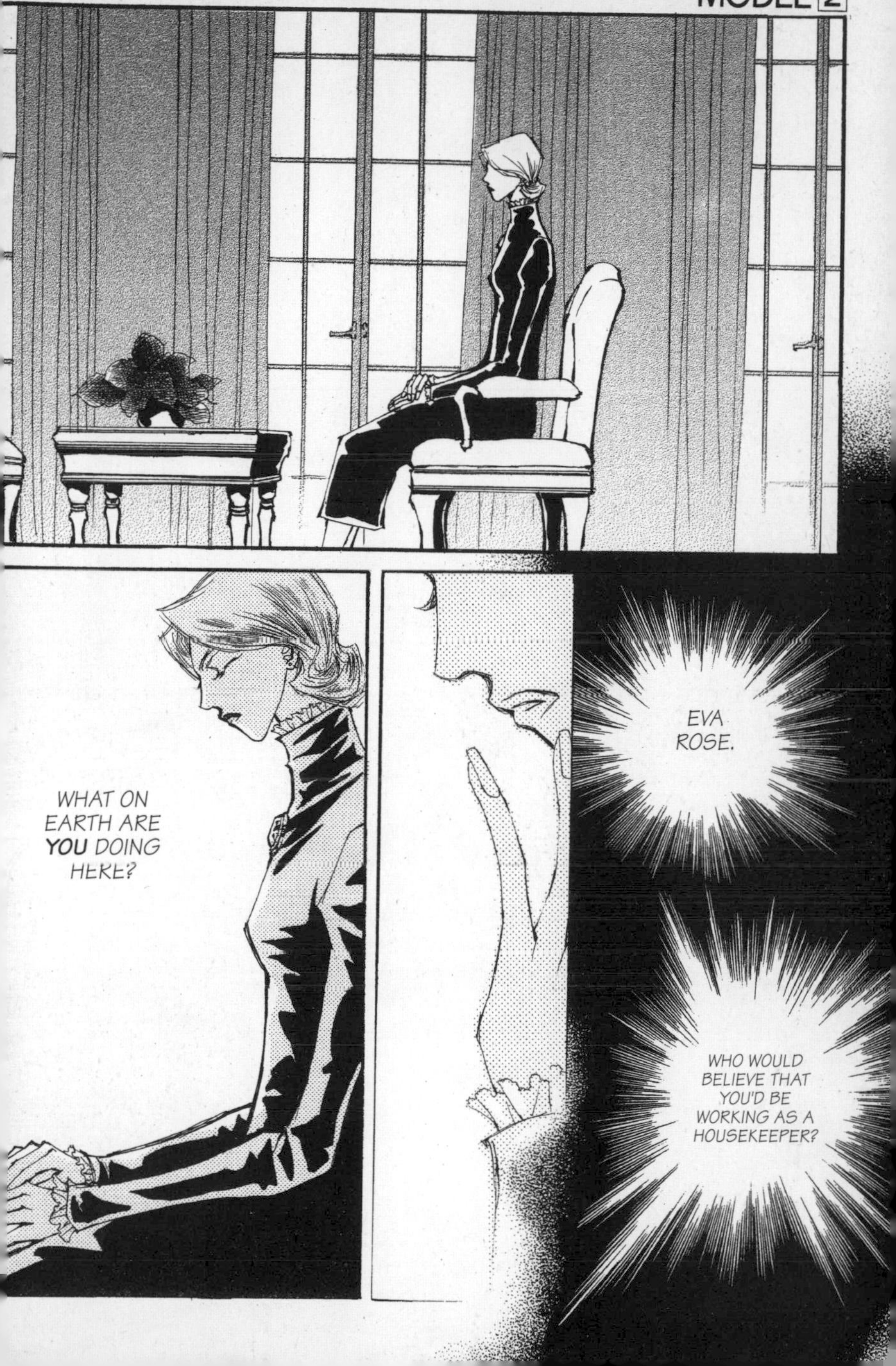
WHAT ON EARTH ARE **YOU** DOING HERE?
EVA ROSE.
WHO WOULD BELIEVE THAT YOU'D BE WORKING AS A HOUSEKEEPER?

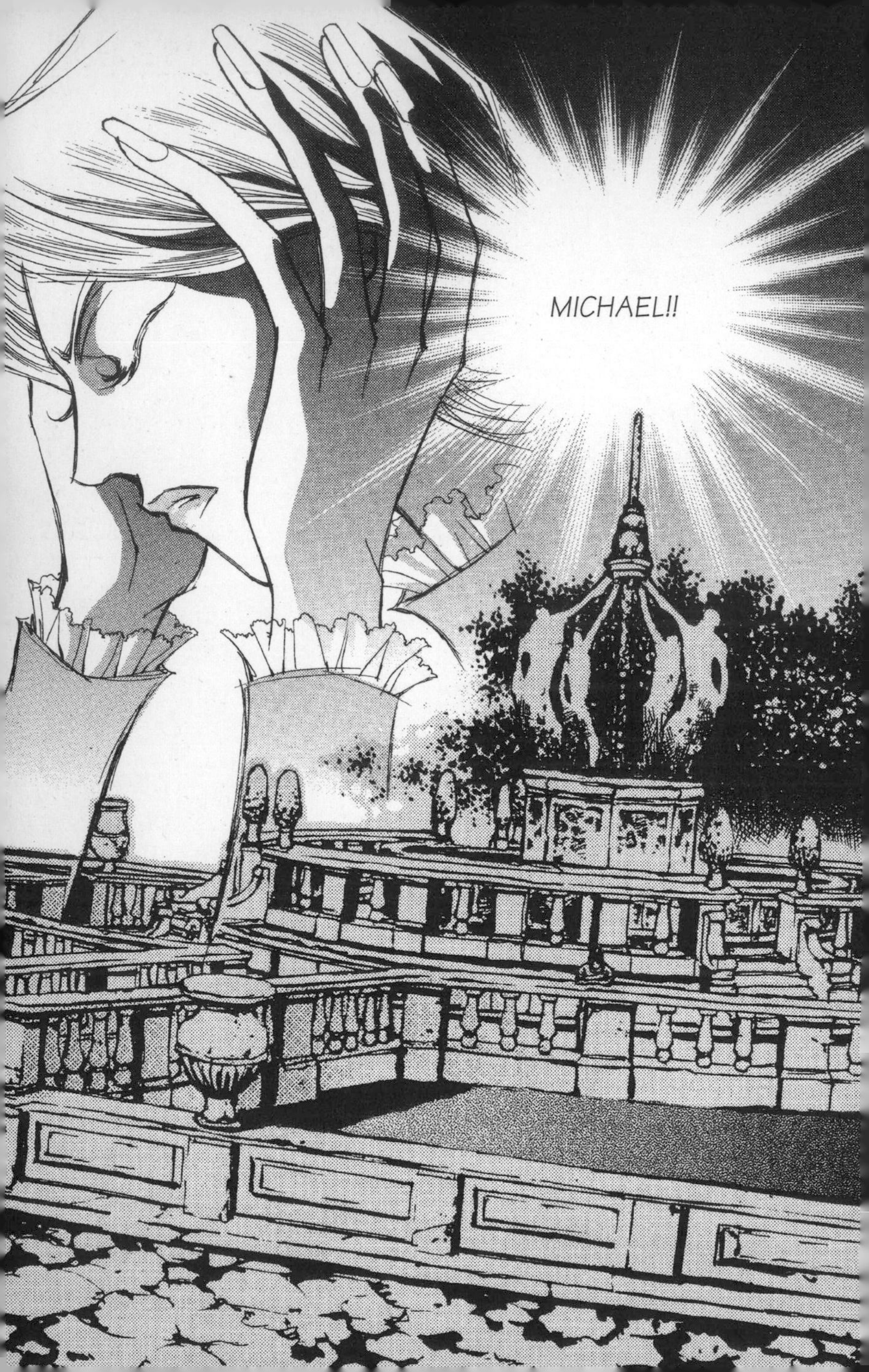
MICHAEL!!

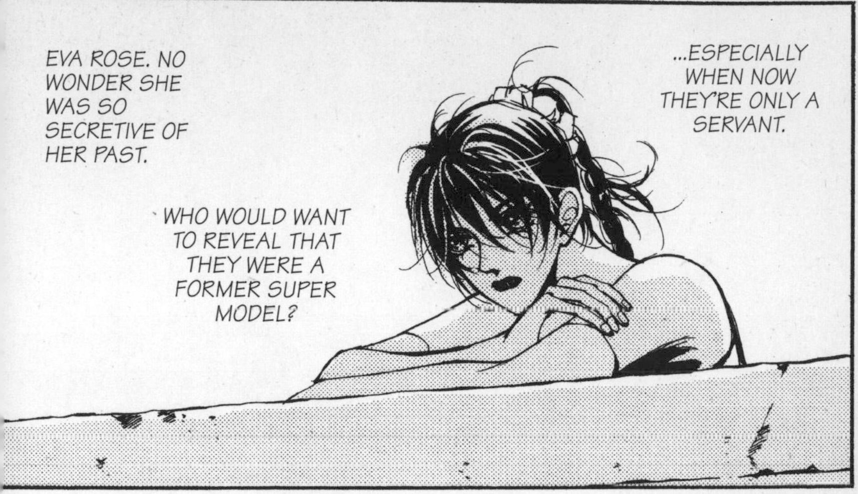
EVA ROSE. NO WONDER SHE WAS SO SECRETIVE OF HER PAST.
WHO WOULD WANT TO REVEAL THAT THEY WERE A FORMER SUPER MODEL?
...ESPECIALLY WHEN NOW THEY'RE ONLY A SERVANT.

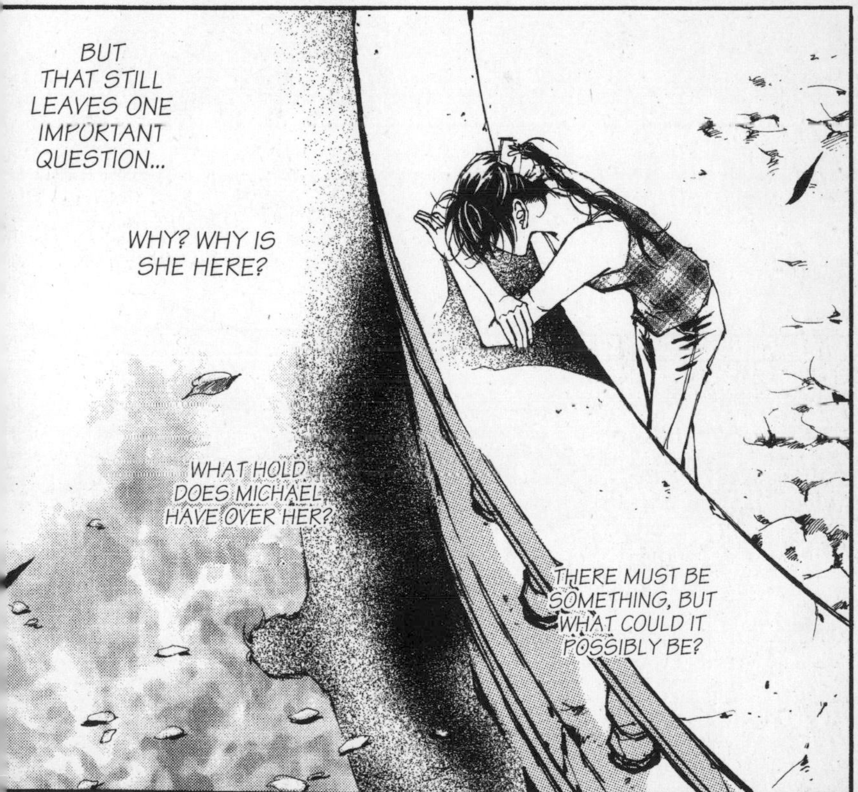
BUT THAT STILL LEAVES ONE IMPORTANT QUESTION...
WHY? WHY IS SHE HERE?
WHAT HOLD DOES MICHAEL HAVE OVER HER?
THERE MUST BE SOMETHING, BUT WHAT COULD IT POSSIBLY BE?

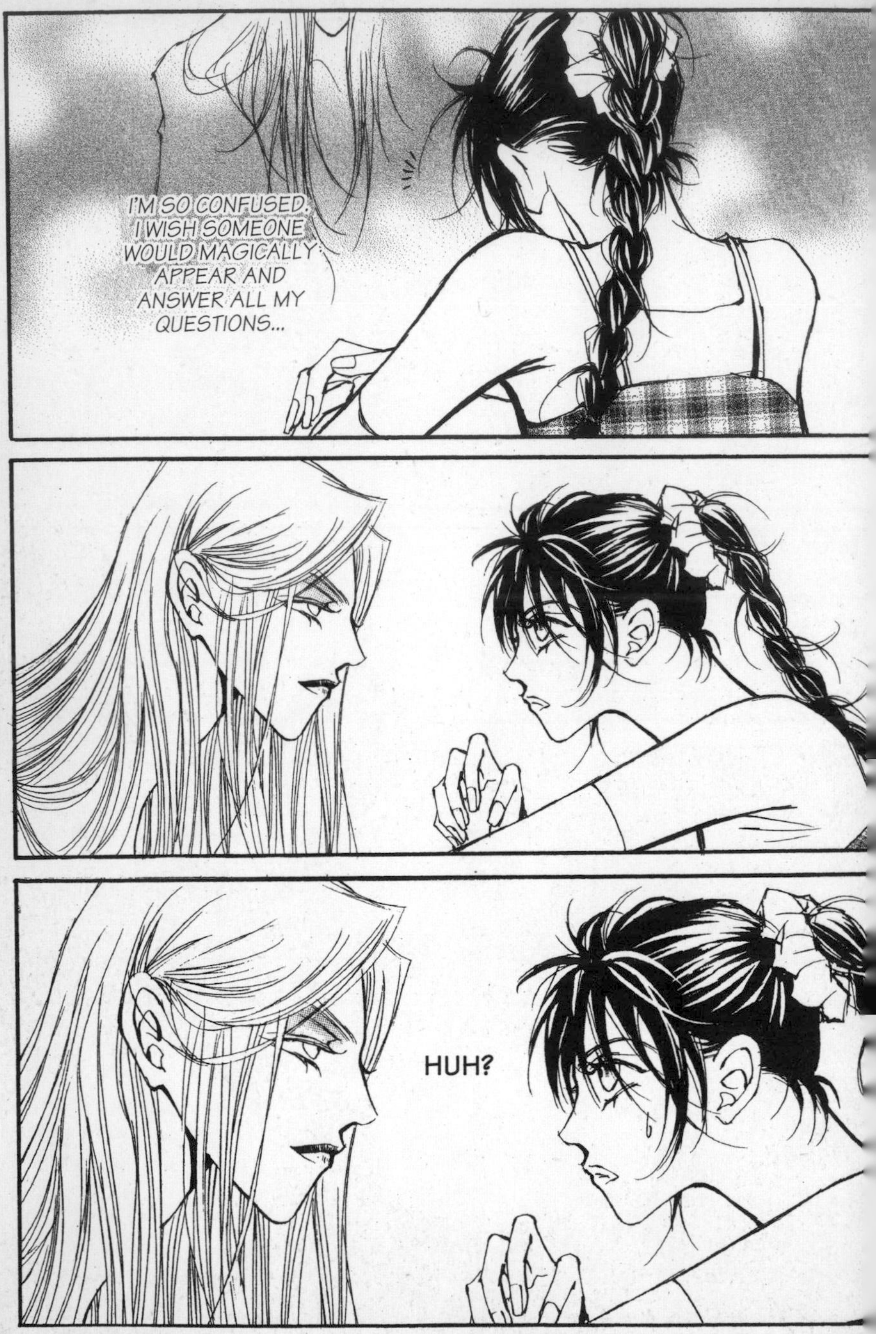
I'M SO CONFUSED. I WISH SOMEONE WOULD MAGICALLY APPEAR AND ANSWER ALL MY QUESTIONS...
HUH?

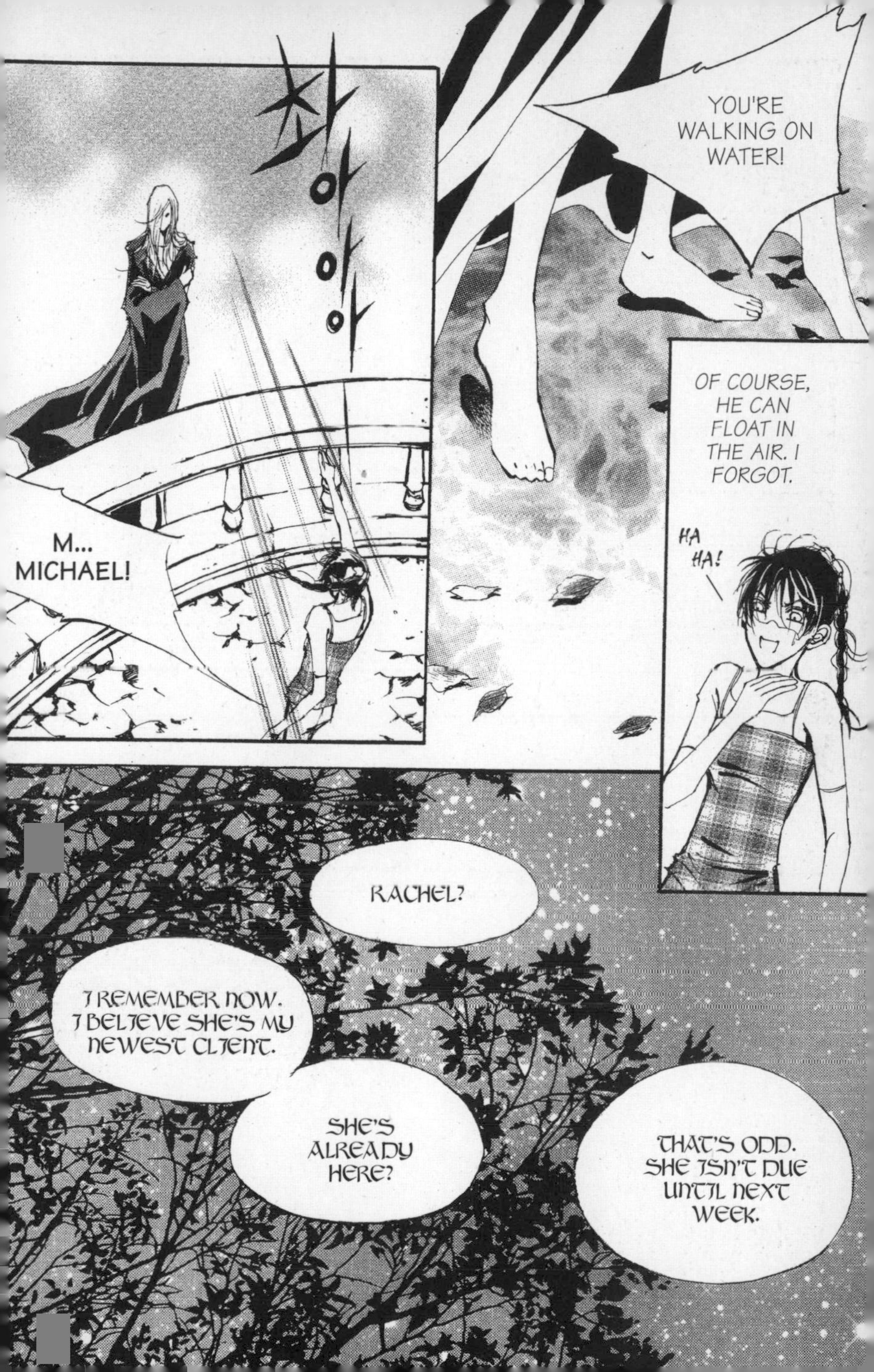
챠아아아
M... MICHAEL!
YOU'RE WALKING ON WATER!
OF COURSE, HE CAN FLOAT IN THE AIR. I FORGOT.
HA HA!
RACHEL?
I REMEMBER NOW. I BELIEVE SHE'S MY NEWEST CLIENT.
SHE'S ALREADY HERE?
THAT'S ODD. SHE ISN'T DUE UNTIL NEXT WEEK.

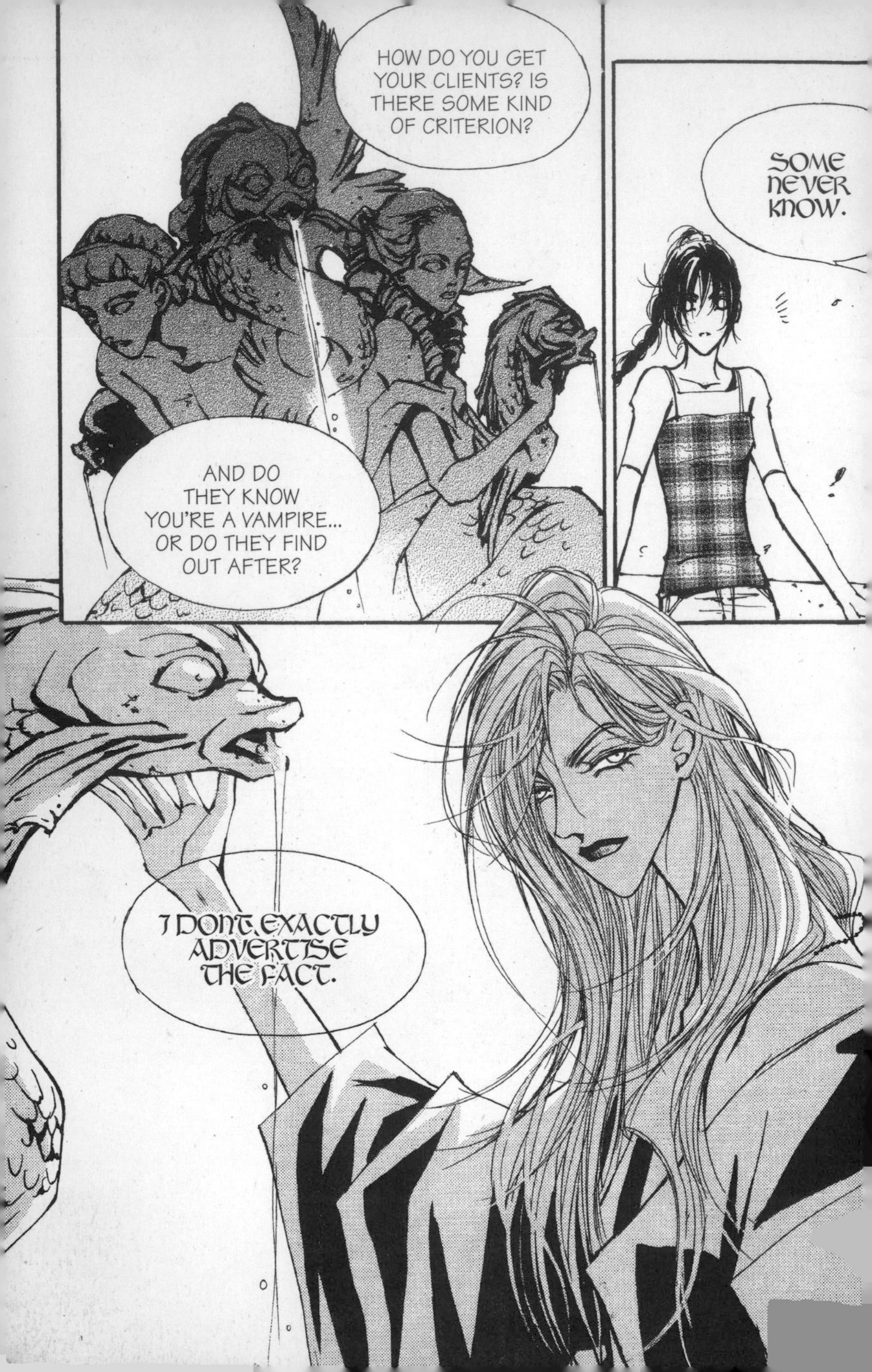
HOW DO YOU GET YOUR CLIENTS? IS THERE SOME KIND OF CRITERION?
AND DO THEY KNOW YOU'RE A VAMPIRE... OR DO THEY FIND OUT AFTER?
SOME NEVER KNOW.
I DON'T EXACTLY ADVERTISE THE FACT.

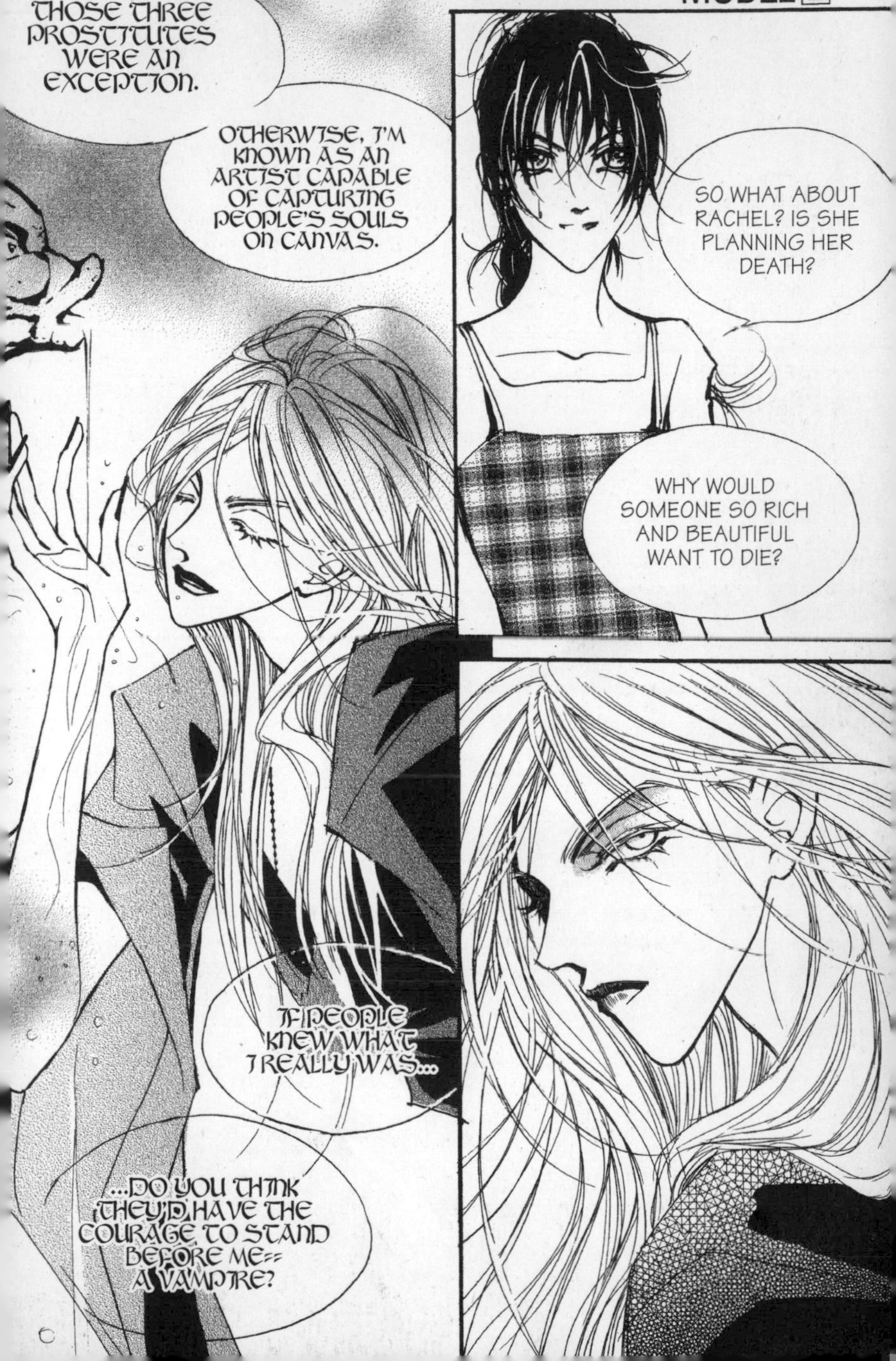
THOSE THREE PROSTITUTES WERE AN EXCEPTION.
OTHERWISE, I'M KNOWN AS AN ARTIST CAPABLE OF CAPTURING PEOPLE'S SOULS ON CANVAS.
IF PEOPLE KNEW WHAT I REALLY WAS...
...DO YOU THINK THEY'D HAVE THE COURAGE TO STAND BEFORE ME-- A VAMPIRE?
SO WHAT ABOUT RACHEL? IS SHE PLANNING HER DEATH?
WHY WOULD SOMEONE SO RICH AND BEAUTIFUL WANT TO DIE?

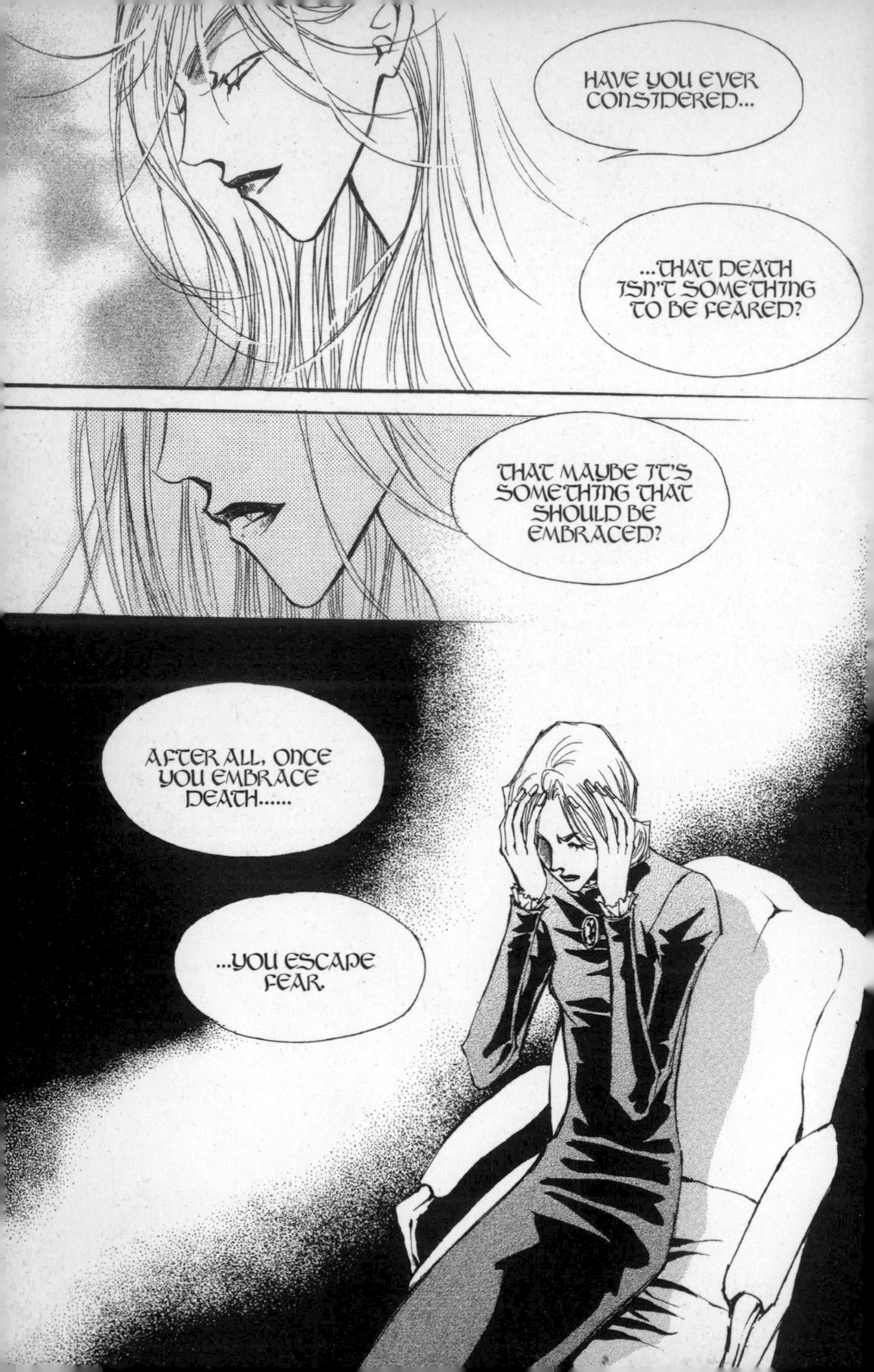
HAVE YOU EVER CONSIDERED...
...THAT DEATH ISN'T SOMETHING TO BE FEARED?
THAT MAYBE IT'S SOMETHING THAT SHOULD BE EMBRACED?
AFTER ALL, ONCE YOU EMBRACE DEATH......
...YOU ESCAPE FEAR.

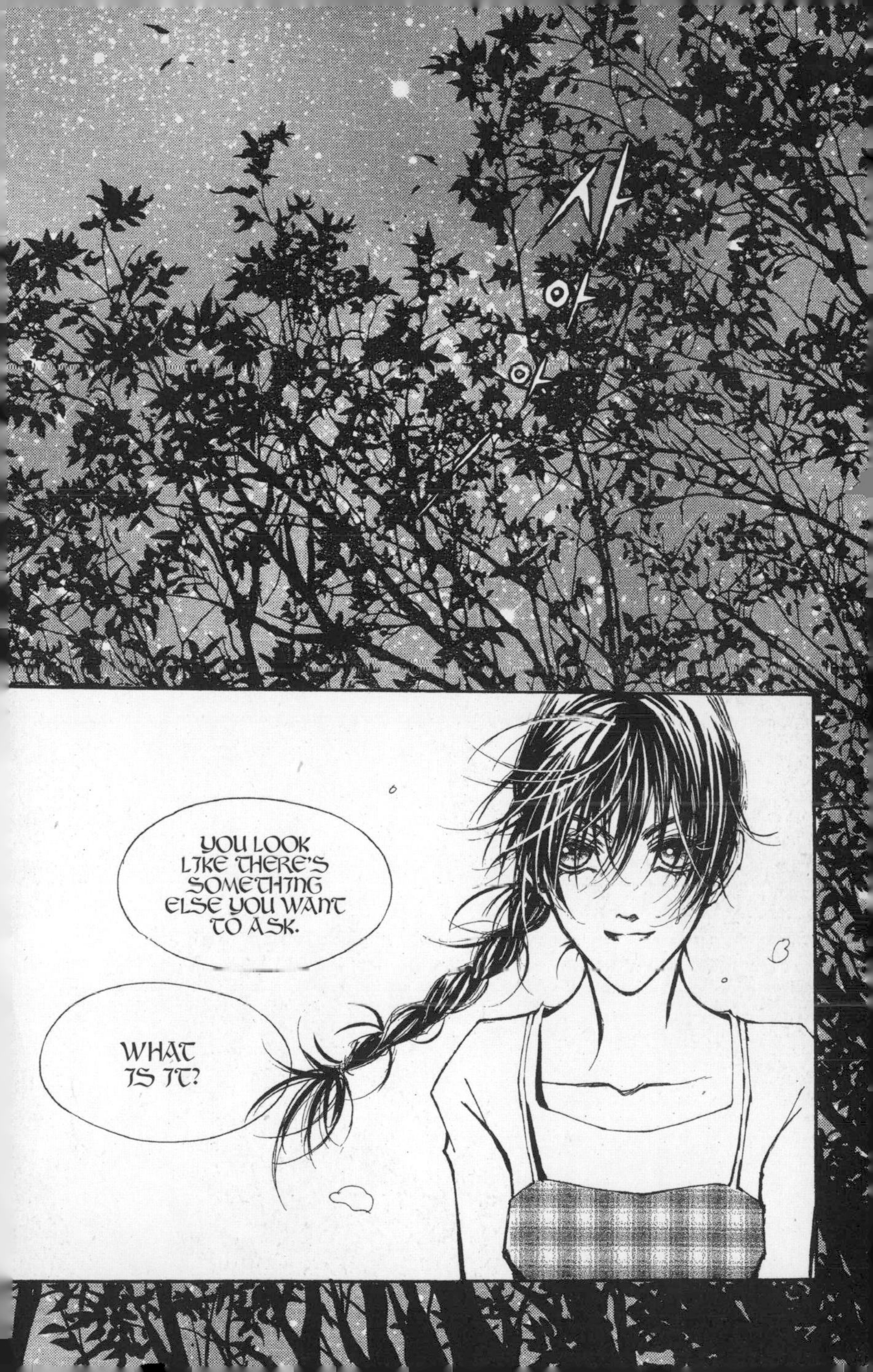
사아아
YOU LOOK LIKE THERE'S SOMETHING ELSE YOU WANT TO ASK.
WHAT IS IT?

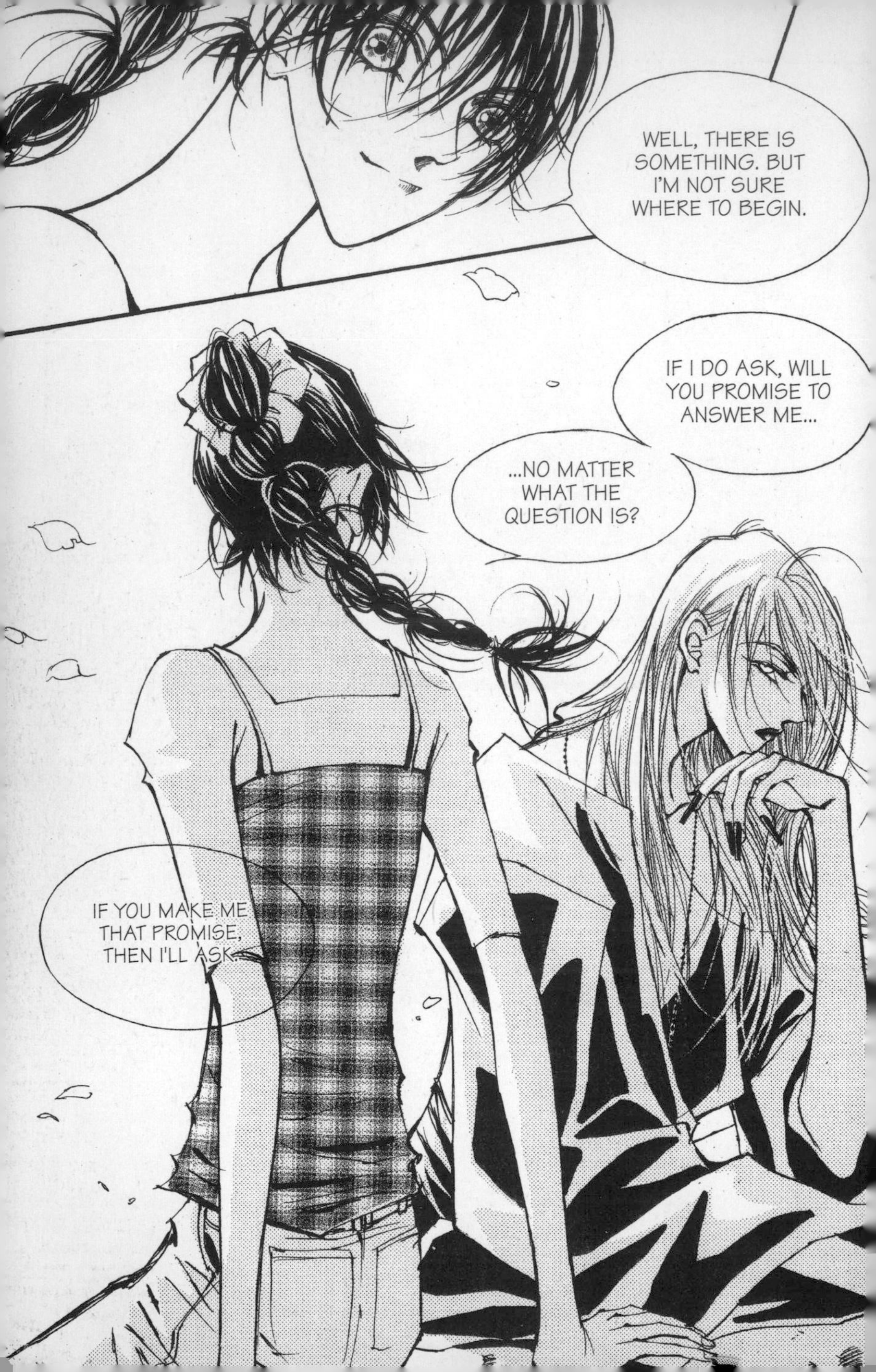
WELL, THERE IS SOMETHING. BUT I'M NOT SURE WHERE TO BEGIN.
IF I DO ASK, WILL YOU PROMISE TO ANSWER ME...
...NO MATTER WHAT THE QUESTION IS?
IF YOU MAKE ME THAT PROMISE, THEN I'LL ASK.

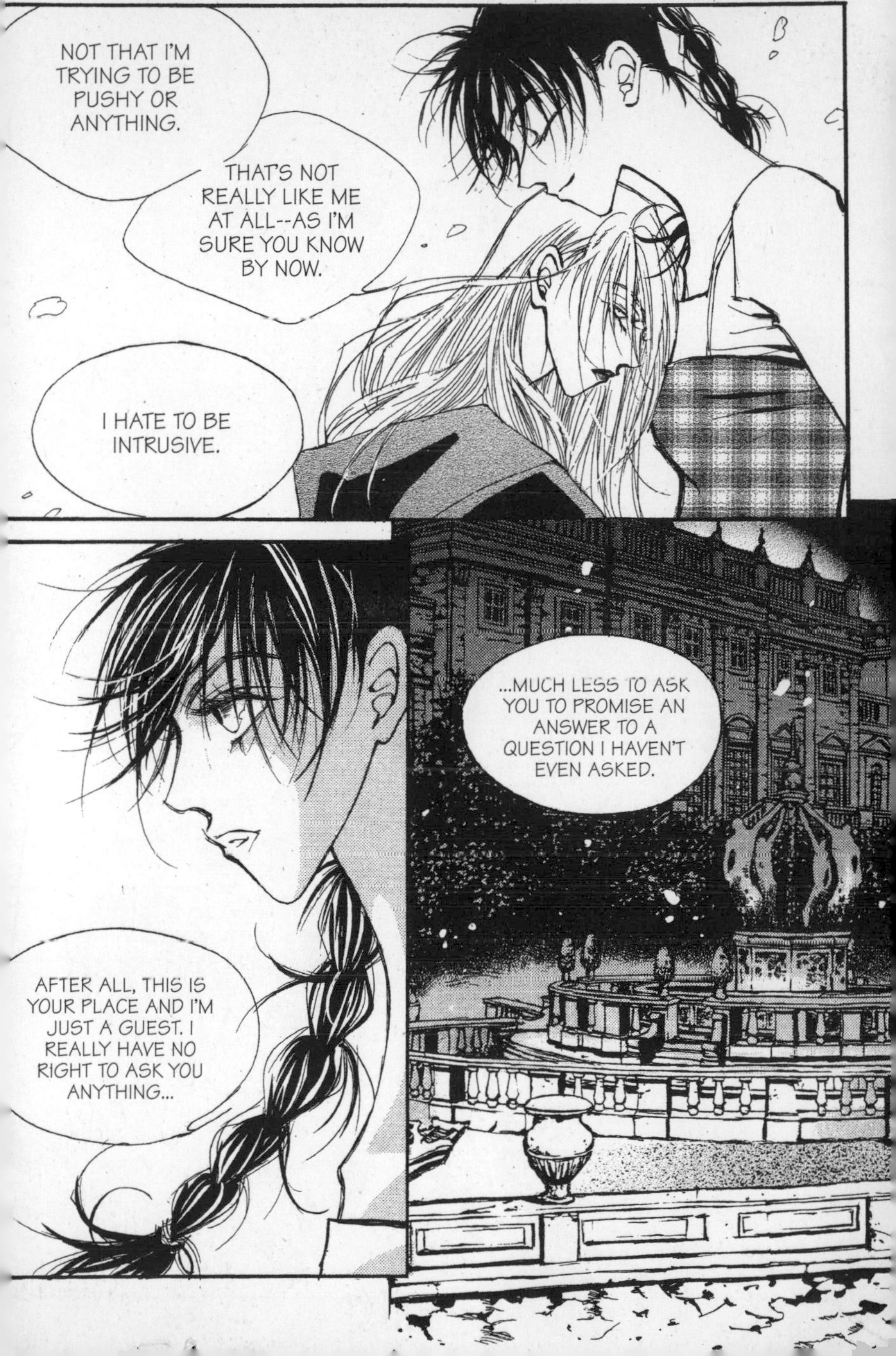
NOT THAT I'M TRYING TO BE PUSHY OR ANYTHING.
THAT'S NOT REALLY LIKE ME AT ALL--AS I'M SURE YOU KNOW BY NOW.
I HATE TO BE INTRUSIVE.
AFTER ALL, THIS IS YOUR PLACE AND I'M JUST A GUEST. I REALLY HAVE NO RIGHT TO ASK YOU ANYTHING...
...MUCH LESS TO ASK YOU TO PROMISE AN ANSWER TO A QUESTION I HAVEN'T EVEN ASKED.

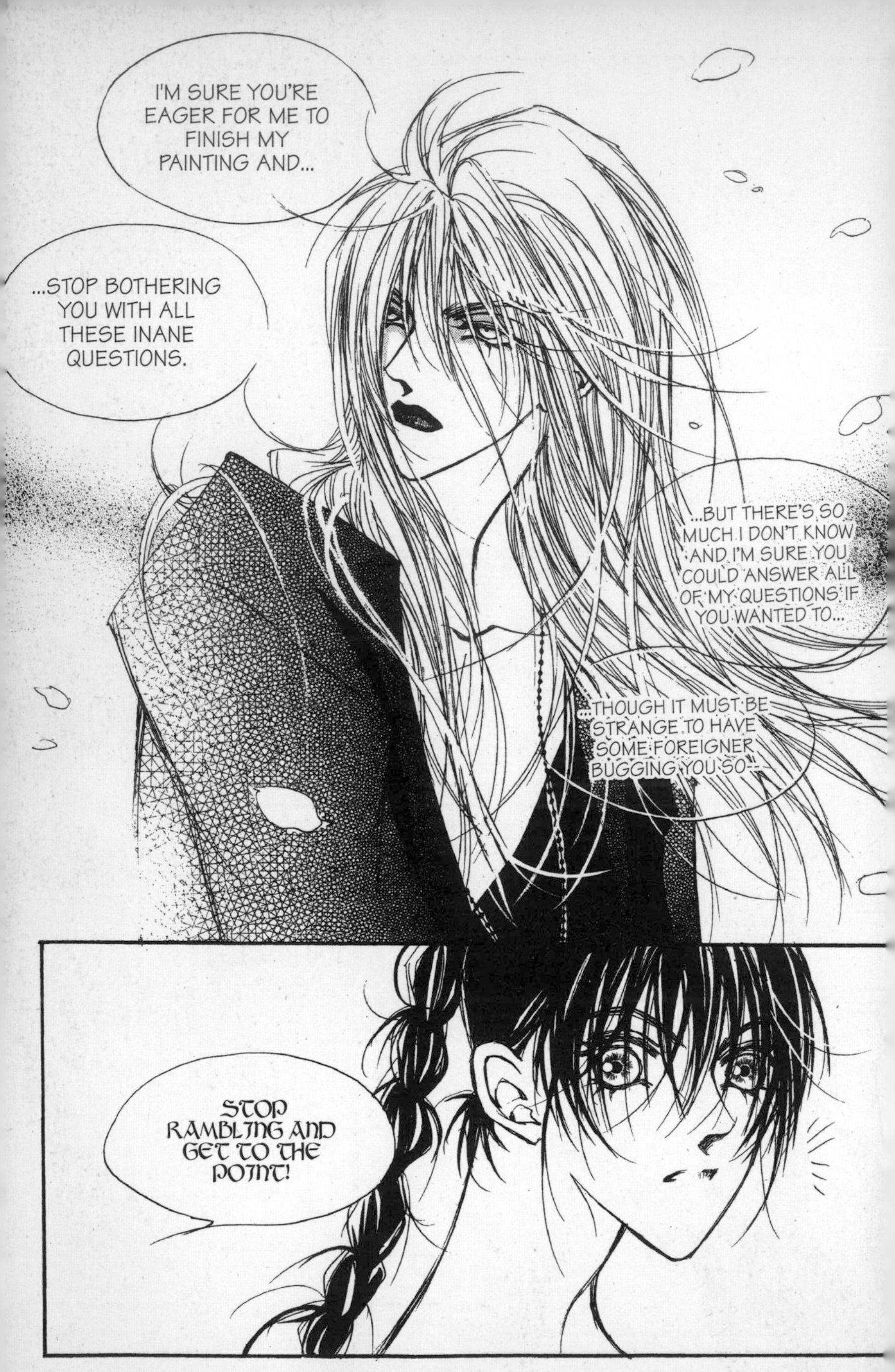
I'M SURE YOU'RE EAGER FOR ME TO FINISH MY PAINTING AND...
...STOP BOTHERING YOU WITH ALL THESE INANE QUESTIONS.
...BUT THERE'S SO MUCH I DON'T KNOW AND I'M SURE YOU COULD ANSWER ALL OF MY QUESTIONS IF YOU WANTED TO...
...THOUGH IT MUST BE STRANGE TO HAVE SOME FOREIGNER BUGGING YOU SO--
STOP RAMBLING AND GET TO THE POINT!

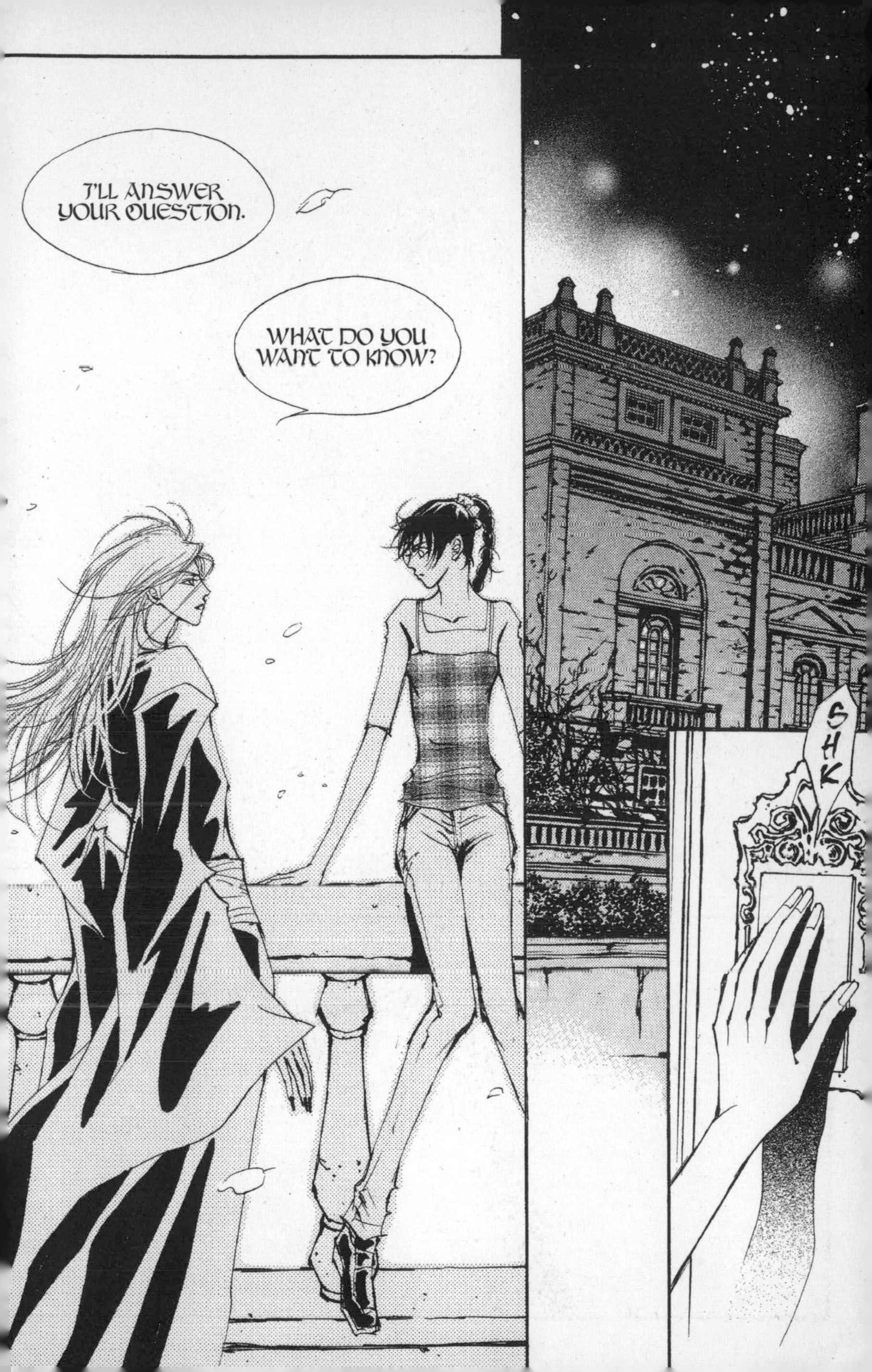
I'LL ANSWER YOUR QUESTION.
WHAT DO YOU WANT TO KNOW?
SHK

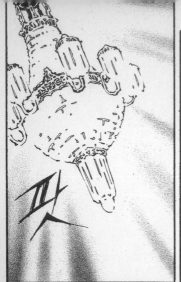

I SEE ANOTHER GUEST HAS ARRIVED.

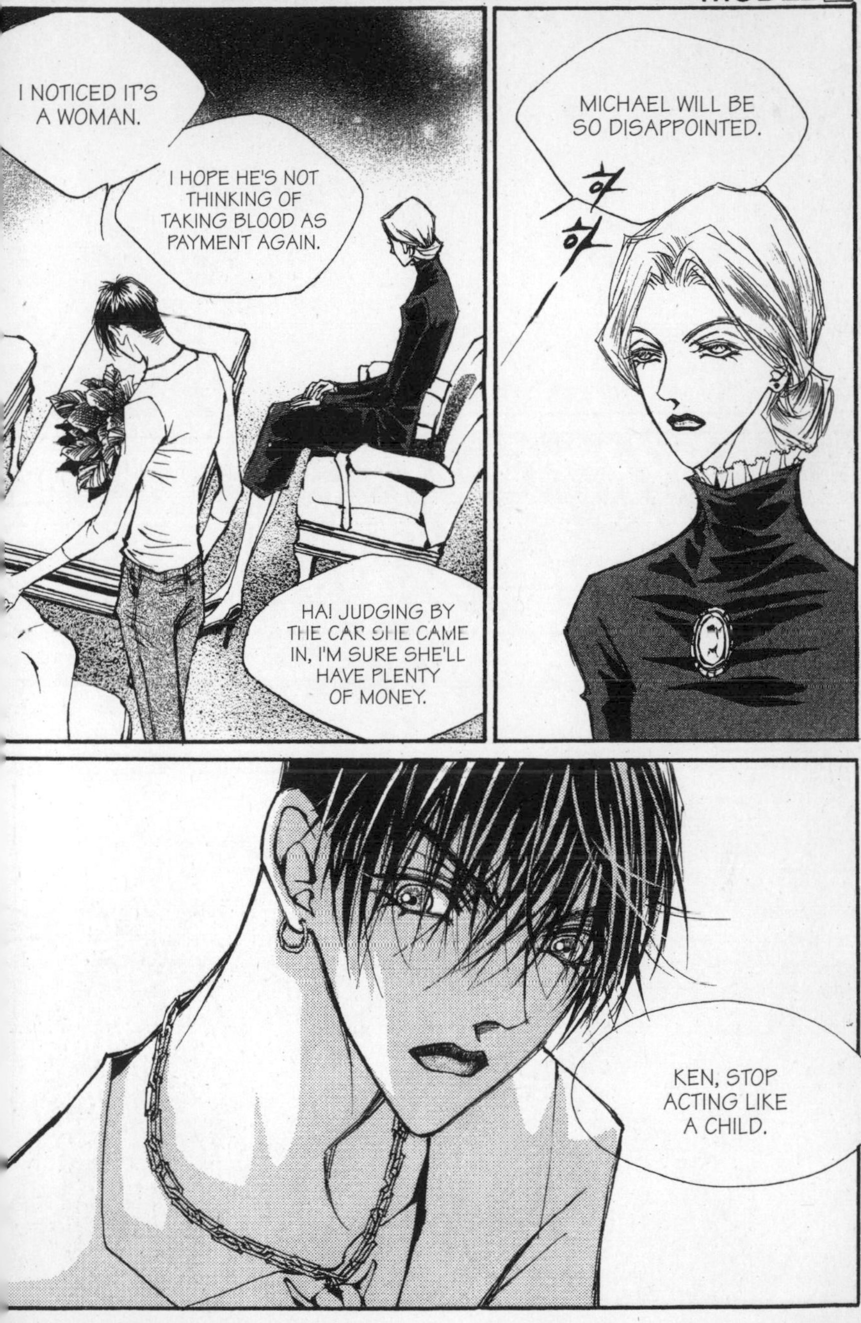
I NOTICED IT'S A WOMAN.
I HOPE HE'S NOT THINKING OF TAKING BLOOD AS PAYMENT AGAIN.
HA! JUDGING BY THE CAR SHE CAME IN, I'M SURE SHE'LL HAVE PLENTY OF MONEY.
MICHAEL WILL BE SO DISAPPOINTED.
KEN, STOP ACTING LIKE A CHILD.

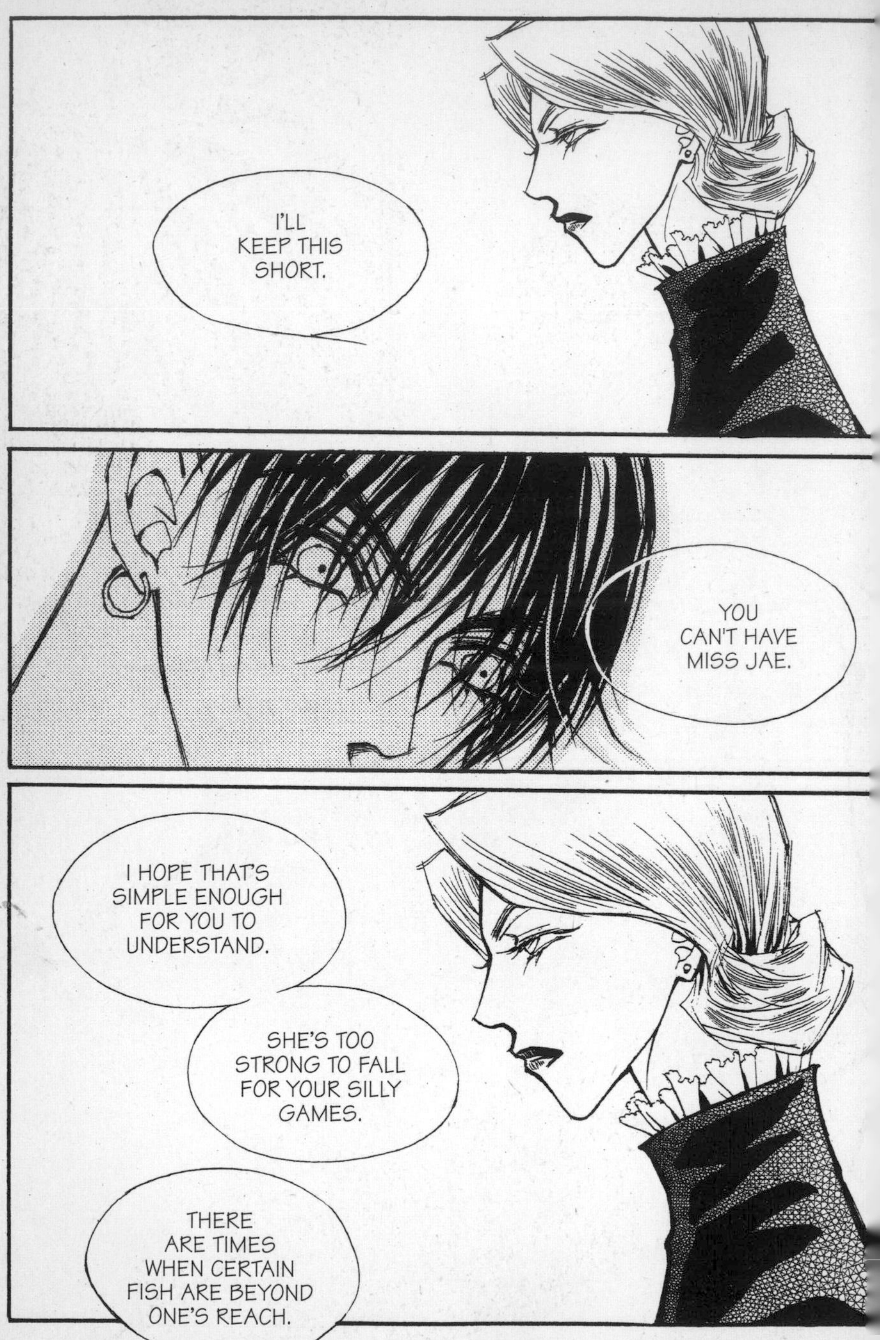
I'LL KEEP THIS SHORT.
YOU CAN'T HAVE MISS JAE.
I HOPE THAT'S SIMPLE ENOUGH FOR YOU TO UNDERSTAND.
SHE'S TOO STRONG TO FALL FOR YOUR SILLY GAMES.
THERE ARE TIMES WHEN CERTAIN FISH ARE BEYOND ONE'S REACH.

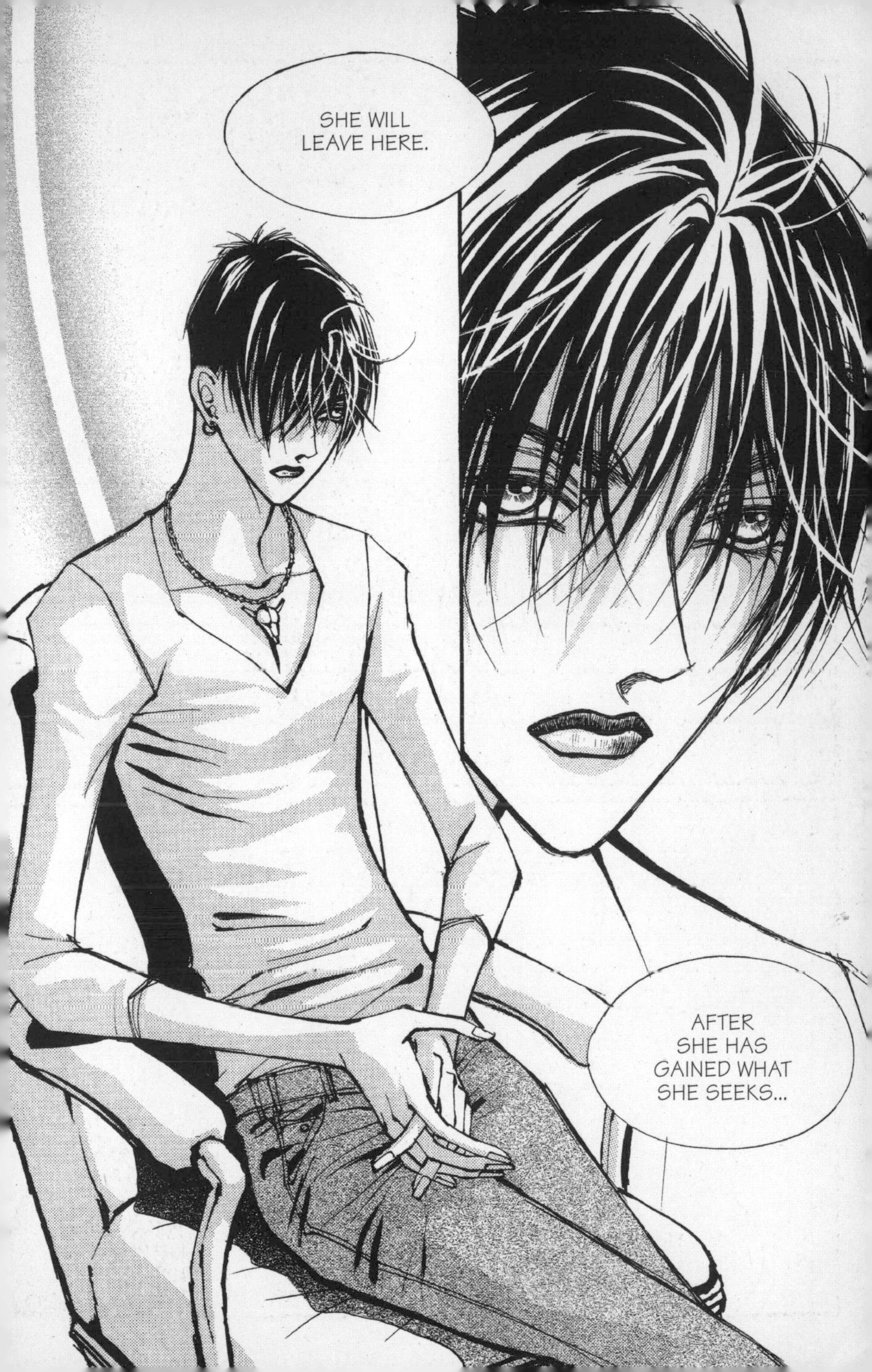
SHE WILL LEAVE HERE.
AFTER SHE HAS GAINED WHAT SHE SEEKS...

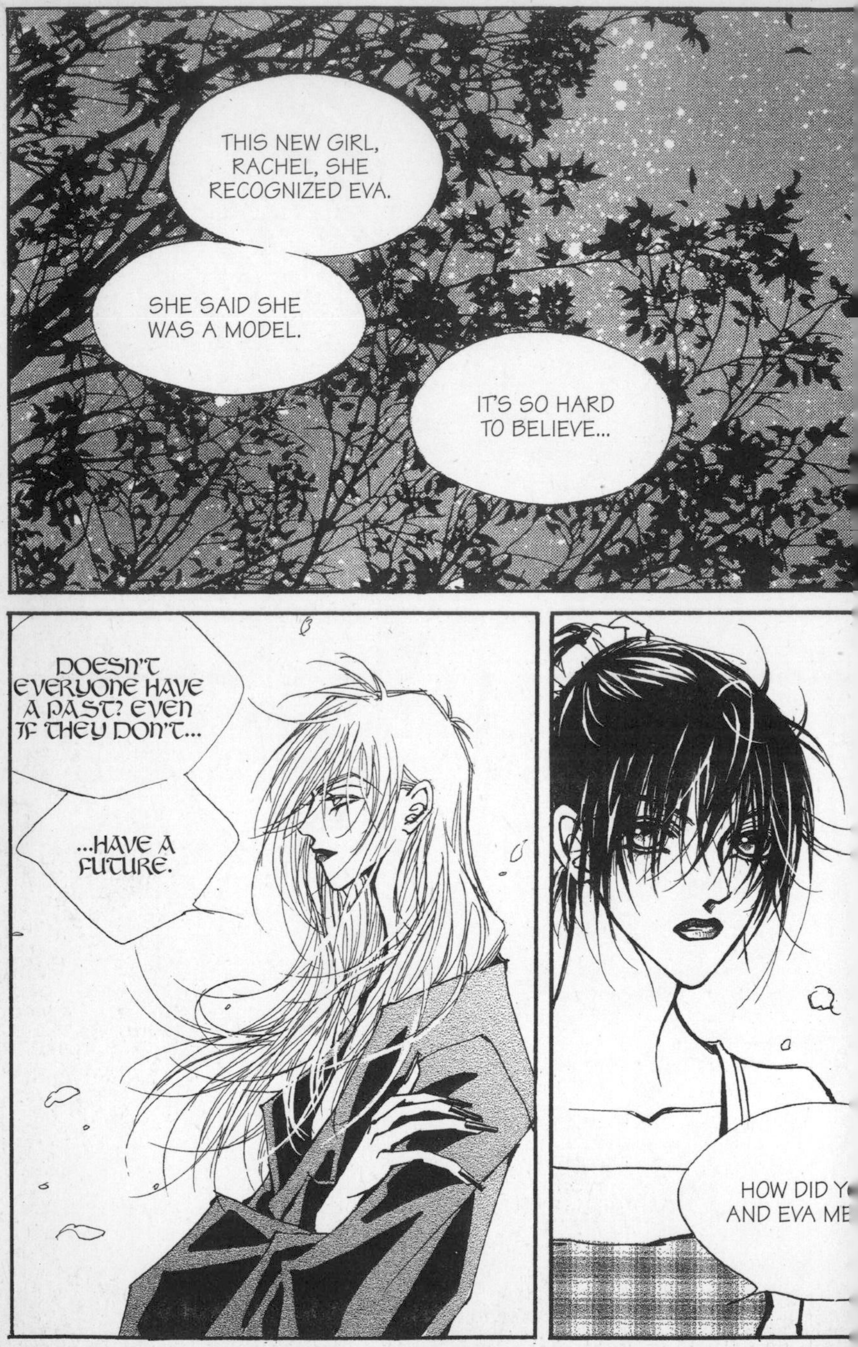
THIS NEW GIRL, RACHEL, SHE RECOGNIZED EVA.
SHE SAID SHE WAS A MODEL.
IT'S SO HARD TO BELIEVE...
DOESN'T EVERYONE HAVE A PAST? EVEN IF THEY DON'T...
...HAVE A FUTURE.
HOW DID Y
AND EVA ME

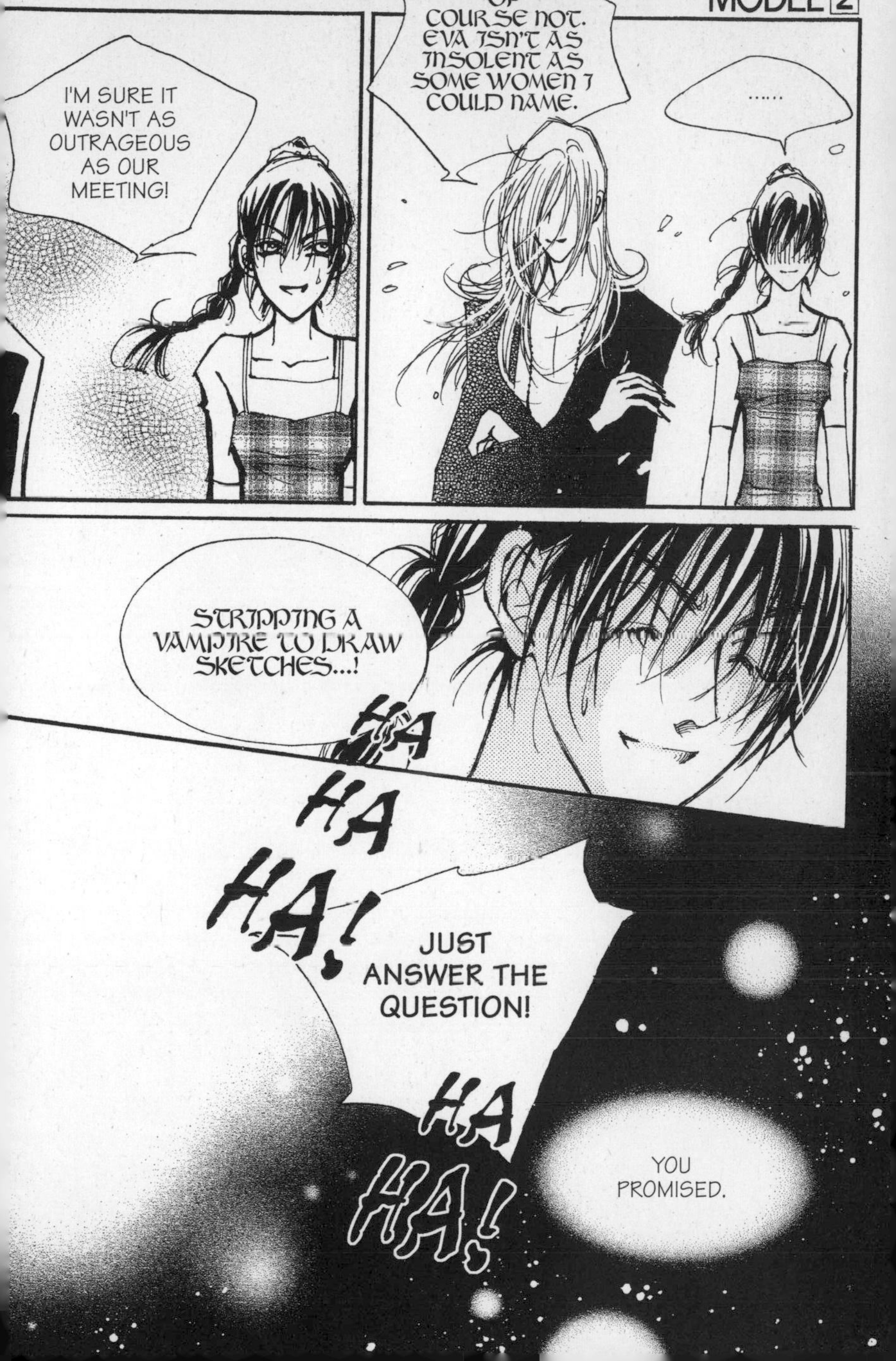
I'M SURE IT WASN'T AS OUTRAGEOUS AS OUR MEETING!
OF COURSE NOT. EVA ISN'T AS INSOLENT AS SOME WOMEN I COULD NAME.
......
STRIPPING A VAMPIRE TO DRAW SKETCHES...!
HA HA HA!
JUST ANSWER THE QUESTION!
HA HA!
YOU PROMISED.

...OF ALL THE QUESTIONS FLOATING THROUGH MY HEAD, I'M NOT SURE WHY I ASKED ABOUT EVA.

SHE JUST HAPPENED TO BE FOREMOST IN MY MIND...

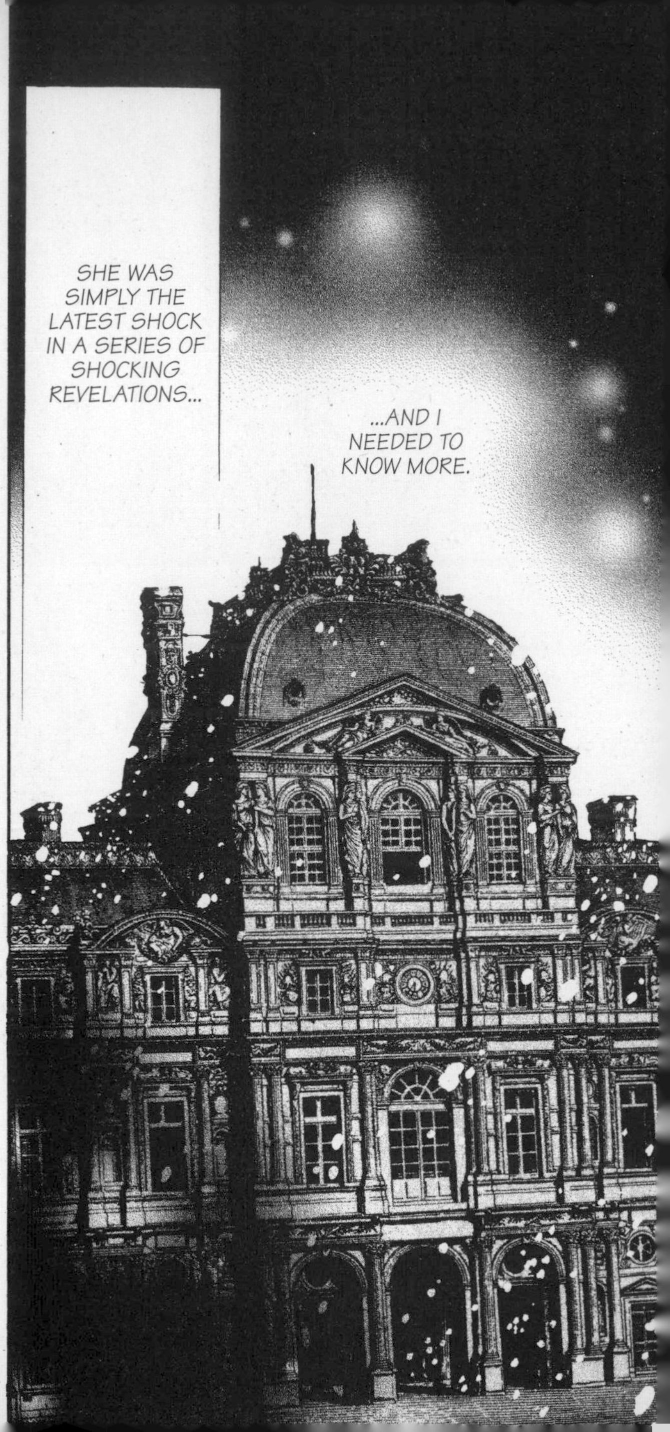
SHE WAS SIMPLY THE LATEST SHOCK IN A SERIES OF SHOCKING REVELATIONS...
...AND I NEEDED TO KNOW MORE.

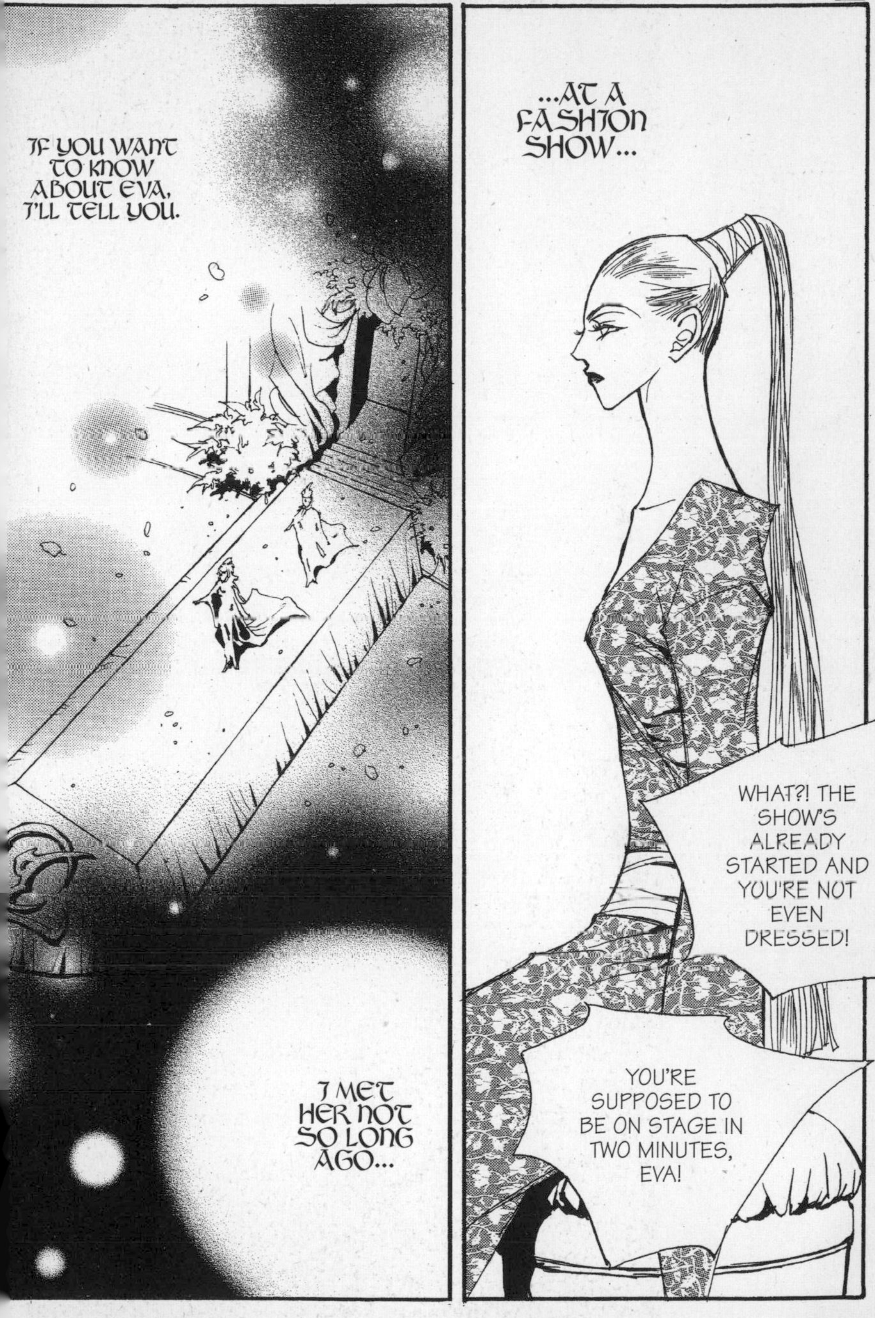
IF YOU WANT TO KNOW ABOUT EVA, I'LL TELL YOU.
I MET HER NOT SO LONG AGO...
...AT A FASHION SHOW...
WHAT?! THE SHOW'S ALREADY STARTED AND YOU'RE NOT EVEN DRESSED!
YOU'RE SUPPOSED TO BE ON STAGE IN TWO MINUTES, EVA!

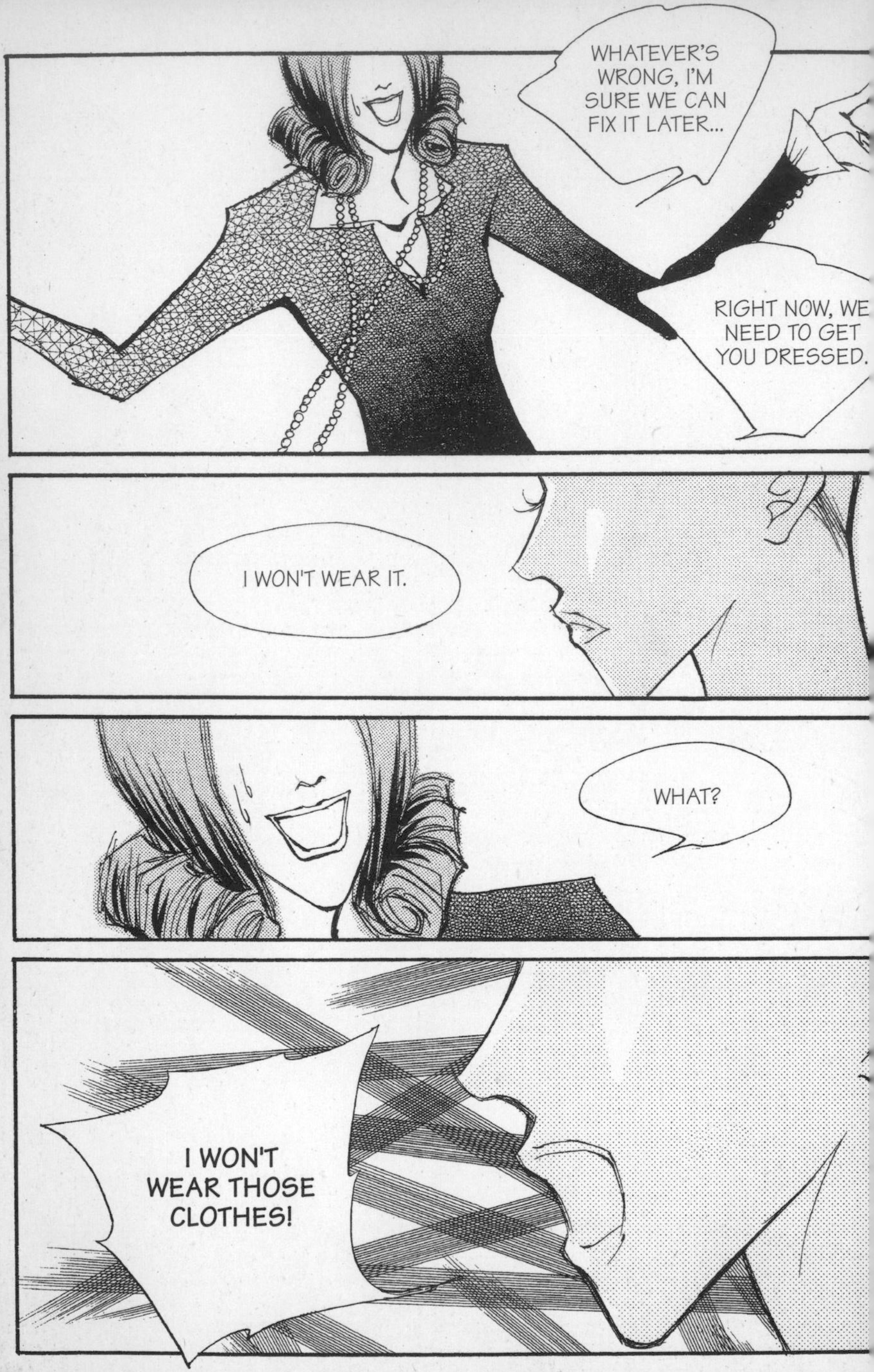
WHATEVER'S WRONG, I'M SURE WE CAN FIX IT LATER...
RIGHT NOW, WE NEED TO GET YOU DRESSED.
I WON'T WEAR IT.
WHAT?
I WON'T WEAR THOSE CLOTHES!

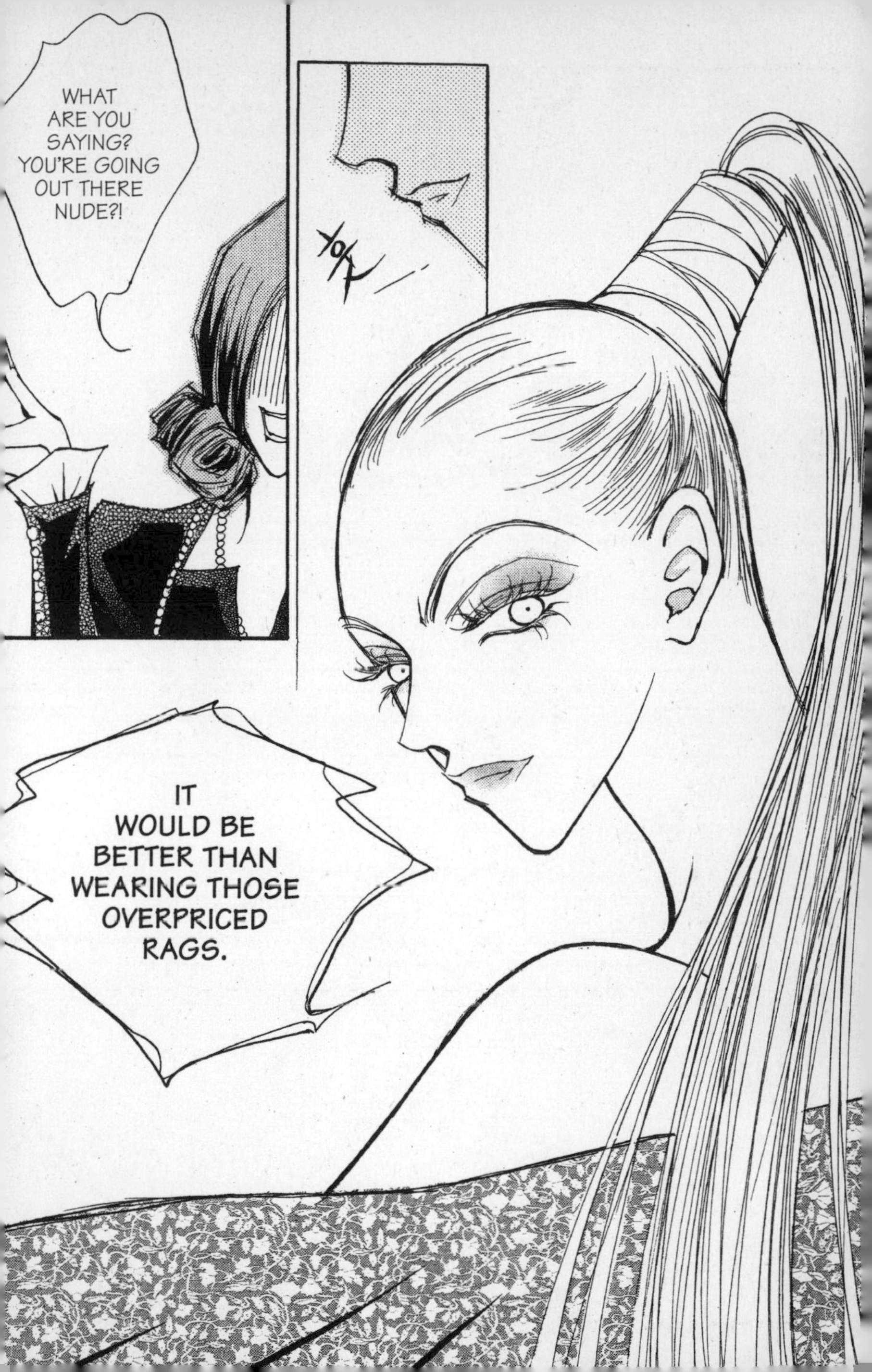
WHAT ARE YOU SAYING? YOU'RE GOING OUT THERE NUDE?!
IT WOULD BE BETTER THAN WEARING THOSE OVERPRICED RAGS.

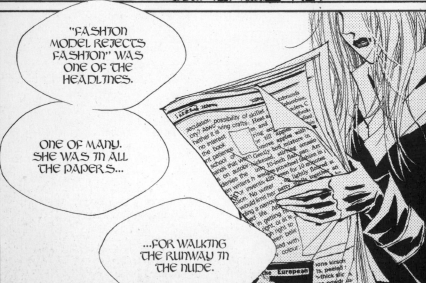

"FASHION MODEL REJECTS FASHION" WAS ONE OF THE HEADLINES.

ONE OF MANY. SHE WAS IN ALL THE PAPERS...

...FOR WALKING THE RUNWAY IN THE NUDE.

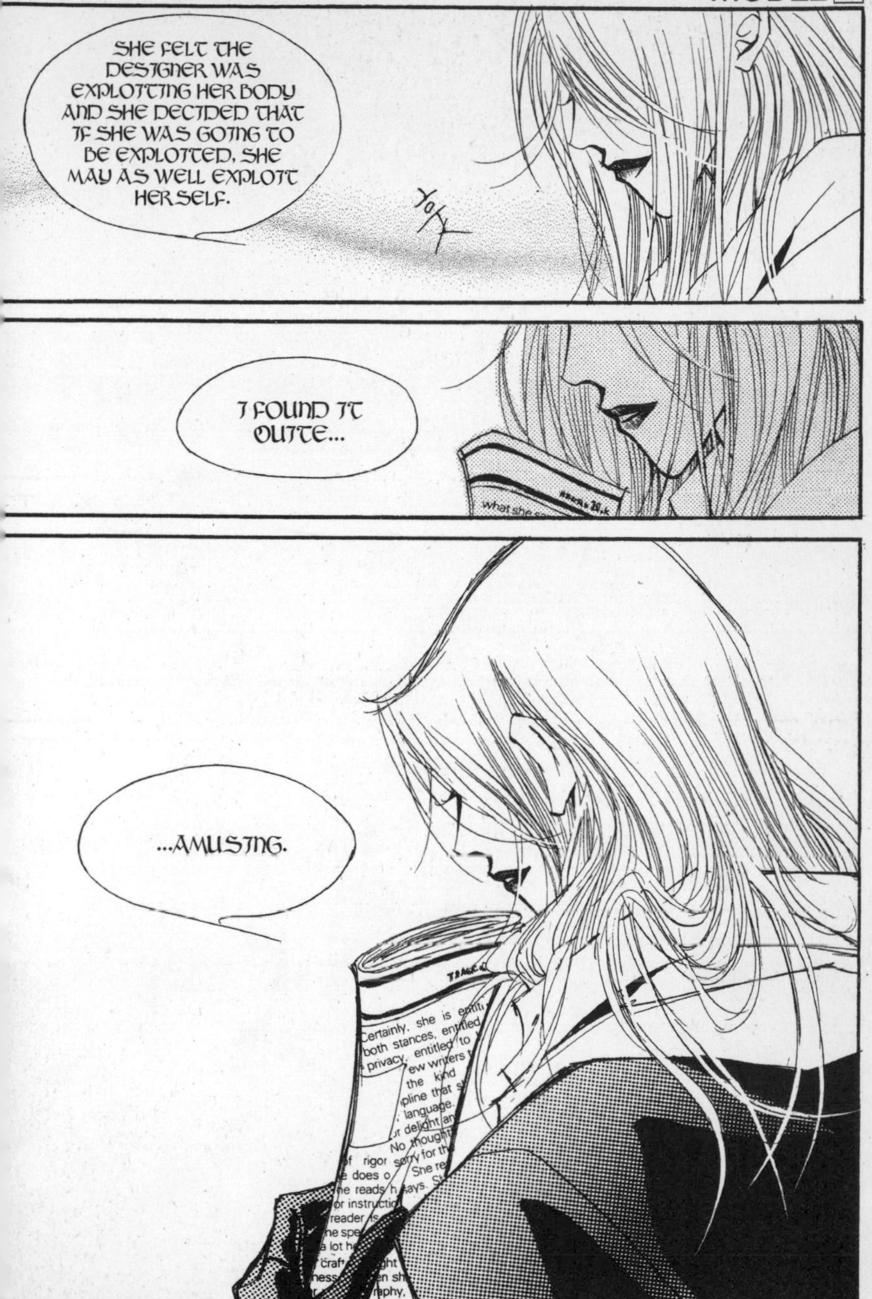
SHE FELT THE DESIGNER WAS EXPLOITING HER BODY AND SHE DECIDED THAT IF SHE WAS GOING TO BE EXPLOITED, SHE MAY AS WELL EXPLOIT HERSELF.
I FOUND IT QUITE...
...AMUSING.

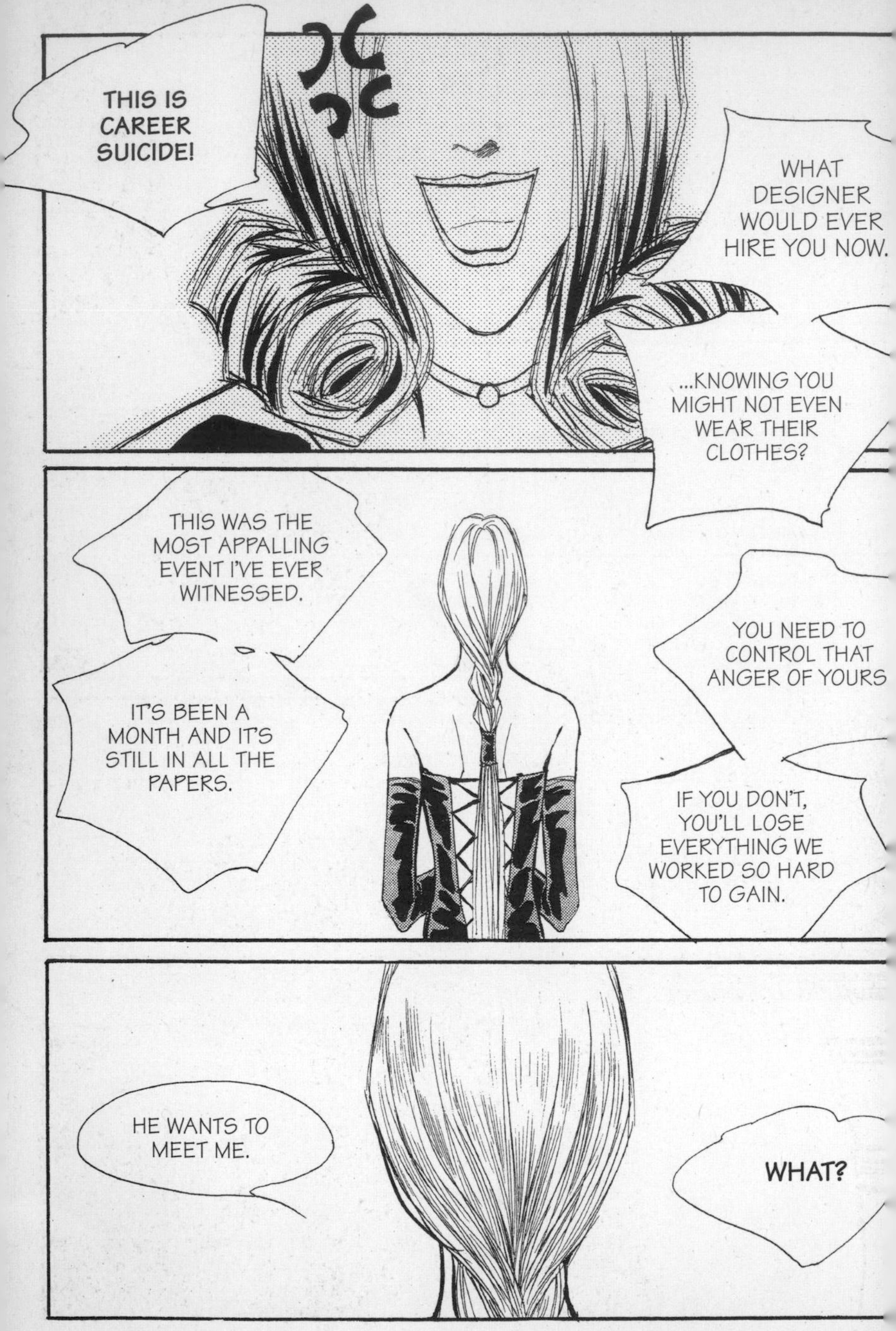
THIS IS CAREER SUICIDE!
WHAT DESIGNER WOULD EVER HIRE YOU NOW.
...KNOWING YOU MIGHT NOT EVEN WEAR THEIR CLOTHES?
THIS WAS THE MOST APPALLING EVENT I'VE EVER WITNESSED.
IT'S BEEN A MONTH AND IT'S STILL IN ALL THE PAPERS.
YOU NEED TO CONTROL THAT ANGER OF YOURS
IF YOU DON'T, YOU'LL LOSE EVERYTHING WE WORKED SO HARD TO GAIN.
HE WANTS TO MEET ME.
WHAT?

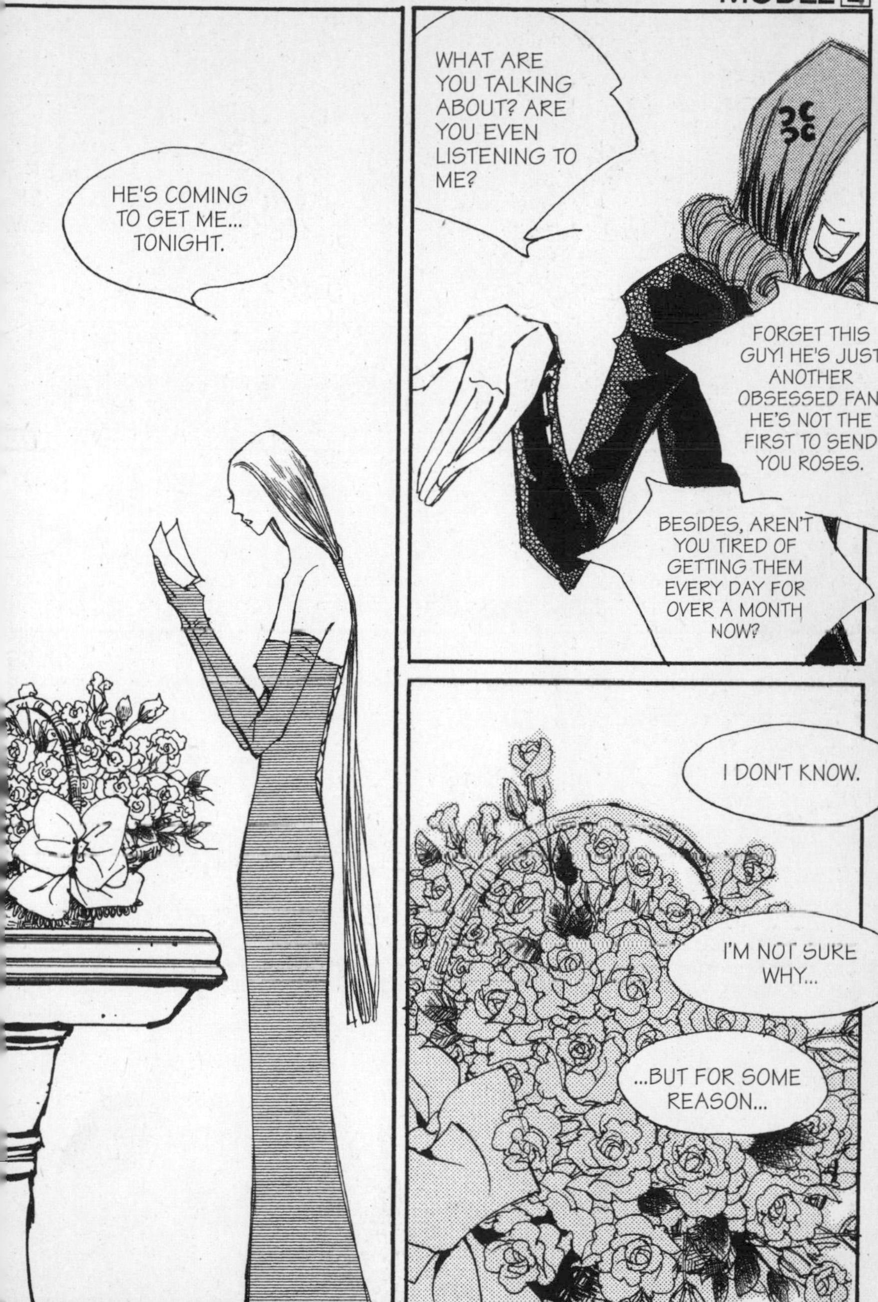
HE'S COMING TO GET ME... TONIGHT.
WHAT ARE YOU TALKING ABOUT? ARE YOU EVEN LISTENING TO ME?
FORGET THIS GUY! HE'S JUST ANOTHER OBSESSED FAN. HE'S NOT THE FIRST TO SEND YOU ROSES.
BESIDES, AREN'T YOU TIRED OF GETTING THEM EVERY DAY FOR OVER A MONTH NOW?
I DON'T KNOW.
I'M NOT SURE WHY...
...BUT FOR SOME REASON...

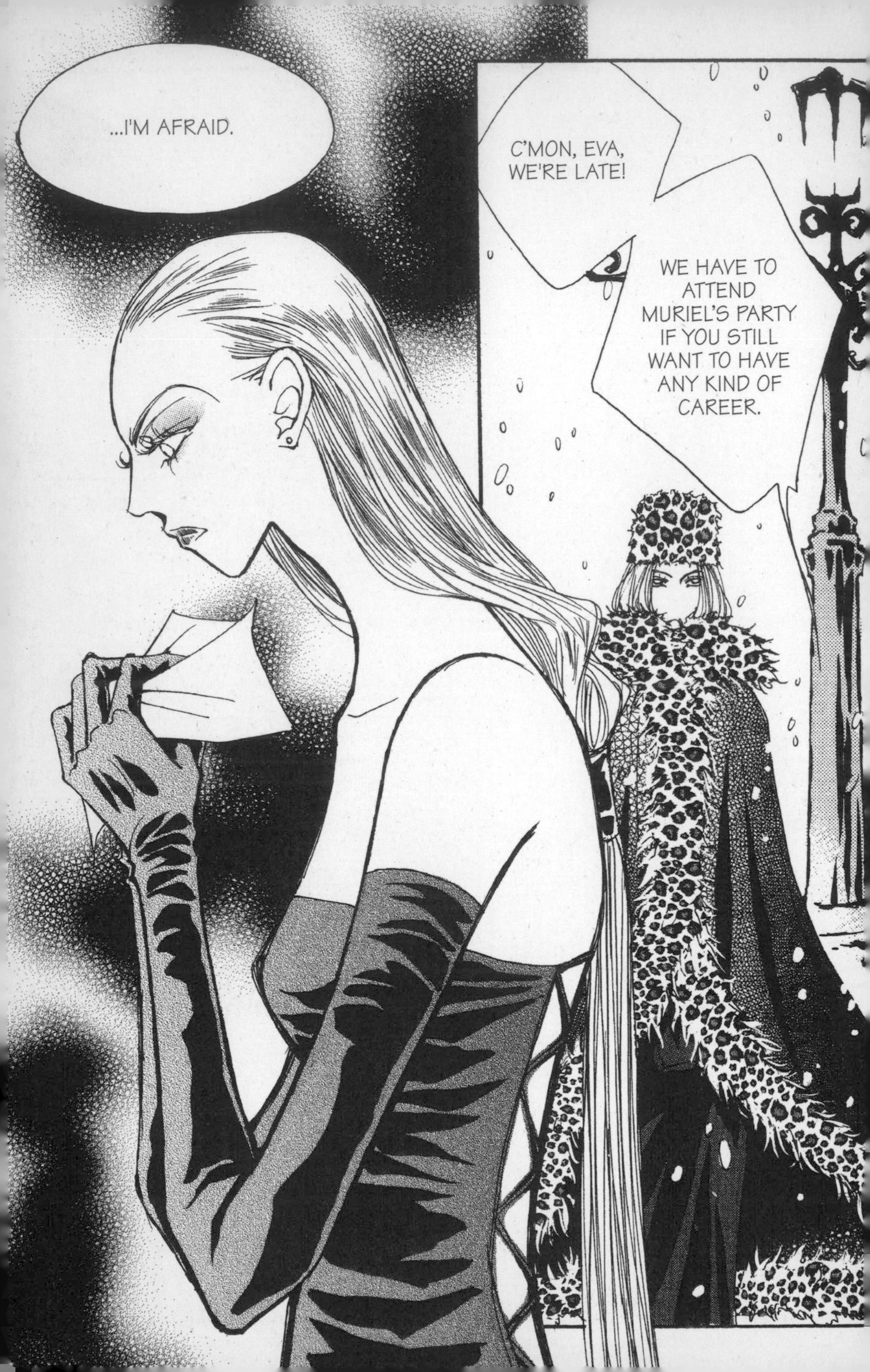
...I'M AFRAID.
C'MON, EVA, WE'RE LATE!
WE HAVE TO ATTEND MURIEL'S PARTY IF YOU STILL WANT TO HAVE ANY KIND OF CAREER.

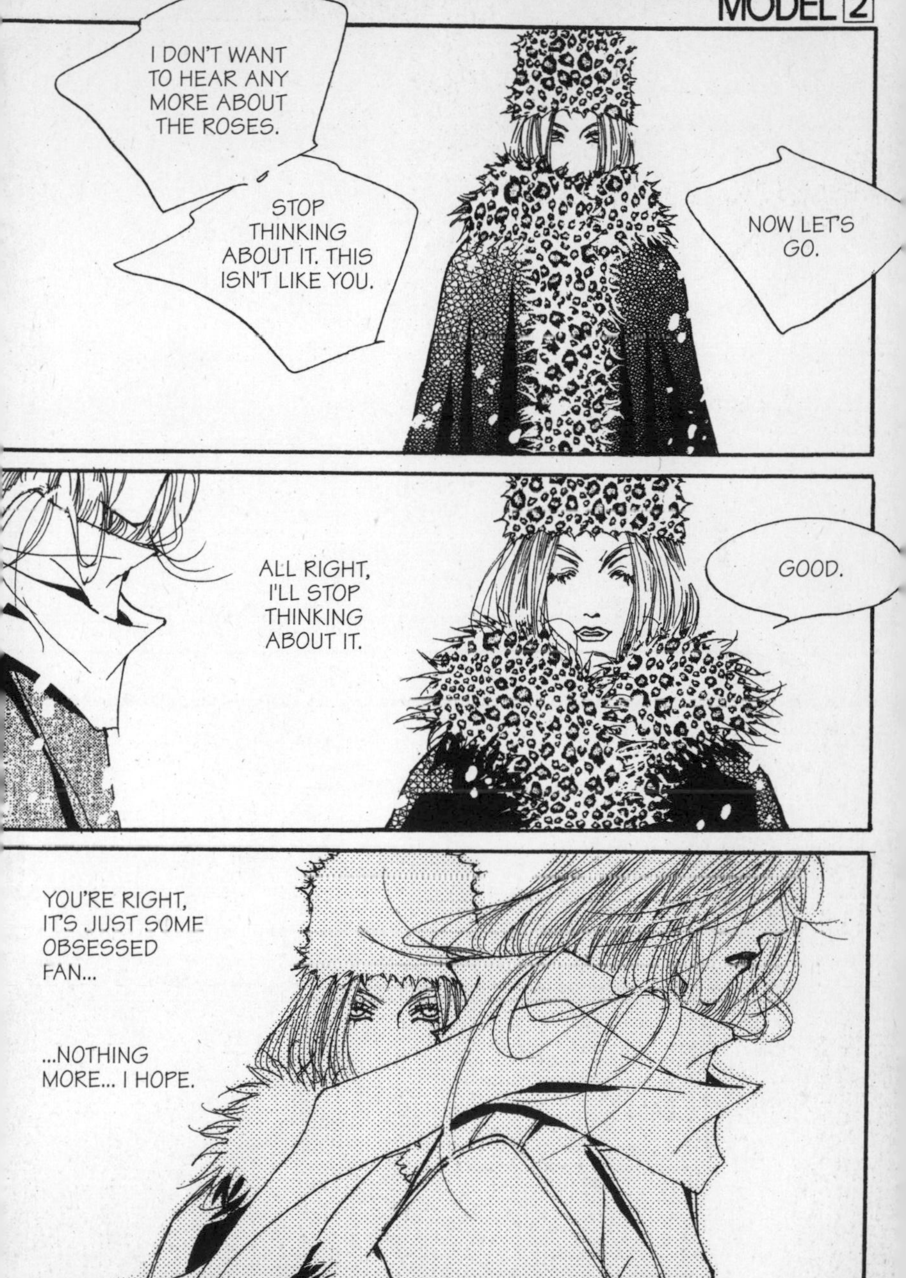
I DON'T WANT TO HEAR ANY MORE ABOUT THE ROSES.
STOP THINKING ABOUT IT. THIS ISN'T LIKE YOU.
NOW LET'S GO.
ALL RIGHT, I'LL STOP THINKING ABOUT IT.
GOOD.
YOU'RE RIGHT, IT'S JUST SOME OBSESSED FAN...
...NOTHING MORE... I HOPE.

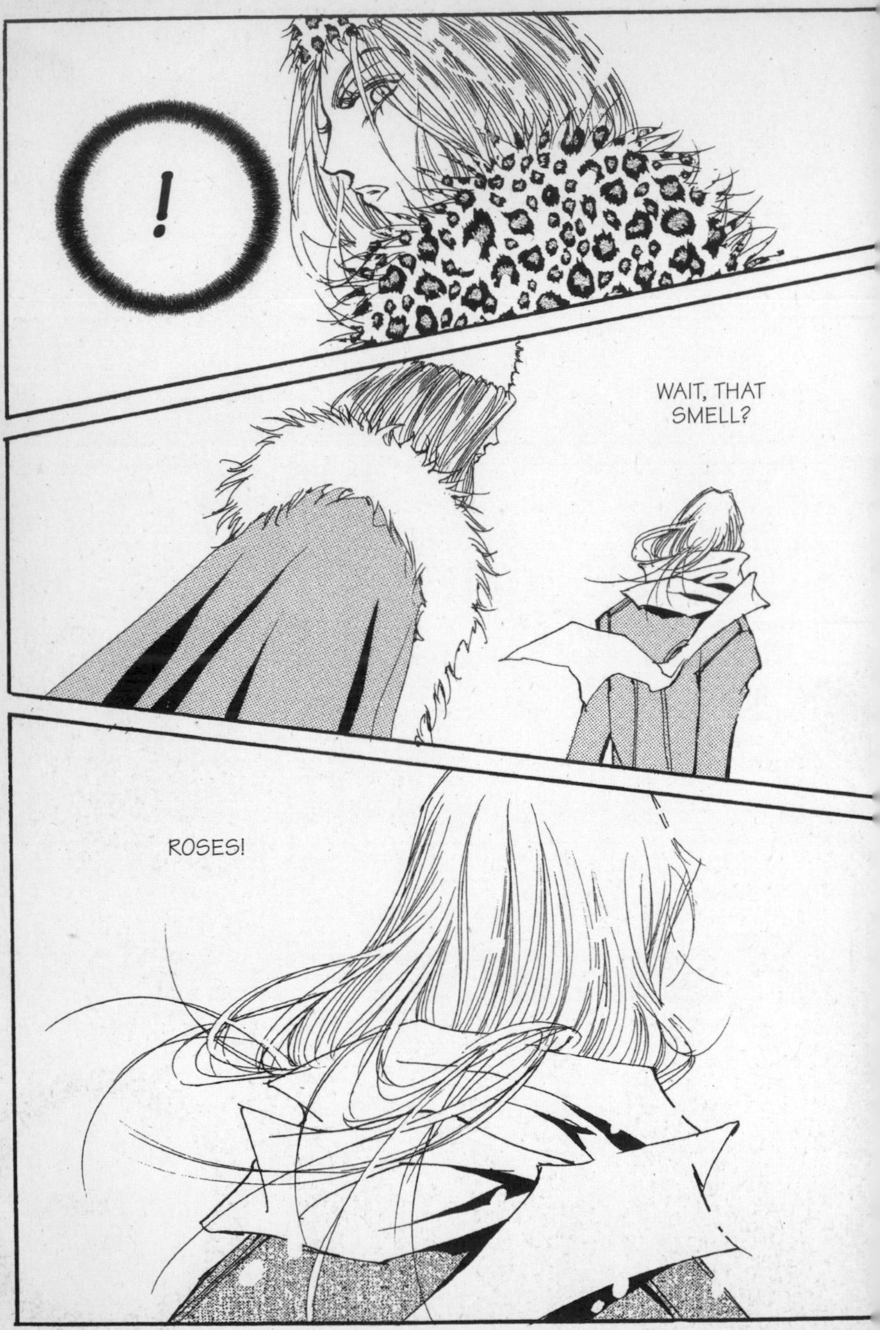
!
WAIT, THAT SMELL?
ROSES!

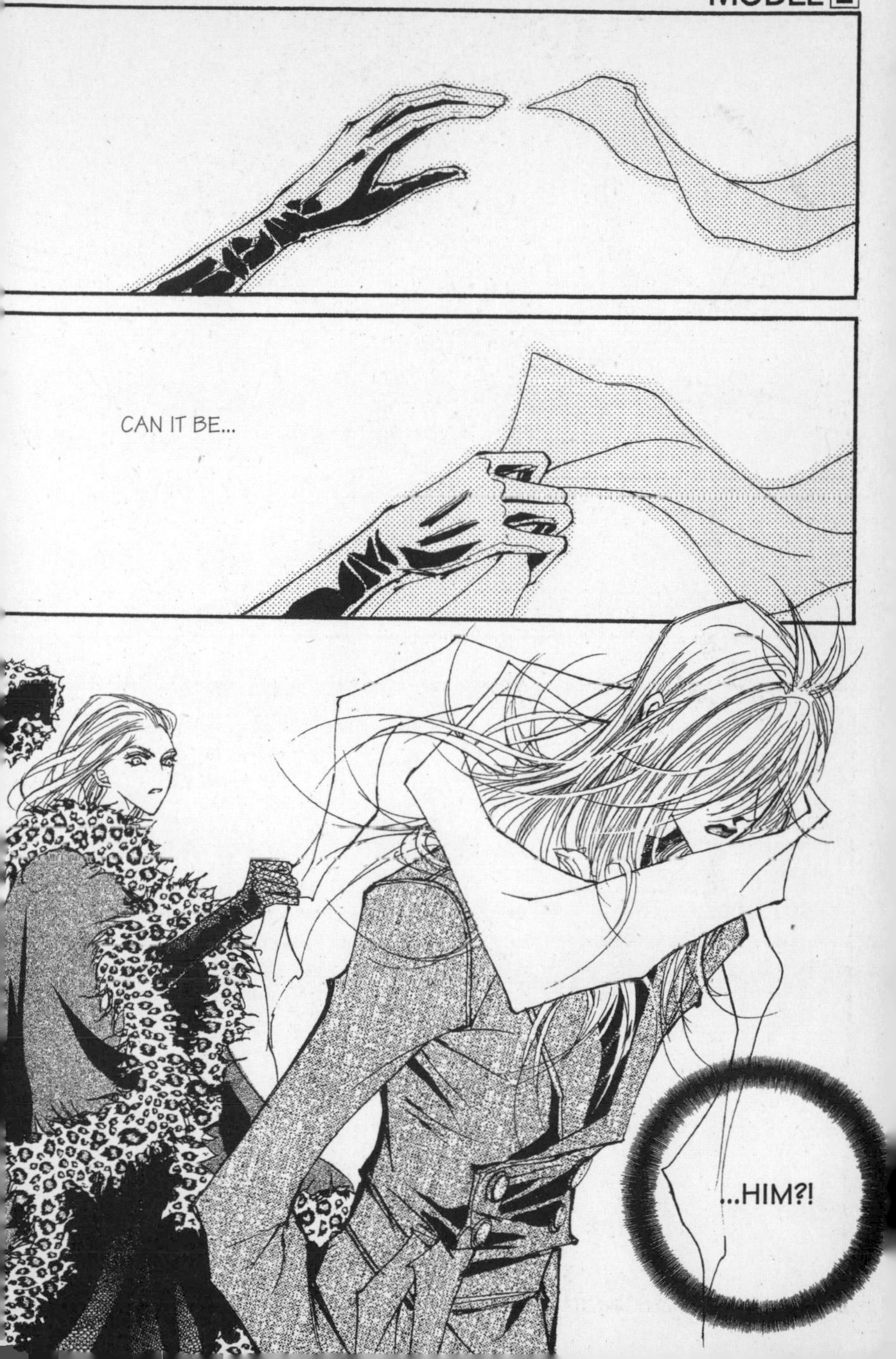
CAN IT BE...
...HIM?!

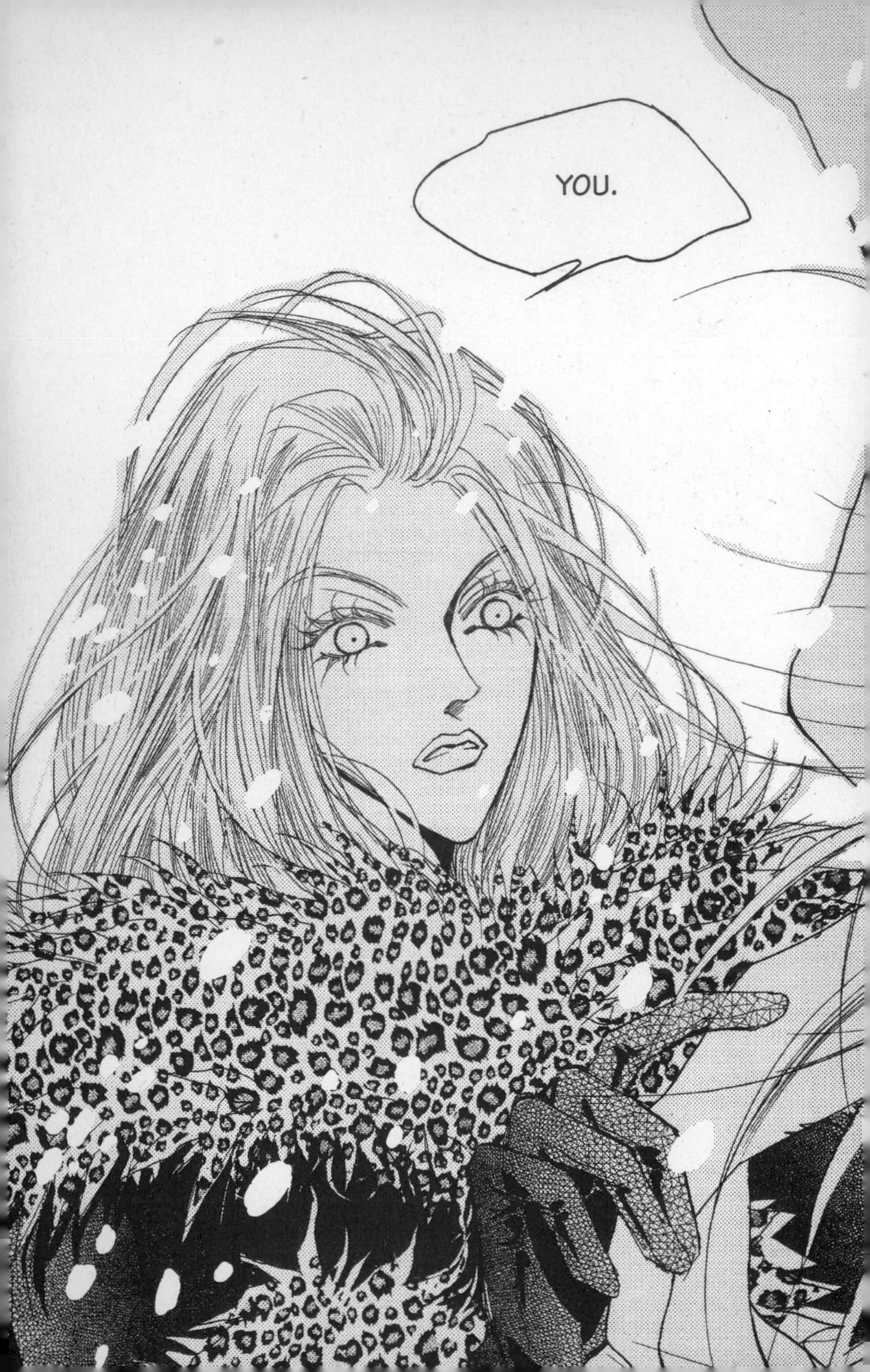
YOU.

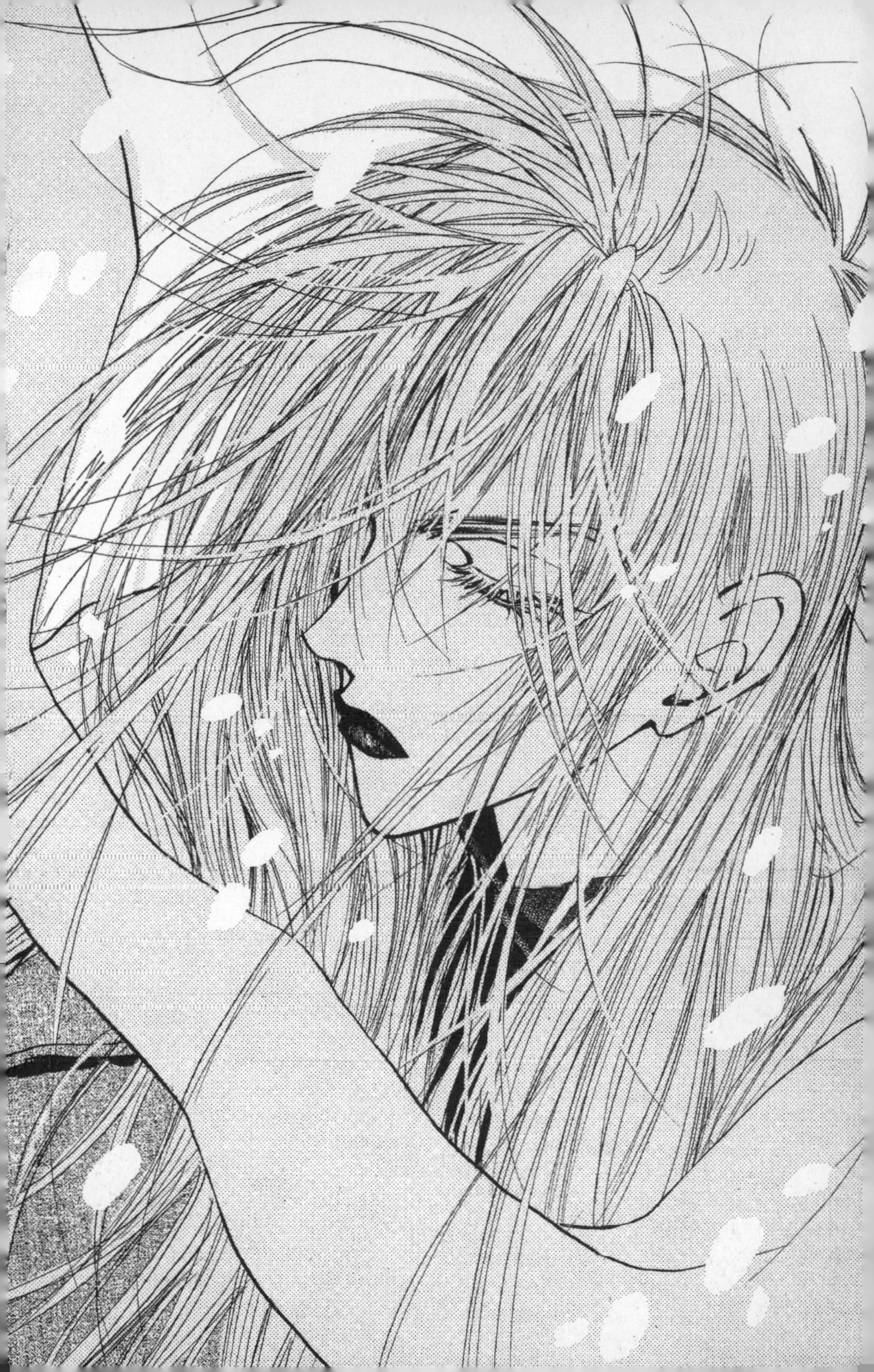

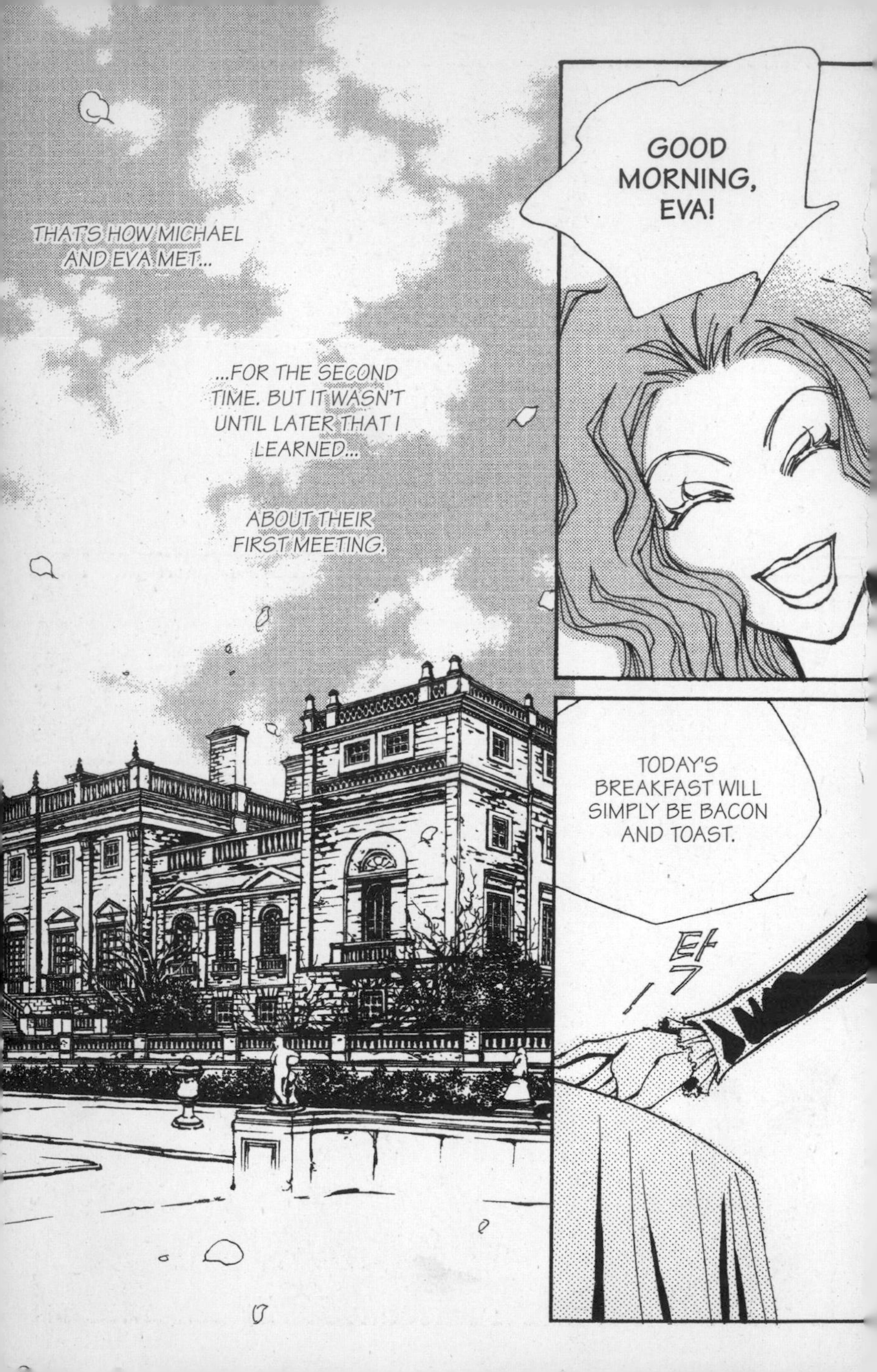
THAT'S HOW MICHAEL AND EVA MET...
...FOR THE SECOND TIME. BUT IT WASN'T UNTIL LATER THAT I LEARNED...
ABOUT THEIR FIRST MEETING.
GOOD MORNING, EVA!
TODAY'S BREAKFAST WILL SIMPLY BE BACON AND TOAST.
탁

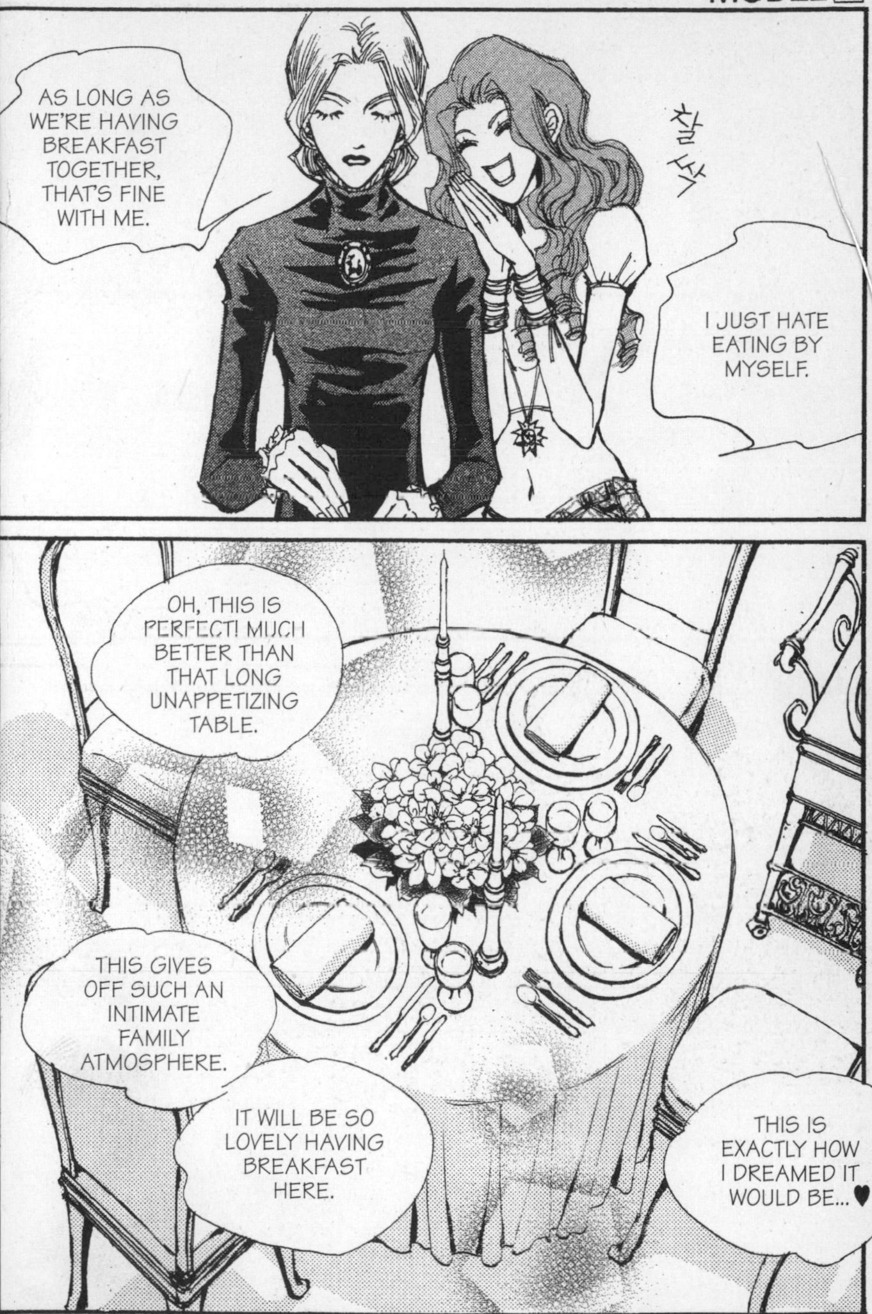
AS LONG AS WE'RE HAVING BREAKFAST TOGETHER, THAT'S FINE WITH ME.
찰싹
I JUST HATE EATING BY MYSELF.
OH, THIS IS PERFECT! MUCH BETTER THAN THAT LONG UNAPPETIZING TABLE.
THIS GIVES OFF SUCH AN INTIMATE FAMILY ATMOSPHERE.
IT WILL BE SO LOVELY HAVING BREAKFAST HERE.
THIS IS EXACTLY HOW I DREAMED IT WOULD BE...♥

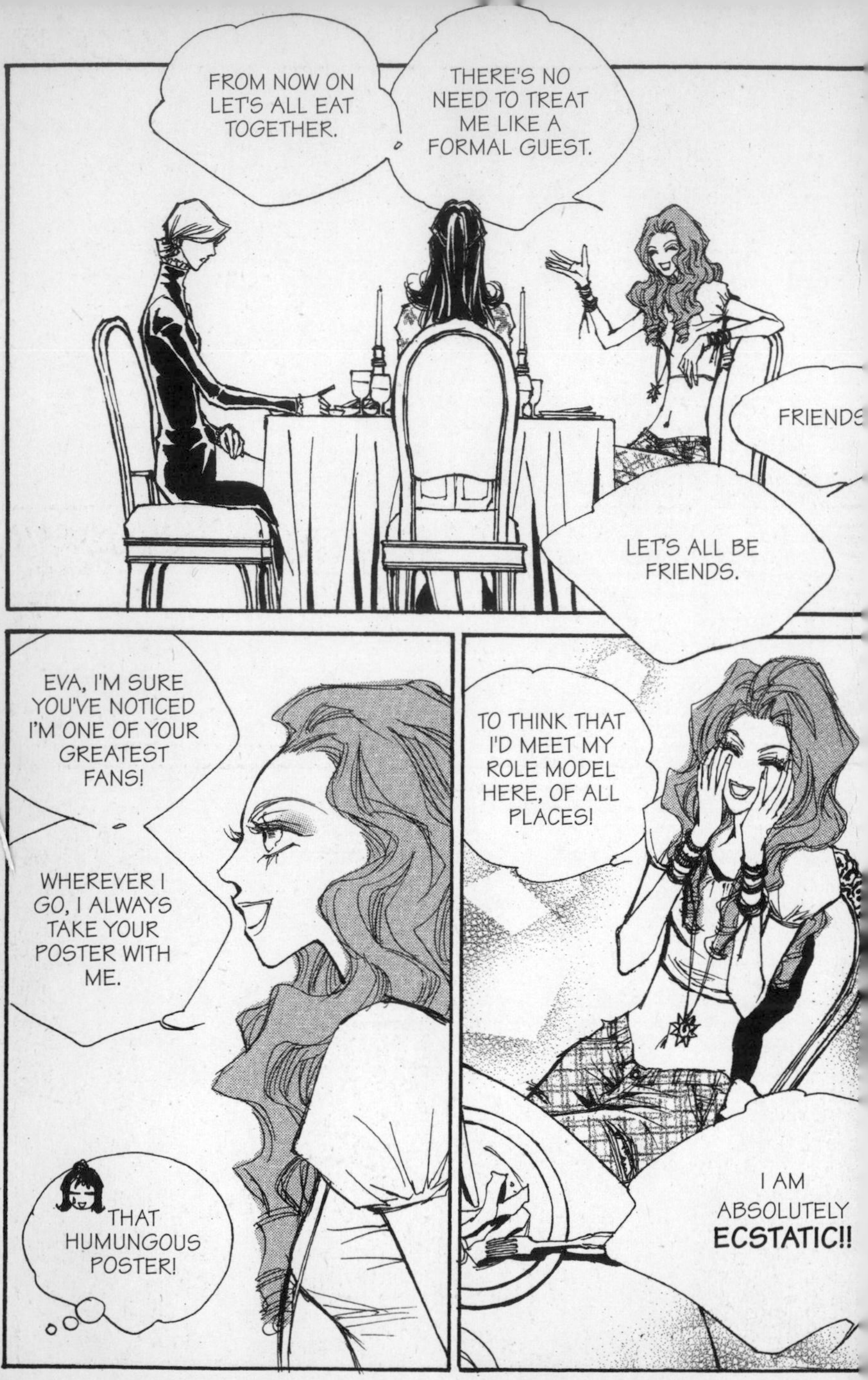
FROM NOW ON LET'S ALL EAT TOGETHER.
THERE'S NO NEED TO TREAT ME LIKE A FORMAL GUEST.
FRIENDS
LET'S ALL BE FRIENDS.
EVA, I'M SURE YOU'VE NOTICED I'M ONE OF YOUR GREATEST FANS!
WHEREVER I GO, I ALWAYS TAKE YOUR POSTER WITH ME.
THAT HUMUNGOUS POSTER!
TO THINK THAT I'D MEET MY ROLE MODEL HERE, OF ALL PLACES!
I AM ABSOLUTELY **ECSTATIC!!**

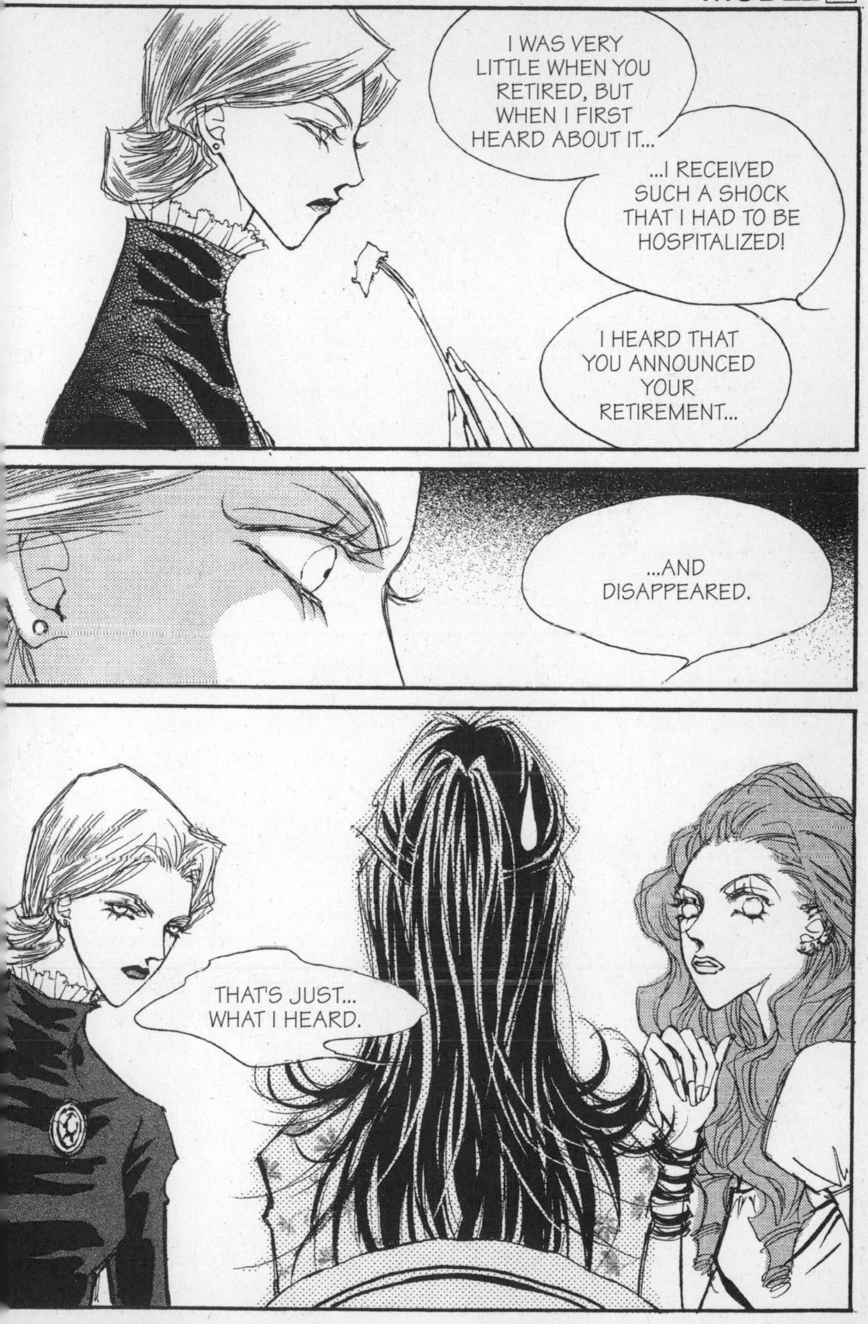
I WAS VERY LITTLE WHEN YOU RETIRED, BUT WHEN I FIRST HEARD ABOUT IT...
...I RECEIVED SUCH A SHOCK THAT I HAD TO BE HOSPITALIZED!
I HEARD THAT YOU ANNOUNCED YOUR RETIREMENT...
...AND DISAPPEARED.
THAT'S JUST... WHAT I HEARD.

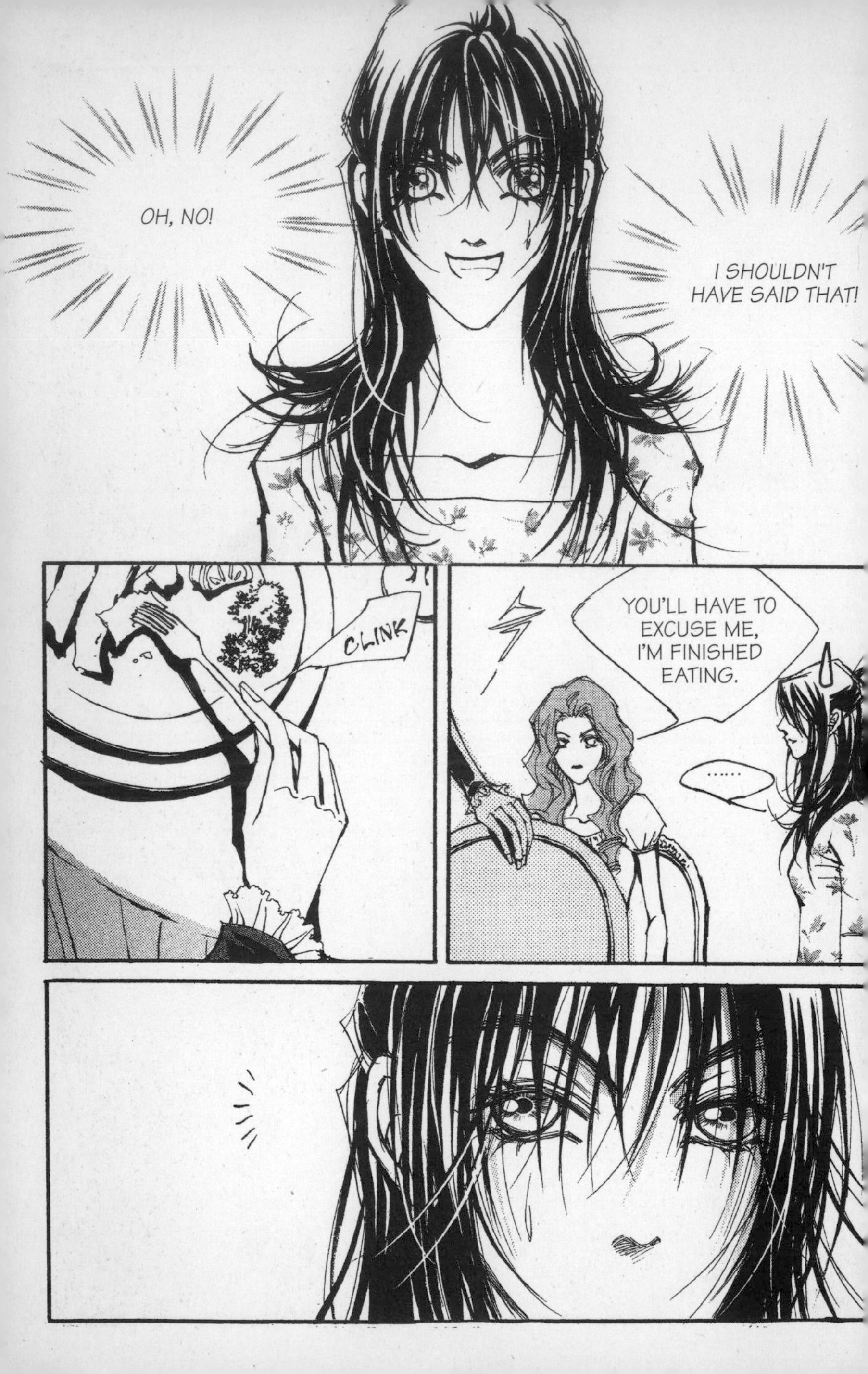
OH, NO!
I SHOULDN'T HAVE SAID THAT!
CLINK
YOU'LL HAVE TO EXCUSE ME, I'M FINISHED EATING.
......

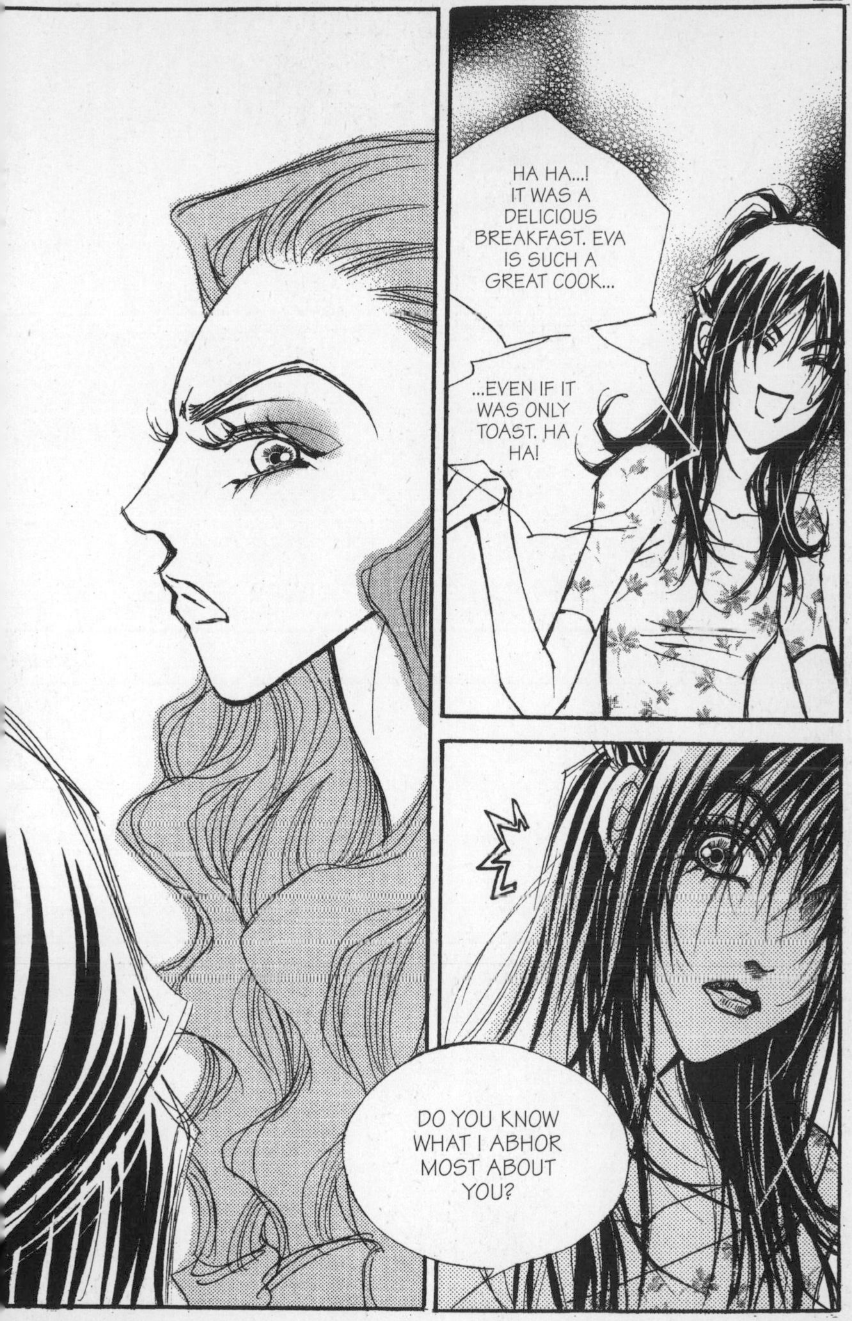
HA HA...! IT WAS A DELICIOUS BREAKFAST. EVA IS SUCH A GREAT COOK...
...EVEN IF IT WAS ONLY TOAST. HA HA!
DO YOU KNOW WHAT I ABHOR MOST ABOUT YOU?

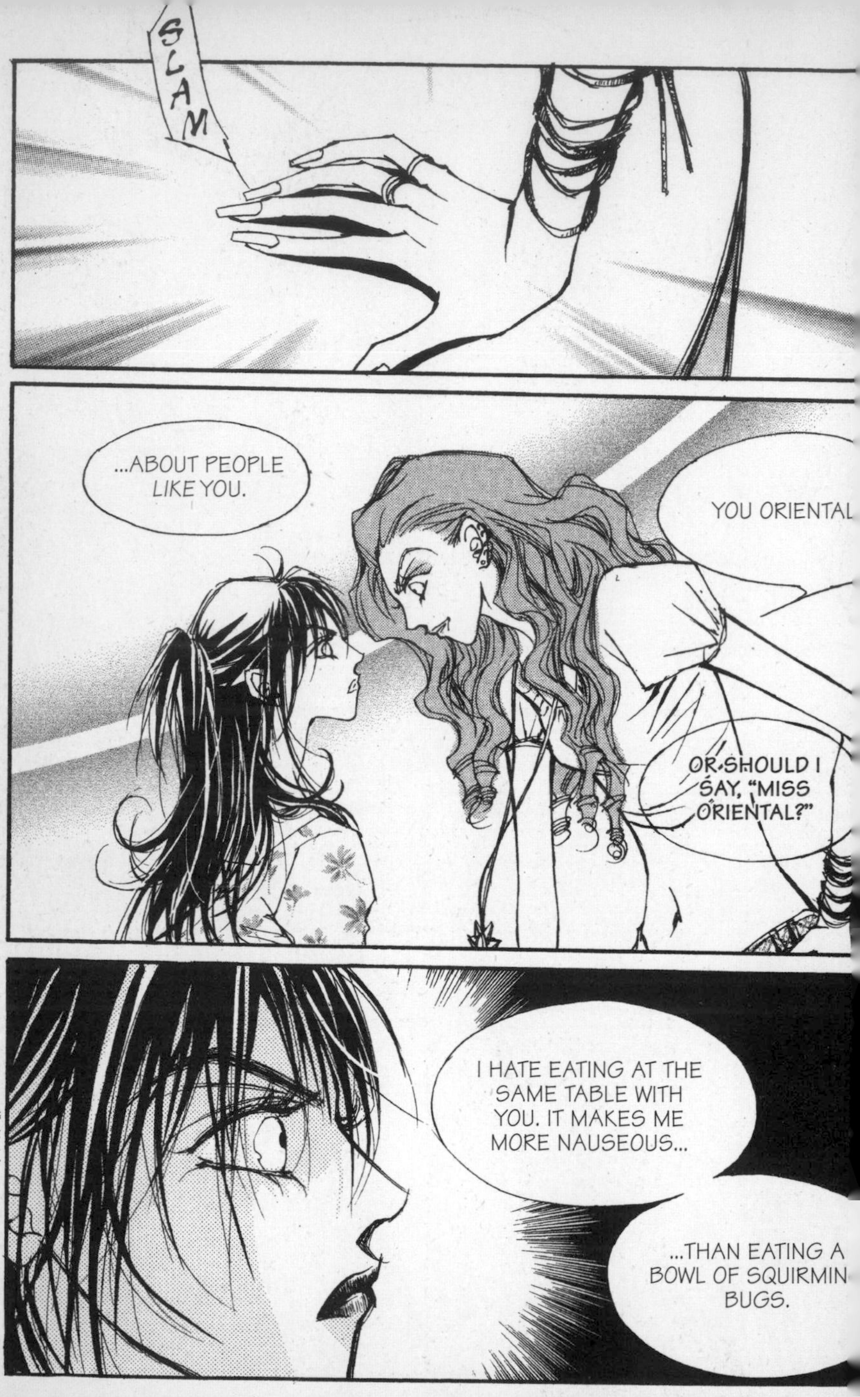
SLAM
...ABOUT PEOPLE LIKE YOU.
YOU ORIENTAL
OR SHOULD I SAY, "MISS ORIENTAL?"
I HATE EATING AT THE SAME TABLE WITH YOU. IT MAKES ME MORE NAUSEOUS...
...THAN EATING A BOWL OF SQUIRMIN BUGS.

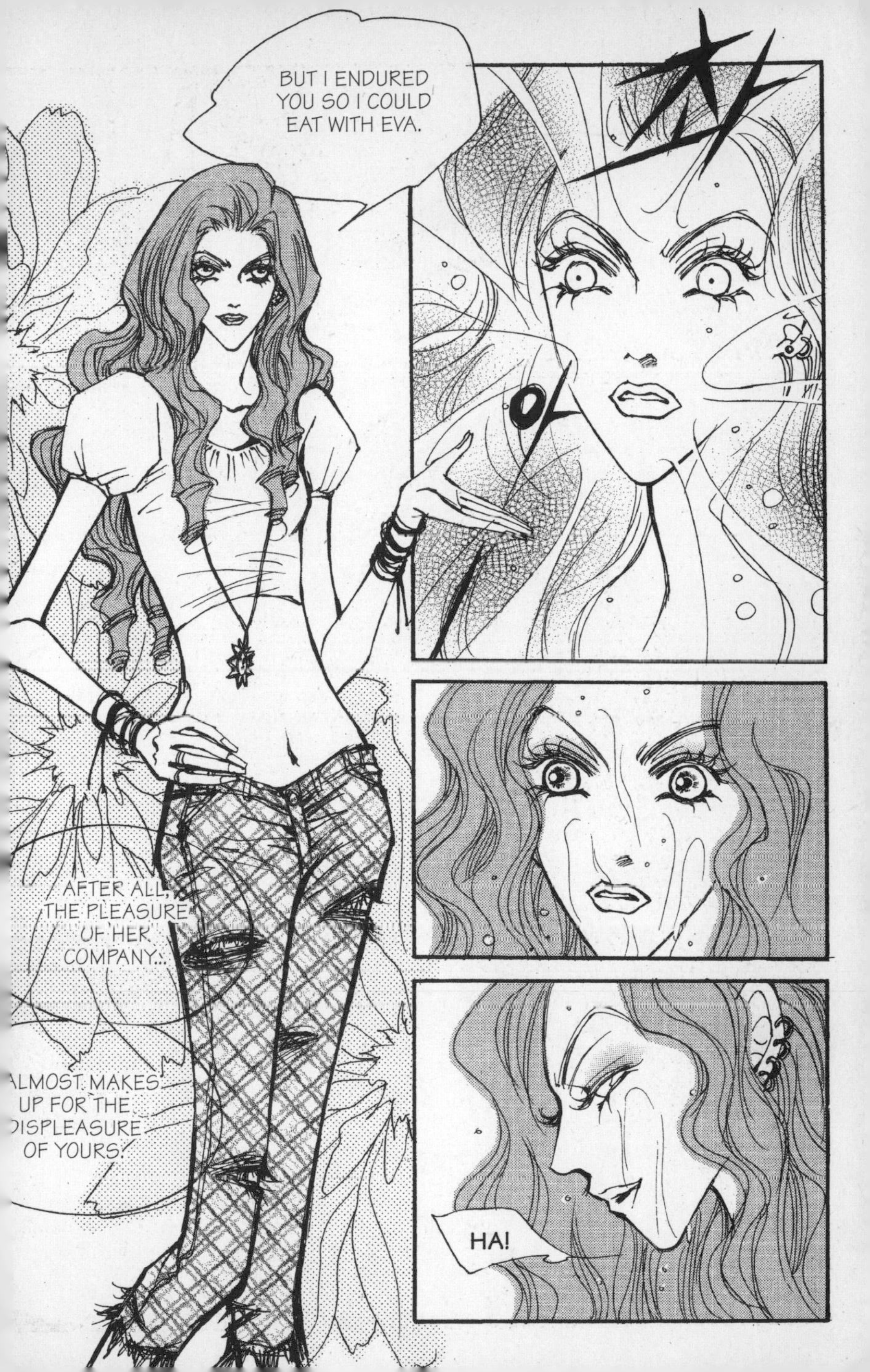
BUT I ENDURED YOU SO I COULD EAT WITH EVA.
AFTER ALL, THE PLEASURE OF HER COMPANY...
ALMOST MAKES UP FOR THE DISPLEASURE OF YOURS.
HA!

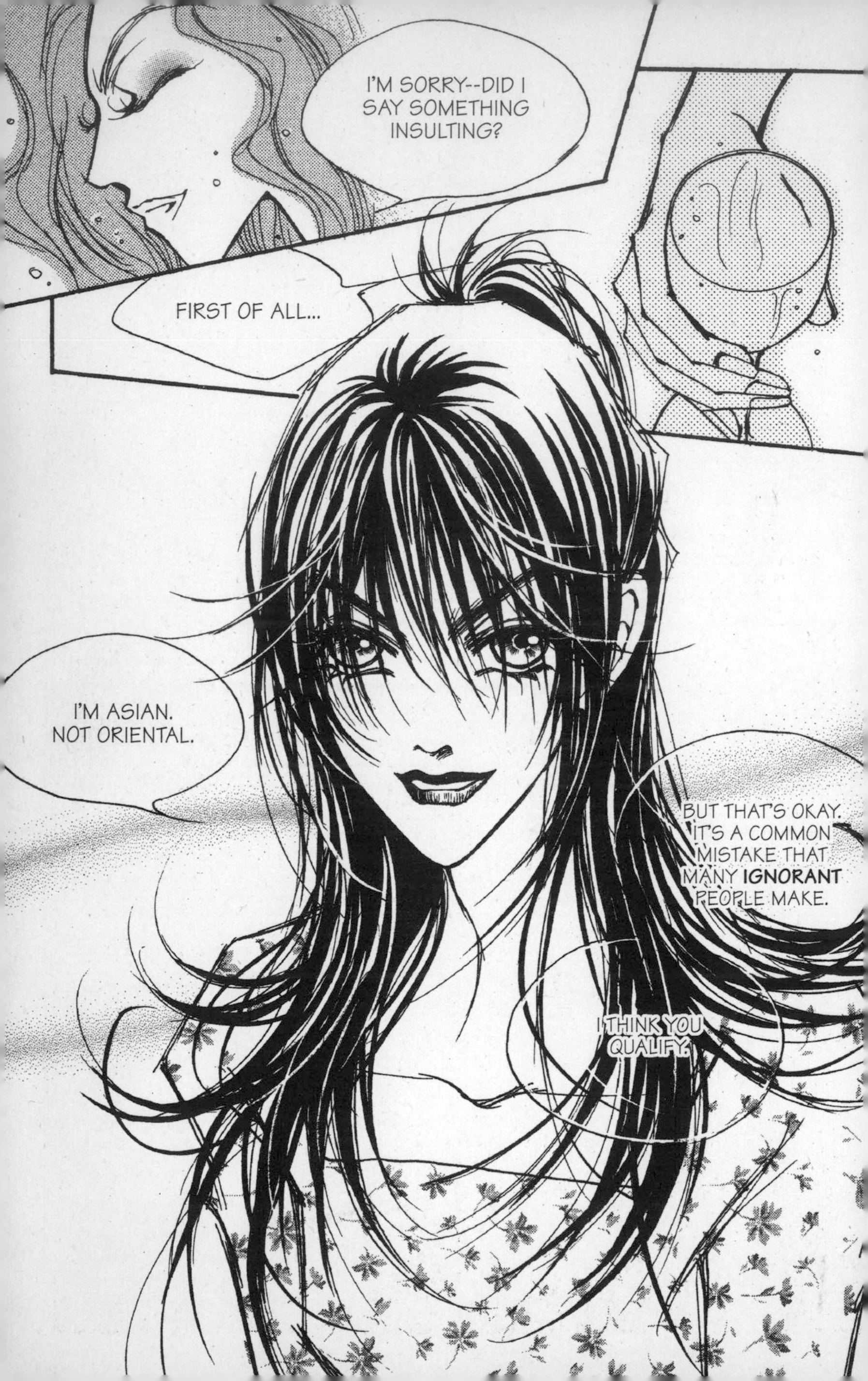
I'M SORRY--DID I SAY SOMETHING INSULTING?
FIRST OF ALL...
I'M ASIAN. NOT ORIENTAL.
BUT THAT'S OKAY. IT'S A COMMON MISTAKE THAT MANY **IGNORANT** PEOPLE MAKE.
I THINK YOU QUALIFY.

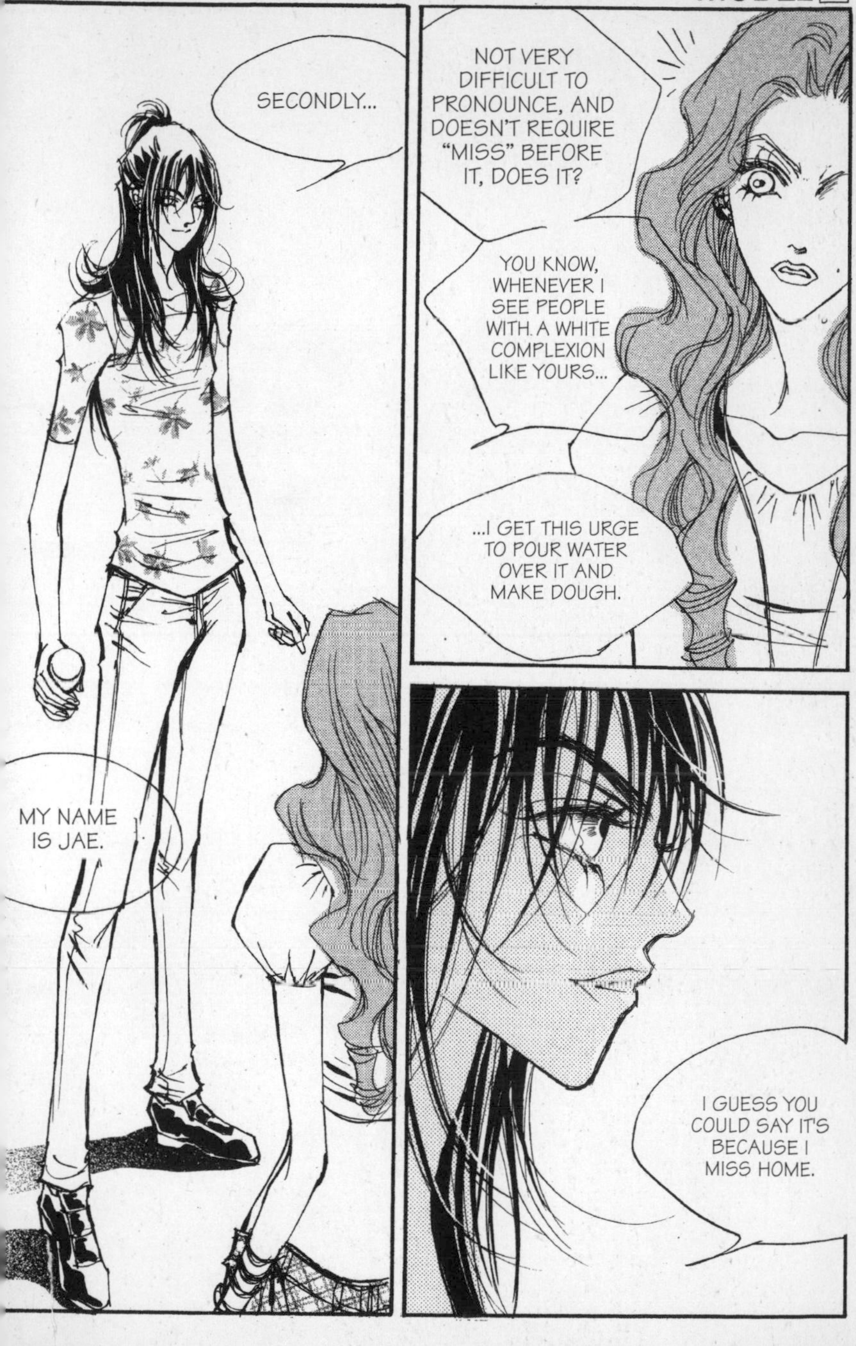
SECONDLY...
MY NAME IS JAE.
NOT VERY DIFFICULT TO PRONOUNCE, AND DOESN'T REQUIRE "MISS" BEFORE IT, DOES IT?
YOU KNOW, WHENEVER I SEE PEOPLE WITH. A WHITE COMPLEXION LIKE YOURS...
...I GET THIS URGE TO POUR WATER OVER IT AND MAKE DOUGH.
I GUESS YOU COULD SAY IT'S BECAUSE I MISS HOME.

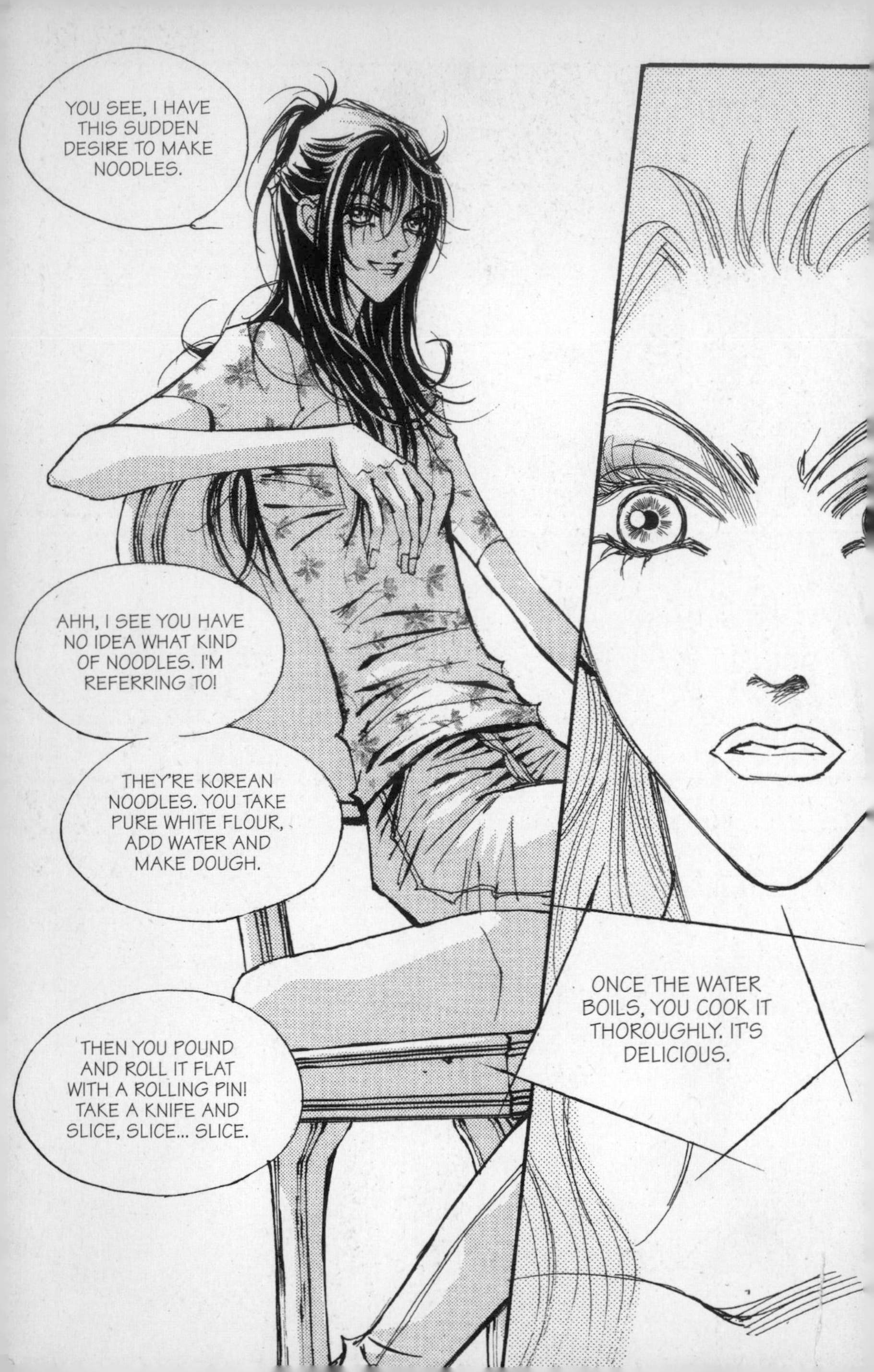
YOU SEE, I HAVE THIS SUDDEN DESIRE TO MAKE NOODLES.
AHH, I SEE YOU HAVE NO IDEA WHAT KIND OF NOODLES. I'M REFERRING TO!
THEY'RE KOREAN NOODLES. YOU TAKE PURE WHITE FLOUR, ADD WATER AND MAKE DOUGH.
THEN YOU POUND AND ROLL IT FLAT WITH A ROLLING PIN! TAKE A KNIFE AND SLICE, SLICE... SLICE.
ONCE THE WATER BOILS, YOU COOK IT THOROUGHLY. IT'S DELICIOUS.

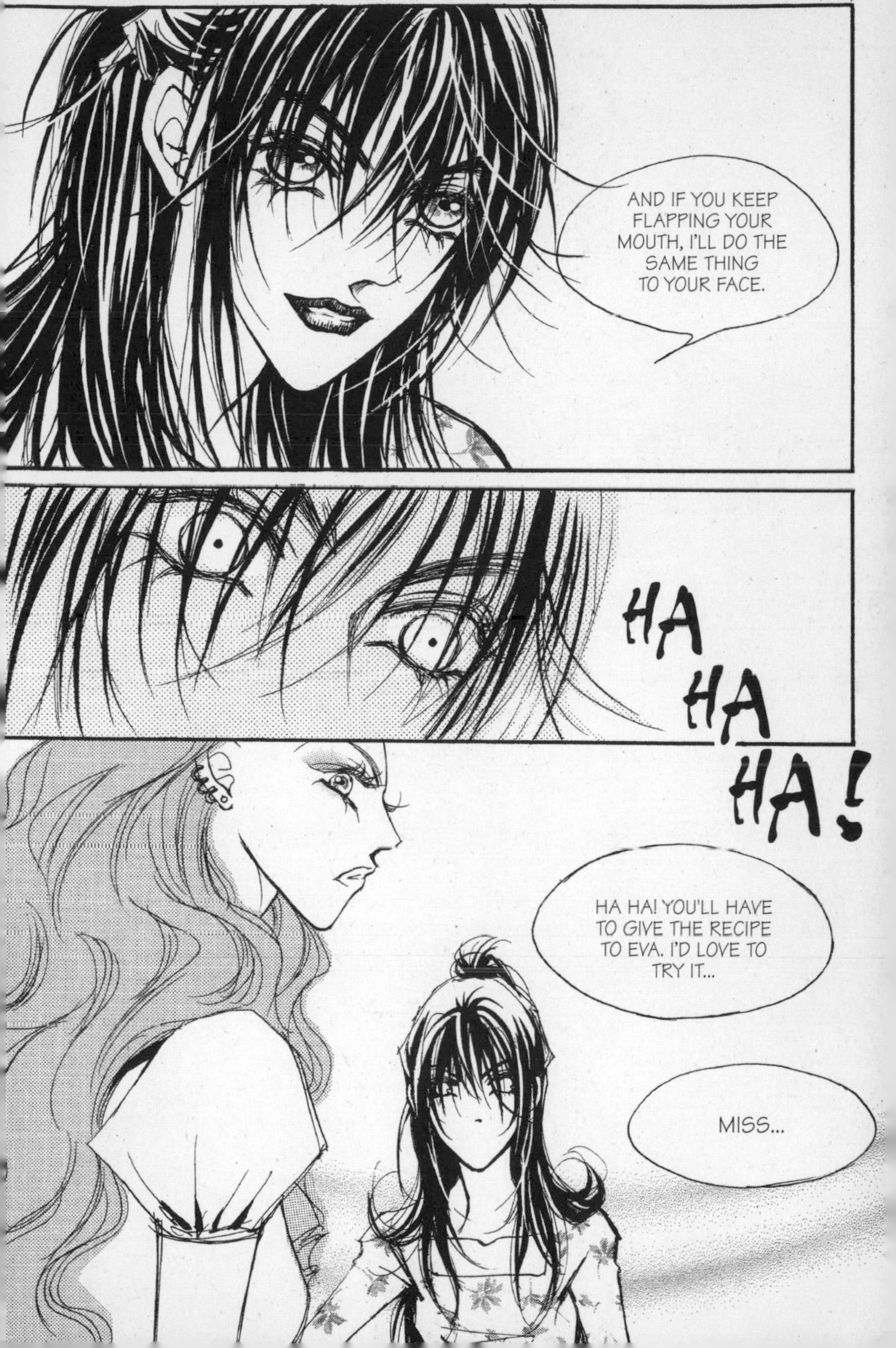
AND IF YOU KEEP FLAPPING YOUR MOUTH, I'LL DO THE SAME THING TO YOUR FACE.
HA HA HA!
HA HA! YOU'LL HAVE TO GIVE THE RECIPE TO EVA. I'D LOVE TO TRY IT...
MISS...

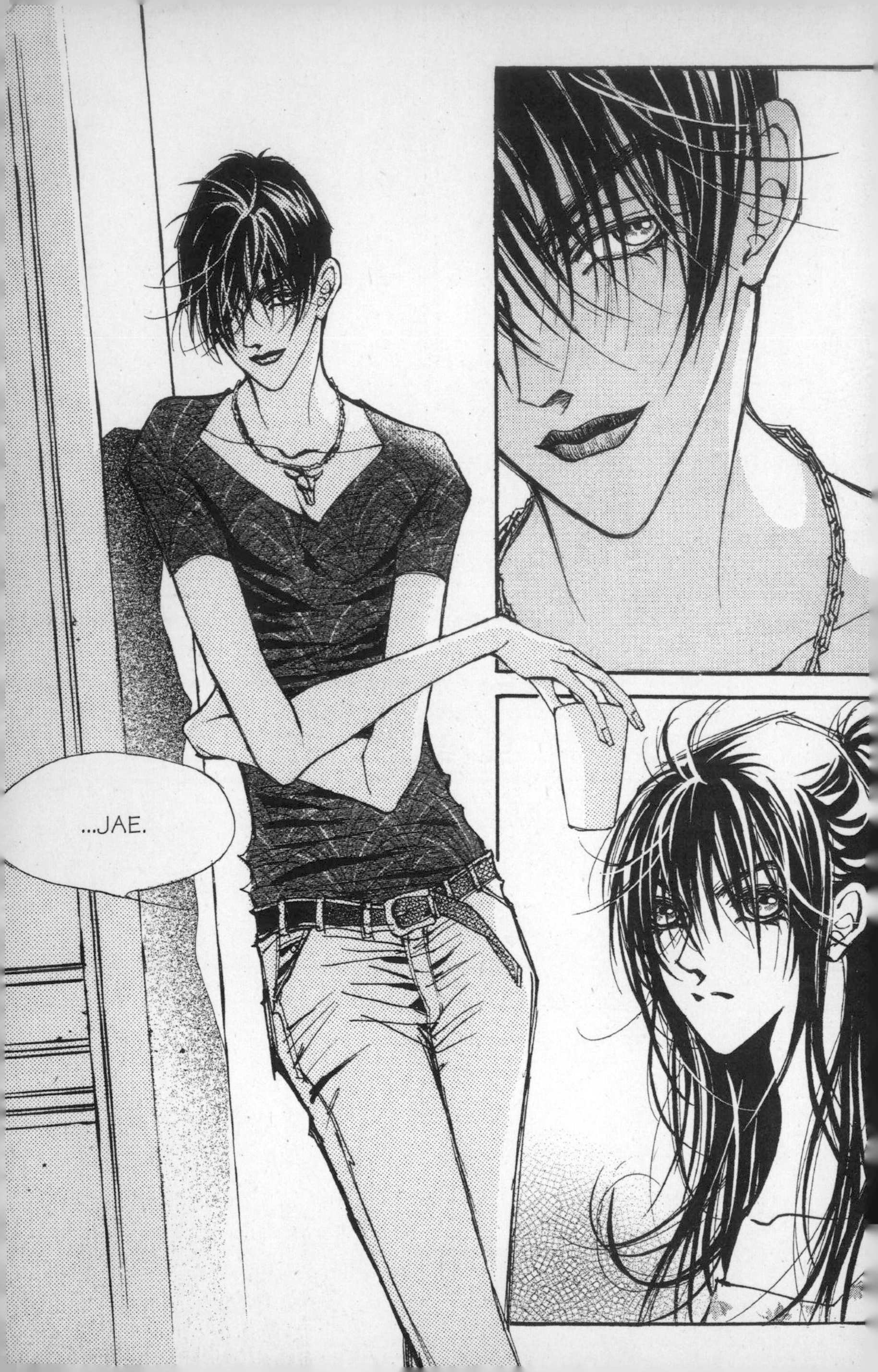
...JAE.

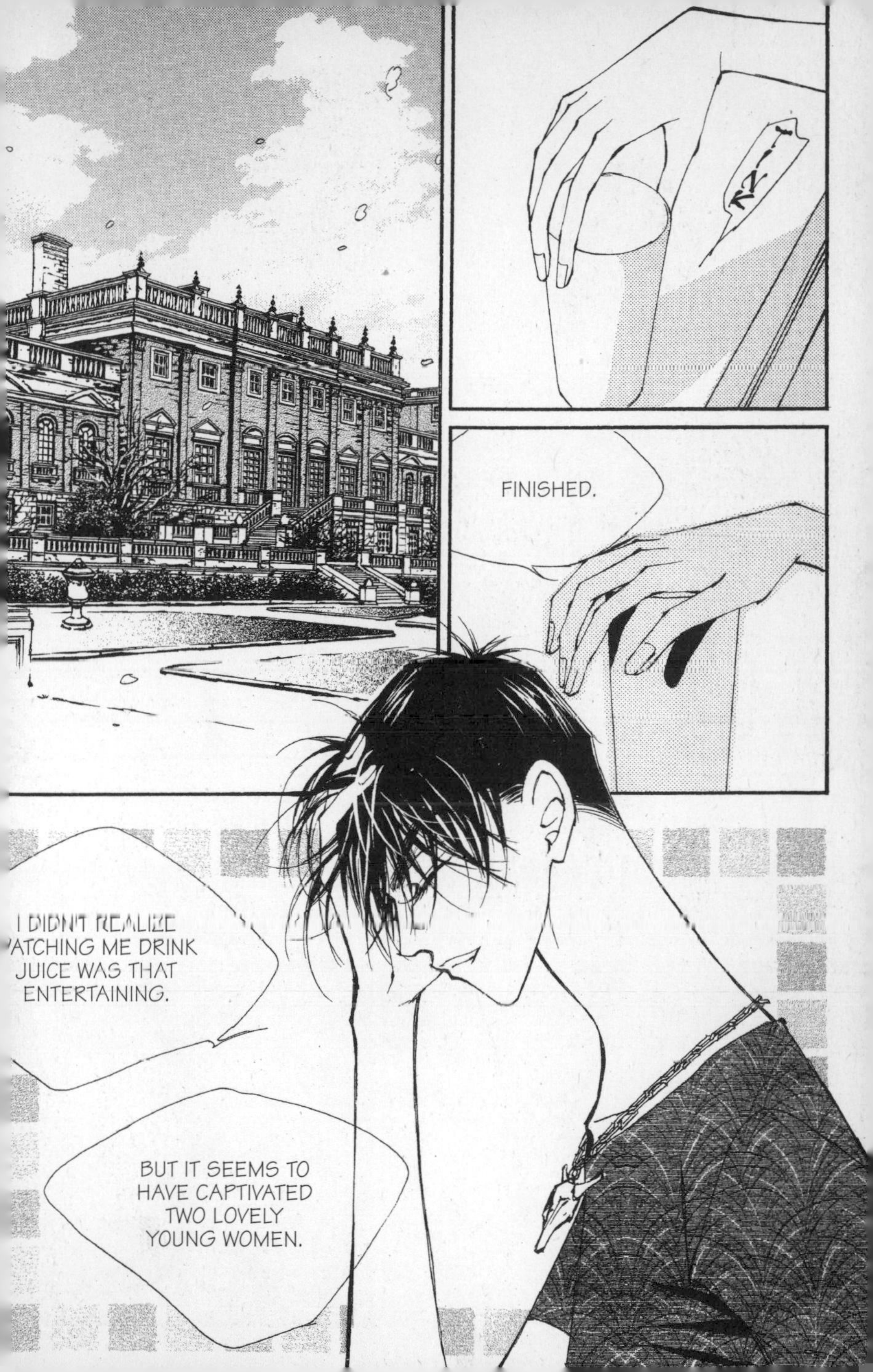
TINK
FINISHED.
I DIDN'T REALIZE ATCHING ME DRINK JUICE WAS THAT ENTERTAINING.
BUT IT SEEMS TO HAVE CAPTIVATED TWO LOVELY YOUNG WOMEN.

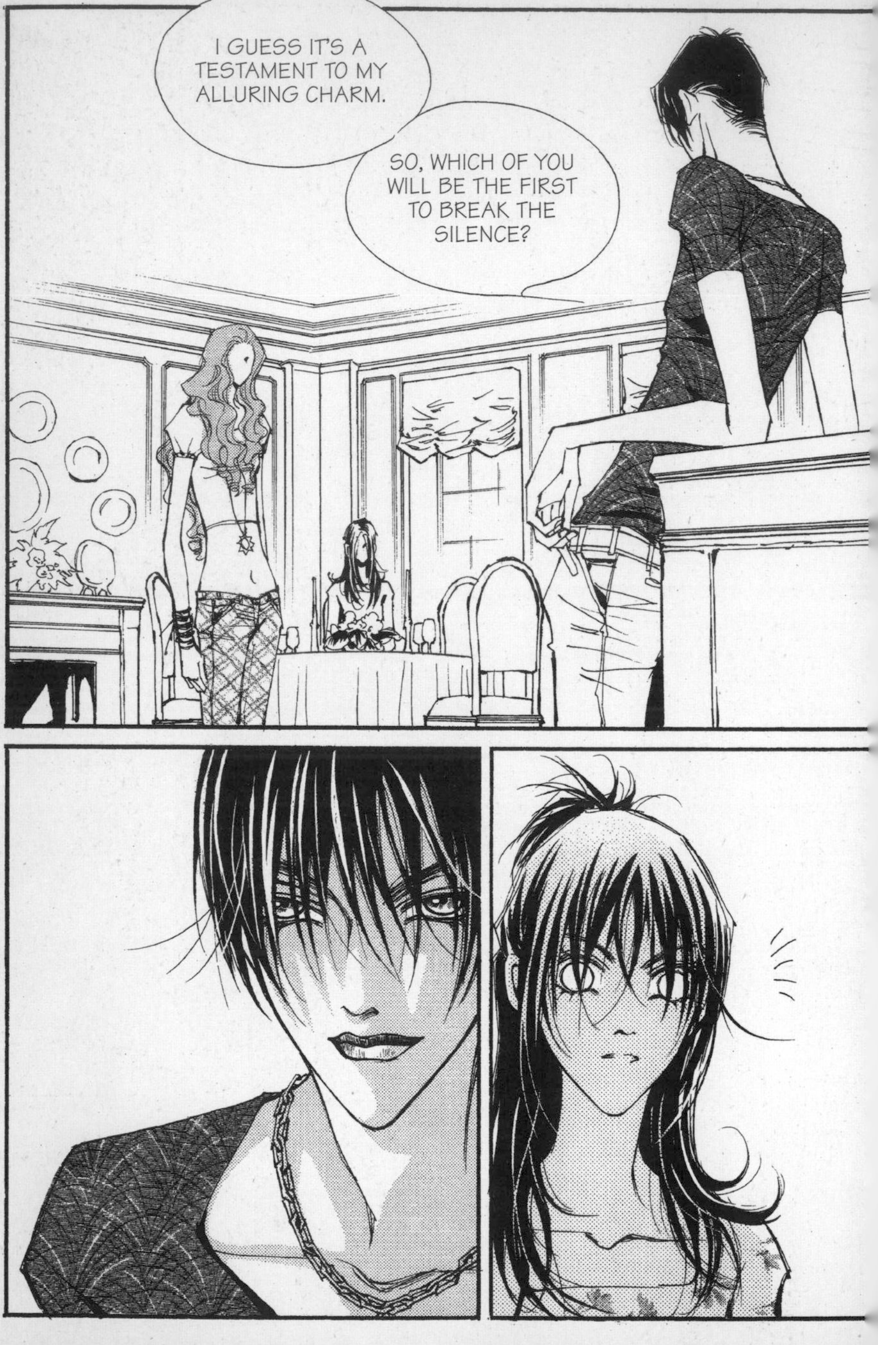
I GUESS IT'S A TESTAMENT TO MY ALLURING CHARM.
SO, WHICH OF YOU WILL BE THE FIRST TO BREAK THE SILENCE?

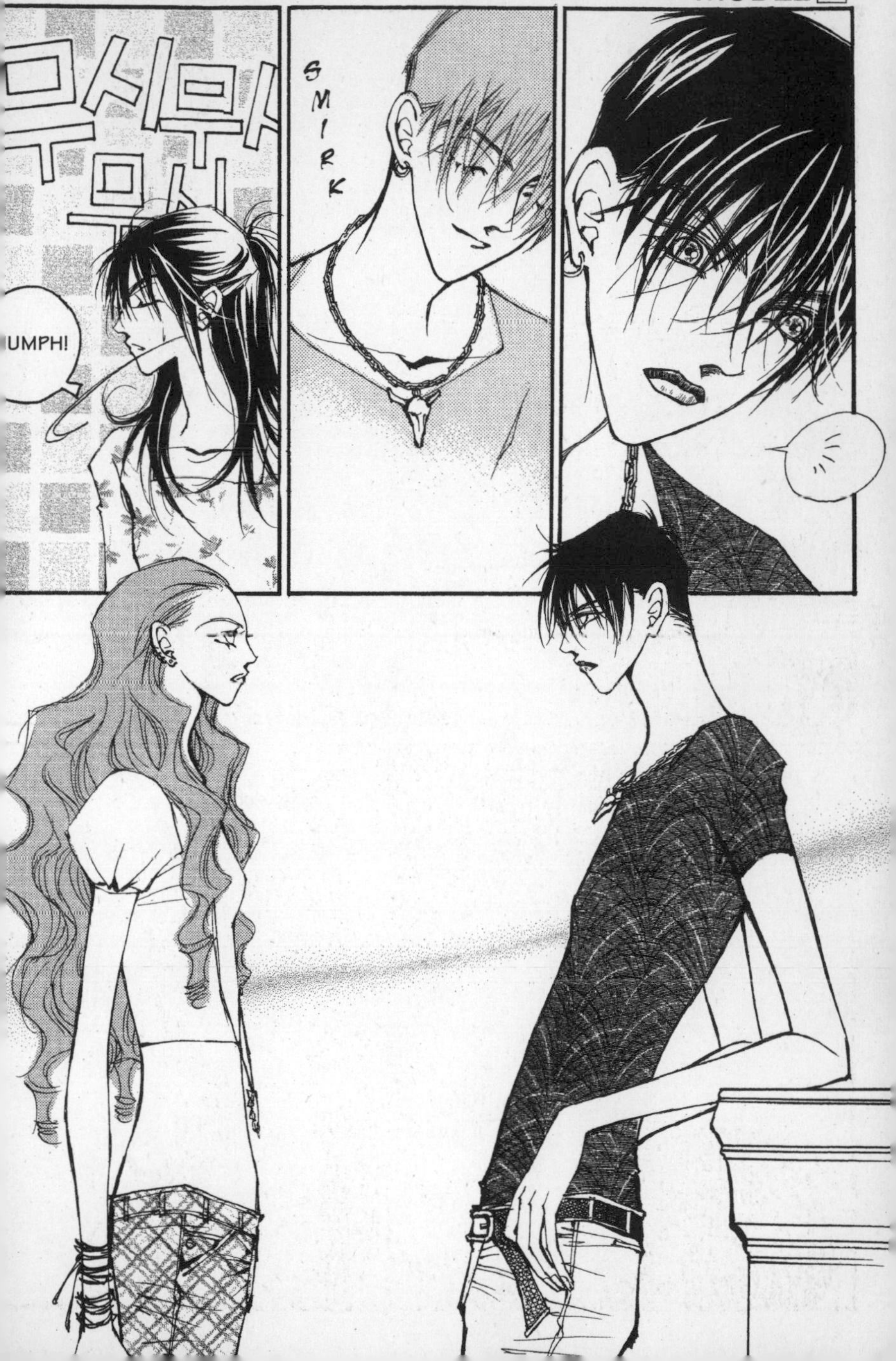
UMPH!
SMIRK

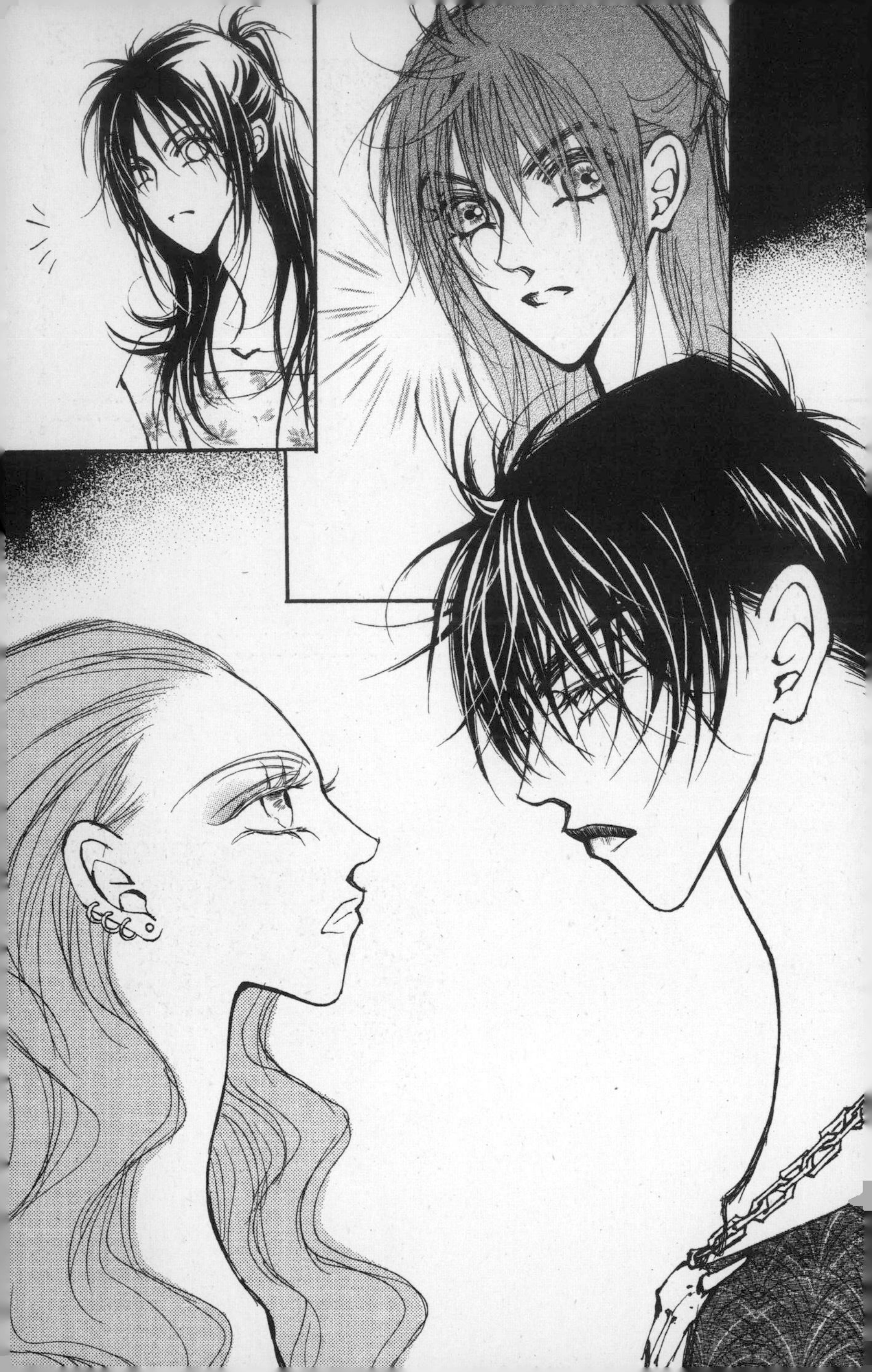

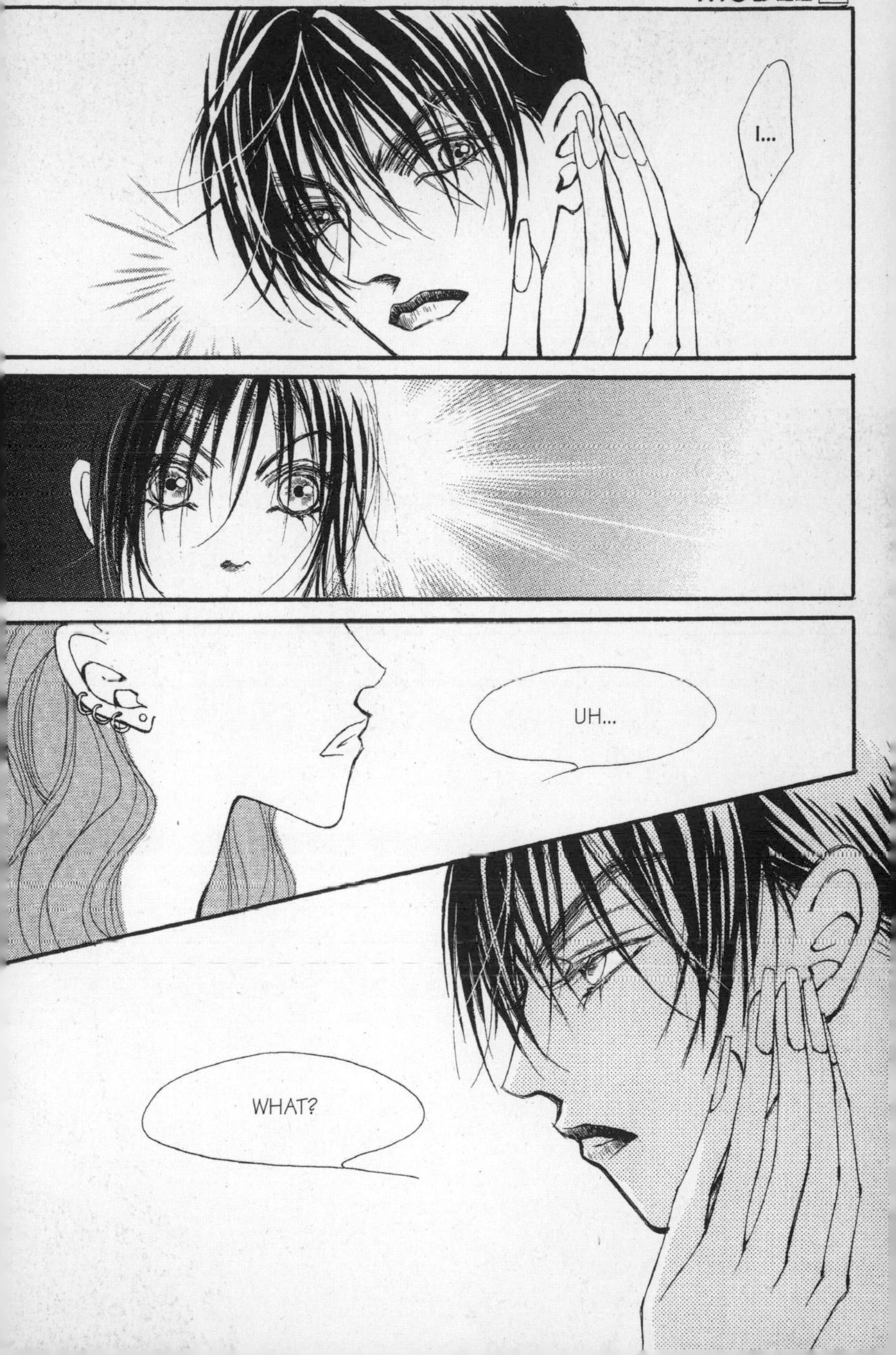
I...
UH...
WHAT?

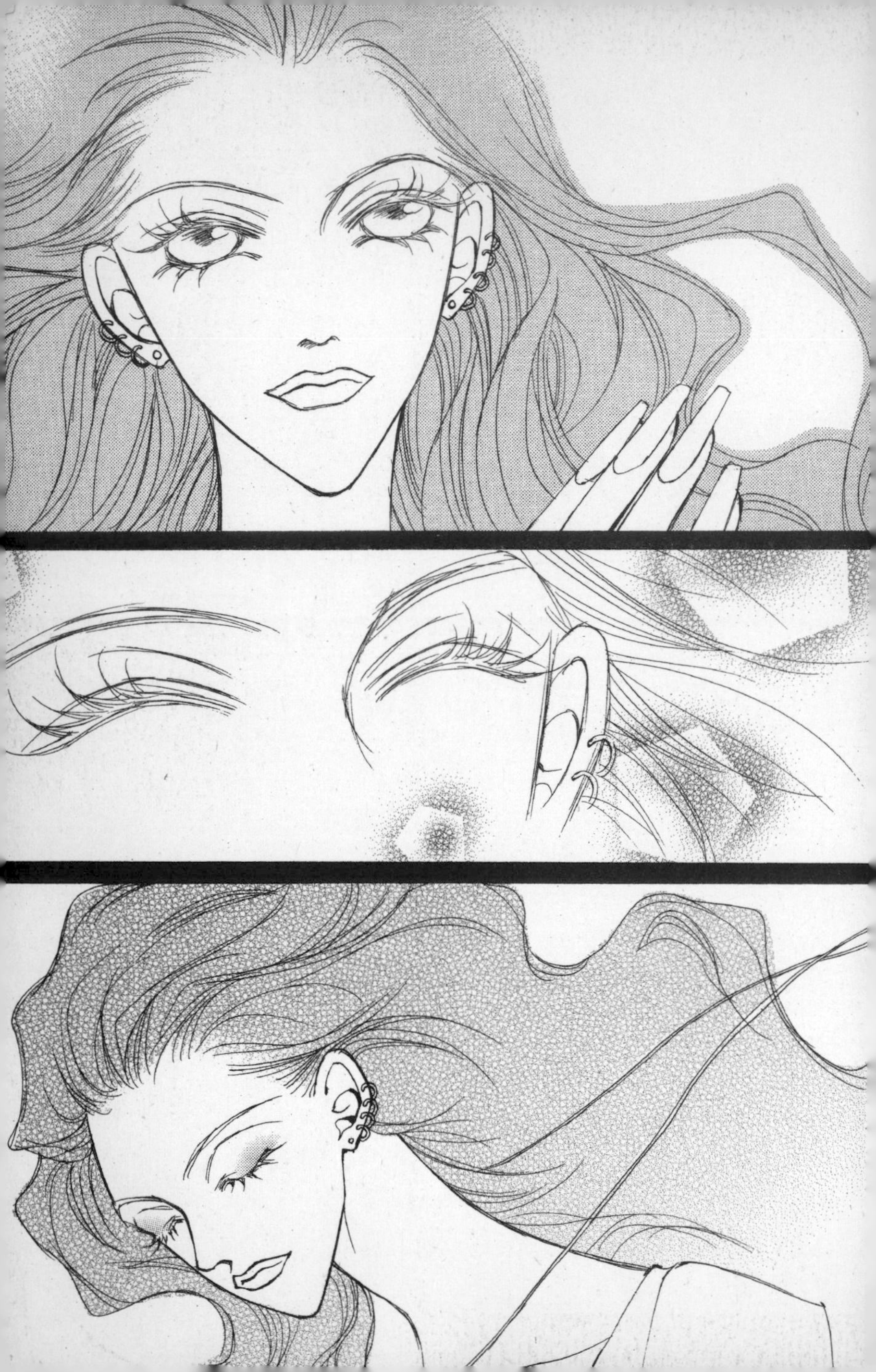

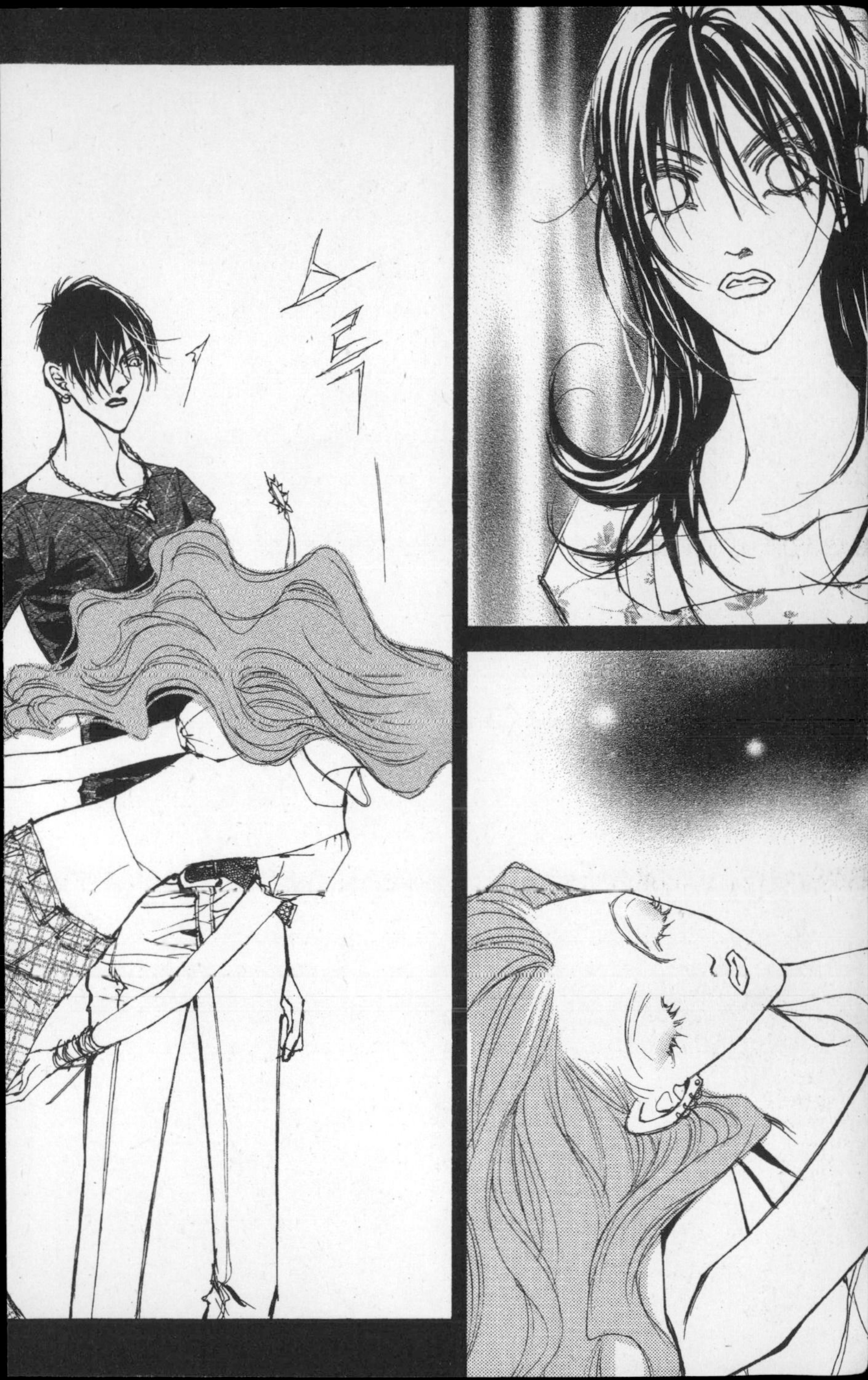
스륵—

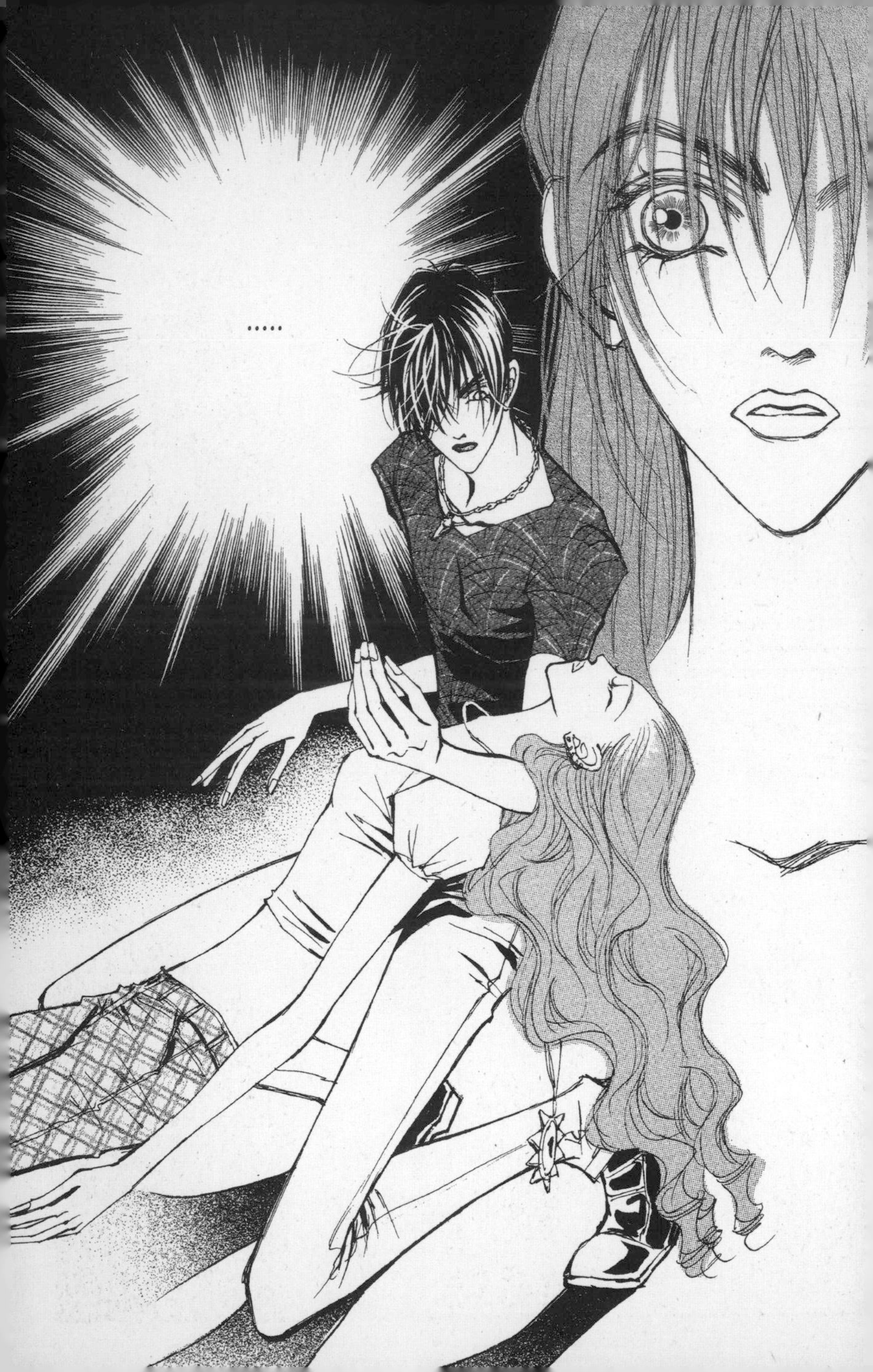
......

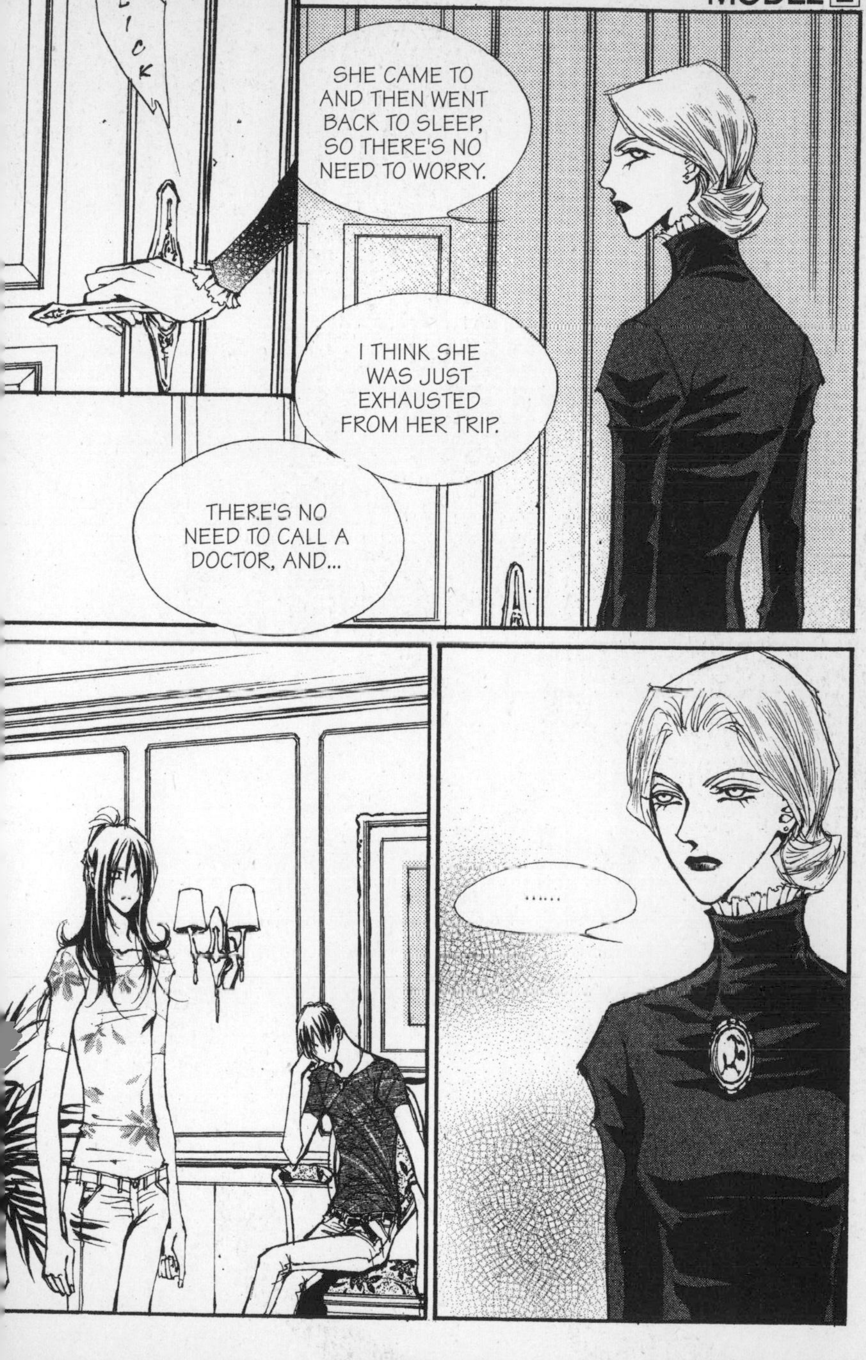
CLICK
SHE CAME TO AND THEN WENT BACK TO SLEEP, SO THERE'S NO NEED TO WORRY.
I THINK SHE WAS JUST EXHAUSTED FROM HER TRIP.
THERE'S NO NEED TO CALL A DOCTOR, AND...
......

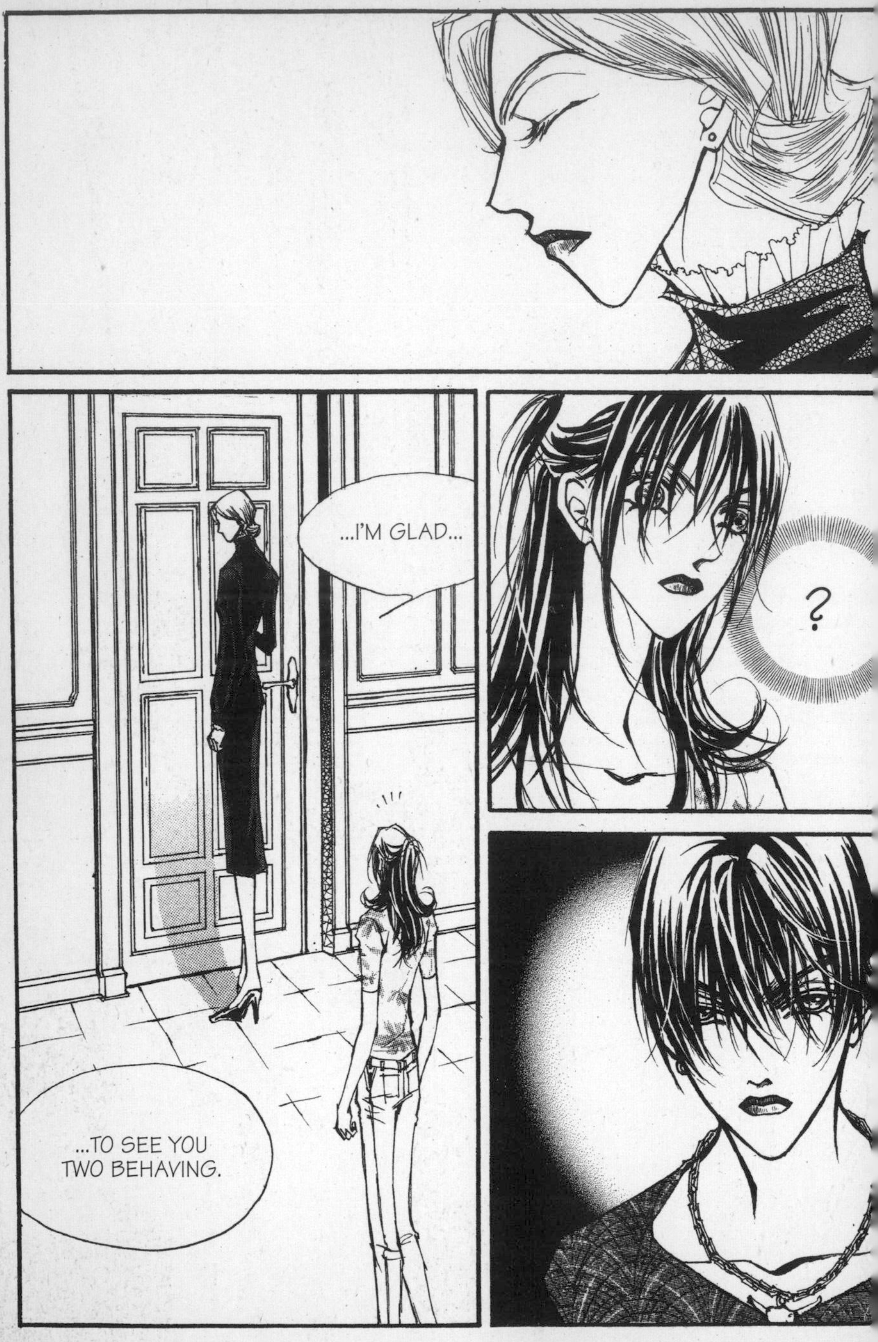
...I'M GLAD...
...TO SEE YOU TWO BEHAVING.
?

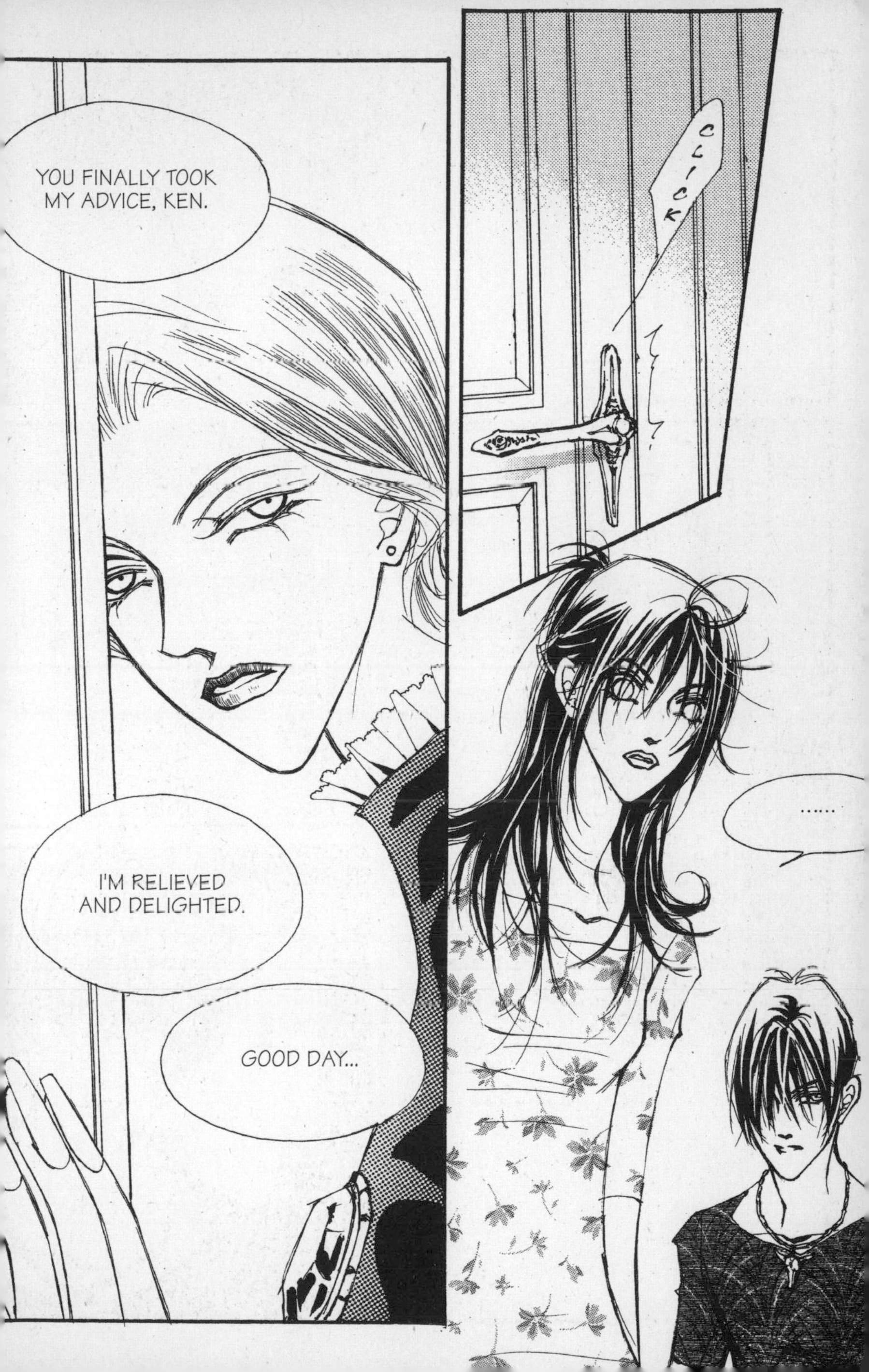
YOU FINALLY TOOK MY ADVICE, KEN.
I'M RELIEVED AND DELIGHTED.
GOOD DAY...
CLICK
......

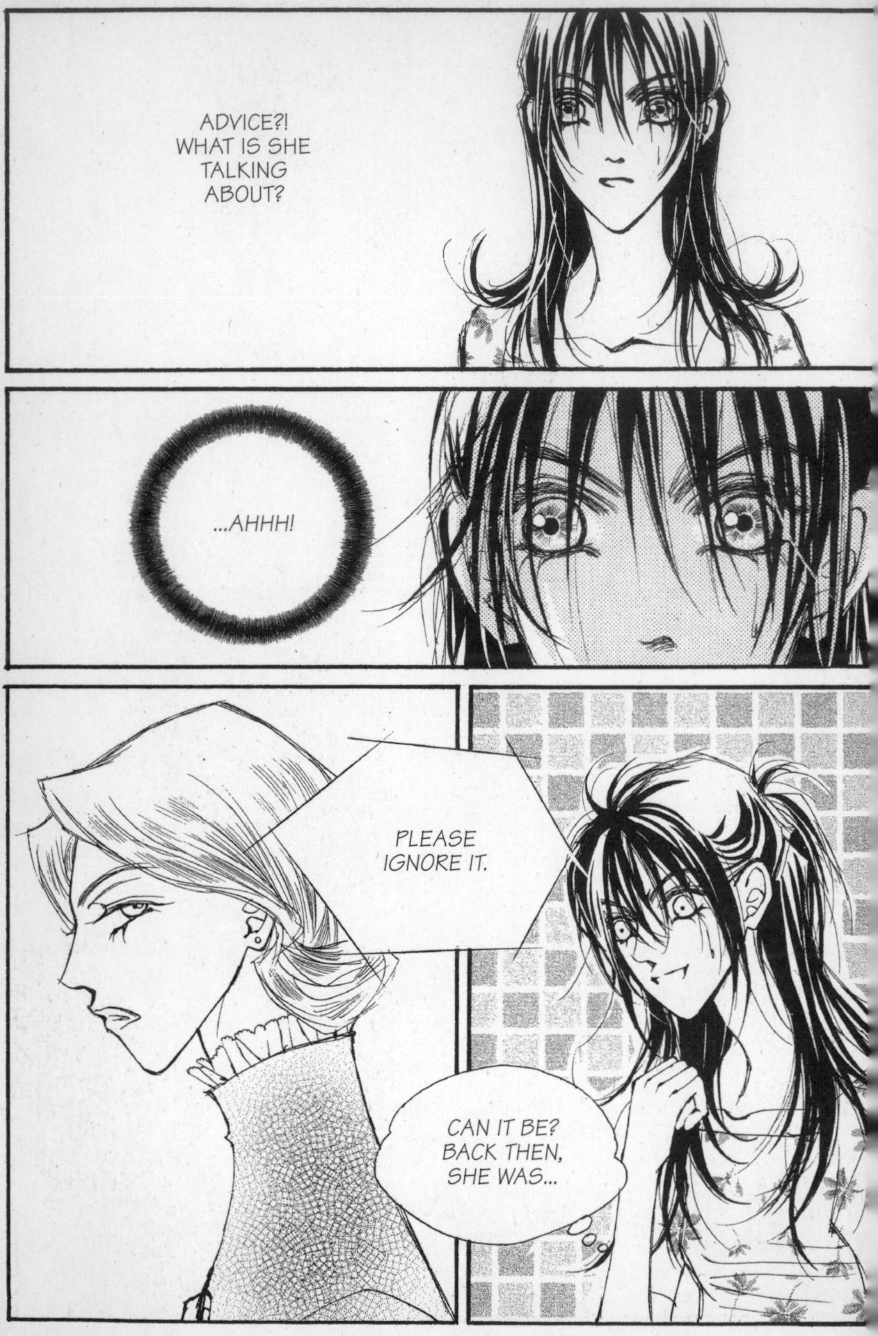
ADVICE?! WHAT IS SHE TALKING ABOUT?
...AHHH!
PLEASE IGNORE IT.
CAN IT BE? BACK THEN, SHE WAS...

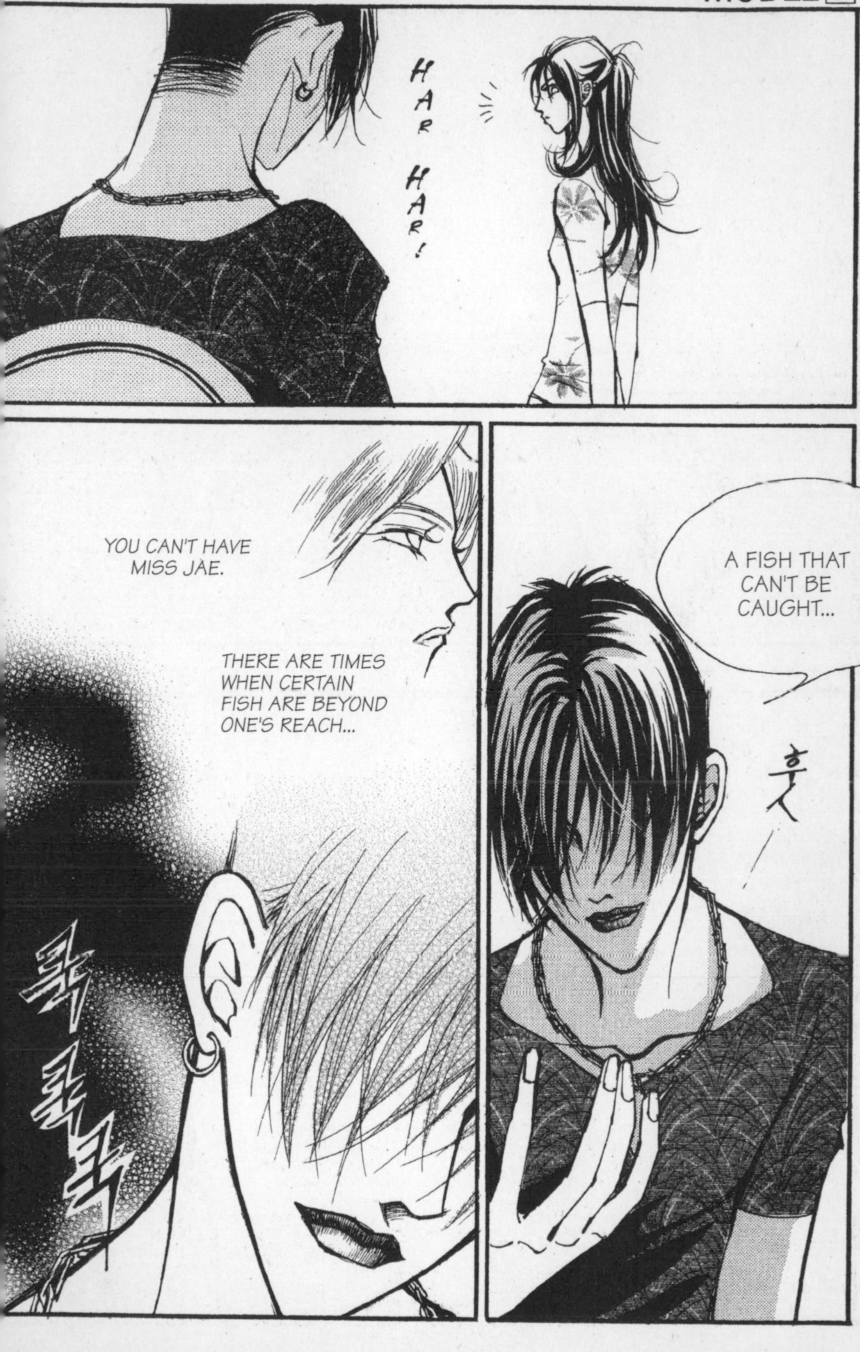
HAR HAR!
YOU CAN'T HAVE MISS JAE.
THERE ARE TIMES WHEN CERTAIN FISH ARE BEYOND ONE'S REACH...
A FISH THAT CAN'T BE CAUGHT...

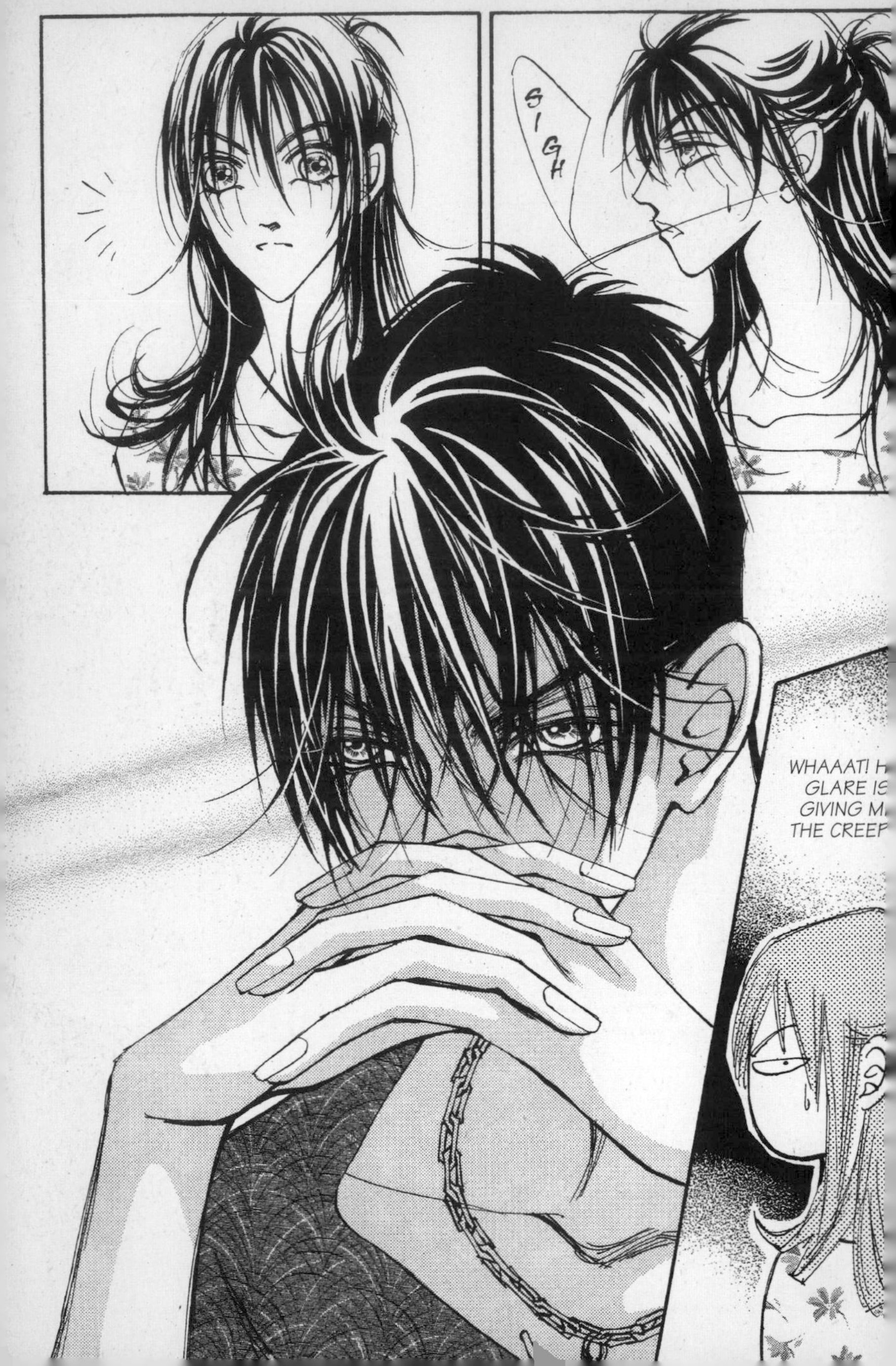
SIGH
WHAAAT! H
GLARE IS
GIVING M
THE CREEP

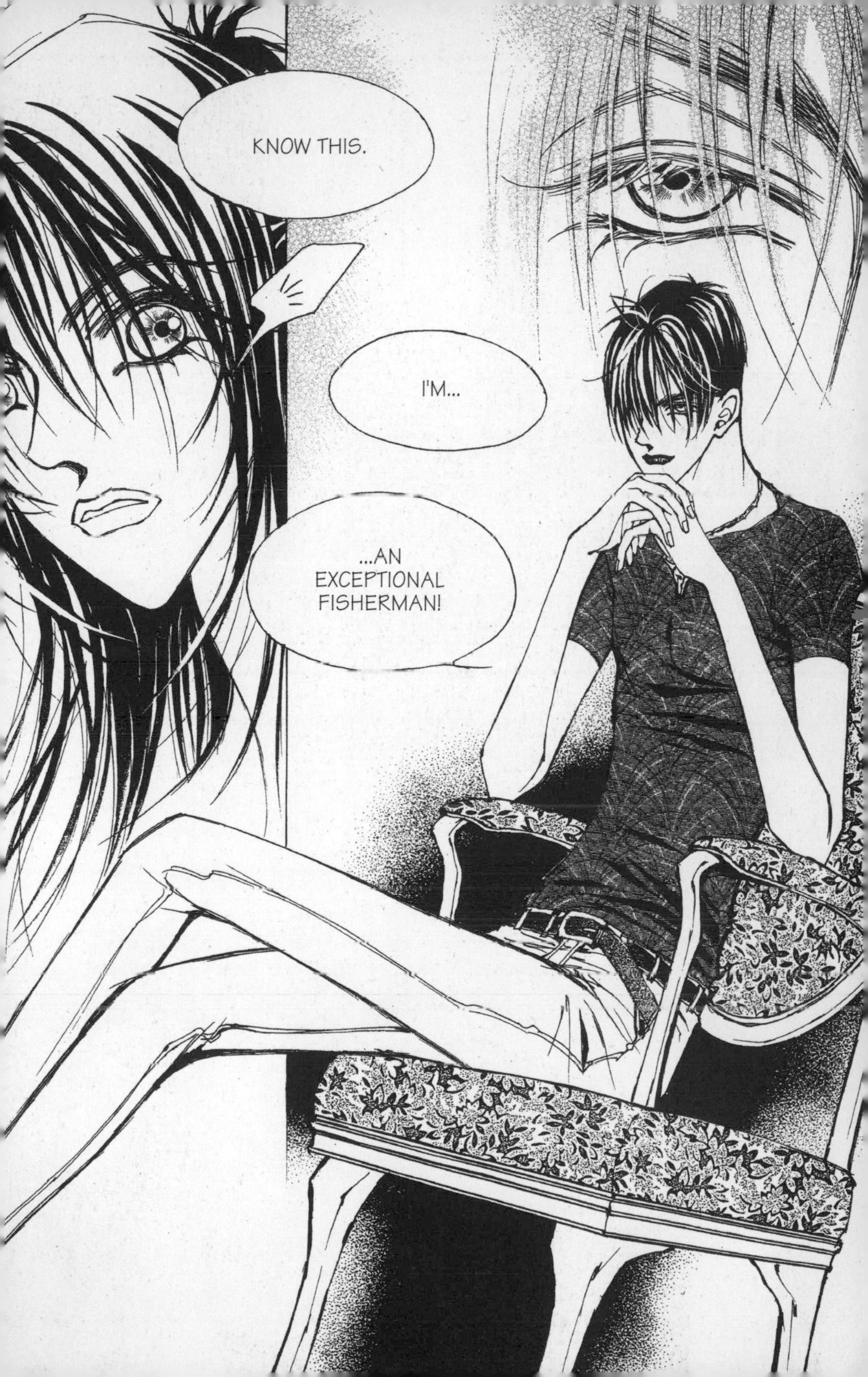
KNOW THIS.
I'M...
...AN EXCEPTIONAL FISHERMAN!

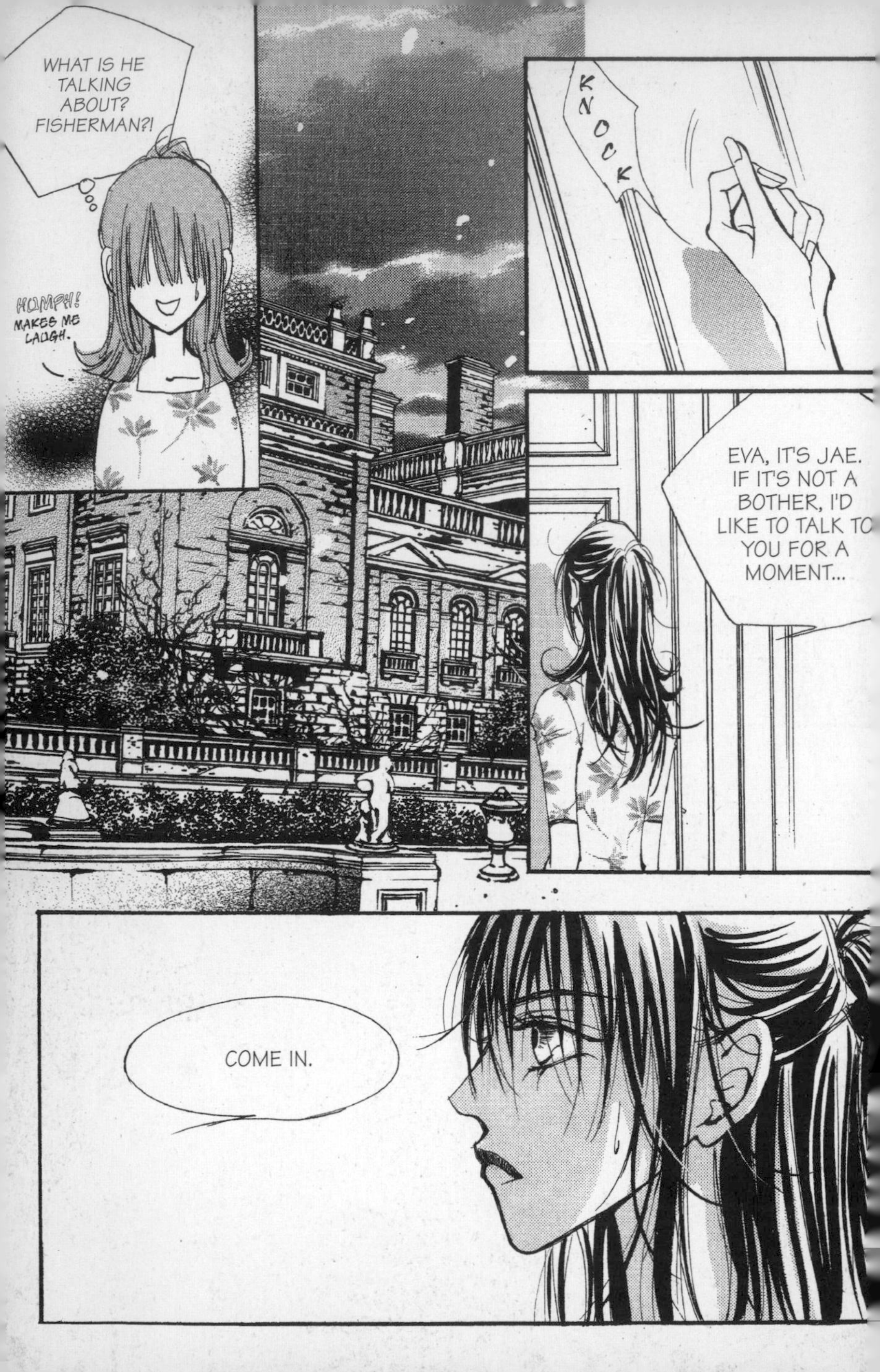
WHAT IS HE TALKING ABOUT? FISHERMAN?!
HUMPH! MAKES ME LAUGH.
KNOCK
EVA, IT'S JAE. IF IT'S NOT A BOTHER, I'D LIKE TO TALK TO YOU FOR A MOMENT...
COME IN.

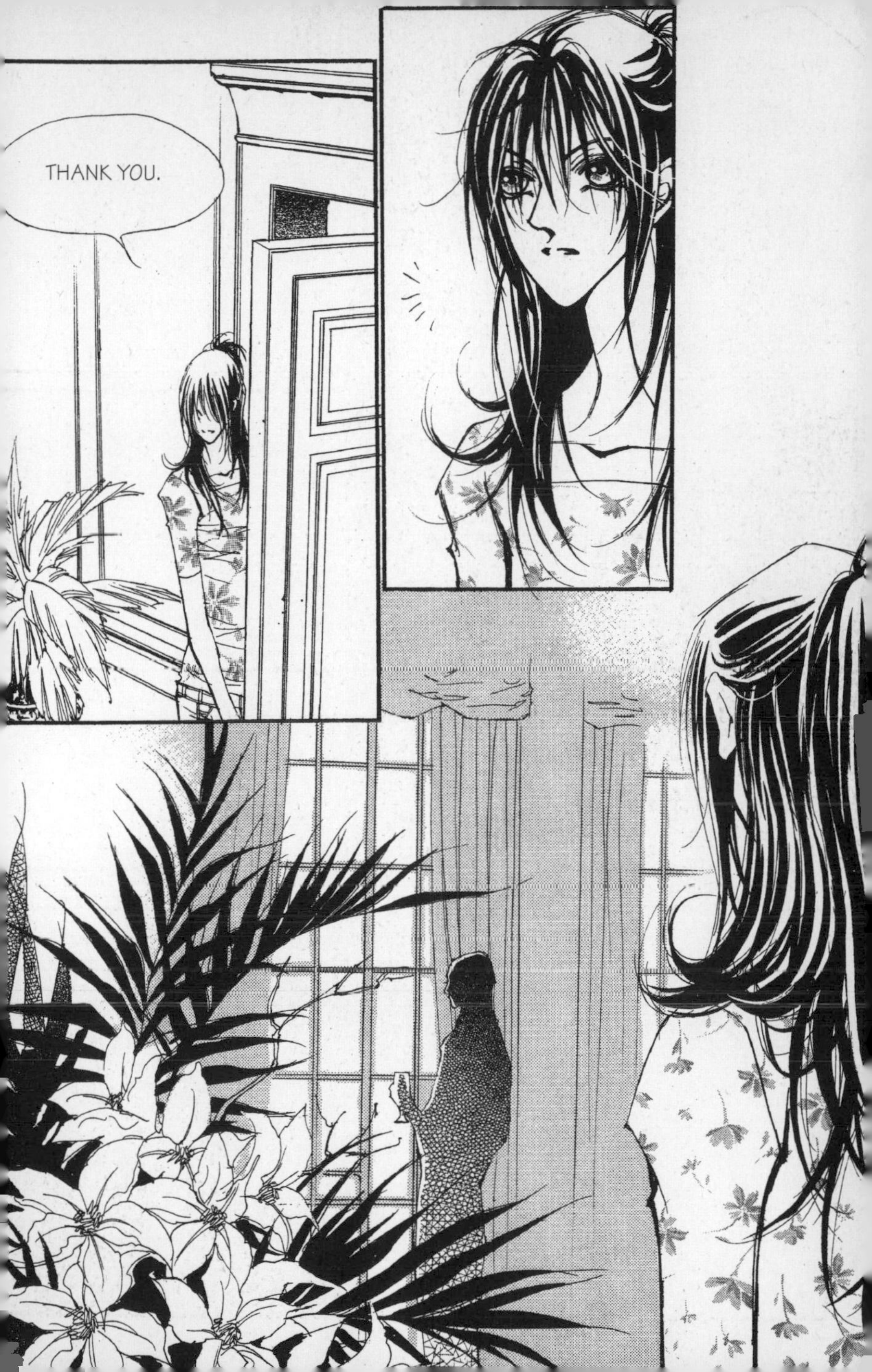
THANK YOU.

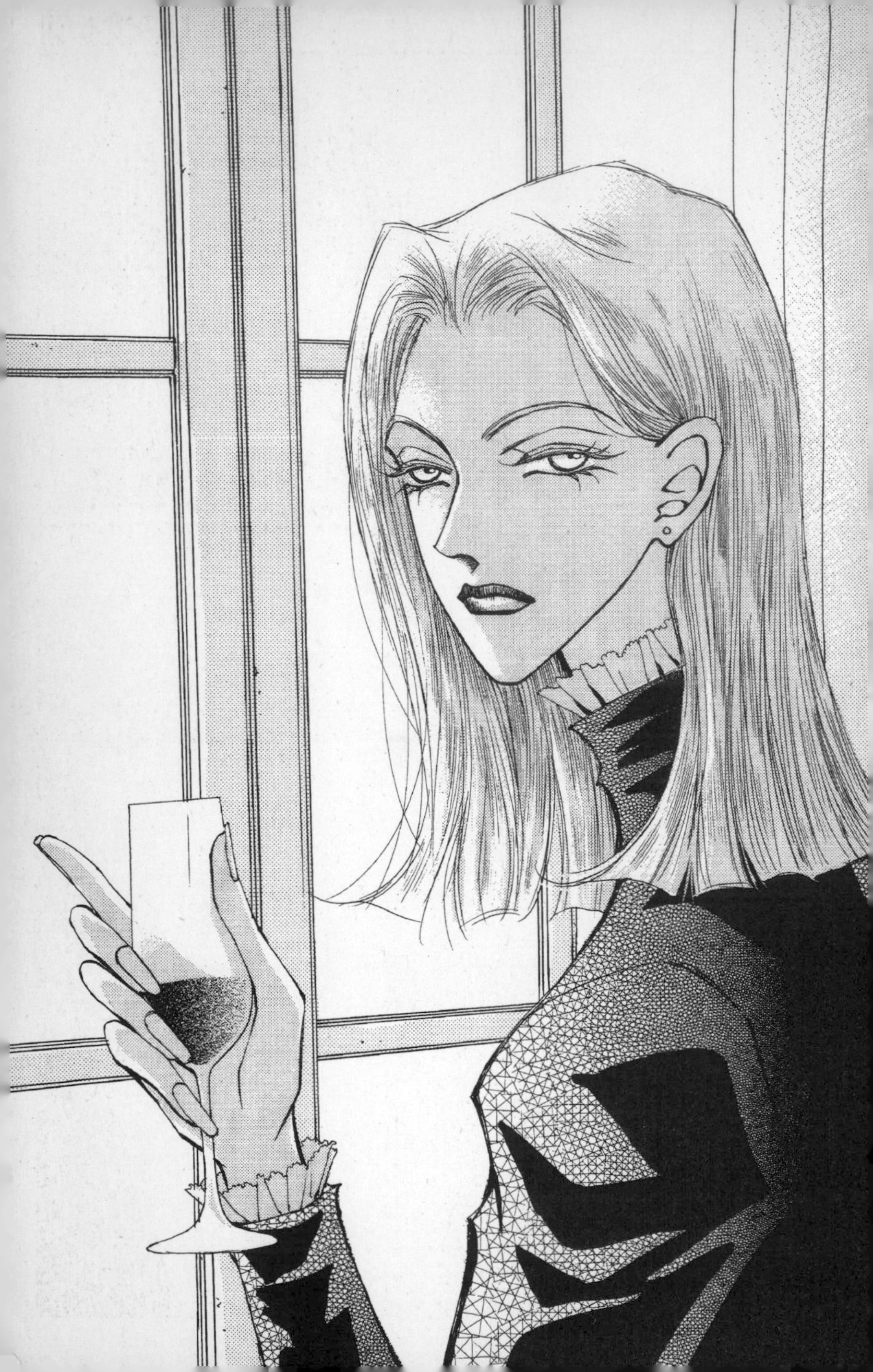

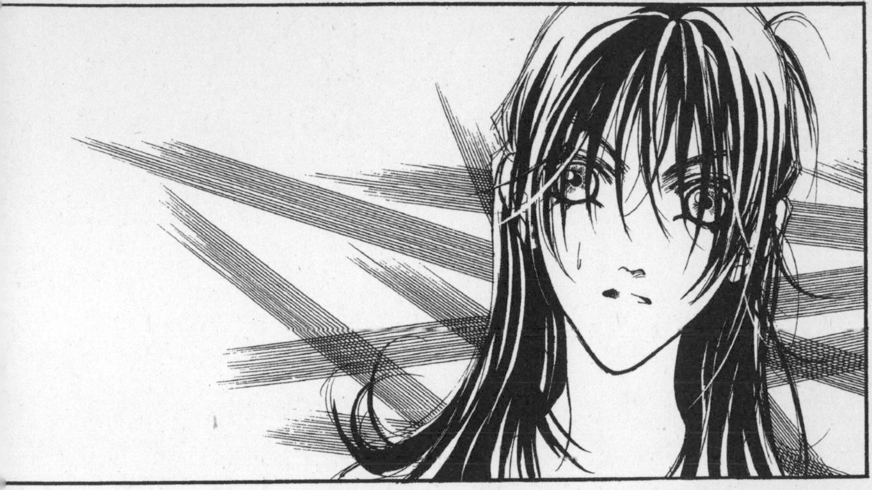

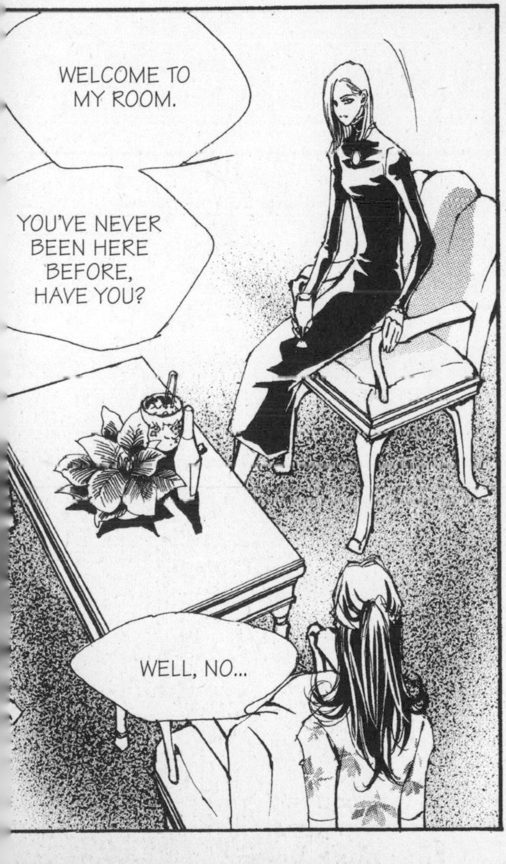
WELCOME TO MY ROOM.
YOU'VE NEVER BEEN HERE BEFORE, HAVE YOU?
WELL, NO...

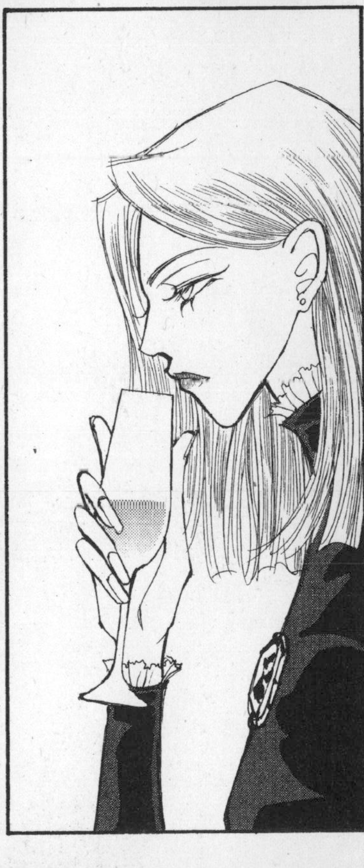

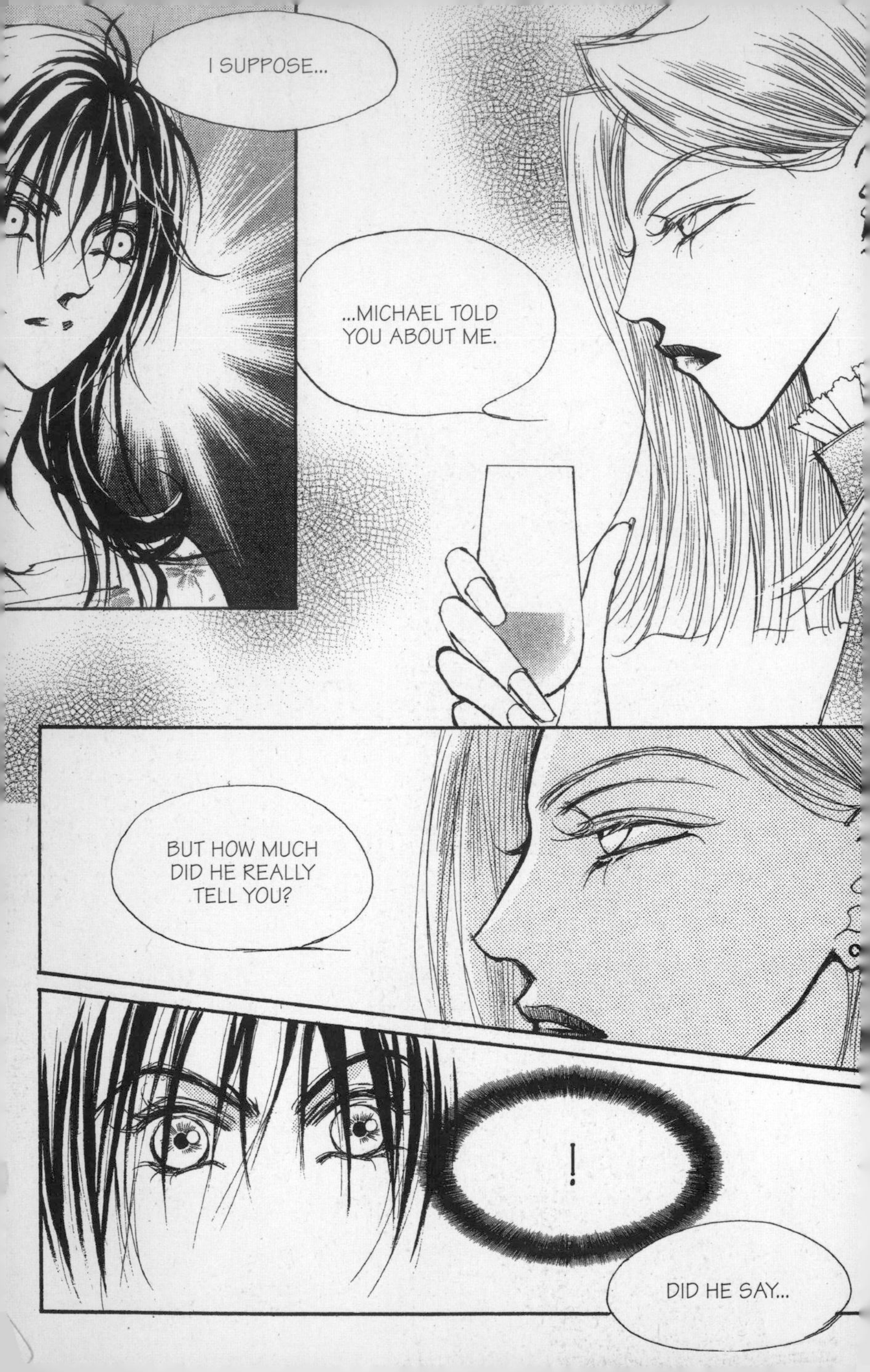
I SUPPOSE...
...MICHAEL TOLD YOU ABOUT ME.
BUT HOW MUCH DID HE REALLY TELL YOU?
!
DID HE SAY...

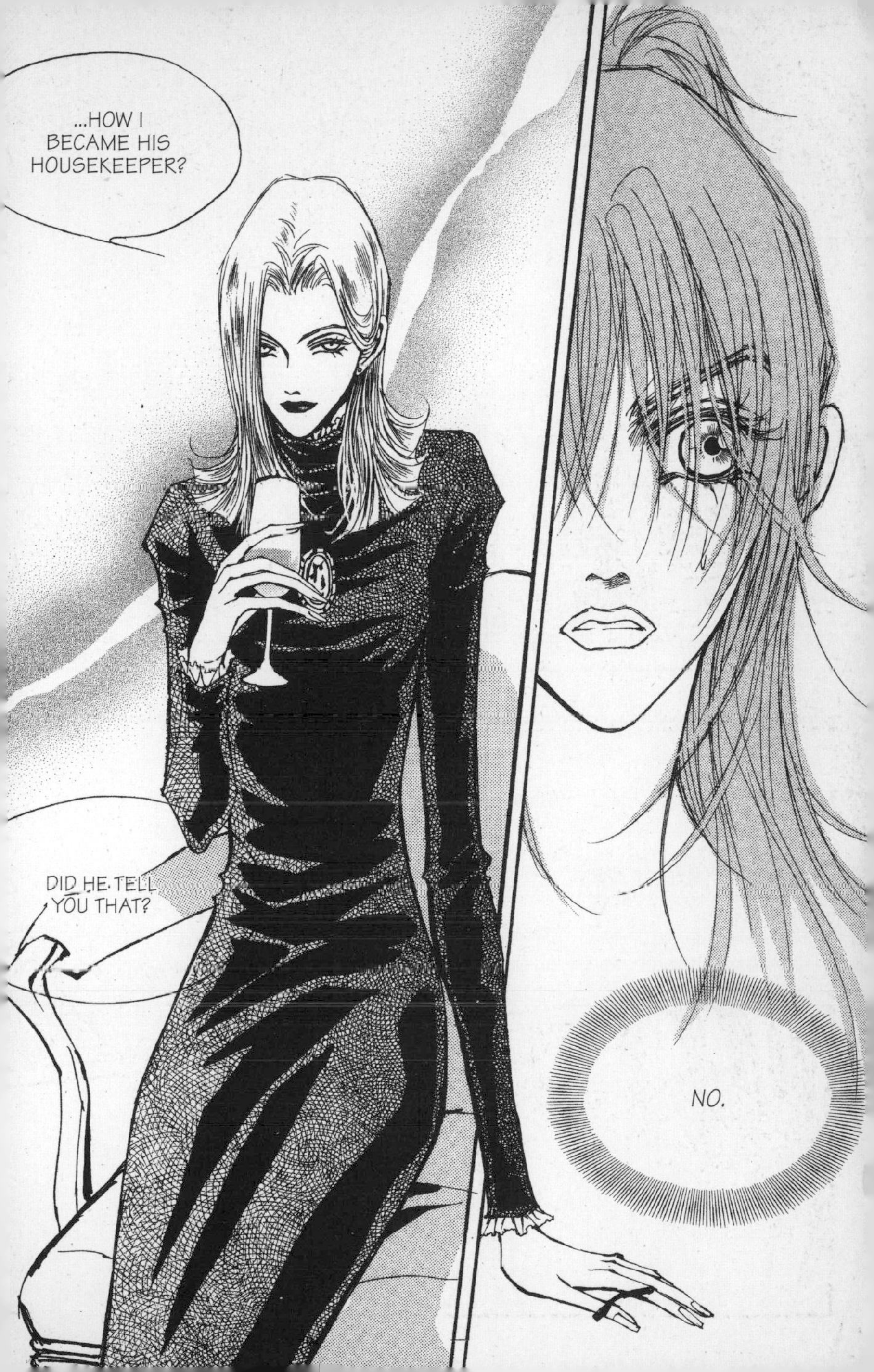
...HOW I BECAME HIS HOUSEKEEPER?
DID HE TELL YOU THAT?
NO.

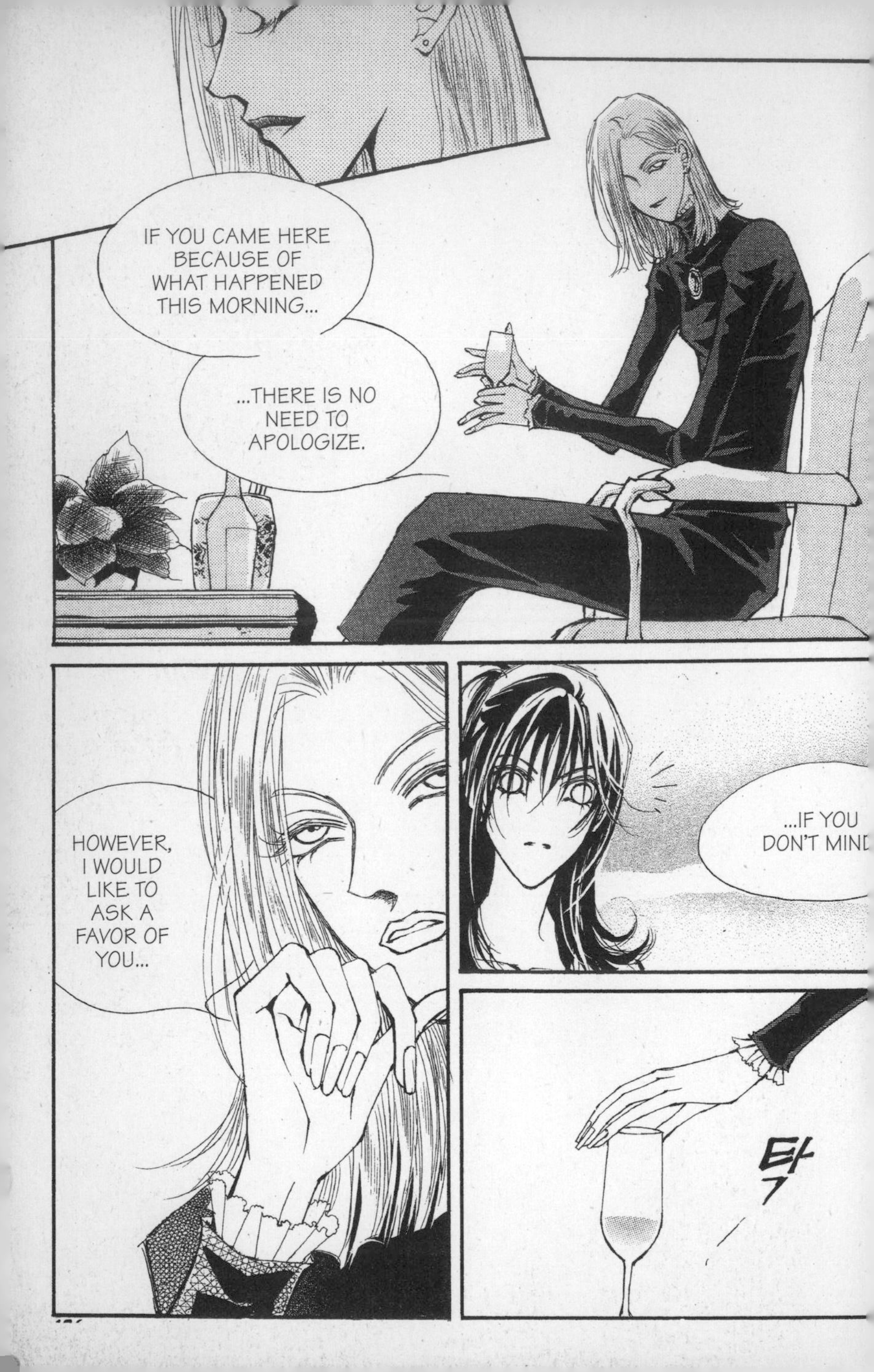
IF YOU CAME HERE BECAUSE OF WHAT HAPPENED THIS MORNING...
...THERE IS NO NEED TO APOLOGIZE.
HOWEVER, I WOULD LIKE TO ASK A FAVOR OF YOU...
...IF YOU DON'T MIND
탁

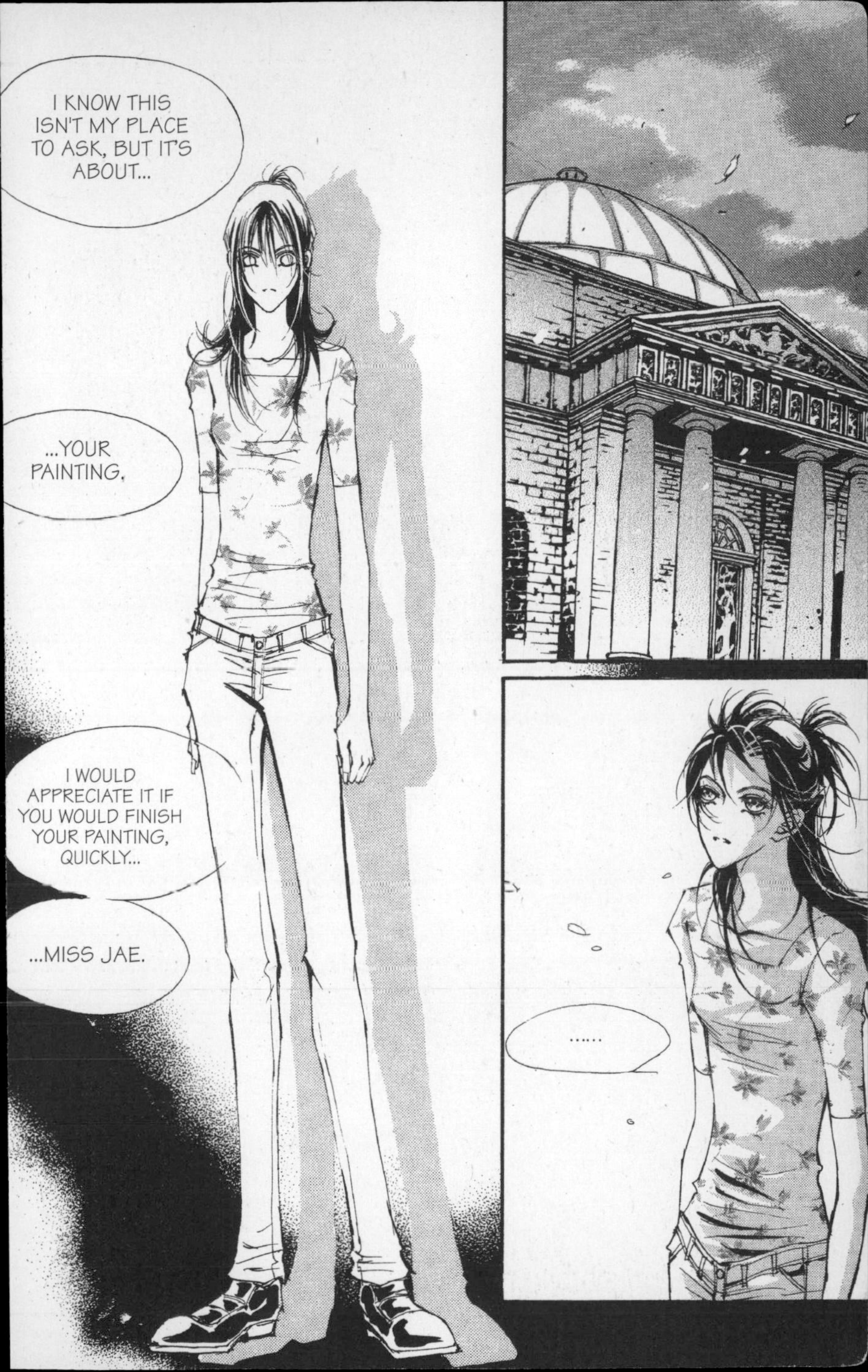
I KNOW THIS ISN'T MY PLACE TO ASK, BUT IT'S ABOUT...
...YOUR PAINTING.
I WOULD APPRECIATE IT IF YOU WOULD FINISH YOUR PAINTING, QUICKLY...
...MISS JAE.
......

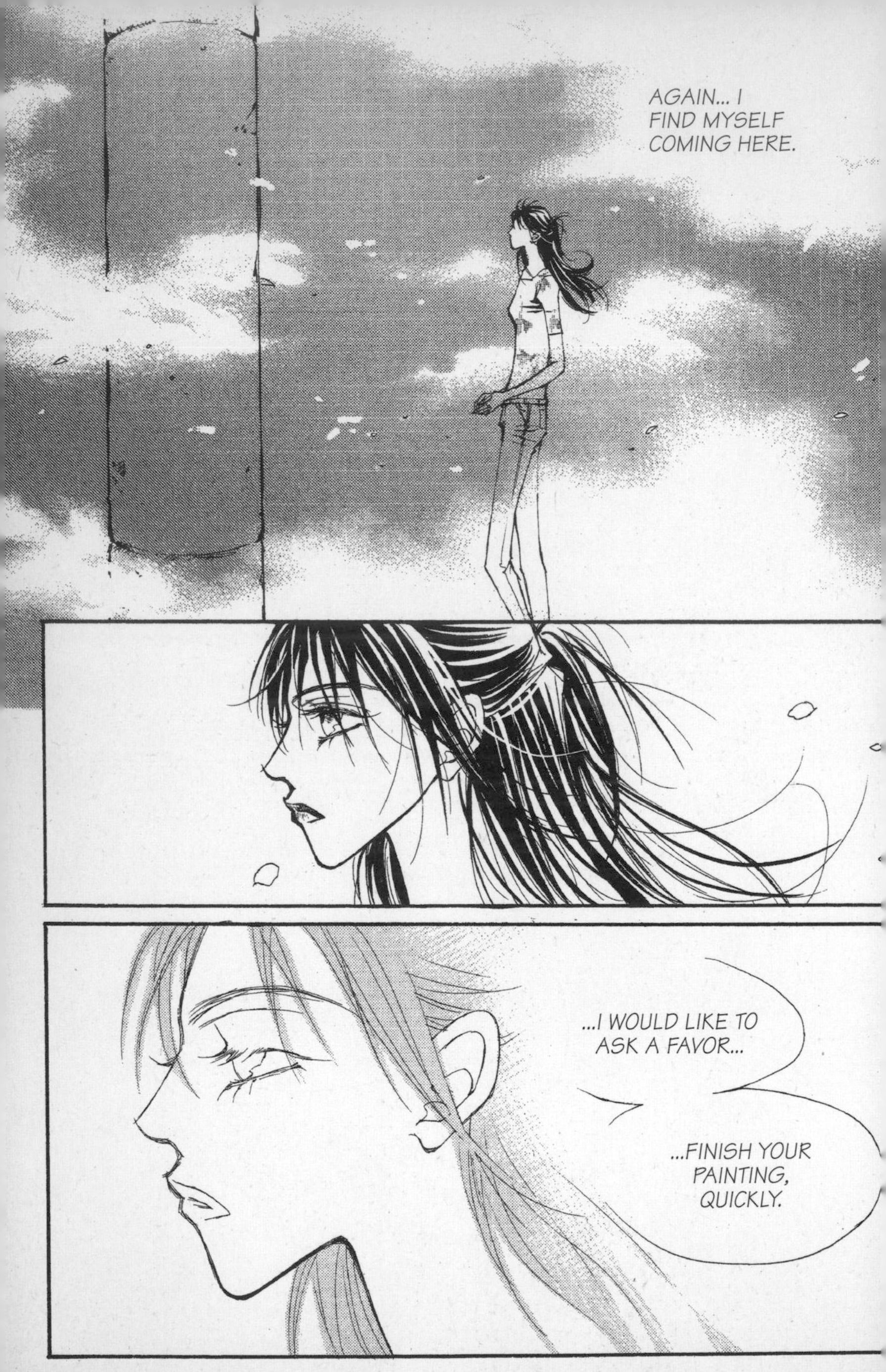
AGAIN... I FIND MYSELF COMING HERE.
...I WOULD LIKE TO ASK A FAVOR...
...FINISH YOUR PAINTING, QUICKLY.

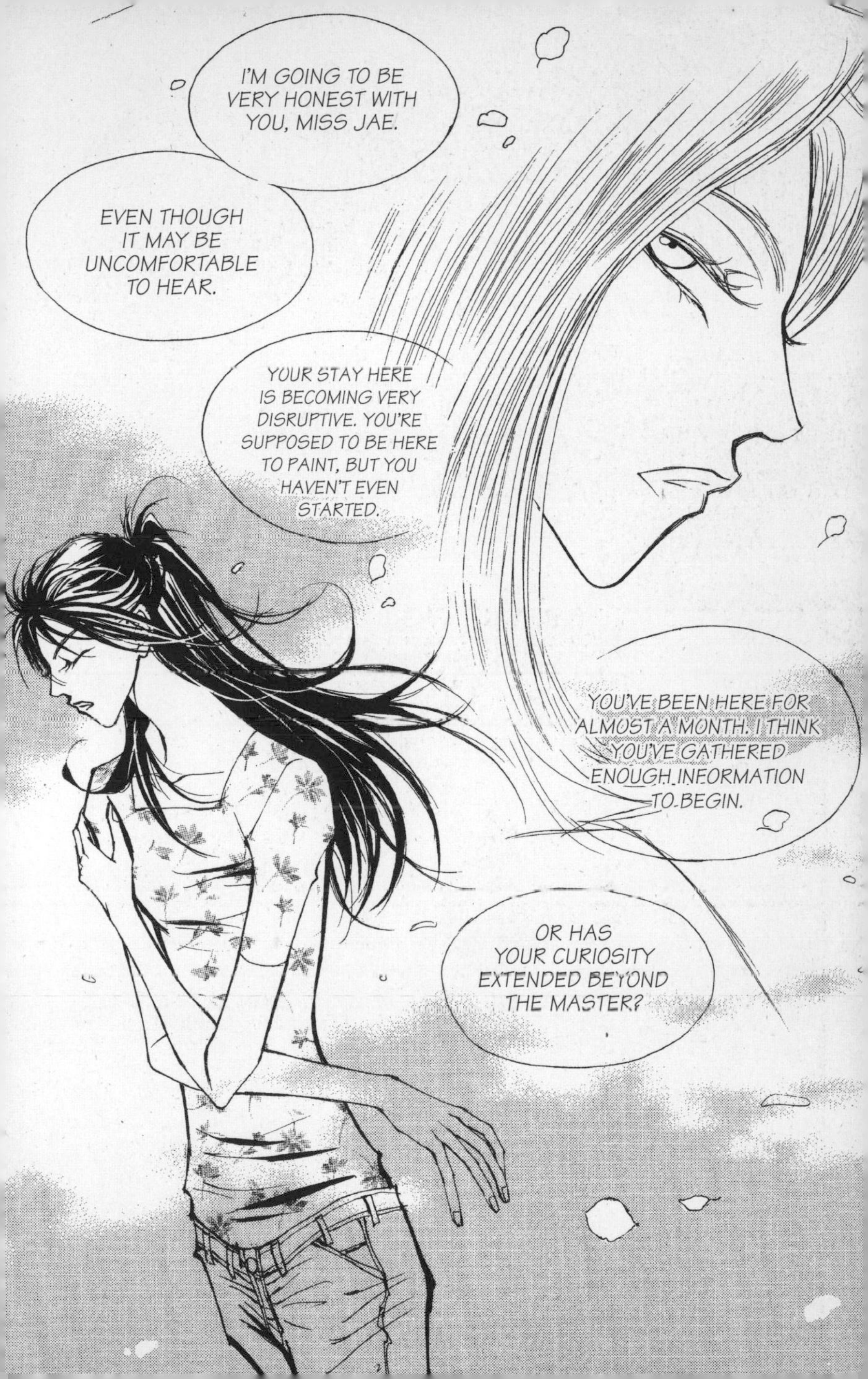
I'M GOING TO BE VERY HONEST WITH YOU, MISS JAE.
EVEN THOUGH IT MAY BE UNCOMFORTABLE TO HEAR.
YOUR STAY HERE IS BECOMING VERY DISRUPTIVE. YOU'RE SUPPOSED TO BE HERE TO PAINT, BUT YOU HAVEN'T EVEN STARTED.
YOU'VE BEEN HERE FOR ALMOST A MONTH. I THINK YOU'VE GATHERED ENOUGH INFORMATION TO BEGIN.
OR HAS YOUR CURIOSITY EXTENDED BEYOND THE MASTER?

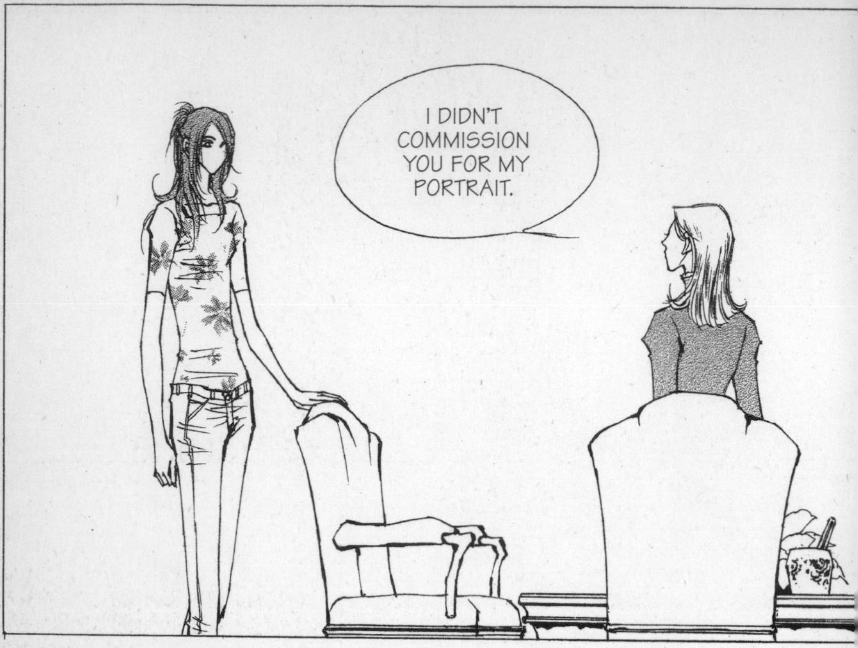
I DIDN'T COMMISSION YOU FOR MY PORTRAIT.

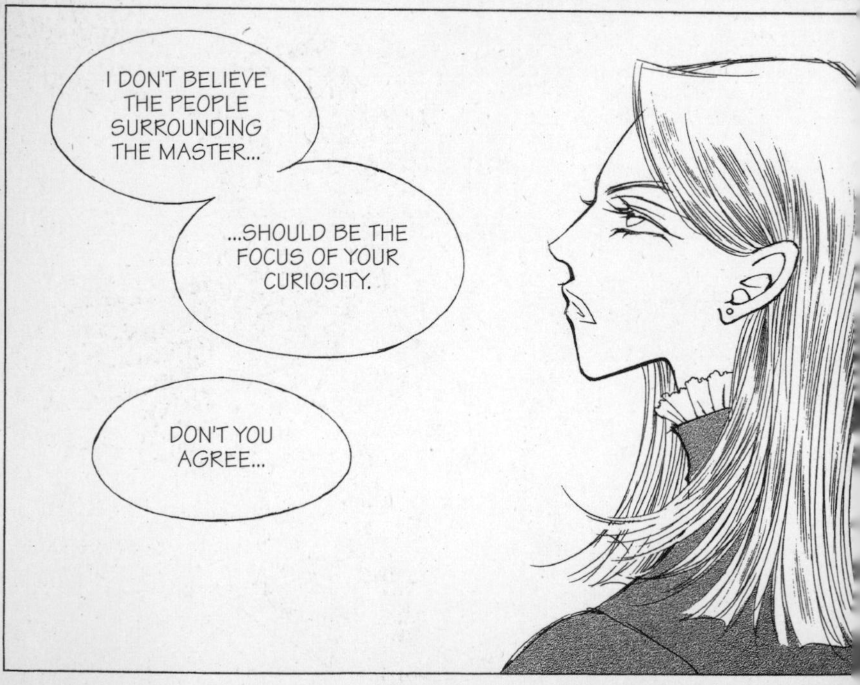
I DON'T BELIEVE THE PEOPLE SURROUNDING THE MASTER...
...SHOULD BE THE FOCUS OF YOUR CURIOSITY.
DON'T YOU AGREE...

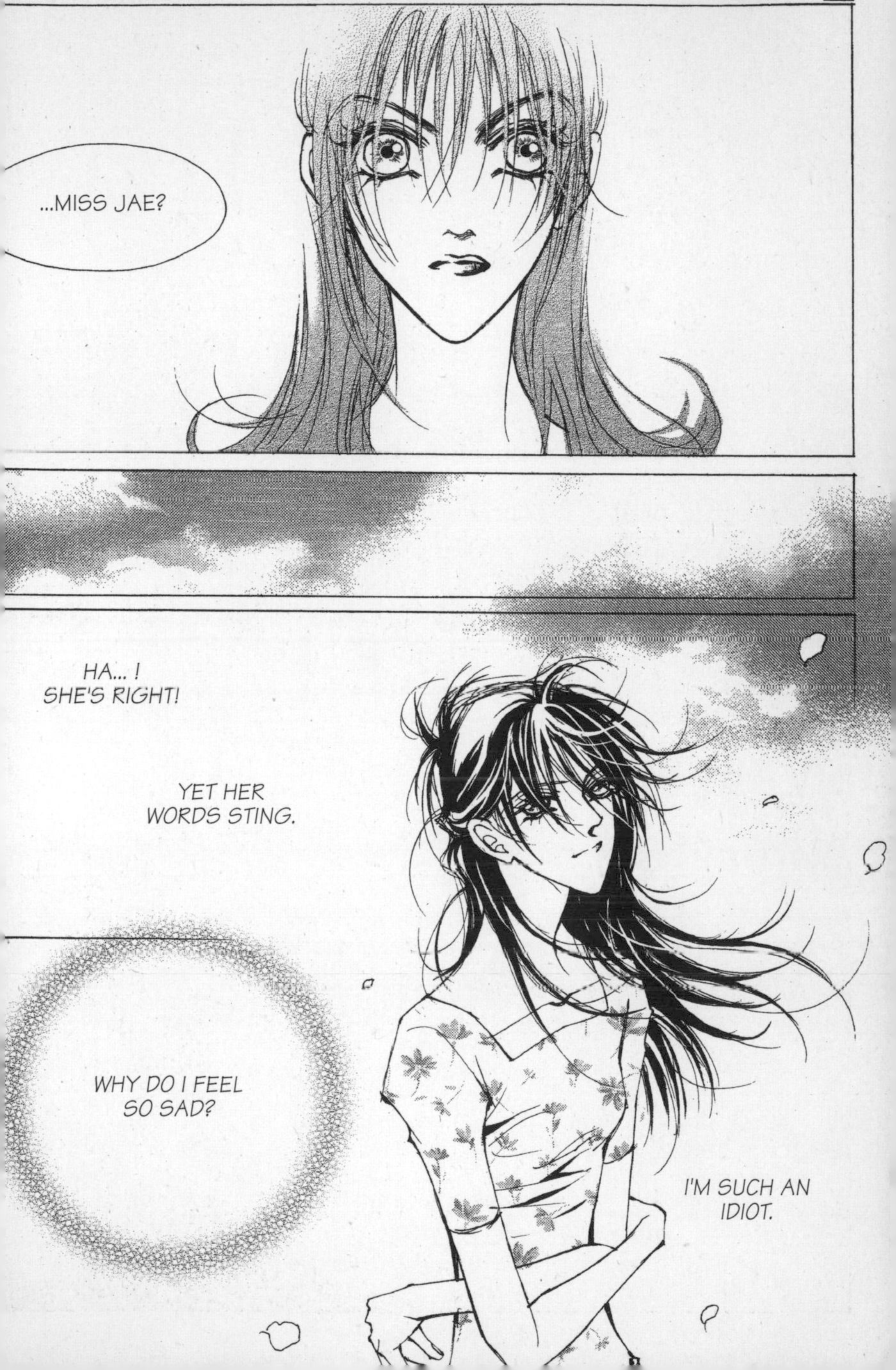
...MISS JAE?
HA... !
SHE'S RIGHT!
YET HER
WORDS STING.
WHY DO I FEEL
SO SAD?
I'M SUCH AN
IDIOT.

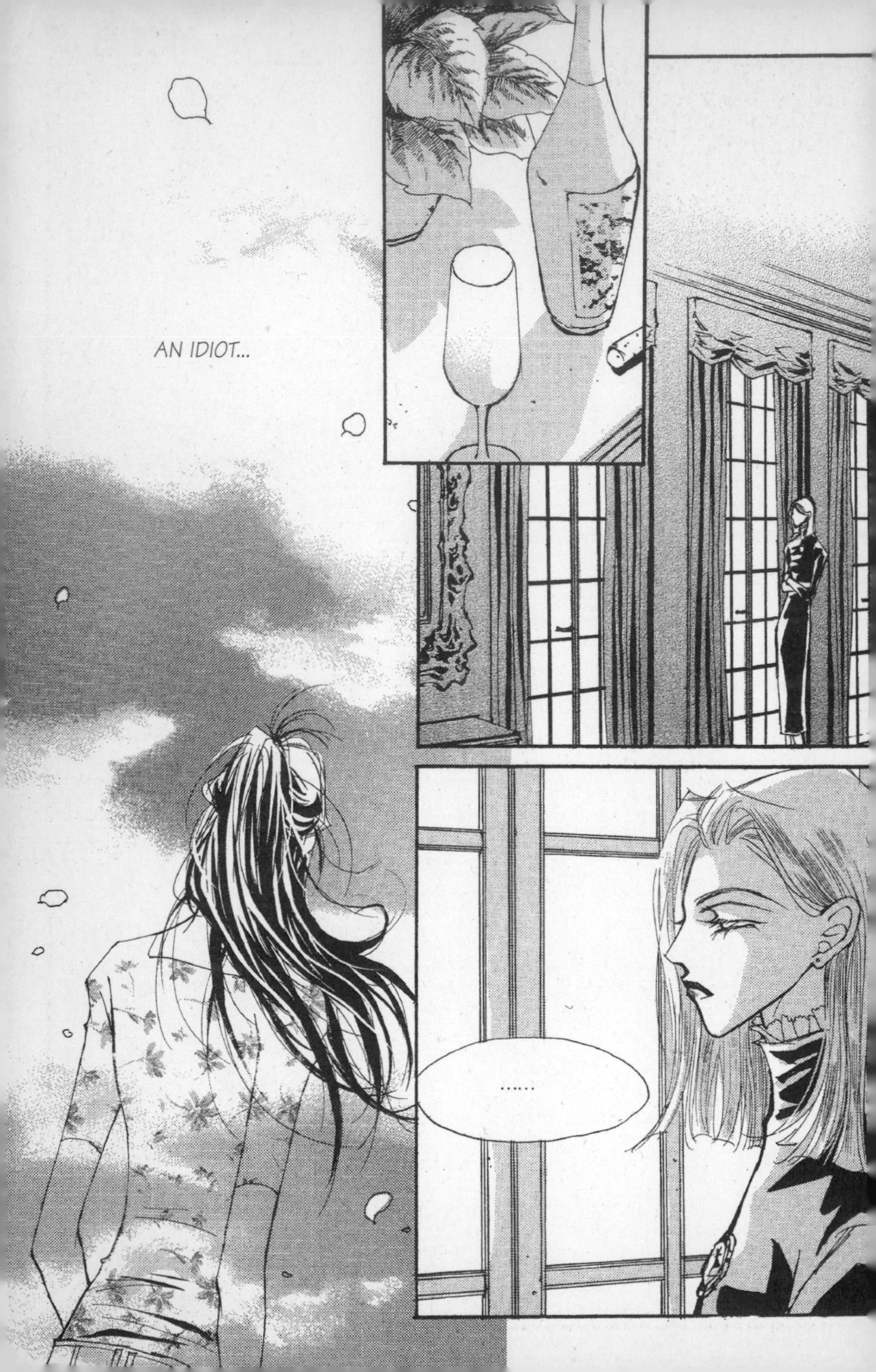
AN IDIOT...
......

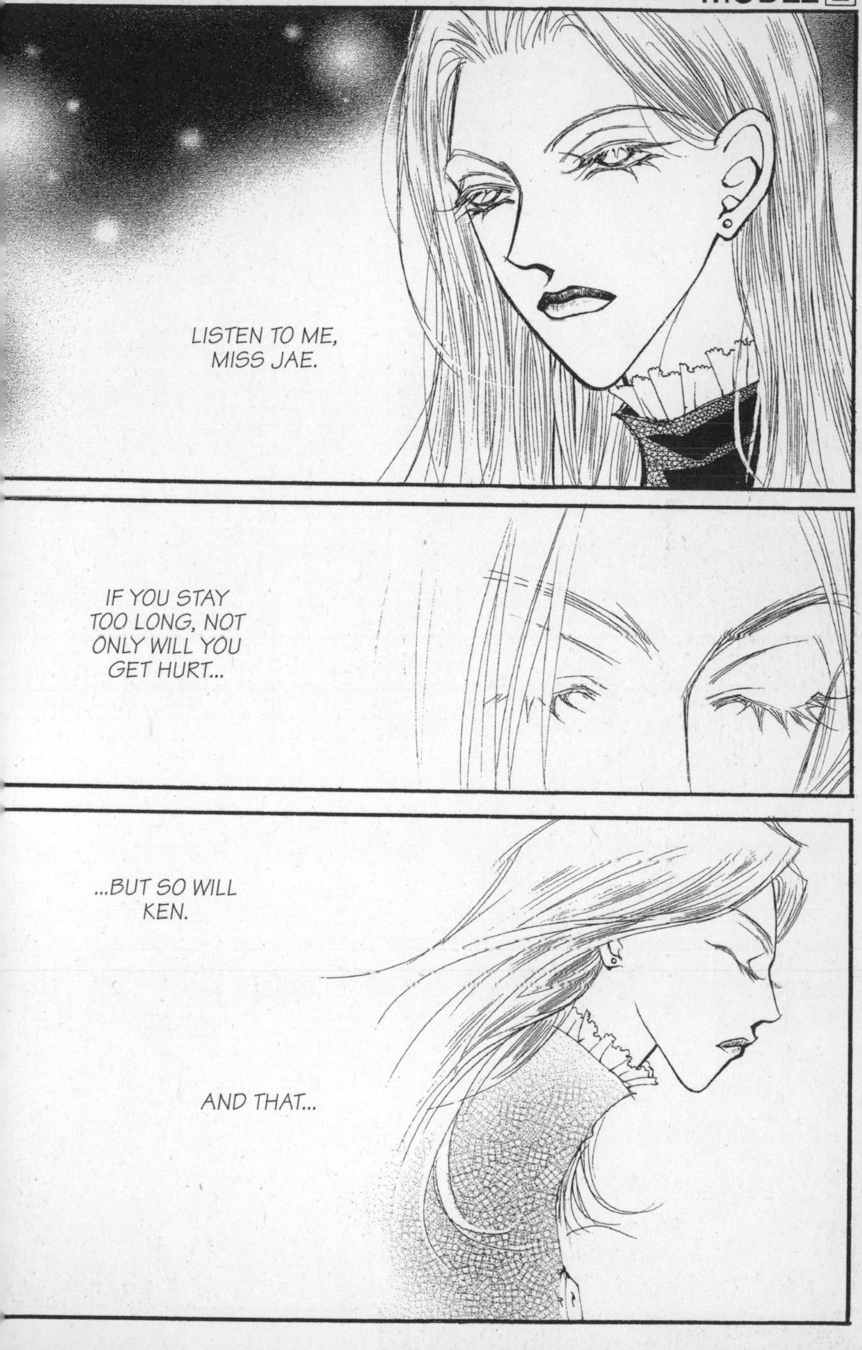
LISTEN TO ME, MISS JAE.
IF YOU STAY TOO LONG, NOT ONLY WILL YOU GET HURT...
...BUT SO WILL KEN.
AND THAT...

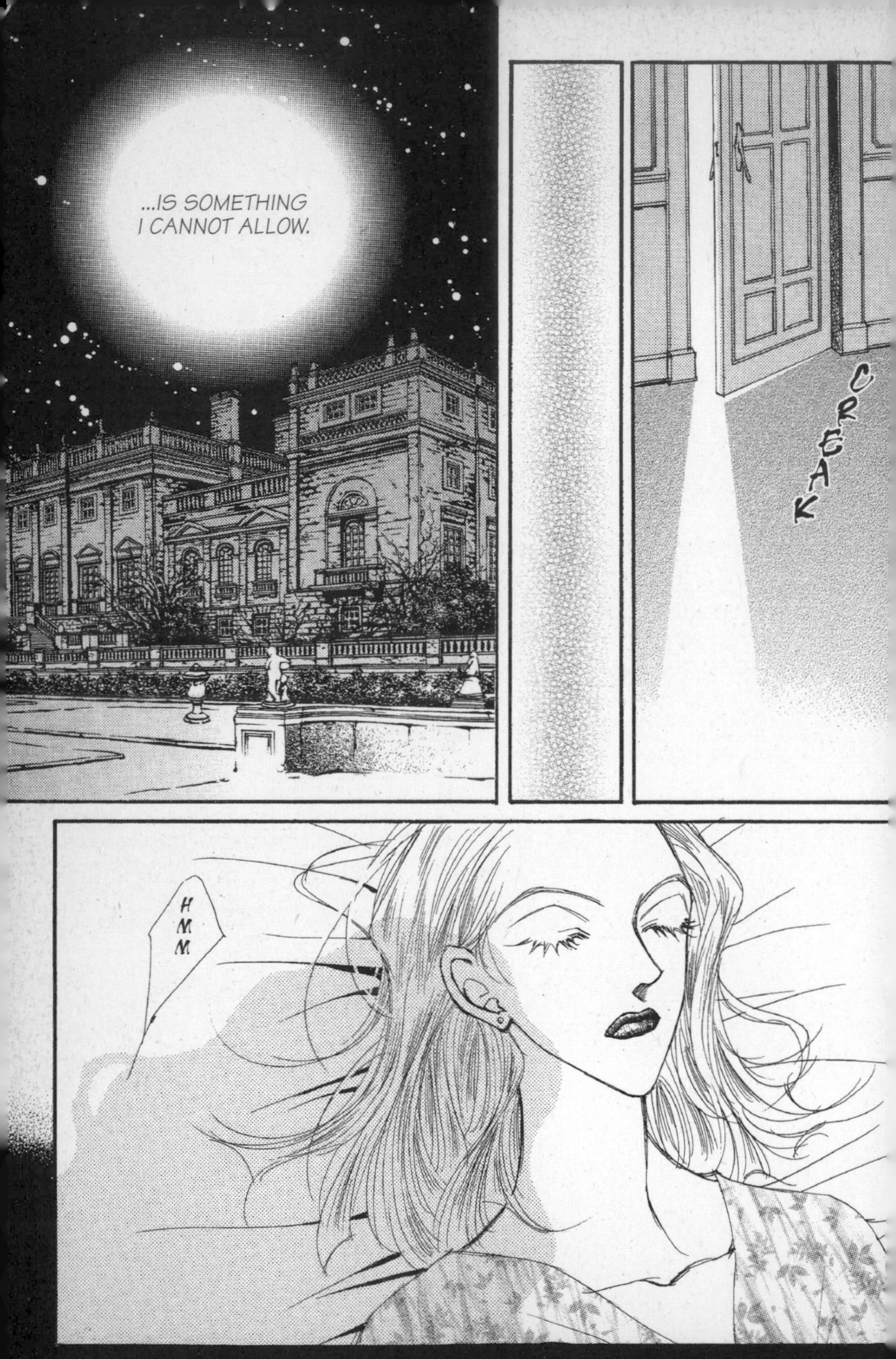
...IS SOMETHING
I CANNOT ALLOW.
CREAK
HMM

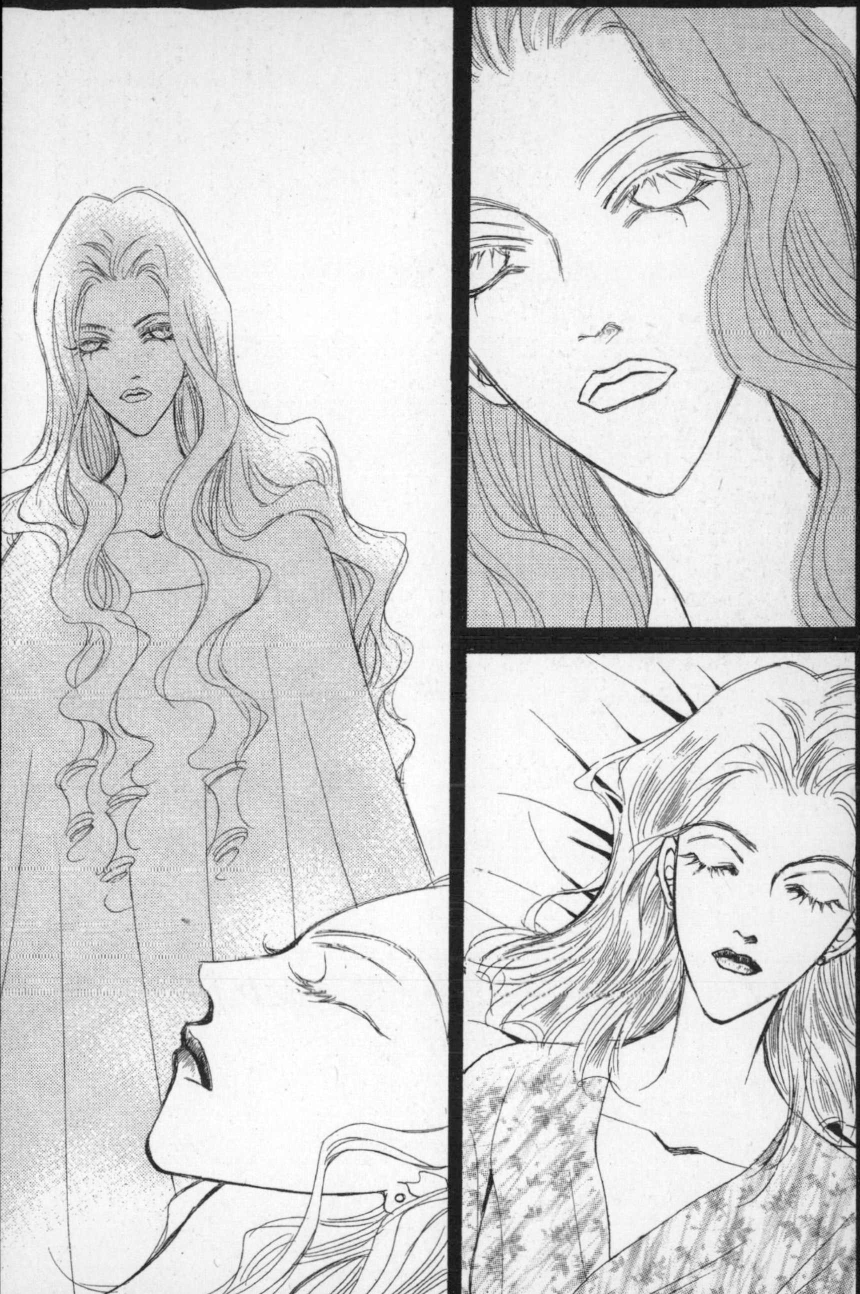

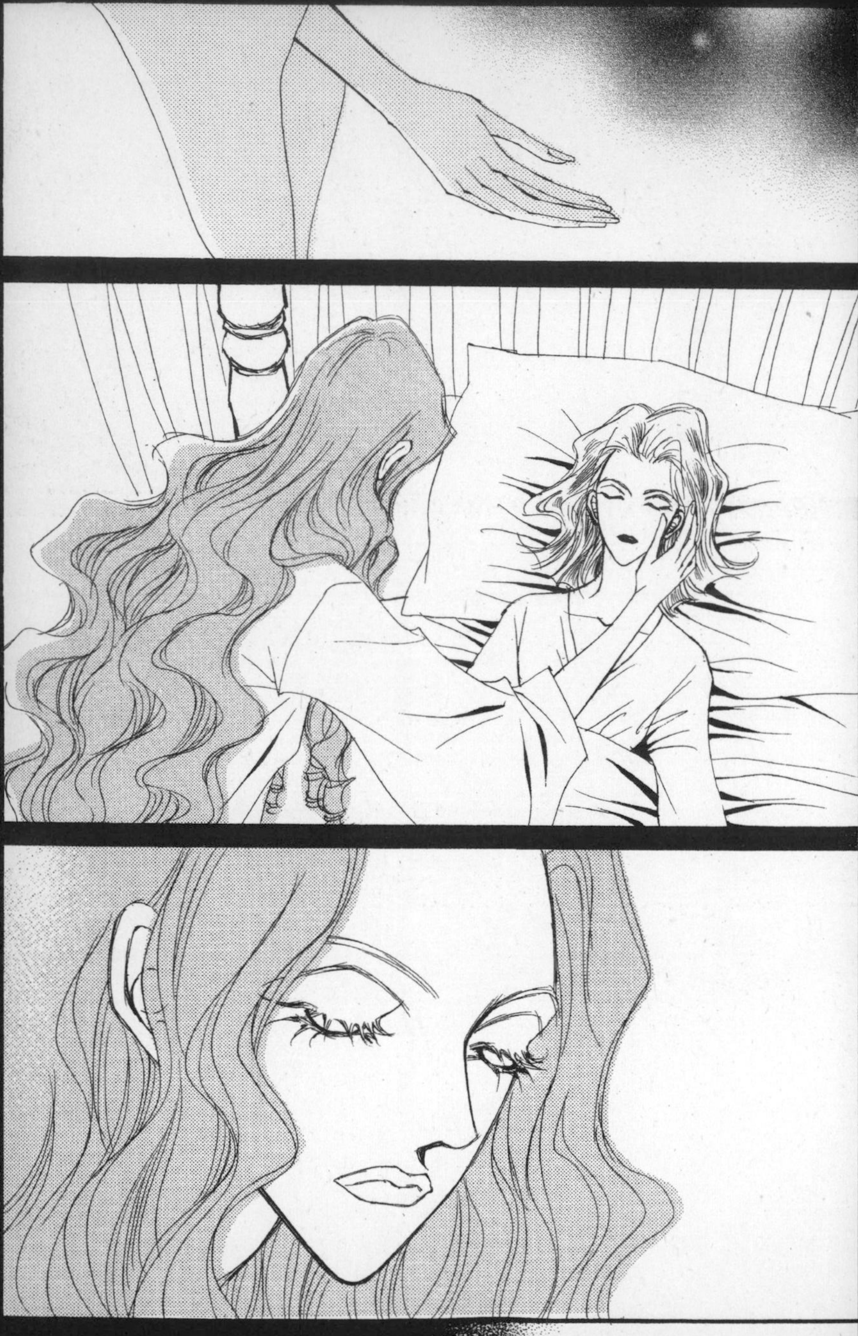

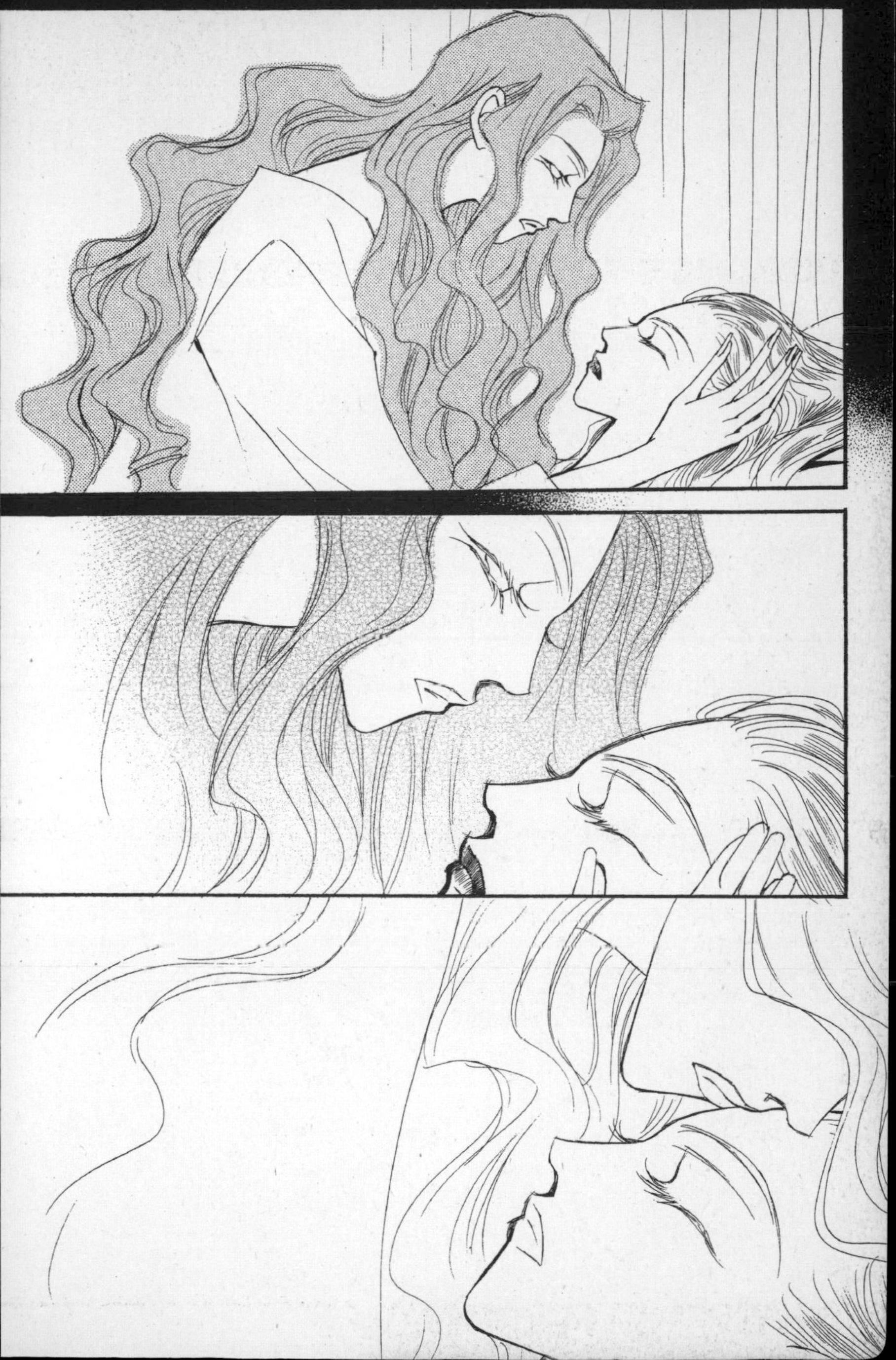

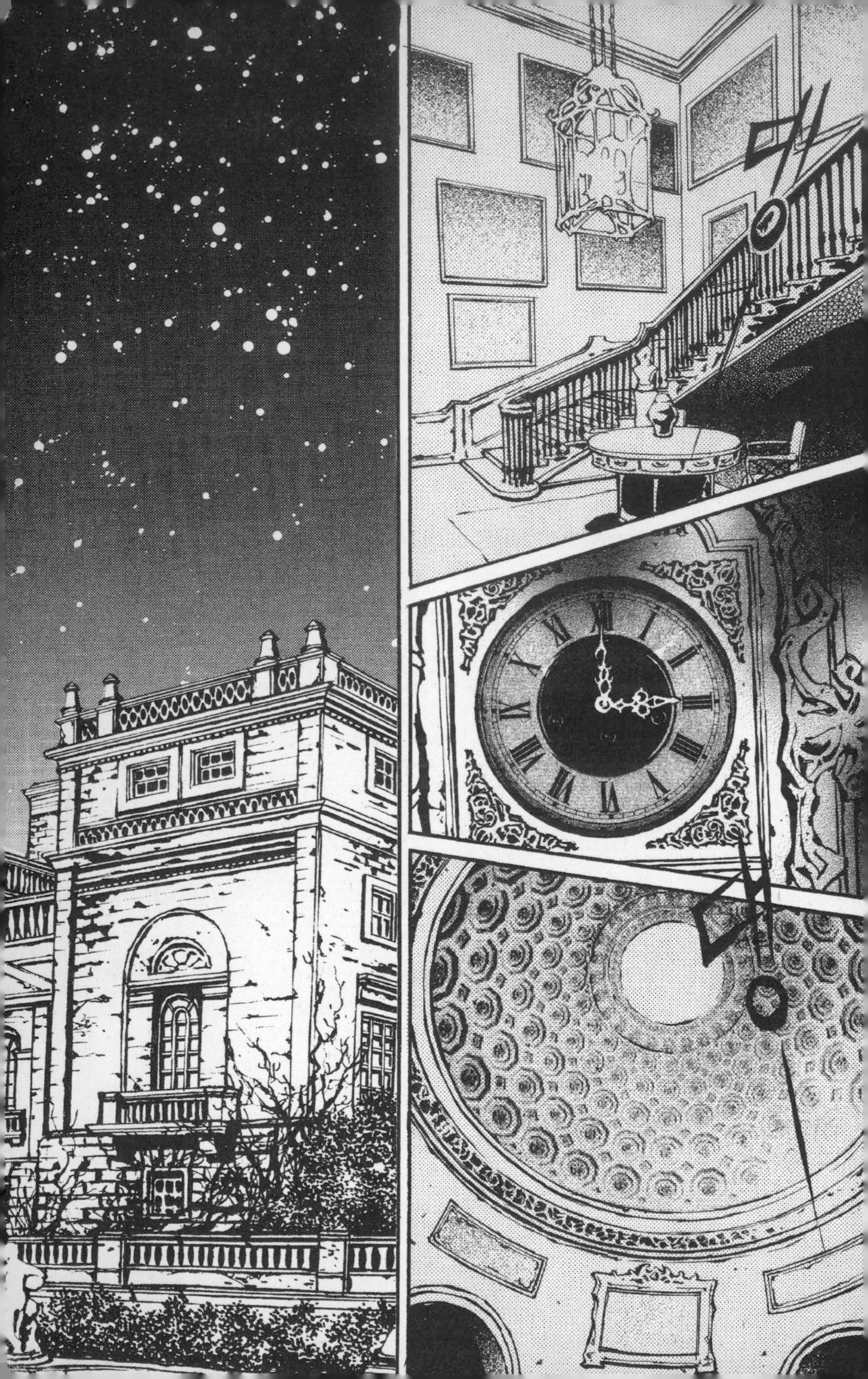

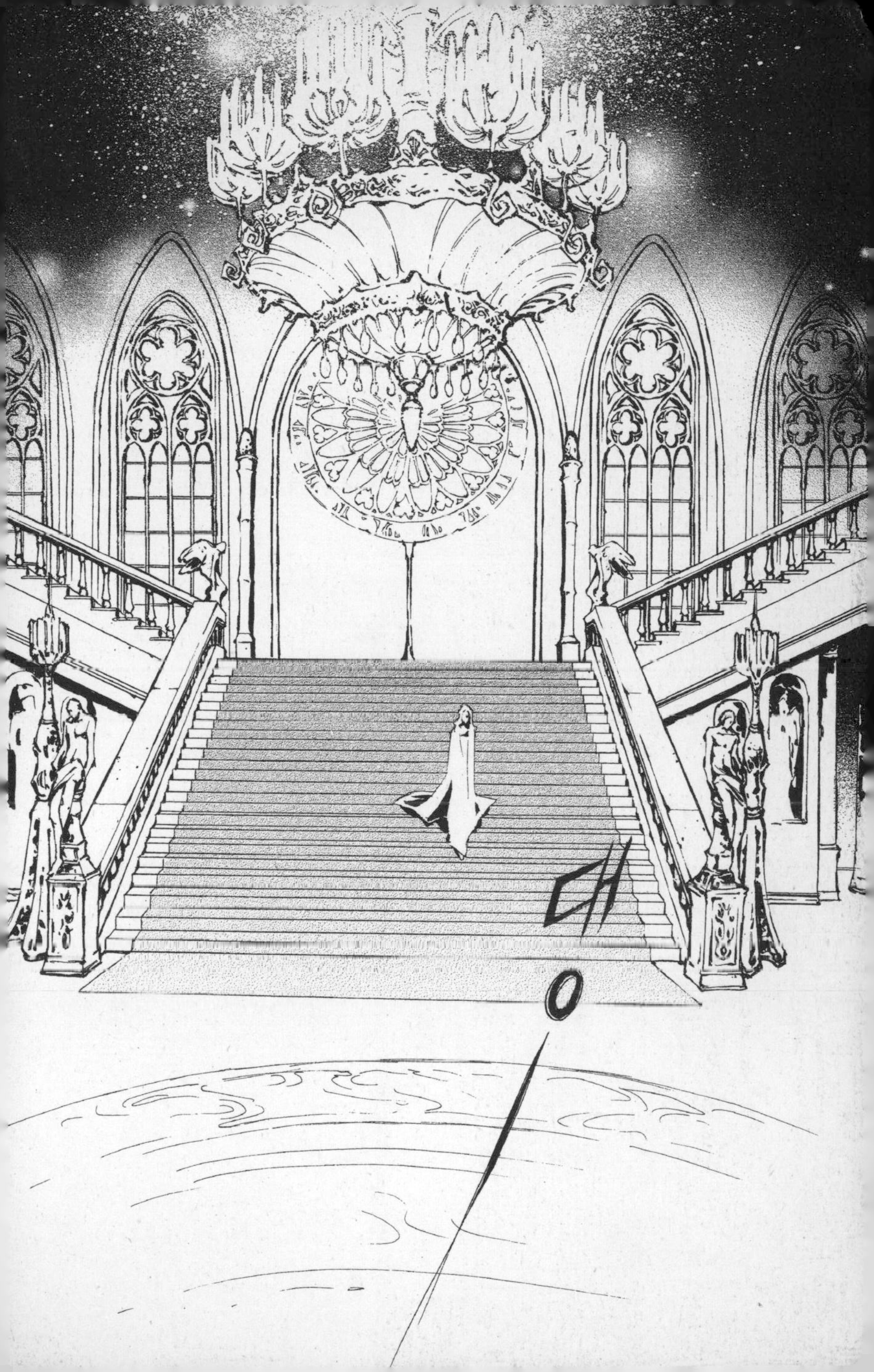
CHO

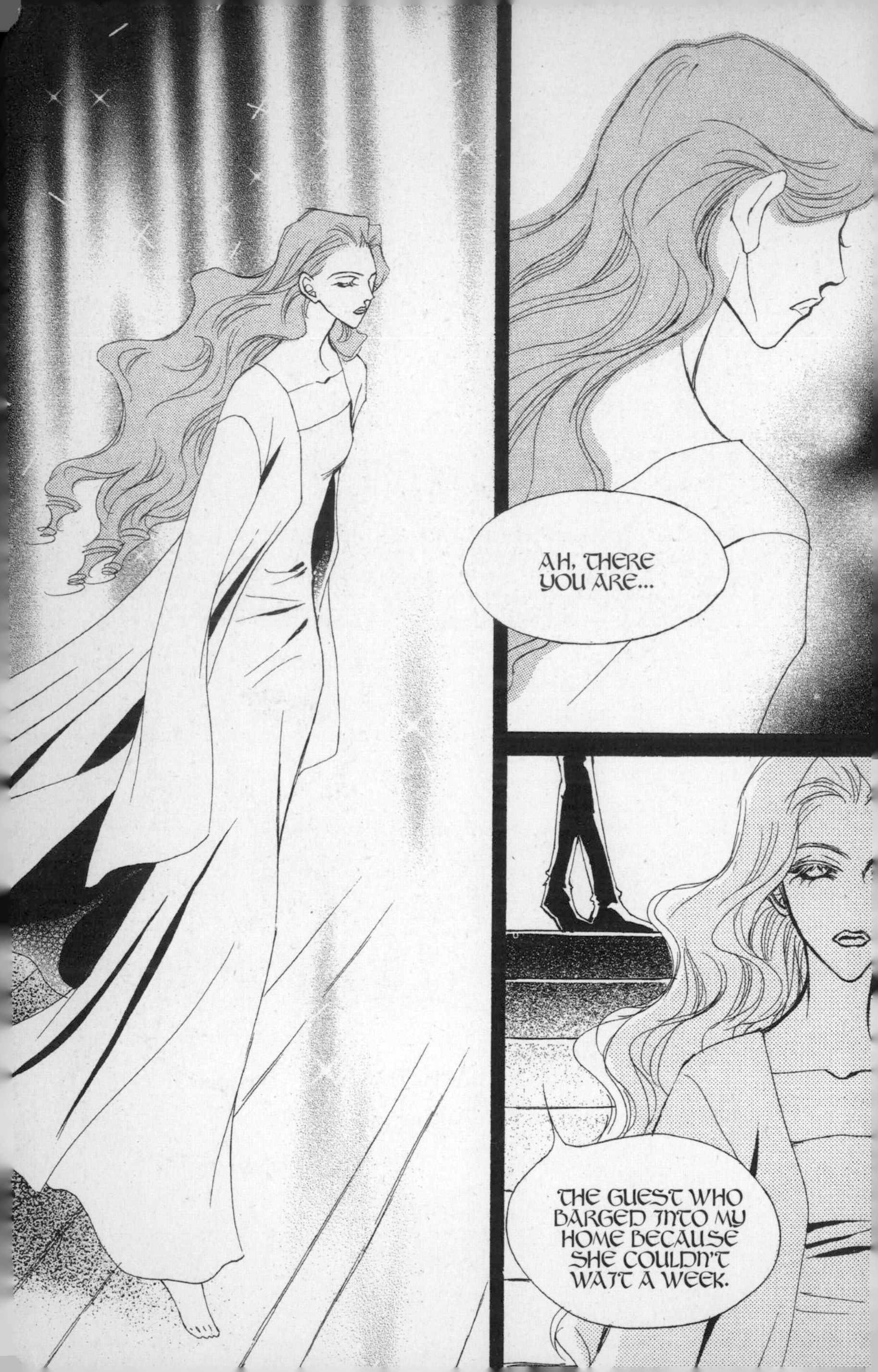
AH, THERE YOU ARE...
THE GUEST WHO BARGED INTO MY HOME BECAUSE SHE COULDN'T WAIT A WEEK.

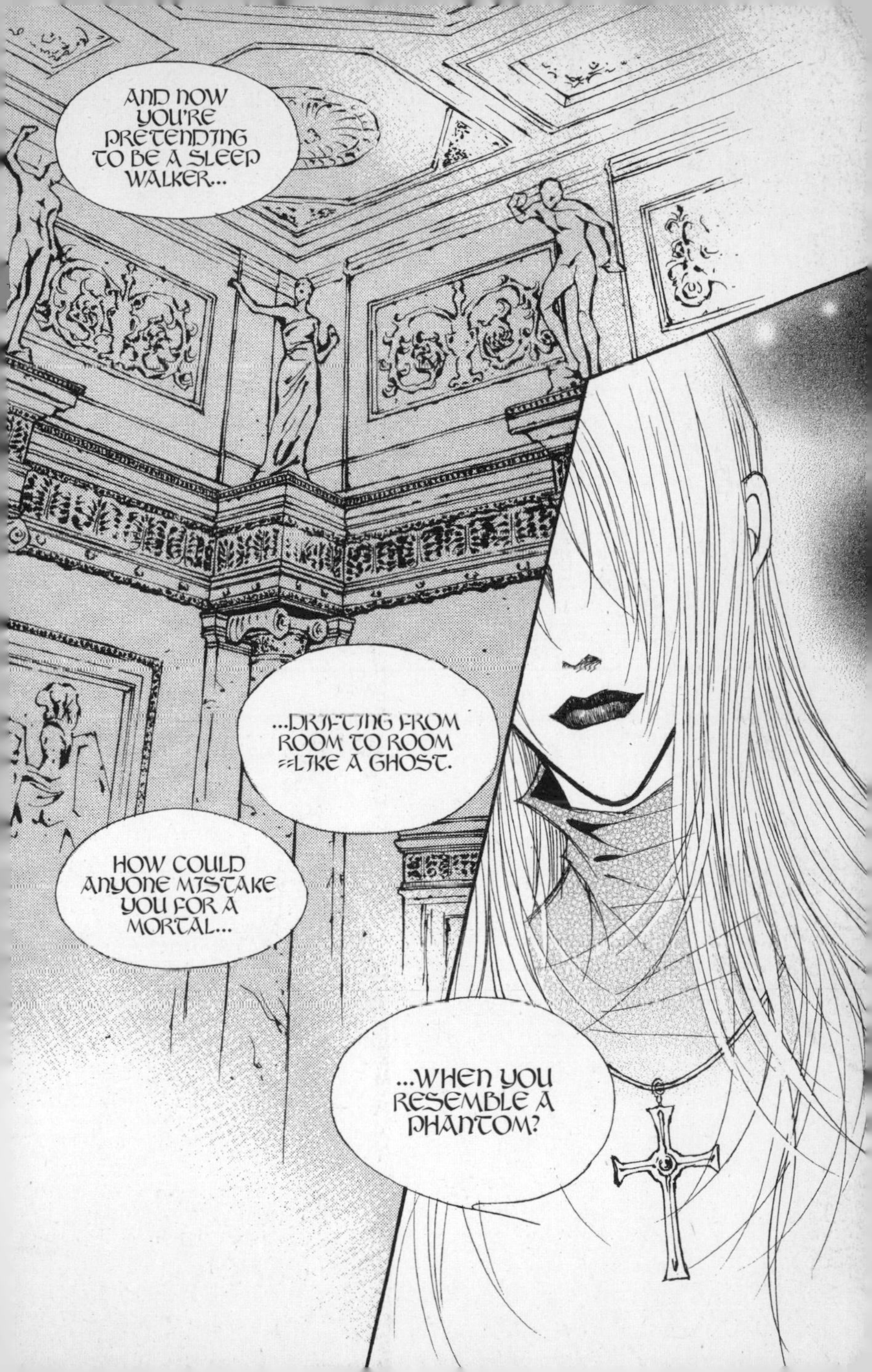
AND NOW YOU'RE PRETENDING TO BE A SLEEP WALKER...
...DRIFTING FROM ROOM TO ROOM ==LIKE A GHOST.
HOW COULD ANYONE MISTAKE YOU FOR A MORTAL...
...WHEN YOU RESEMBLE A PHANTOM?

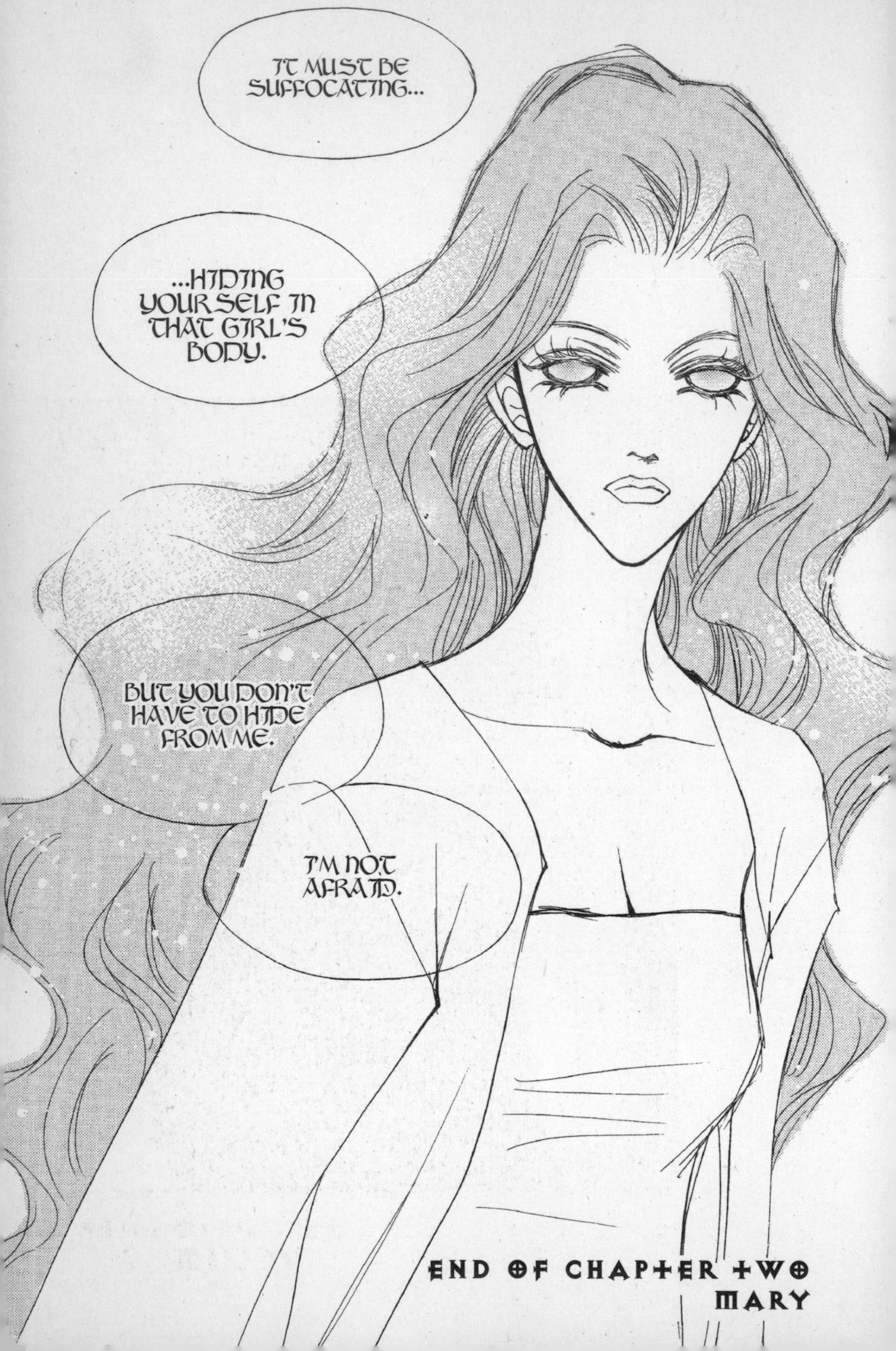
IT MUST BE SUFFOCATING...
...HIDING YOURSELF IN THAT GIRL'S BODY.
BUT YOU DON'T HAVE TO HIDE FROM ME.
I'M NOT AFRAID.
END OF CHAPTER TWO
MARY

**END OF MODEL
VOLUME 2**

MESSAGES FROM THE MAUSOLEUM

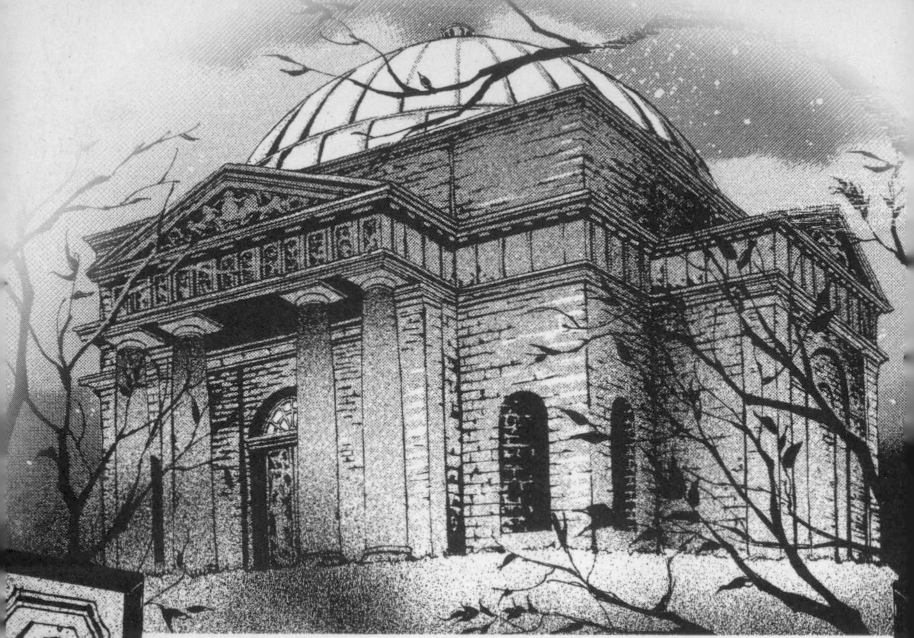

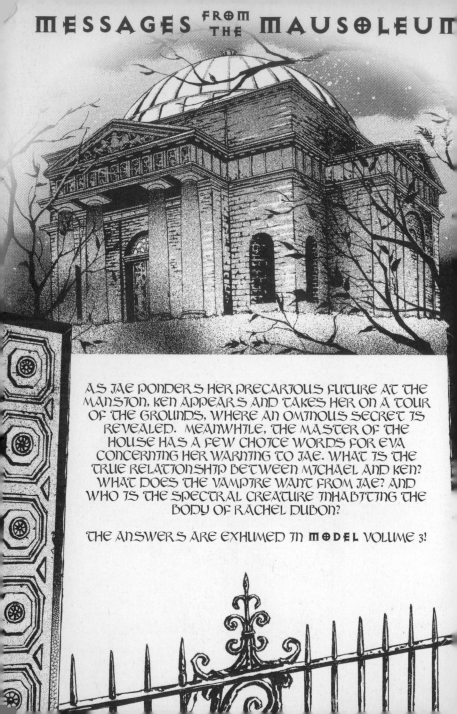

AS JAE PONDERS HER PRECARIOUS FUTURE AT THE MANSION, KEN APPEARS AND TAKES HER ON A TOUR OF THE GROUNDS, WHERE AN OMINOUS SECRET IS REVEALED. MEANWHILE, THE MASTER OF THE HOUSE HAS A FEW CHOICE WORDS FOR EVA CONCERNING HER WARNING TO JAE. WHAT IS THE TRUE RELATIONSHIP BETWEEN MICHAEL AND KEN? WHAT DOES THE VAMPIRE WANT FROM JAE? AND WHO IS THE SPECTRAL CREATURE INHABITING THE BODY OF RACHEL DUBON?

THE ANSWERS ARE EXHUMED IN **MODEL** VOLUME 3!

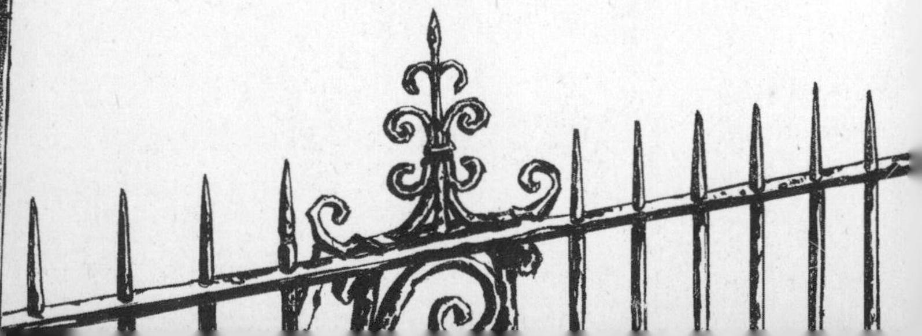

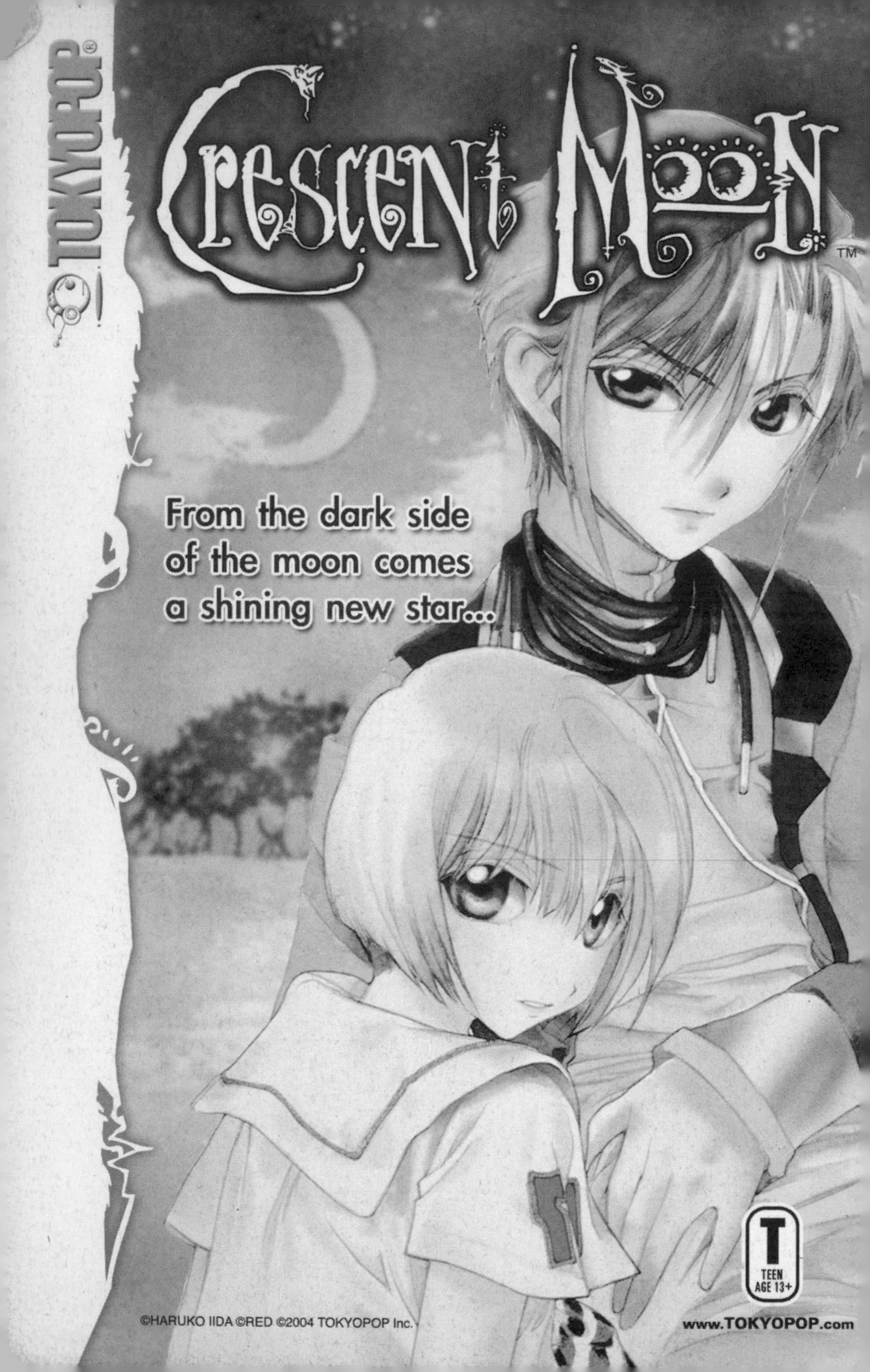
TOKYOPOP®
Crescent Moon™
From the dark side of the moon comes a shining new star...
T
TEEN AGE 13+
©HARUKO IIDA ©RED ©2004 TOKYOPOP Inc.
www.TOKYOPOP.com

DEMON DIARY ™

Art by Kara
Story by Lee Yun Hee

Can Harmony Be Reached Between Gods & Demons?

TEEN
AGE 13+

www.TOKYOPOP.com

TOKYO
BABYLON™

Welcome to Tokyo.
The city never sleeps.
May its spirits rest in peace.